AGAINST SILENCE

The Voice and Vision of Elie Wiesel

We have 613 commandments. The last one is probably the most important because it includes all the others: *Kitvu lakhem et hashirah hazot.* "You must write this poetry." To be Jewish means to be a poet. There is poetry in the Jewish existence, and we are commanded to see its poetic dimension. We are to write it down in order to share it with as many people as possible; every Jew is commanded to read the Torah, to write it, and thus to transmit it.

— Elie Wiesel

VOLUME III

AGAINST SILENCE

The Voice and Vision of Elie Wiesel

Selected and Edited by Irving Abrahamson

HOLOCAUST LIBRARY
New York

ISBN 0-8052-5050-6
Printed in the United States of America

To Gwen Hirsh and to the Memory of
Morris Henry Hirsh

_____

VOLUME III

Section 12. Television Scripts

Section 13. A Drama

Section 14. Stories

Section 15. The Books: Genesis and Commentary

Night

Section 16. Open Letters

Section 17. Jewish History and World History

Section 18. President's Commission on the Holocaust

Section 19. United States Holocaust Memorial Council

Section 20. Explorations and Explanations

Section 21. Quotes and Comments

SECTION 12

Television Scripts

THE ITINERARY OF ELIE WIESEL: FROM SIGHET TO JERUSALEM

WIESEL It all began here, it all ended here. Children became old men overnight, and Sighet turned into Jerusalem — Jerusalem up there in heaven.

ANNOUNCER "The Itinerary of Elie Wiesel: From Sighet to Jerusalem."

WIESEL That's where the town of my childhood seems to be now. Not here, but up there, in a Jerusalem of fire, hanging onto eternal memories of night.

NARRATOR Transylvania: a Rumanian, Hungarian, Austrian province. Occupied by the Turks, the Russians, the Germans. Coveted by all the tribes in this part of the world.

Despite the diversity of tongues spoken, despite the variety of regimes succeeding one another, it was a typically Jewish region, just as its villages and hamlets were typically Jewish, too.

Jews lived here for so many centuries that their presence was an integral part of the landscape. Jewish farmers, Jewish innkeepers, Jewish landowners, storekeepers, merchants: there was no village without its Jews.

Elie Wiesel's grandfather, Dodye Feig, lived in Bitchkev. His uncle, Isroel Feig, owned a small grocery store in Kretchenev.

(Wood-carver working)

A celebrated rabbi, a kabbalist, known for his piety and powers, he lived in Sapinka. Jews in the hundreds, Hasidim, would come to see him, pray with him, sing with him.

Now the entire region is almost *Judenrein*, empty of Jews. A history of some 900 years came to an end.

(Music)

WIESEL Sighet and Jerusalem — at times it seems to me as though I have written all my life only about one or the other, about one within the other.

Jewish children of Sighet in 1944 lived in Sighet, and dreamed, and dreamed of Jerusalem. Is Sighet, Sighet? It is not.

NARRATOR These pictures were taken somewhere in Poland, but they could describe what took place throughout Europe as well.

(Music)

In his first memoir, *Night*, Elie Wiesel tells of the Jews leaving their homes, their belongings, their hopes. He tells of their journey toward the unknown, the arrival at Birkenau.

He tells of what happened to the child he had been. He says, "Never shall I

The Eternal Light, National Broadcasting Co. Television Network, May 21, 1972.

[1]

forget that night, the first night in camp, which has turned my life into one long night, seven times cursed and seven times sealed. Never shall I forget that smoke.

(Drums and music)

"Never shall I forget the little faces of the children, whose bodies I saw turned into wreaths of smoke beneath a silent blue sky. Never shall I forget those flames which consumed my faith forever.

"Never shall I forget that nocturnal silence which deprived me, for all eternity, of the desire to live. Never shall I forget those moments which murdered my God and my soul and turned my dreams to dust.

"Never shall I forget these things, even if I am condemned to live as long as God himself. Never."

(Drums and music)

WIESEL Fifteen thousand Jews lived here once upon a time. Today, fifty families. Once upon a time we had here a vibrant Jewish community, scores of rabbis, houses of prayer and study, sages and troubadours, poor beggars and merchants. Today — nothing. Fifty families.

Today, a cemetery. The cemetery probably is what Sighet maintains Jewish. The cemetery is where I feel at home. Stones. Letters. So many stones and so many letters.

What remained of the community that I have known? Stones. What remained of the tales that I have heard? Letters. Only letters.

(Music)

This street had many names. Before the Holocaust, it was called the Jewish Street. Now it has been renamed again and again for the third time, *Strada Traian*. The last indignity: The Jews of Sighet are not even remembered except in the cemetery.

NARRATOR George Dabala, stationmaster in Sighet, was a high school student in April, 1944. He remembers the ghetto; he remembers the freight cars.

DABALA *(In Rumanian with narrator voice-over in English)*

These cars were used for shipment of livestock and material. These cars carried six to eight cattle each. But over fifty Jews were crammed into each car. Many friends watched the departure of the trains, and I remember many Jews crying and asking for help. None of my schoolmates ever returned.

NARRATOR Dr. Ion Octavian Vlad was doing his internship in the Sighet Hospital in 1944.

VLAD *(In Rumanian with narrator voice-over in English)*

In May, 1944, the deportation of the Jews began. I remember a Jew called Shloime Perl who was hidden in the neighboring mountains. We decided to hide him in the hospital. Today he is seventy years old and still lives in Sighet. My fear was overcome by the thought that many Rumanian citizens had helped to hide Jews, and I thought of what Shakespeare said: to be or not to be a man.

WIESEL My *heder*, my teachers, my friends, my *Shabbat*. I would come here and sing and pray and dance. I would come here and hope. I would come here and plead with the Messiah to come.

I would come here. Now, closed is the *heder*, closed the *bet hamidrash*, gone are the Hasidim.

(Hebrew chanting)

One synagogue — the only one left. Gone are the melodies of *Shabbat*, gone the rebbes and the Hasidim, gone the *yeshivah* students, gone the troubadours, gone their songs, gone the messengers and their tales.

And yet I still see them. But I'm alone to see them. I listen to them and I hear their voices, and their voices are from far away. At times their presence becomes so real that I want to stop one of them, any one, and give him a message. "Go and tell these people, go and tell your companions and mine, tell them they are taking the wrong road. The path leads into night. Yours and mine."

But I keep quiet. I'm afraid of waking the dead. It is dangerous to wake the dead. Their memory is better than yours.

(Rural countryside sounds)

NARRATOR A house at a street corner, a house which Elie Wiesel was reluctant and even afraid to visit. The last time he was inside he was a pious, quiet teenager, with his faith intact in God and man alike. He went through it now, pale, nervous, his lips tight. He came out. We have never seen him as shaken up.

WIESEL What then is a house? A house is a word, the first word. A dream. The first dream. The first steps from outside. The first song ever heard. The first tale ever told. A house is a beginning; it is an opening to life.

I was afraid to come back, and to see this house. I was afraid perhaps because here more than anywhere else, with the only exception of Jerusalem, everything is called back into question.

When I first came back, this gate was different. It was an old, wooden gate. I remembered the squeak of it. Now it's in stone.

Except inside, in the house, everything is the same. The furniture. Even the wallpaper. And it is so much the same that at times I am afraid that perhaps the door might open and a young boy that used to look like me will come out, and he will ask me very innocently, "Tell me, what are you doing here, stranger? What are you doing in my dream? In my tale?"

Where is the boy? And where is the old man? Where are the rabbis? Are they laughing? Is anyone laughing?

The last image I had of this house was twenty-six years ago. I was standing there in the street, with all of the Jews of this street. It was spring, almost summer, between Passover and *Shavuot*. The first transport of Jews was to leave Sighet. I remember it vividly, to the point of killing all other words in my mouth and all other images.

I remember that night which began — which is still lasting in a way. They were all here: the Zlotchever Rebbe and Shloimele Heller, the *dayyan*. And they were all here, even the chief rabbi. I saw them with their bundles on their shoulders. And they were so thirsty and already so tired.

They were sitting here on the cobblestones because the Hungarian gendarmes were driving them mad with waiting and fear. And they were so thirsty that my sister and I went to the well and brought them water. Then, three days later, I was myself among then. I still am.

NARRATOR Another person who dreams of Jerusalem in Sighet is a Jew named Moshe Kind. He serves as the *shoihet*, as ritual slaughterer. With him Elie Wiesel spoke of his past and future. *(Conversation: Elie Wiesel and shoihet in Yiddish, narrator voice-over in English)*

"Where were you born?" "In Mesiv." "How many Jews lived there before the war?" "A total of around 1,200 souls." "How many Jews are there today in Mesiv?" "Today there are no Jews." "What was your father's occupation?" "He was a butcher." "Did you have brothers or sisters?" "I had one sister." "Is she still living?" "No, she was deported to Auschwitz." "And yourself?" "From us they took my father and my mother and my wife and two little children. My wife was pregnant at the time. And my sister and four children." "And you, yourself?" "I was taken to the work brigades in a town of Kleinverdan."

"How long were you there?" "Two years. I remained alive, and my brother-in-law also." "If you could have one request of God, what would it be?" "That the Messiah should come." "When? Tomorrow?" "No, yesterday would have been late already."

"I know that after the war many Jews returned to Sighet and many traveled on. You could have kept going too, to Israel. You didn't go. Why not?" "I wanted to go. I inquired of the chief rabbi of Rumania, Rabbi Rosen, 'I beg of you, Rabbi, let me go to my family.' So he answered, 'Reb Moshe, you would leave the Jews here as sheep without a shepherd?'" "So you have remained here. Tell me, you walk down the street and you see the synagogue of the Hasidim of Wizsnitz. But there are no more any Wizsnitzer Hasidim there. Doesn't this sadden you?" "Indeed, that does sadden me. The loss of our brothers, the synagogues, the school children."

"How then do you understand the ways of God? So many righteous people, so many innocent children. Why?"

"We cannot question such things. It is written, 'You are God's children.'" "Is God such a father? So you remain an optimist. You have retained your faith in God?" "Yes." "And the Jewish people?" "The Jewish people will certainly blossom again, and they have blossomed. Everything will turn out well." "*Shoihet*, do you think we will meet again?" "Certainly, if God wills it, in Jerusalem at the Western Wall. We will yet be able to kiss the earth of the Holy Land in Jerusalem."

Sighet is not in Sighet. But then where is it? In Jerusalem? Yes. Here in a place called *Martef Hashoah* — the Cave of the Holocaust — where all the Sighets of Eastern Europe have been absorbed.

WIESEL I remember that for many, many years, I was looking for my town and had not found it. I still look for it. I don't know where it is, but I know its name. And I remember that in 1967, when I attended the third ingathering of exiles, when all the people, from all over the world, from all over history, converged upon Jerusalem to fight for Jerusalem's survival, I remember I was astonished. How did they do it? How did Jerusalem survive? How did the Jewish people manage to gain its victory and its purity? And then I understood. I understood that Jerusalem was the only place that took them in, the only place where all the names that were erased from Jewish history by the hand of the murderer or his accomplice — all the names that so many enemies throughout the centuries wanted to see disappear, vanish, go, shamed — the only place in the world where all these places and all these names and all these dreams were taken in was here.

But what is a Jewish town? A Jewish town is a name, and names — only here can you find them. And there are so many that they invade your dreams, and you are haunted by them. My problem and yours, the problem of someone who tries to make words, is how to make names not come alive — this is impossible — but how to make them sing.

NARRATOR Tears enough to fill heaven and earth. Babi Yar and Ponar, Treblinka and Auschwitz, each a gate to the kingdom of fire. Kretchenev and Bitchkev, Sapinka and Tzanz. Look at these names, remember these places. Tell their tales and remember that the true tale cannot, and will not, be told.

(Elie Wiesel speaking with little girl)

But a town means also, and above all, people. So in Israel, Elie Wiesel searched for Sighet in people. Some work on kibbutzim, others are civil servants. They all belong to a society called the Sighet Society. They even publish their own periodical. Those who came from there will not forget it. But how about their children?

Elie Wiesel spoke to them, two of them, Aryeh and Irit Schon. Their father, their grandfather came from Sighet. What do Aryeh and Irit know about Sighet? Not much. They know it was a Jewish town. But then, they explain, neither their father nor their grandfather talks about it.

(Gunshots)

Then came the Six-Day War. It reminded Elie Wiesel of his past. Once again his people were alone. Once again mankind kept silent. Was the Temple going to be destroyed again, for the third time?

(Gunshots and moving artillery)

Elie Wiesel came to Israel while the fighting was still raging. In liberated Jerusalem the storyteller stood in front of the Wall and whispered a prayer to himself. To his childhood, to his mother. To those who were left behind, over there in the other kingdom of Jewish history, that of darkness.

His prayer became a tale, *A Beggar in Jerusalem*.

(Crowd sounds, cheering)

The War of June, 1967, brought together men and women from all horizons, from all corners of Jewish history. It even brought together a city, eternally divided: Jerusalem, symbol of man's quest for unity.

Professor Moshe Lazar, dean of arts of Tel Aviv University, has been among Elie Wiesel's oldest friends. They met in 1945, in France, in a children's home. In 1948, in Paris, they went together to a recruiting center for the newly-formed Israeli Army. Both volunteered. Professor Lazar was accepted, his friend not — for medical reasons.

WIESEL Moshe — you are among my oldest friends. You were born in a place named Satu Mare [Satmar], very near Sighet, where I was born. You left it, I left it, and you came to Israel; you chose Israel the nation, Israel the country. For some strange reason, I chose the Diaspora. Moshe, you became a soldier; I did not. Did you ever kill?

LAZAR Oh, yes, I killed. I killed in '48, I killed in '56, and I killed in '67. But the war of '67, which was the shortest, compared to the two others, was the worst I had. You remember, you came after the Six-Day War, and you met me when I was burned completely by the sun and disgusted by the smell of death and the fear of being killed. And for five months, even after I met you, I was unable to write, to read, or to do anything. I had to justify myself, to find a new justification: Why go on teaching, why go on dealing with literature, if at any moment it doesn't mean anything?

WIESEL You know when you killed or simply you know that you killed?

LAZAR I even know when I killed.

WIESEL Do you know whom you killed?

LAZAR No, I don't know whom I killed. But I can imagine.

WIESEL Have you had any desire to find out — after all, such a metaphysical thing? You became God when you killed.

LAZAR No.

WIESEL Are you afraid to know?

LAZAR No. I am always one with myself in what I am doing. And I — you know it — I went to the war because I had to go. And I did not have to justify myself. Since I'm living in Israel, I don't feel anymore need to justify my destiny here and to justify what I am doing. It's far harder to justify what is the meaning of my life in the world, in existence in general. But I don't have problems to justify my being here.

WIESEL It's not a matter of justification; except in France when we studied together, you wrote poems and I wrote the music for them. Wouldn't it be much more simple and much more human to go on, you writing poems and I writing music, rather than killing and speaking of death?

LAZAR I think on this we agree. There is another point on which we agree, and it's related to what we said just a few moments ago, that for both of us, I think, since '45, questions were more important than answers.

WIESEL Moshe, there is something terrible after all. I am telling tales, I am telling stories. I have questions. I try to share my questions with others, perhaps with your students, but somehow I always believed that at least you have some answers. Now you tell me that you have none. What have we been doing, you and I, for twenty-five years?

LAZAR Well, like I said, not the answers are important but the questions. And there's a play about Christopher Columbe by Ghelderode, where he says: "Tomorrow I will know that the earth is spheric, but I will be less happy." So you don't have to know to be happy. If you know, it's finished. You have to start always new peregrinations, new navigations. And look for other earths, other worlds. And if once I thought that scholarly work is my kingdom, it finally becomes my exile. And maybe where people think I am in exile, it's my kingdom.

WIESEL The same with me but the other way around. But, Moshe, you and I know that man's goal is not exactly to look for happiness.

LAZAR No, happiness is maybe a moment like this, when we meet again.

WIESEL It's more than that. Tell me, I remember in '47, I went through a terrifying crisis of faith. You were then even more religious than I. Personally, I never speak about my relationship to religion, because whatever I would say I would lie. Perhaps you feel the same. In that case you will not answer me. Do you still believe the way you did then?

LAZAR No. It's right: I was very religious before I came to Israel. And somehow, the country, the people, the hills, the sky, all that was abstract and metaphysical in the Bible. . .

WIESEL Became real.

LAZAR Became real. And God has become part of those trees here or those hills, and I lost my faith somehow. At least the faith in a dogma or in practicing religion.

WIESEL What is *Shabbat* to you? You used to sing *Shabbat* in Versailles, you used to sing in my choir, "Oh, *Shabbat*, the Queen, *Shabbat* is coming." Do you miss it? I must tell you I do. I miss nothing else — not even *Shabbat* in Versailles. You know, I think I could do really without all the big holidays. I know how to behave. What I miss is the *Shabbat* in Sighet. Nowhere on earth will I ever feel this kind of *Shabbat*, not even in Jerusalem. Don't you miss *Shabbat*?

LAZAR I miss in a certain way the *Shabbat* we used to have in France, sitting even after midnight and speaking and dreaming about other worlds. About the Queen of *Shabbat*. And then we were speaking about kingdom and exile, like we are speaking now. And it seems like nothing has changed. And it's twenty-five years ago.

WIESEL Nothing has changed?

LAZAR I don't know.

WIESEL What is *Shabbat* to you now?

LAZAR *Shabbat* to me now is friends, the possibility to go away from the scholarly work, to go away from the daily world, and to find this same silence which is surrounding us here.

WIESEL I could join you in that. *Shabbat* is friendship — more than that, really. It's a kind of nostalgia, very, very tender melancholy.

I had a rebbe who used to quit *Shabbat* with a song, a Yiddish song. He sang: "If I would have the strength I would run in the streets and cry aloud '*Shabbat*, Holy *Shabbat*. . . .'" And he used to sing it.

Who is your rebbe?

LAZAR Who is my rebbe? You. At least in this field. You taught me to sing, twenty-five years ago, and you taught me a lot of Hebrew songs and songs in Yiddish, which were a big part, a great part of your world.

WIESEL Tell me, twenty-five years ago, we were at the crossroad — you to go to Israel and become a soldier, I to become a writer, a novelist. Would you take the same decision?

LAZAR I don't know if I would take the same decision, but I'm sure that I would have gone the same way, and you also.

WIESEL I think so.

NARRATOR When asked where he feels most at home, Elie Wiesel answered, "In Jerusalem, when I am not in Jerusalem." Except that no matter where he is, he is in Jerusalem. To him Jerusalem is a song, the most beautiful of all. The princes and the beggars, the children and their heroes, the saints who died too young, and those who will never die: they are all here in Jerusalem — the City of Peace in a world that needs peace more than anything else, the city which moves man to sing and rejoice, in defiance of death.

WIESEL The itinerary of a Jewish writer today begins, has to begin, somewhere in the Carpathian Mountains, in Sighet, has to go through many stations like New York where I live now; Paris where I had my formative years, where I studied; Moscow, Leningrad — the places where I discovered the Jews of Silence who are silent no more. But naturally, it is always Jerusalem that stood before the eyes of the storyteller, Jerusalem that was the substance of his tales, the tale of his tale. The truth is that I knew Jerusalem before I knew Sighet. I knew how to pronounce the word Jerusalem before I knew how to pronounce Sighet.

The fact is also that for a while I thought I was in Jerusalem before I had really reached Jerusalem. That was a strange Jerusalem, a dark Jerusalem, a horrifying Jerusalem. Some twenty-six years ago, I remember. I remember 1944 — a Jewish child, very pious, full of dreams, and full of piety, so naive that he still believed in man and words and dreams. I remember that child because he was one of many, many children and one of many, many people who one night arrived in a strange kingdom — a kingdom of night, a kingdom of fire. He was young, very young, and he saw at midnight thousands of people speaking all tongues, engaged in all trades, from all origins, from all the countries on earth. And all of them converged upon that kingdom.

I didn't know what it meant. I still didn't know that man could turn a kingdom into hell, into a hell of inhumanity, and reduce people to numbers or objects. I was so naive that for a moment I had a strange feeling that perhaps I was in Jerusalem, perhaps the Messiah had come. Perhaps the Messiah had come to deliver his people and all peoples, and all of them had come to greet him. All of them had come to see him, to welcome him, to pray and to sing his glory, to worship what he worships.

Then I found out, of course, that was not Jerusalem: that was the dark side of Jerusalem. And if there was a Redeemer, he stayed there, among the victims. If there is a Redeemer, he had to be there.

Then some twenty or so years later in 1967 I happened to be here at the Wall, on the very spot Golda Meir, the prime minister, described so movingly, where she described her tears. Naturally, we all cried. We all did; we couldn't hold back our tears.

But believe me, for a moment, for a fraction of a second, I wanted to laugh. When I saw that day so many Jews, young and old, speaking all tongues, who had seen all things in life and beyond, people who were pious, and paratroopers with tears in their eyes — and they were rushing to the Wall, throwing themselves to the Wall to speak to the Wall, because the Wall alone heard us for two thousand years: again I had a feeling, well, this is Jerusalem — the real Jerusalem, the unreal Jerusalem, the eternal Jerusalem, the Jerusalem of all cities. And perhaps the Messiah had come.

And I wanted to laugh, I wanted to laugh so hard that never before had any human being such a desire to laugh. We laughed and we cried. And Jerusalem remained Jerusalem, although something of Jerusalem remained there, burned in the ashes of the dark Jerusalem.

ELIE WIESEL'S JERUSALEM

One enters Jerusalem as one enters a dream — breathless: a dream filled with anguish, joy, wonder, and beauty — beauty above all; a dream filled with colors, images, memories; a dream filled with your own past — a past as rich as the past of mankind.

This city — symbolically and ironically called the City of Peace, Jerusalem, *Yerushalayim* — has invited many invaders, many conquerors. Who didn't want to conquer Jerusalem? The Byzantines and the Turks and the Mamelukes and the Arabs and the Crusaders. And now Jerusalem, the City of Peace, has re-become Jerusalem, has reconquered its own tale, and we all are part of it.

In the beginning there was Jerusalem. A journey through this eternal city means a journey to its origins. Here, more than anywhere else, you experience a sense of return. You walk through the Damascus Gate into streets and alleys filled with sunshine or shadows; you cut through crowds of merchants or worshipers, and you look at them and at yourself as though you all belonged to another era; a walk in this city of eternity leads you back in time…back to a child's spellbound and spellbinding city where all men are mysterious sages and princes.

I remember: legends and promises, prayers and benedictions, long ago and next year, David and the Messiah, exile and homecoming. What would I, a Jew, be without this city, the most Jewish of all, the most universal as well?

All my memories are linked to its own: the laws, the rituals, the Temple, the priests, the prophets, the catastrophe, the surviving stones — the Wall.

I remember my first discovery of the Wall. It was during the Six-Day War. The war was still on and we had just arrived at the Wall.

I remember moving my lips, and what I said then I have been saying ever since: that I belong here in this very place. We all do. I remember the words. Here I am, and I said my name, and I remembered my father. My father. I remembered my mother. I remembered my teachers, my friends. I said, "I am the eye that looks at the eye that is looking. I shall look so hard that I shall be blinded. So what? Then I shall sing. I shall sing with such force that I shall go mad. So what? Then I shall dream." I shall dream. I shall dream my own dream, the dream of my people, which is the dream of mankind. I have never felt what I felt here.

Here at the Wall, you remember. Here at the Wall, you cannot but remember. And I see before my eyes the kings and the prophets, the poets and the beggars — all those Jews and non-Jews, who throughout the centuries were looking for some

Canadian Broadcasting Corp.-TV, Easter, 1979.

consolation, for some comfort, for some hope, and would come here to speak about it.

Once after a sleepless night, I heard the muezzin's call to prayer. . . . And I felt...envy.

The Temple Mount is where the First and Second Temples stood. But this is also where the Moslems constructed the Dome of the Rock when they conquered Jerusalem from Byzantium in the seventh century. The dome stands on the foundation stone, the foundation of the world. The site is holy for both Jews and Moslems. There are many legends attached to it, as there are many legends attached to any building, any stone, any shadow, any tree in this city. Legend has it that Mohammed the Prophet flew from here when he ascended into Heaven.

Legend has it that Abraham prayed here. Solomon prayed here. David prayed here. Elijah prayed here, and, of course, the Prophet himself.

Furthermore, legend has it that when Cain and Abel quarrelled and fought, when one killed the other, it is here that their battle took place. This is, therefore, probably the holiest place in the world.

Only once since it was built did it yield its authority to another power, to another religion. That was during the Crusades in the eleventh century, when the Crusaders called it *Templum Domini*. Their control didn't last long. And for the last 1,300 years the beautiful building has remained almost as it was then.

Jerusalem has known more than one beginning. Here images and words and customs may remain unchanged for decades or even centuries. Meah Shearim, a hundred years old, is an enclave in time, an enclave in Jerusalem. Somehow it reminds me much more of my old hometown than of Jerusalem. Because here people are still very religious, extremely religious, and whatever they do now, they have been doing for the last 2,000 years, and perhaps more so.... The houses here are exactly the same as those I knew as a child: small, poor, clean. But the people are fervent. They are extremely fervent. On Friday everybody goes to the *mikveh* to be purified for the coming of the *Shabbat*. Small children prepare their home for *Shabbat*. The mothers prepare the meals for *Shabbat*. Some of these people do not recognize the authority of the State of Israel. Some maintain that since the Messiah has not come yet there should be no state at all. And they are violently opposed to the political entity of Israel. However, they are a minority, and although they do not recognize us, we recognize them.

Old Jerusalem. New Jerusalem. Then. Now. The same vitality, the same energy, and perhaps the same miracles. Now you need them when you cross the street. But then everything is a miracle. Everything relates to miracles. And everything in Jerusalem calls for miracles.

There is something strange about Jerusalem, something unique about it. When I visited the city for the first time, I felt that actually it was not the first time, that I had been here before, many times before. But now every time I come back to Jerusalem, I feel it is the first time here. And this strange sensation penetrates your whole being; it is only in Jerusalem that it takes hold of you. When did I first see Jerusalem? I try to remember. At home in my little town in Sighet somewhere in the Carpathian Mountains, what I knew about Jerusalem was that it was more than a city, more than a place, more than a concept. It was simply something that cannot be told.

At one point I thought it is a book, because I always read about it in books. Then I thought it is a chant, for always we sing about it — on Saturdays, on the Sabbath, and on the Holy Days and three times a day, in our prayers. Then I thought it is a memory. There is a custom that when we say grace, all knives should be removed from the table. Why this custom? First, because every table in a Jewish home is supposed to be the altar, and the altar is something sacred in the Temple, and therefore a knife, which can kill, should be taken away, put aside. But there is another more plausible reason: in our prayers, after the meals, we speak and we sing about Jerusalem and we pray God to rebuild Jerusalem. Our teachers and masters were afraid that perhaps we would be overtaken by so much longing, by so much melancholy that unwillingly, unwittingly a person might take the knife and kill himself. Therefore the table must be cleared like an altar, with no knife before our eyes.

In the beginning there was Jerusalem. Within its walls you are obsessed with history. Geographically the city is almost insignificant. Historically it surpasses in its significance all other cities. It is like a Dina Recanati sculpture, one of her gates: it is an opening, an offering. No other city has such evocative power to bring the past back to life. Just walk and walk. And listen. Someone is singing, and you think of David. Someone is questioning, and you think of the poet Judah Halevi. Someone is getting ready for battle, and you think of the Zealots in the mountains. Someone is conjuring the heavens in the name of hope, and you think of Rabbi Akiba. Samuel and Isaiah, Elijah and Jeremiah, Zedekiah and his underground tunnels, Bar Kokhba and his military strongholds, Herod and Agrippa: somehow they all invade your memory as it touches that of Jerusalem, the most faithful of cities.

In Jerusalem a Jew feels more Jewish, and a Christian more Christian. The Via Dolorosa, the road that Jesus Christ followed when he went to the cross in Golgotha, is for Christianity probably the most holy of all the roads in its history. Here in Jerusalem, for the first time in perhaps 2,000 years, all religions are respected by all who are still somehow in faith, and believe in faith, and believe in the same God. No place is more sacred, more important than the Holy Sepulchre for Christians. As a Jew, I can only speak about it from the outside, with respect for those who respect their religion. And mine....

In ancient times, on the holiest day of the year, on *Yom Kippur*, there was a watchman whose task it was to stand on the walls and wait for the first light. When he caught that light, he would shout, *"Barkai! Barkai!"* meaning the light has arrived. He has seen the light. And then he set into motion the process, the mechanism of all the things that were supposed to happen that day and did. We have seen that light sometimes in the morning, we have seen it sometimes diffused, and often we have caught its reverberations later in the day. But, for us, the light really is expressed in words, and we remember only the tales of that light, the tales of those days. These tales mostly are sad tales, because what marked our imagination, what marked our memory was the destruction of this beautiful city, and the beauty of that city.

When you look around Jerusalem and see its caves and walls, you realize that this city is a city of height and a city of depth. Somehow, here you feel more humble than ever. At the same time you feel more proud than ever. You feel humble because the city is older than you, because the city is richer than any human being can ever hope to become. I can hear, literally, at night Zedekiah, the last king of the First Temple, as he was walking through the cave, the secret cave, to escape the siege, and to be free to fight again. I can hear the Babylonians as they took him prisoner. I can hear Jeremiah as he was lamenting before and during and after. You can hear in this city, you can hear the sounds.

You can almost hear the silence that preceded those sounds, and the silence that succeeded them. All the tales of Jerusalem, most of them, are tales of sadness, except when you speak of the first light. The first light of Jerusalem contains so much beauty and so much hope that all you can do is try to take it in you and give it to others. Therefore Jerusalem to me has been and is this light, not only for my people but for the world and mankind.

There is strength in these walls, there is power, there is beauty. There is also something majestic in these walls. I wish I could say they are 2,000 or 3,000 years old, but they are not. Suleiman the Magnificent built or rebuilt them between 1537 and 1541. Here and there we find some remnants of stones, of rocks, part of the walls built by Herod and Agrippa. The walls, as we know them, were important because Jerusalem, somehow exposed to so many enemies and invaders, needed protection, natural protection. And the walls were here to offer that protection, except that the protection was not absolute. Somehow the enemy always managed to get through, to destroy them, to destroy the inhabitants, to destroy the culture inside those walls. But because of the importance of the walls, there are certain Jewish laws which pertain to cities within walls, just as Jerusalem used to be and is still today.

Pagan temples replacing synagogues, churches built upon synagogues, monuments erected on houses of study and prayer: all attempts to tamper with the Jewish soul of the city ended in failure. Throughout the centuries Jerusalem has remained the symbol of Jewish endurance and continuity, the symbol of new beginnings. When Jews pray they turn towards the Holy Land. When they pray inside the Holy Land, they turn towards Jerusalem. No city is linked to as many customs; no city has inspired so many legends. Though afflicted and wounded, Jerusalem has outlived its enemies: it is older than they.

On June 7, 1967, Motta Gur and his paratroopers rushed through The Lions' Gate to reconquer and liberate the Old City. All the other gates remain open as well, except for one, the Gate of Mercy, which is to remain bolted until the very day of the coming of the Messiah. For let anyone but the Messiah enter it, and the earth will shake to its foundations.

Others have entered this city through other gates. Some remain. Some remember Suleiman the Magnificent, so do we. Has Jerusalem changed since? Have its people changed since? Jerusalem changes and changes and stays the same.

Jerusalem everywhere loves to acquire new layers but never gives up the old. For us Jews the old layers are as important, if not more important, than the new ones, for they remind us of our beginnings, of the Jewish beginnings of Jerusalem.

Students of Slobodka and their teachers, beggars in Warsaw and their benefactors, poets and their leaders, masters and disciples, rich and poor, young and old, we have been waiting for redemption which in our vocabulary was linked to a return to Zion, which to some had a practical political dimension as well, for, above all, what is Zion if not a return to beginnings?

1917. The Turko-German armies are defeated, the British are victorious, and in Jerusalem General Allenby, the conqueror of Palestine, accepts the surrender of the notables. In the triumphant British Army there are three battalions of Royal Fusiliers; one raised in Palestine, one in Britain, and one in America but trained in Canada. Three men who later became famous in the State of Israel served in the American and British and Palestinian battalions: Prime Minister David Ben-Gurion, President Itzhak Ben Zvi, and Prime Minister Levi Eshkol. Levi Eshkol and David Ben-Gurion took leave without permission and were demoted from corporal to private. Still, later they fared rather well, for they became prime minister and defense minister of the sovereign State of Israel.

They believed that in the beginning there was Jerusalem, that in the beginning there is Jerusalem, that Jerusalem is the beginning. Therefore in this city everything seems possible. In this city human miracles are forever possible. Anwar L. Sadat's visit to the Knesset in this city was a miracle accomplished by all of us. The fact that he chose Jerusalem was no accident. It had to be in Jerusalem, for only Jerusalem could inspire such need, such desire for peace. The fact that he came, of course, was important, but what was equally important, if not more so, was the way he was received in this city. Thousands of Jews, men and women and children, some of them orphans or widows, some of them wounded, mutilated, hurt by this very man, came to applaud and encourage and love. This is the miracle of Jerusalem, the beginning of an era that could be something we have been longing for and we love: peace.

The tents of the Bedouins who come to Jerusalem seem to come out of ancient history. The Bedouins belong to the present and the past at the same time. They are peaceful people, extremely peaceful, and Israel has absolutely no problem with them. Their tents can be found just a few feet away from the Hebrew University, one of Israel's five universities. Thousands of students from all over the world come here to study — anything from nuclear physics to humanities and, of course, the Bible and the Talmud. And the Talmud today means Saul Lieberman, the greatest scholar of many generations. When he explains a Talmudic passage, especially in *Talmud Yerushalmi*, you are transported back to those times. His words come to life, and when I think of *Yerushalayim Shel Maalah*, the Heavenly Jerusalem, I see him in it, building Jerusalem with words. *Mishkanot Sha'ananim*, the Dwelling Place for peace and rest, is where artists, scholars, and writers with international reputations are invited from all over the world to come to spend time and write and reflect. It is a real honor to be here, to be invited by the mayor and the city of Jerusalem to stay here. Here you can work, create, and people expect nothing from you. The place was built by Sir Moses Montefiore, a century ago or so, as an old age home. Now it has been converted into this artists colony. Sir Moses Montefiore is remembered here with very deep affection. He traveled a lot. He went to Morocco, to Eastern Europe. He frequently visited the Holy Land in his *carrosse* to help Jews everywhere financially and politically. And therefore the whole neighborhood, the whole quarter, is called *Yemin Moshe*, Moshe being for Moses. When you see the windmill, you realize also that he built it for one reason: to provide work for people who would live here. And now people work, create, meditate, and try to do something which they do wherever they are — except here they do it better and, in a way, truer. Samibak, a great artist obsessed with the Holocaust universe even here, or here especially — the ghetto, fear, death, the broken covenant — Samibak remembers the ghetto, Lithuania, the violation of the most urgent of commandments, "Thou shalt not kill." Yehuda Amichai a young scholar, André Neher a philospher, Haim Gouri a poet, Israel Adler a musician — they all meet in *Mishkanot Sha'ananim* simply to be with their friends from abroad, to remember, to compare notes and souvenirs, and to chat. And there, Teddy Kollek is in the middle, always in the middle. He is Jerusalem's dynamic, energetic mayor, always looking for new projects and new parts and for someone to pay for these projects, always finding something to repair, to correct. From early in the morning to late at night, you can see him walking the streets or sitting in his office. No one has done so much to modernize this ancient city.

"Wherever I go," said Rebbe Nahman, the great storyteller of the Hasidic movement, "my steps lead me to Jerusalem." As for me, I could say that whenever I speak, I speak about Jerusalem. There is something about this city that cannot but move you to smile, to weep, but surely to remember. I knew its name before I knew my own. The first lullabye was about Jerusalem. The first tale I heard was about Jerusalem. The first prayer I uttered was to Jerusalem.

The Talmud says that should a man lose his way in the desert or anywhere else and not know where to pray, how to pray, he should in his mind concentrate on Jerusalem. That means that Jerusalem is also in our mind, Jerusalem is in our heart. This is the center. This is the bearing. Whenever I feel lost, I think of Jerusalem and feel stronger and know where to go — and sometimes what to say.

I remember very beautiful tales, and some of them I try to repeat in my own words, with my own *niggun*, with my own song, in my own tales.

What is Jerusalem if not a tale of my tales? The dream of my dreams? What is Jerusalem if not the memory which is more than my own? A Jew in Jerusalem sings of Jerusalem. A Jew in Jerusalem recalls Jerusalem, and his mind reflects Jerusalem. A Jew in Jerusalem weeps over Jerusalem, and he is told by Jerusalem: "Do not cry, do not cry. Why not sing? Why not sing?" And the Jew says: "One does not learn how to cry, one cries as one lives. But one must learn how to sing, and I have no one to teach me." So the Jew in Jerusalem continues to cry for Jerusalem until he is told again: "Do not cry. I shall teach you how to sing here or, rather, I shall teach you how to sing again of Jerusalem, for Jerusalem." With rare and tragic interruptions, there have always been Jews in Jerusalem. Recent excavations have shown that the earliest settlers here — dating back to the seventh century before the Common Era — were Jewish. However, some sites are lucky and others are not: the Jewish Quarter of the Old City somehow always suffered and endured all the invasions and the cruelties of the invaders.

When the Jews came to Jerusalem from all the lands of persecution, from Spain, from Portugal, from the Inquisition in those places, they built subterranean synagogues with magical and ancient names — Rabbi Yohanan ben Zakkai, the Ramban — all full of wonder and piety. They were all destroyed again and again, but rebuilt again and again. In 1948 the Jordanians destroyed all these synagogues. They destroyed the entire Jewish Quarter. In 1967, when the first paratroopers entered the Jewish Quarter, many of them wept because they saw the sanctuaries in ruins.

But now they have all been reconstructed. Weddings are celebrated in the Yohanan ben Zakkai Synagogue. Tours take place every day. Strangers come from faraway lands to see the miracle of reconstruction. For this is the miracle of Jerusalem: we can build upon ruins.

When I come here I remember that Jerusalem has been destroyed seventeen times and seventeen times reconstructed. In this house of study, a *yeshivah* near the walls, students young and old explore the depths and the colorful evocations of the Talmud and the Bible and the Prophets. And they bring me back sounds and melodies from my childhood. Just as we in our town repeated Talmudic sayings, examined laws, they here let themselves be carried by Talmudic legends. We have all been singing the same songs. We have all tried to capture the same truths. We have all tried to be in Jerusalem, except over there we were in Jerusalem away from Jerusalem, and here they are in Jerusalem. And still they speak about it with love and affection, and, above all, with longing. And their longing is a melody. What a melody!

Perhaps I should say it publicly: I love Jerusalem. You cannot not love this city. But at the same time one must say that one can never leave it either. Once you have entered Jerusalem, Jerusalem stays with you, as you stay with it. Once you have been to Jerusalem, you have become its pilgrim, and even more so now, its messenger. Once you have been inside its walls you know that wherever you go, wherever your steps may lead you, you will always now go back to Jerusalem, for from now on you will stay inside its memory, inside its tale. Forever.

SECTION 13

A Drama

A BLACK CANOPY
A BLACK SKY

CAST

  MENDEL

  SARAH

  MAGGID

  BOY

  NARRATOR

THE TIME: Early in 1943.

THE PLACE: Somewhere in a Polish ghetto; an underground bunker. A lamp hanging from the ceiling spills a dull, dusty light into the bunker. In that light, the frightened Jews who fill the bunker are felt rather than seen. A young couple — Mendel and Sarah — are the only people seen immediately. But to one side, leaning against the wall, the Maggid can be made out. Mendel and Sarah sit on a wooden bench before a wooden table, trying not to look at each other. Mendel keeps looking at his wristwatch; Sarah bites her lips, as if trying to keep from speaking.

MENDEL Where is she? She's been gone more than an hour. Something must have happened to her.

SARAH Be patient, Mendel.

MENDEL Was I wrong in letting her go? Maybe I shouldn't have. She might have gotten caught.

SARAH Patience, Mendel, patience.

MENDEL After all, she went to see Edek, and who knows whether he is trustworthy. He might be a traitor!

SARAH Edek belongs to the Polish Resistance movement. The Germans are as much his enemies as they are ours. He gave his word he'd get us out of here. For money, true, but he did give it.

MENDEL Do you know Edek personally?

SARAH No. But Chava has met him several times. And I have faith in her intuition; she sees through everyone's mask.

MENDEL (*Sighs*) It's getting late.

  (*A man's voice is heard in the background quietly reciting the evening prayer. An old woman is heard giving the amens. Outside, night has already fallen. Since the Germans do not enter the ghetto after dark, the immediate*

Elie Wiesel's first play, performed in 1968 to mark the twenty-fifth anniversary of the Warsaw Ghetto Uprising.

[19]

danger has passed — perhaps until morning. The Germans know that the Jews in the ghetto have formed a defense organization — not to do battle now, but perhaps later, at a more opportune or more desperate time. Mendel and Sarah have remained in the bunker to make sure that the last German has left the ghetto with the coming of night.)

MAGGID *(Comes forward)* You think Edek will save us all? Me, too? Even though I have nothing to offer except my hunger . . . and my learning. Do you really think Edek will pull me out of this even though I have nothing to pay him with . . . and you, too?

SARAH Don't worry. If everything goes as it should, we should be free tomorrow; in the forest, perhaps, with the partisans.

MENDEL *(Deep in his own thoughts)* Chava should have been back already.

SARAH It's only been an hour since she left.

MAGGID Who is Chava?

SARAH *(Not wanting his interruption)* If you would be patient, you would find out. Chava is his bride-to-be.

MENDEL *(Indicating Sarah)* She's her sister.

MAGGID *(Interested)* When will the wedding take place?

MENDEL Wedding? Are you out of your mind? Who can think of weddings when all the earth, heaven itself, is a cemetery?

MAGGID So. . . it's possible to erect a *huppah* even on the field of the dead. As a matter of fact, this is often a good way to avert the evil decree.

MENDEL It is either too early . . . or too late.

SARAH *(Cupping her ear)* Shsh . . .

(Everyone freezes. Mendel looks to the door; the Maggid looks up towards the ceiling, to hear every possible sound from outside the underground bunker.)

I thought I heard steps. I must have been wrong.

MENDEL Something must have happened to her.

MAGGID *(Continuing as if there had been no interruption)* Maybe we could have the wedding tonight. We could put up the *huppah* right here. I have my *tallis* and, thank God *(Indicating people in background)*, we still have a *minyan* of Jews. I will perform the marriage. For nothing. It will be my *drosheh-geshenk* — my gift to the bride.

MENDEL Stop this foolishness, this nonsense. This is neither the time nor the place to speak of marriages or other empty rituals. We have more important problems on our minds.

SARAH *(To Mendel)* Don't aggravate yourself, Mendel. He doesn't mean any harm.

MENDEL *(Doesn't answer but rises and paces around the bunker)*

MAGGID You see? He's a real bridegroom, so nervous he can't sit still.

SARAH *(Quietly)* It *is* getting late.

MAGGID Young brides like to make you wait.

MENDEL If I had known that you talk so much, I wouldn't have brought you to the bunker.

MAGGID It is my duty to speak out. I am a *maggid*, a preacher-rabbi. True, a *maggid* without a congregation and without a *shul*. The Germans killed my congregation and leveled my *shul*. Who is left to hear me, then, if not you? Who will listen to the *maggid*'s words, if not you? *(Quietly, with horror)* We may be the last worshipers. This might be the last wedding between two Jews.

MENDEL Are you crazy? There are dozens of bunkers in this ghetto and dozens of ghettos in the country. . . .

MAGGID I know . . . I know . . . But . . . have you seen the others? . . . No. Neither have I. And we can swear only to what we ourselves have seen, not to what others say they have seen. So how do we know that we are not the last witnesses?

SARAH *(Weakly)* Chava is our representative to the defense organization. She has visited other ghettos; she is in contact with other groups in other bunkers.

MAGGID When did she leave here?

SARAH Just before you arrived.

MENDEL I warned her to hurry. We are running out of time. Every minute counts. Every minute could be the last.

SARAH Mendel, I beg of you, try to be calm, Chava must have been delayed.

MENDEL *(Quickens his pacing, hands behind his back)*

MAGGID *(To Sarah)* Chava is your sister?

SARAH *(Pause)* Uh, yes.

MAGGID An older sister?

SARAH Uh, it's hard to tell.

MAGGID Does she look like you?

SARAH Uh, more or less.

MAGGID Don't you agree with me, Sarah, that we have the wedding tonight? We can't delay it. Mendel and Chava must be man and wife when we leave this bunker.

SARAH *(Deathly pale)* Why?

MAGGID To show the world. To inscribe ourselves in history. To show God himself that we Jews refuse to lose our belief in ourselves. That we Jews will persist; we *will* reach into the future, if necessary over our own dead. To show that on the very threshold of destruction, we sanctify life through the fulfillment of the commandments. This marriage, in this besieged underground bunker, this affirmation of life, will be our answer to our enemies.

SARAH *(Sighs deeply)* We can't talk about it.

MAGGID Good. We'll wait until Chava returns. The bride does have something to say about her own wedding.

SARAH *(Leans toward the Maggid and whispers)* Please. Do me a favor, talk about something else. Better yet, don't talk at all.

MENDEL *(Tiring, he stops pacing and returns to his place near Sarah. He stares into nothingness, then:)* You talk nonsense while I, in my thoughts, go to funerals. Funerals? No, not even that sorry satisfaction. Tens, hundreds of my relatives have gone to their death. I did not even accompany them on their last journey. Even so, they did not halt for a moment so that, perhaps, I could catch up. They are in the other world, now. But my eyes continue to see their last walk.

MENDEL Funny, I never used to believe in the other world. Now I believe. Oh, yes, now I believe. Look into my eyes, and you will learn what is happening in that other world. Look, and you will see that even there they lead holy old men and innocent children to the slaughter. Do you understand what I am saying to you? There are no more hiding places in this world or that. There is nothing. No way out. Even after death one cannot hide from evil.

SARAH *(Tries to comfort Mendel, she puts her hand on his: her face is like a broken mirror.)*

MAGGID I come from a town near Kolamai. It was a great big lively community. We had rabbis and scribes, students and beggars, merrymakers and musicians, teachers and laborers, real solid citizens, and ragged, hungry pious ones. I knew them all, and they all knew me. I used to go from one *shul* to another, from one home to another, warning them that there will be eventual punishment for evil deeds. Twice a year, on *Shabbes Shuvah* and *Shabbes Hagadol*, they all came together in the old *shul*. They all came, all — you hear? — to that great hall, and there my preaching tore from them bitter, heart-rending tears. Now I know that that was a mistake. I should not have castigated them. They deserved better treatment; they earned other words. One moment of the shattering fear that is the breath and blood of every person in the ghetto is penance enough for all their sins. Now I would like to ask them to forgive me. But . . . there's no one to ask. They are all dead. The slaughter of the Jews of my town took several days. And where was I? At the cemetery. That was my sanctuary. The corpses protected me. But they did not protect the other Jews, the living Jews of my town and theirs. Later, when I went into town and discovered what had happened, I ran back to the cemetery and began to shout at the buried dead. Listen, I said to them: Why didn't you protect your relatives from the slaughter? Why only me? Why didn't you protect your heirs, your *Kaddish*-sayers? Why didn't you have pity on *them?* Since that time, I go from one cemetery to the other, berating the dead. I have become the preacher to the dead Jews.

((The Maggid's speech is interrupted by a knock on the door. Mendel and Sarah freeze, then look at each other.)

MENDEL *(Whispers)* Who could it be?

(There is another knock.)

SARAH *(Also whispering)* That's the signal. It's a friend.

MENDEL Chava . . . ?

SARAH *(Shakes head indicating no)*

(The Maggid walks to the door and opens it. A young boy, twelve or thirteen years old, skinny, tattered, is seen in the doorway. He enters.)

MENDEL *(Gently)* Did you see. . . ?

SARAH *(Interrupts)* What's happening outside?

BOY Today's action is over. The Germans have left. We are now in the *shul* courtyard.

SARAH Are there many dead?

BOY A lot.

MAGGID Who?

MENDEL . . . Chava . . . !

MAGGID The Rov? The head of the *yeshivah*?

BOY *(Matter of fact)* The Rov . . . and his students. When they came out to be led
away, they brought their *tallesim* and *tefillin* instead of food and clothes.

MENDEL Chava! What happened to Chava?

BOY Who is Chava? I don't know her.

SARAH *(To Mendel)* She will be here soon.

MAGGID The Rov. . . . Did he speak? Did he say anything as he was taken away?
Did he leave us a legacy?

BOY He came out of the *bet hamidrash* silently, as if to prepare the way for the
students. A German hit him with his rifle. The Rov kept right on walking. A
second German tore off his hat and threw it into the mud. The Rov bent down
to pick up his hat, but the German gave him another blow with his rifle-butt.
So the Rov took a handful of mud and smeared it on his head. Then he went
on — with head covered. The Rov.

MAGGID You saw it all?

BOY Yes, with my own eyes, from my hiding place.

MAGGID What else did you see?

BOY Men . . . many men. Women . . . many women. A crowd. Children . . .
silent children. All being taken away.

MAGGID How many?

BOY A lot.

MAGGID Names. . . . Do you remember their names?

BOY Some. Moshe . . . Chaim . . . Itzik . . . the red Pesah . . . Yonkel the crip-
ple. . . .

MAGGID *(Insistently)* More. . . .

SARAH Let him alone.

MAGGID More . . . we must remember.

SARAH Why? For what? Let him alone.

MAGGID *(Piteously)* Their names . . . these dead must be remembered . . . every
one.

(They eye each other. Mendel is lost in his own dream.)

BOY *(Licking his lips)* I have a message . . . from David.

MAGGID David? Which David?

SARAH Our David. Everyone's David. The leader of the Jewish Resistance.

BOY David wants you to know that today's battle was the beginning of the end.
We have decided to fight.

MAGGID With what? With our nails?

BOY With our nails, if necessary.

MAGGID Are you crazy? Do you hope to defeat the German army?

BOY Defeat them? No. But we do hope for the privilege of fighting.

SARAH What other orders did David send?

MENDEL *(Dreamily)* What could have happened to Chava?

BOY *(Disregarding Mendel)* Do you have any weapons?

SARAH No.

BOY Not even one revolver?

SARAH No.

MENDEL Maybe Chava. . .

MAGGID *(To himself)* I have given myself to prayer throughout my life. Could it be for nothing? Maybe . . . for nothing.

BOY Without weapons you don't have a chance. David says it would be smarter to sneak out of the ghetto, across to the Aryan side. If you have friends there. *(With emphasis)* Good friends.

MAGGID Friends? *(Laughs bitterly)* On the other side? We? Maybe you'll take me with you when you go back to David. In my later years, perhaps I'll become a soldier.

BOY Impossible.

SARAH Tell David. . . No, tell him nothing. . . . We were children together. We went to high school together. The last time we saw each other. . . When was that? . . . When we entered the ghetto. . . . Now David is our general. . . Odd. . . Tell him. . . . Does he have enough fighters?

BOY No . . . but we have still fewer weapons. We have five men for every gun. But we'll find a way out.

MAGGID I would gladly go with you, my son. But you don't need me. Besides, I have to perform a marriage here soon.

BOY *(Looks at the Maggid as if at someone without sense. He waits a moment to see if Mendel or Sarah have anything more to say. He walks to the door.)* It's getting late. I have five more bunkers to find, So . . . good night . . . and . . . *(At a loss)* be well.

SARAH Good-bye . . . good luck.

MAGGID *(Gently)* What is your name, son?

BOY I do not know my name. . . I am afraid to find out.

MAGGID Do you think we will ever meet again?

BOY No.

MAGGID *(Wondering)* Where do you get your assurance, your calmness?

BOY Even if we survive this war, even if we save ourselves, I will no longer be me. . . . Maybe you will be me.

MAGGID *Kholileh*. . .

MENDEL *(To Boy)* If you meet Chava on the way . . . a young woman with blonde hair and gray eyes and a slim figure, tell her to hurry up.

BOY Blonde hair, gray eyes? . . . it's dark outside.

MENDEL Nevertheless . . . it will be impossible to miss her . . . tell her. . .

SARAH They're waiting for you, son. Good luck.

(The Boy leaves the bunker. The Maggid bolts the door after him.)

MAGGID *(Turning to Mendel, his face alight)* I forgot. . . I forgot to recite the blessing over the boy, that he live until the Messiah comes. How could I have forgotten. Maybe you know where he went. I might catch up with him. It is very important that I recite this blessing.

MENDEL You mean this blessing could help?

MAGGID It might. . . Then again, it might not. That's God's province, not mine. I know only that I must recite the blessing for him.

SARAH *(Shaking head, no)* It's either too early . . . or too late.

(Mendel covers his face with his hands. The Maggid breathes heavily; he walks around the bunker, looking for his audience, his congregation of Jews from yesterday, from today, from tomorrow. Throughout the following speeches, the Maggid describes visions, not of hope, but of despair.)

MAGGID You don't believe in the coming of the Messiah? Me, I believe! *(Recites)* "I believe in perfect faith in the coming of the Messiah." Perhaps there will be no one left to redeem when he finally comes, but he'll come. I see sunny, golden times ahead for our people.

MENDEL Stop that foolishness!

SARAH Shsh. . . Don't yell. We mustn't raise our voices.

MAGGID *(Anguished)* You don't believe me? I don't even believe myself. But I see. . . I see visions . . . not of us . . . but of those who will come after. . . . I see Jews marching in the streets with flags and music; but we will not hear that music. . . I see proud Jews; but we shall not see their pride. . . I see victorious Jews; but we shall not share their victories. . . I see a time when young Jews will throw fear into our enemies. . . when the entire world will say of us, again: an Eternal People. . . I see the time when the world will listen to Jewish voices, reckon with what they say; but these will not be our voices. . . I see. . .

MENDEL *(Interrupts)* Stop it . . . that's enough . . . end it right there. It's night. Outside one can't even see his own shadow, but you can see tomorrow.

MAGGID Shadows have nothing to do with tomorrow. I tell you . . . and I swear by all that is holy . . . that I *do* see better times ahead . . . a brighter future.

MENDEL You're crazy! All right, that's your business. But don't try to make *us* insane. Do you hear me!

SARAH Mendel . . . Maggid . . . Mendel . . . we must not yell. We'll be heard outside. Maggid, I'm pleading with you.

MAGGID Do you think I want to speak? I wish I could seal my lips. But what can I do when the words tear themselves out of my throat despite my efforts. I tell you that our people stands on the threshold of glorious times. You don't believe it? . . . I don't believe it myself. But . . . I see it. I know that this is an empty dream . . . impossible. But the visions I see are greater than logic.

MENDEL *(To Sarah)* Visions . . . dreams. . . He is out of his senses.

SARAH Is it any wonder? Who today is strong enough not to lose his mind? Who today is adaptable enough to retain his sanity?

MAGGID I know. . . I know. . . Don't explain it to me. You think I don't know the truth? The world burns and our people lie beside their own gravestones. Abraham, our Father Abraham, take your only people and bind them as sacrifices in a new *Akedah*. But this time, no angel of the Lord will interfere to forbid the spilling of our blood. No good will come out of this sacrifice. . . I know, I know . . . it's all over; it's all lost. The Merciful One has divorced himself from His people, from His world. So I'm back where I started from: there will be no more *huppahs*. There's no reason to hold one up; and no one to be married under it. The dead are free from all the commandments. So the *maggid* of the dead has no one to preach to; there's no one to listen, and no reason to hear.

MENDEL *(Beside himself)* Be still, I tell you, be still. If not, I'll throw you out.

SARAH Let him speak, Mendel. Leave him alone. Have mercy on him.

MENDEL I just can't stand it anymore. He keeps on talking, talking. When's he going to stop? *(Pause)* And Chava still isn't here. Where is she? Damn it.

SARAH Calm yourself, Mendel. She'll be here. Perhaps her negotiations with Edek are taking more time. Perhaps she's looking for a new hiding place for all of us. It's not easy . . . you know that better than I do.

MENDEL She's always taking care of others.

SARAH That's the kind of girl she is. Would you want to change her?

MENDEL No . . . but. . .

SARAH So you do want her to change?

MENDEL No . . . but. . .

SARAH *(Sadly)* You love her because she is what she is and who she is. So be patient. Have faith. She'll return. If not now . . . then later . . . tomorrow . . . perhaps even later than tomorrow.

MENDEL What are you saying? . . . Tomorrow? I don't want to wait until tomorrow. I don't want to wait at all. If she isn't back in one minute, I'll go look for her. I'll find her. I'll bring her back.

SARAH It makes more sense to wait here, Mendel. Believe me, it's smarter. You could very easily get lost. You might miss each other in the dark. She'll arrive and not find you. It's better to wait. . .

MAGGID I'll wait. I'll outlive the war. The *maggid* in me will remain a *maggid*. When it's over, I will go to every cemetery where Jews are buried and ask the dead not to disturb the rest and the joy of the Jews who will live in peace with themselves from then on. I'll tell our dead: If you don't obey me, no Jew will ever be rid of his guilt-feelings. If you don't obey me, every Jew's *Kiddush* wine will be bitter with tears. So leave them in peace, I'll tell the dead: Do the living a favor, even if they are not worthy; do more for them than they did for you; help them far more than they helped you.

MENDEL *(Interrupts angrily)* You won't remain quiet . . . No? . . .

SARAH Mendel. . .

MAGGID *(Continuing)* Be gracious, O dead, to the Jews of tomorrow. Don't deny them their joys; don't deny them their *Bar Mitzvahs* and their marriages, their hopes and their freedom. This is what I will ask of my dead congregation.

MENDEL *I* am not dead, and I will not listen to you.

SARAH Unfortunately.

MENDEL *(Runs to door, opens it)* I am going to find Chava.

SARAH *(Runs after Mendel. It is too late. She returns to the table, falls onto the bench, defeated.)*

MAGGID *(Soberly)* You think he really believes he'll find Chava?

SARAH No.

MAGGID Where is she?

SARAH I don't know.

MAGGID Does he know?

SARAH No.

MAGGID So what will happen?

SARAH Nothing. . . Either he'll come back after a bit, or they'll catch him. In the long run, it's all the same. Sooner or later, they will catch us all.

MAGGID And Chava? What of her?

SARAH Nothing.

MAGGID Isn't she in danger?

SARAH No, she's in no danger.

> *(The Maggid wants to say something but holds it back. Sarah looks into his eyes with a sad smile.)*

SARAH You still don't understand our secret? Chava doesn't exist. I never had a sister. Mendel does have a bride — and I am she. He thought up Chava a few months ago. He was captured and was being taken to his death. He thought that I, too, had been captured. He was wounded and, quite literally, crawled back out of the grave. But he could not face the idea of my death. So he told me that I, Sarah, was dead. But that his bride, Chava, lived.

> *(Sarah stops talking. The Maggid closes his eyes and becomes motionless. Sarah shakes him by the shoulder.)*

SARAH Tell me the truth, Maggid. Is Mendel right? Was I killed? Am I dead? And am *I* out of my mind . . . not he?

MAGGID *(Eyes closed)* I don't know any more. I can no longer tell reality from dream. And I am afraid to know. I know only that from now on I'll look for you in all the graves, in all the fields of the dead. I know only that coming generations will bring to you the whole round world as a gift.

SARAH Talk to me of today, not tomorrow. I do not have the strength to last until tomorrow. Tell me what is happening now, what will come one minute from now, no more.

MAGGID I don't know. . . I am afraid to look ahead.

SARAH I beg of you. . .

MAGGID I am afraid to look upon what I see.

SARAH Tell me . . . what do you see? . . . Tell me, whom do you see?

MAGGID I see a black *huppah*. . . a dreadful black *huppah*.

SARAH What else . . . whom do you see?

MAGGID The black *huppah* stands under a sky of black stars.

SARAH What else do you see?

MAGGID I see the groom. . . He is alone. . . All alone.

> *(A sudden silence falls. The Maggid's face flames. Sarah's face is lit by*

bright rays of broken light. She springs up with a heart-rending scream and runs out, screaming.)

MAGGID *(To himself)* It is later than I thought.

(Slowly, the dusty light dims until it is black. In the background, the hidden Jews are heard, but the words are indistinguishable. We will never know what they said.)

SECTION 14

Stories

THE SERMON AT HELL'S GATE

Although I did not grow up a Gerer Hasid, on the High Holy Days I worship at the Gerer *shtibel* in Manhattan. On those occasions I want to be among people who continue to believe and pray as they did in the past, in the old style of Eastern Europe. Among the Gerer, there is no rabbi delivering sermons, no guard demanding tickets, no synagogue president asking for money — just a few dozen Jews whose faith is ardent.

This year, on the second day of *Rosh Hashanah*, a Gerer Hasid told me the following tale: A few days before *Rosh Hashanah*, 1944, the final transport from the ghetto of Lodz arrived at the Zigmar-Schoenau concentration camp in Lower Saxony. Weak with hunger and clad in rags, the Jews prepared for the High Holy Days. Several young men decided to form a *minyan* rather than pray alone, knowing that to do so was punishable by death.

That evening after roll call, hundreds of Jews — young and old, pious and non-observant, even *kapos* — streamed towards the designated barracks for *Maariv* prayers. At first they prayed softly, but the prayer soon turned into a lament, each man remembering his home, his loved ones, the High Holy Days as they once were. They wept, mourning both the dead and the living. It seemed that the fountain of tears would flow until the Almighty took pity on His people.

Before the closing prayers, Shimon Tsuker, a Gerer Hasid, suddenly stood up. He felt compelled to speak; the Gerer Rebbe had appeared to him.

"Brothers!" he cried out. "It is *Rosh Hashanah* and although we are all bereaved, beaten, and starving, we should do as we did in bygone days — after prayers, go to our parents, our wives, our children, and our friends with good wishes for the new year. Let us follow this custom in our thoughts. Let each of us think of our beloved and send them our words." Hearing this, the people broke into mournful weeping.

Shimon Tsuker continued his discourse: "Soon we have to recite the *Kiddush*, but we have nothing over which to say the blessing. Not even a morsel of bread remains from today's meal. Let us lift our soup bowls to our eyes and fill them with our tears. Over these tears we will say *Kiddush* for the Almighty."

Twenty years later in the Gerer *shtibel* in Manhattan, Shimon Tsuker stands beside me, praying with fervor. Then, like Reb Levi Yitzhak of Berditchev, I asked of God: What other people would pray to You and crown You King of Kings though they languished in the shadow of death?

Jewish Daily Forward, October 5, 1965.

A *HANUKKAH* STORY

It happened in the kingdom of night, somewhere on the unclean earth of Auschwitz. December winds raged through the camp, transforming it into a snow-capped cemetery. The gaunt, starved prisoners marched out to work, knowing that many of them would be carried back to the ovens. It was plain to nearly everyone that only a few chosen ones would live to see the spring.

Each of us thought the same thoughts: How to obtain a warm shirt or a second pair of rags to cover our legs, even if it meant trading one's bread ration. Only my neighbor, the former head of a Polish *yeshivah*, had something else on his mind.

When I first noticed his worried expression and restlessness, I was certain that, like everyone else, he was trying to "organize" a jacket, a coat, a scarf. Then he confided to me the cause of his despair: he was having difficulty finding a suitable customer for his portion of bread.

"What are you looking for," I asked, "a shirt or a scarf?"

"Heaven forbid!" he said in astonishment. He was searching for eight potatoes and some oil to fashion into *Hanukkah* candles.

At first I thought he had lost his mind — "*Hanukkah* in Auschwitz!" I said in disbelief.

"Especially in Auschwitz," he replied. "If one gives up one commandment, even a minor one, sooner or later one will give up a more important one. It is best, therefore, not to overlook any mitzvah." He then asked, "Is not *Hanukkah* the holiday which symbolizes Jewish self-sacrifice? For twenty generations, Jews have been lighting candles to recall the heroism of Judah the Maccabee, a man prepared to die rather than betray the teachings of Judaism. Is this the moment to spurn his example? The flame of faith must be kept burning in the Jewish people."

I argued in vain that the lighting of *Hanukkah* candles is not a mitzvah worth dying for.

"If I thought any of us could outlive the enemy," he responded, "perhaps I would do things differently. But if we are going to die anyway, why do what the murderer wants? Why not die for a mitzvah?"

Other inmates tried to dissuade him. They quoted from the works of early and later rabbinical authorities, cited lines from ancient tractates, but the former *yeshivah* head countered every argument. Still, he had neither potatoes nor oil. Finally, a merciful kitchen worker, a pious man, brought him two raw potatoes and a little cup of oil. My neighbor gave the potatoes to an artisan, who fashioned

Jewish Daily Forward, December 10, 1969.

them into candles. The next day, following roll call, our block was ready to celebrate the first night of *Hanukkah*.

The news spread quickly through the camp. Many came to recite the blessing and to marvel at the old-new miracle of Jewish strength and perseverance. When the eighth candle was lit, the entire block participated in the ceremony. Everyone listened to the blessing, responded with a loud "Amen," and sang the popular melodies of *Hanukkah*.

For a long time, we warmed ourselves at the thought of those candles, reminded of another generation of Jews who had the courage to believe that they would be victorious over their enemy.

I do not know if my neighbor survived. I lost sight of him during the evacuation of Auschwitz. But his act of bravery will always remain with me.

THE OWNER

Reb Mendel of Kotzk used to say: "Often when I walk in the forest, I see a castle. The castle is burning, and I see a man at a window; and this man at the window is shouting, 'People, there is fire in the castle! People, the castle is burning.'" Then Reb Mendel interpreted his vision. "Yes," he said, "the castle is on fire, the forest is on fire, the Holy Word is on fire. But there is an owner of the castle, there is someone there. Someone we can't see, but someone we must hear."

Is there an owner in the castle? To my generation this question was put very cruelly, very often. The child that I was, drunk with fervor and drunk with prayer, later on grew to doubt whether there was anything there but fire. Not Holy Fire, but simply fire. Not the fire of the Burning Bush, but the fire of the Holocaust.

Adapted from *Teachers' Study Guide: Jewish Legends*, 1968.

MOSHE THE WATER CARRIER

Somewhere in the Warsaw Ghetto ten Jewish hostages were about to be executed, and one of them, nicknamed Moshe the Water Carrier, began laughing with all his might. It was the holy day of *Purim*, and on *Purim*, which is a joyous holiday, the Jews are supposed to laugh and to drink in celebration of the miracle which befell the Jewish community of Shushan over two thousand years ago. Much like Hitler, the evil Haman had planned to exterminate all the Jews, but they were saved by God and by Mordecai and Esther. So to drink and be joyous on *Purim* is as important as it is to fast on the Day of Atonement.

But the Germans were laughing as well, and they said to Moshe, "Now you will pay for what you once did to Haman and his children."

Standing on the gallows, Moshe the Water Carrier continued to laugh, and he laughed with all his might. He said to the Germans, "I pity you." Everybody thought he had gone mad. Perhaps he had. Perhaps his madness was a necessary madness, a human madness. And he laughed again and said, "I pity you, because my laughter is not like yours. You see, today I am Moshe the Water Carrier, but tomorrow I shall be Moshe the Martyr."

In *Teachers' Study Guide: Jewish Legends,* 1968.

A SPARK OF HOLINESS

One day the evil spirit came to God and said, "Master of the Universe, what is the difference between this group of people who are pure and these who are impure?" And God answered "They, the pure ones, protested. The others did not protest." "So," said the evil spirit, "had they protested, would You have listened to them?" And God said, "No." "Did they know that?" asked the evil spirit. And God said, "No, they didn't know it; therefore they should have protested — protested against Me, against man, against everything wrong — because protest in itself contains a spark of truth, a spark of holiness, a spark of God."

Therefore, little does it matter whether our protest is heard or not. Protest we must to show that we care, that we listen, that we feel.

In *Teachers' Study Guide: Jewish Legends*, 1968.

DO NOT BE AFRAID, MY SERVANT JACOB

A friend of mine happened to be in a small Russian city on June 4, 1967. You remember our fear, our anguish, because then Israel was alone, but not only Israel: we were alone. Suddenly we felt the cycle beginning again: the same words were being used, the same images were being invoked, the same dangers were threatening every one of us. On that day every Jew was directly linked to Israel. The end of Israel would have meant the end of the Jewish people. I am convinced of that.

My friend, an Israeli diplomat, did not know anybody in that Russian city. It was Sunday afternoon. He went to the hotel. How could he sleep? His children were at the front, his family in a kibbutz. And so he listened to the radio. The first news bulletins came early, about three or four in the morning: stupidly, both the Russians and the Arabs believed that the Arabs had won. That is why Jordan's King Hussein entered the war. Radio Moscow began flashing news bulletins: Tel Aviv is burning — the Egyptian army is already in the Negev — Jordan is cutting through Jerusalem — it is finished. I can imagine what my friend, alone in a strange, hostile city, must have thought, what he must have felt. A Jew in distress wants to be with other Jews. He went to the synagogue and found it packed with people — young, old, children, women, all together. And the *hazzan* was reciting *tehillim*, Psalms. It is the old weapon of the Jew — *m'zogt tehillim*. My friend was not religious, though he has since developed an understanding of religion, a sensitivity to it. He heard *tehillim*, but, not knowing what they were, he stood in a corner. At that time Israelis in Russia always wore the Israeli emblem on their lapel so they could be recognized by other Jews. Someone saw him and noticed the emblem. Suddenly the congregation stopped reciting the *tehillim* and spontaneously formed a circle, like *hakafot* on *Simhat Torah*. They put him on the *bimah* and simply shook his hand. Children and their grandparents, men and women — everyone felt the need to come up and shake his hand. As they came by he noticed they were whispering something to him again and again. At first he did not understand. He thought they were speaking a dialect he did not know. But then, as in a dream, he thought he *did* understand the words. They were Hebrew words: "*Al tira avdi Yaakov* — Do not be afraid, my servant Jacob." My friend thought he had gone mad. Fearing that Israel had been destroyed, he stood there in silence as the Russian Jews of this city came up to console him! *They* were comforting *him!*

Adapted from lecture, Congregation Shaarey Zedek, Southfield, Michigan, February, 1971.

He told me later that this repetition — *Al tira avdi Yaakov, Al tira avdi Yaakov* — went on for hours. Later, back on his kibbutz, he still heard the same words. They replaced all other words in his memory and in his mind. He could not hear anything but this *Al tira avdi Yaakov*.

Al tira avdi Yaakov is also part of the *zemirot shel Motzei Shabbat*. When the *Shabbat* leaves, we sing all kinds of *niggunim* to try to recapture the *Shabbat*, the sanctity, the simplicity of *Shabbat*. One of these is *Al tira avdi Yakaov*. I know at least three melodies for it, and they are all beautiful — Wizsnitz, Modzhitz, and Rizhin. But the most beautiful melody I know — because every time I retell it I shiver — is the monotonous repetition heard by my Israeli friend in that Russian city: *Al tira avdi Yaakov*.

THE HAUNTED HOUSE

I didn't know it when I arrived in Spain, but someone was awaiting me there, someone and something in Toledo.

In Toledo I was shown a synagogue which used to be a church during the Inquisition. This synagogue has Hebrew letters on the walls. The man who showed me the synagogue told me a true story: When the synagogue was transformed into a church they put a cross in it and all the other things that usually are to be found in a church, but somehow the Hebrew letters always appeared again. And no matter what they did throughout the centuries the Hebrew letters always came back. Frightened, the priests then decided to leave the church. Therefore the house of prayer was no longer a church, but then there were no longer Jews to make it a synagogue. What remained of the synagogue in Toledo, as I have seen it, is nothing but a house full of memories, haunting memories, and Hebrew letters on the wall.

Adapted from *The Eternal Light*, February 14, 1971.

THE LAST *MAGGID*

I believe that we can be very good Jews in the Diaspora, provided we maintain a link with *Klal Yisrael* and a deep loyalty, a total commitment to the State of Israel. Yet, I do not feel good about living outside of Israel, especially since I met a strange old Jew.

I am a teller of tales. That is the only claim I make for myself. Therefore I feel close to the *maggidim*, those anonymous wandering preachers and storytellers who went from town to town, from village to village, telling tales — always the same and never the same — thus creating links between people and communities, Jews and their destinies, sometimes embodying their very destinies. I remember these *maggidim*, how they would tell stories on *Shabbat*. I can see them, I can hear them now. They had a very deep impact on me and on my voice. They were always tall, nameless, and mysterious, so that to me they were always the same *maggid*. Only his tales changed. Thanks to him I would visit faraway places without ever leaving my own home. I became acquainted with Vilna and Slobodka, Lizensk and Berditchev, Lemberg and Medzebozh, simply by listening to his stories about their Jews and their masters. Thus, in my mind, *Shabbat* remains associated with stories and legends. All the *maggidim* are gone now — all except one. Let me tell you the story of Moshe the Shoihet, a ritual slaughterer.

Last year we went back to Sighet, my hometown, to film an NBC television program titled, "My Itinerary — From Sighet to Jerusalem." Why not "to New York"? I do not know. Maybe because everybody for many years was convinced that I was an Israeli, and I never denied it because I did not want to insult anyone. Golda even once offered me a job in the Foreign Ministry. Yet when I have to decide an itinerary, it must end in Jerusalem. It must. Therefore — from Sighet to Jerusalem.

The day before we left for Sighet, I received a telegram from the film director who had arrived there two weeks earlier. It read: "Dear Mr. Wiesel: We found Moshe." Moshe the Madman is in my vocabulary, in my mythology, and I always write about him in all of my books. But he had died. I was frightened. The next day we met Moshe, and then I realized it was not the same Moshe.

Five years ago I was in Sighet for one night, and in one of my tales I describe my return to that Sighet. While I was at the cemetery lighting candles, I heard someone behind me say *Kaddish*. I turned around and I saw a Jew, a magnificent-looking man, with a grey-white beard and *payes*, and melancholy blue eyes, the eyes of a sad child. He was dressed like a Hasid, in a gray-black kaftan. And he said *Kaddish*. And I said to him, "Who are you?" He said, "My name is Moshe."

Adapted from address, United Jewish Appeal, New York, December 14, 1972.

"What are you doing here?" He said, "I am a *shoihet*." I was so struck by that meeting that afterwards I wrote about it.

But I became convinced that this is one of the stories that is both true and not true, that I had invented Moshe. Now I realized I had not invented him. He was there. I spoke to him, and I decided to include him in my program. I shall tell you why.

We walked around Sighet together. And I came to my home, which I had not seen since I left it in 1944. It was a shattering experience, you can imagine. There are certain themes and certain experiences that make you change whether you want it or not, when you must reevaluate your relationship with the surrounding society, with man and with God and with yourself. This was one of these moments. I remember I entered our home. It was just as I had left it. The furniture: in the same place. The wallpaper: the same. The stove — I remember the discussions we had at home about buying the stove — it was there: the same. I was almost afraid that if I opened another door, the young child that I was would come out and greet me and say, "Stranger, what are you doing in my dream?"

What made me realize that I was not at home? A spot on the wall. When the Wizsnitzer Rebbe died in 1936, we received his photo. He was a beautiful man. I remember putting the nail in the wall and hanging the rebbe's picture on the wall. The nail was still in the same spot — with a crucifix on it. And when I saw it, I realized if there is no room for the Wizsnitzer Rebbe in my home, there is no room for me either. And I ran out of the room, out of my home, out of my childhood.

Moshe showed me the town. I asked, "How many *bet hamidrashim*, how many synagogues do you have here?" He said, "One." We used to have hundreds. It was a Jewish town. *Shabbes* was *Shabbes*. Even the non-Jews observed *Shabbes*. He showed me the only synagogue — of all things, the Reform synagogue. That was the first time I entered it, because as a boy I was too religious to enter it.

"Tell me, Moshe," I said, "I am going back to New York soon. There are fifty Jews left in Sighet out of 15,000. Maybe you need something, some help? I know some people, UJA, Joint. I can help you."

He said, "No, we do not need anything — except there is a hole in the ceiling of the *shul*. Please, do something so it should be repaired. Because after all — it is the last *shul* in Sighet, the last."

So I had an idea. I said, "Moshe, I'll call the crew and have them film me interviewing you. At one point I will ask you, 'Moshe, what is your greatest wish?' and you will tell me, 'I want the hole to be repaired.' I guarantee you that within twenty-four hours you will have a new ceiling."

He said, "What is television?"

Go and explain to a Hasidic Jew — the last Hasid in Rumania — what television is. I said, "Well, it's something that if you speak here, people in America will see you."

"Well, then it's a miracle."

"Yes, it is a miracle."

"Just like the rebbe's miracles."

"Yes, except the rebbe does not know how television works."

I did not know at the time that the president of the Jewish community was a Communist, and that he did not want to give Sighet a bad name. People would say that the Communist regime cannot even repair a hole in the ceiling and I did not know that he had threatened Moshe: "If you tell tomorrow that we have a hole, you will go to jail."

The day of the taping was very moving. We talked in Yiddish about Hasidism, Jews, rebbes we have known. We did not talk about the Holocaust — strange, really. The fifteen-man film crew, all non-Jews, did not understand a word we said, but they were filming and crying. From time to time my wife explained a few words to them. They felt something very important was going on there — the last Hasid. The last Hasid. And I asked him, "Tell me, Moshe, what are you doing here alone?"

"Well, you see, Israel needs young people, so I sent them my four sons, and they serve in the Tank Corps. My four sons need a mother — I sent them my wife. But I am old. What am I supposed to do in Israel? Israel does not need me. The Jews here need me."

"They need you?"

"Yes. I am a *shoihet*. There are still some Jews who eat only kosher. Three Jews in Sighet eat kosher, so I go from village to village, like the former *maggid*, and I bring them kosher meat. They need me."

"Moshe, if you had one wish, what would it be?" And I was convinced he would say, of course —

He looked at me and he said, "*Mashiah zol kumen* — the Messiah should come."

His answer was so unexpected that for a very long moment I could not ask a question. I was dumbfounded. I finally said, "Moshe, maybe you'll settle for something less?"

But he was stubborn, and he said, "No." At the end I said, "Moshe, you are a Wizsnitzer Hasid. I am a Wizsnitzer Hasid. If it had not been for the war we would not have met. Moshe, do you think we will see each other again?"

And then he broke down. He said, "Of course. I will — I must go to Israel. I want to see Jerusalem. I want to cry in Jerusalem. I want to sing there." He spoke with such fervor and such passion and with such pain that I could not help but ask him again. I said, "Moshe, now tell me the truth. Why didn't you go to Israel?"

And he said something which really brought tears to my eyes. He said, "Maybe I wasn't worthy of it."

Well, then I thought of all the Jews I know — Jews in America and France and Belgium and everywhere — who go to Israel whenever they feel like it. They are worthy, and this *tzaddik* is not?

Often I recall my conversation with Moshe, the last *shoihet*, the last Hasid in Sighet. In a way I see him as the last *maggid* of my childhood. Thus he is linked to the last *Shabbat* I spent in Sighet. I recall him so as to capture his fervor, his piety, his love for Jews and Jerusalem — for it is this fervor that makes Jerusalem what it is and *Shabbat* what it is.

THE PRICE OF COURAGE

I was in Israel during the Yom Kippur War, as I have been there during all the wars, except in 1956, when I was in the hospital. Never did I come back with such a heavy heart. Something happened on that *Yom Kippur*, something new, something unprecedented. Maybe it was the solitude. Maybe it was the surprise, maybe it was the inner weakness. I have never seen Israel as sad, as melancholy. Maybe it had to do with the blackout, but then there was a blackout in 1967 too. Maybe it had to do with the casualties, but there were casualties in 1967 too. I do not know.

Then the names began to appear. I read the stories. A woman lost her husband in 1967. Ten days later she gave birth to a son. She remarried. She lost her second husband now. And ten days later she gave birth to another son. I know cases of people who have lost two or three children. I know the case of a former army officer who was sent to the Sinai to inform his third son to come home because his two brothers had been killed. And when the father came back he was alone. I read of a *brit milah*, a circumcision, in which the child was named after his father.

Behind every story is another story of extraordinary heroism, of extraordinary courage. This war, as I was told in Israel, was a war of soldiers, of eighteen and nineteen-year-old youngsters, not of officers. And when the onslaught came, they tried to maintain the line of defense with their bodies. That is why the number of victims is so high: 1,850 and more.

When I arrived in Israel, I immediately went to Tel Hashomer, the military hospital. Before going to the front I wanted to see the suffering. Before seeing courage, I wanted to see the price of courage. I will never forget what I saw that day: hundreds of severely burned men. Not one of them moaned.

In each room the head medical doctor introduced me to the soldiers and officers. In one ward he took me to meet a young officer, blind, eyes bandaged, face burned — faceless. He asked the doctor if we could come closer. So I came closer. And he said, "I want you to know I am glad you came." For a moment I was afraid that under his burns was someone I knew. No, he was a stranger. I said, "Why?" He said, "Well, because I read some of your writings." I had tears in my eyes. I did not know what to say. Nor did he. So for a very long moment we were quiet. Then this faceless soldier wanted to say something else but couldn't. In the end all he could utter was the Hebrew sentence, "*Kol hakavod* — All honor to you." This remark is usually addressed to Israel's Defense Forces: "*Kol hakavod leZahal.* — All honor to the army." I felt like taking my head in my hands and weeping. He gave his face, he gave his sight, he gave his blood for Israel. All I gave were words, words — and *he* compliments *me* for coming? In that hospital I received the most precious compliment of my life.

Adapted from lecture, Congregation Kol Ami, Chicago, Illinois, November 22, 1973.

BRINGING THE MESSIAH

Madmen have always occupied me. Not madmen who kill but mystical madmen intoxicated by God. Rather than provoke solitude, they try to combat it. They are very beautiful madmen.

As a Jewish child in Europe I had two very close friends. We wanted to live so intensely that we would bring the Messiah. You must understand what the mystical theory proclaims: God is in exile, but every individual, if he strives hard enough, can redeem mankind and even God himself. The three of us were going to bring the Messiah, as simple as that.

After a couple of months, one of my friends went mad. And then a second. They wouldn't speak, couldn't speak. I think I know why: they were just terribly sad that they could not bring the Messiah. I am convinced I would have gone mad, too, if the Germans hadn't come to our little town.

Washington Star-News, May 7, 1974.

THE REPORTER

Don't ask me how I became a journalist. I don't know. I needed to do something, so I became a reporter and managed to fool everybody. I wrote about politics but understood nothing about politics. I still don't. I wrote about anything under the sun, because I had to, without understanding what I was writing. Somehow it was read, or not, but I had to go on.

What is a reporter? The definition of a reporter reminds me of a shoemaker in my hometown. He was named Haskall — Haskall the Schuster. We also had a good *hazzan* a good cantor, so I thought. So he thought. One *Shabbat*, it was *Shabbat Rosh Hodesh*, the *hazzan* came home and was very unhappy. His wife asked, "Why are you so unhappy?" He said, "Can you imagine? Today I felt it. I felt that I gave the best — the best I had. I have never prayed as I prayed today. I have never had a voice such as the one I had today. I felt the prayers. They went up straight to the Celestial Tribunal. I felt it. And then, imagine, when I left the synagogue, Haskall the Shoemaker approached me and said, '*Hazzan*, today you were not so good.' Can you imagine?" To comfort the unhappy *hazzan* his wife said, "Don't pay any attention to him. What does Haskall the Shoemaker know about music, about *hazzanut*? *Di gantze shtot redt, zogt er oych* — The whole town talks — so he just repeats."

Well, that's how I was a reporter. I reported — that is, I repeated what others told me.

Adapted from lecture, 92nd Street YMHA, November 3, 1977.

THE INTERVIEW

One day my editor in Israel — I worked for an Israeli paper — decided that since France had a Jewish prime minister who was a great man — Mendès-France brought peace to Vietnam — I had to interview him. I was ready, but he was not.

I sent letter after letter — but nothing doing. He gave no interviews. Mendès-France was known for two things then: one, he didn't drink wine, and in France not to drink wine, well, you must be a Jew not to drink wine. I am convinced that is part of the anti-Semitism...And the second, he didn't give interviews. But my editor wanted an interview. Every morning around six I used to get a telegram: "What about the interview?" And I would cable back: "I want, but he doesn't." Finally, the telegrams became a joke.

One day I wrote a letter to Mendès-France saying: "Mr. Prime Minister, please, you must give me an interview, because if not, one of two things will happen. Either I will be fired, or my paper, sending me so many telegrams, will go bankrupt."

And then he answered me with a handwritten letter, very beautiful, saying, "I cannot give you an interview, but should one of the two things happen, then call me and I'll give you a job." I did not get the interview.

But I published the letter.

Adapted from lecture, 92nd Street YMHA, November 3, 1977.

THE NEW LAW

A strange, beautiful legend in our Midrash says that ever since the Prophet Elijah ascended into heaven, all he does is go around the world as a chronicler, collecting tales of Jewish suffering. And when the Messiah will come, we are told, Elijah will give him his chronicles, his book of Jewish suffering, and that book will become the new *Sefer Torah*. That book will become the Torah, the New Law, the Messiah's Law. Thus the Messiah will remember our suffering.

I know few legends as beautiful and as poignant.

Not one tear should be wasted. Not one sigh should go astray. Nothing should be lost.

Adapted from lecture, Schara Tzedek Synagogue, Vancouver, B.C., May 6, 1978.

APPEARANCE AND REALITY

Recently, I met again with some close friends, and they said that my visits to their city — and everywhere else I go — must be like the visits of the *maggid*, the itinerant lecturer in Eastern Europe. I do not like to use the word "preacher" with respect to him. I am not a rabbi. Rabbis should preach. I do not. I like to teach, to share. It suddenly occurred to me that actually I like the idea of being a *maggid* because I used to like the *maggid* when I was a child. I always looked forward to his coming. It was always a special element in our life to hear this wonder tell stories from faraway countries, knowing that tomorrow he would be gone.

But as I thought about him I asked myself: Do I *look* like a *maggid*? Surely not. Anyone who comes from Eastern Europe will agree with me: I do not look like a *maggid*. A *maggid* looked like a *maggid*. He had a beard and *payot* and a hat and a kaftan. He looked the part. How can I be a *maggid*?

Then I remembered a story. In Jerusalem a certain professor of ethics had a very brilliant student. But the brilliant student was poor. So one day the professor said to him, "You know, you are brilliant, and I see now that you are going to need a lot of money because you have expensive tastes and you will need money to satisfy them. So I have an idea: Don't work. Marry a rich girl." The student was outraged. He said, "Professor, how can you say such a thing! How can you teach ethics and teach me to do such an unethical thing!" The professor listened to his student, and then he said to him, "It so happens that my colleague in the next room teaches mathematics. Does *he* look like a triangle?"

Well, perhaps one can fulfill the part of the *maggid* — and not look it.

Remarks, Congregation Am Shalom, Glencoe, Illinois, November 11, 1979.

THE STORY OF A STORY

When I was your age, my son, I heard this tale from my father, who heard it from an unknown beggar who had come into our village during a cold, winter night:

There once was a poor, unhappy man. Not knowing which way to turn in his sorrow, he sought advice from Rebbe Israel Baal Shem Tov. The rebbe welcomed him warmly and said, "Stay with me, at my side; look and listen and, above all, be silent."

Time passed slowly. Our hero, still poor, still unhappy, did not leave the master's side for many weeks, many months. From dawn to dusk, often late into the night — and even until dawn — he sat with the rebbe, listening to him speak in his wisdom, listening to those who confided in him, only listening.

One day, after the morning prayer, the master turned to him, smiled, and said, "Now you may leave. Start your journey today. You will go from village to village, from marketplace to marketplace, and everywhere you will tell and retell the tales you have learned here. They will bring you good fortune and happiness, you will see. Go."

Thus the hero of our tale became a teller of tales and nothing else. In every village he would recall the teachings of his master and spin breathtaking stories for the men and women — and children, of course, — who gathered around him to listen. They showed their gratitude by giving him a warm meal, some old clothes, or even, on rare occasions, a small coin. Thanks to him and his tales, their existence seemed less dreary and their future less gloomy. Thanks to him and his wondrous parables and anecdotes, his listeners came to believe that miracles were still possible, that men, women, and especially children can still dream strange and sunny dreams.

After many years the teller of tales arrived in a lost village. He walked immediately to the inn where, according to his custom, he went from table to table telling local people and visitors his most moving stories, hoping to earn a few coins, which he desperately needed. But his listeners were either misers or penniless. Or was it that they were deaf or drunk? Sadness came over our hero. He was hungry and thirsty, and his purse was empty. So in his heart he silently asked his master, "What shall I do, Rebbe? What am I to do? You promised me good fortune and happiness. What has become of your promise?" On the verge of tears, he barely heard the innkeeper say to him, "I have an idea for you. Our village lord is crazy. I mean he's crazy about stories. He pays money for stories: one piece of silver for a story he has heard only once, one golden coin for a story he has never heard."

In *Wonders: Writings and Drawings for the Child in Us All*, 1980.

[49]

Without wasting a second, our teller of tales ran to the palace and asked to be received. When the servant heard what his trade was, he immediately showed him into a room where the village lord was already waiting with food and drink on the table. "Please begin," said the village lord. Summoning all his talent, all his memories, our hero began. Unfortunately, his host knew all his stories. Our hero felt uneasy. He shut his eyes and implored his master to come to his aid. He remembered an old parable, another one, and yet another about sick people in need of recovery, lonely people in need of beauty — all for naught: the host knew them all. Drained by his efforts, the visitor felt too weary to rise and take leave. For a long time he remained seated, facing the village lord who grew impatient, even exasperated. Then, all of a sudden, in a sort of daze, the teller of tales recalled an incident he had long kept buried in his memory: Rebbe Israel was talking with a stranger in tears, comforting him, saying, "Do not be sad. You have made many mistakes and have committed many sins, but you will repent, will you not? You will do your part, and God will do His. He will forgive you, I promise you." The stranger whispered, "How will I know that I have been forgiven?" "It is simple," replied the illustrious wonder-rebbe. "One day someone will tell you this story; on that day you will know."

The teller of tales fell silent. Overwhelmed, the village lord burst into tears of gratitude and gave him one hundred gold coins. And from that day on they remained friends, bound by their common knowledge of the Baal Shem Tov.

The teller of tales continued to wander around the world and tell his stories — all but one, the most beautiful of all, which he kept for you, my son, for you alone.

THE FORGER

I have a special feeling for Rebbe Nahman of Bratzlav and his stories. The greatest tales in Hasidic literature are those of Rebbe Nahman. The greatest stories in Jewish literature are those of Rebbe Nahman. I would even say that the greatest stories in literature are those of Rebbe Nahman.

To this day, two hundred years after his death, the Hasidim of Rebbe Nahman believe he is still their rebbe. Thus other Hasidim call them "*di toite Hasidim* — the dead Hasidim" — because they believe in a rebbe who is dead. Why do they believe he is living? As he lay dying, his Hasidim began to cry. And he said, "Why are you crying? I am not leaving you." They took it literally — that he was not leaving them. And so to this day they speak about him in the present tense: "the Rebbe says," "the Rebbe writes," "the Rebbe hears." Rebbe Nahman also told them he would pull anyone out of hell who would come and spend time at his grave and say a chapter of Psalms. Therefore Bratzlaver Hasidim from all over the world go to Russia to say a chapter of Psalms at their rebbe's grave. They seek to do so even today.

Two weeks ago I received a telephone call in New York from the Bratzlaver Hasidim: "You must do something. Something terrible has happened to a Bratzlaver Hasid from Israel." What had happened? Since the Israelis cannot go to Russia, a Hasid of Bratzlav had borrowed an American passport from a friend, forged the passport, and gone to Russia to spend time at the grave of Rebbe Nahman.

Though the Bratzlaver Rebbe often accomplishes miracles, this time the Russians had arrested his Hasid and accused him of espionage. I told them I could not go to the White House and plead for somebody who had forged an American passport. But I did. What choice did I have? A Hasid was in trouble. Believe it or not, the Russians freed him.

I have nothing but admiration for the Bratzlaver Hasidim and the Bratzlaver Rebbe. But then, I am also a Hasid, though not of Bratzlav.

Adapted from lecture, Niles Township Jewish Congregation, Skokie, Illinois, December 7, 1980.

[51]

JEREMIAH'S LESSON

Jeremiah predicted the catastrophe; he lived through the catastrophe; he remembered the catastrophe; and he taught about the catastrophe. There are many legends about him in the Talmud and Midrash. One of them tells us that as the Temple was burning he went to Abraham, Isaac, Jacob, and Moses, to our common ancestors, and, waking them up, he said, "Do something! Do something! Speak to God! Move heaven and earth! Do something!" In other words, he wanted our past to protect us. They looked at him angrily and said: "Jeremiah, you were alive when all this was happening. Why didn't you prevent it?"

Adapted from address, first workshop meeting to establish United States Holocaust Memorial Museum, National Portrait Gallery, Washington, D.C., September 22, 1982.

MIAMI: DISTANT ECHOES

Having spent all of my youth in the shadows of the Carpathians, I am always drawn to mountains, for I love their silence and their dizzying mysteries.

They are not like the sea or, rather, like the seashore. A wretched tourist, I am not made for vacations. I do not swim, I do not play tennis, and I know nothing of golf. Sunbathing, endless conversations about tans and the weather and the price of rooms and hotel service, about low and high politics and the news of the day: all this holiday chatter, this forced restfulness and programmed, commercialized "happiness" is not for old-fashioned puritans like me.

And yet — do not laugh — I never leave for Miami without a certain keen pleasure. I manage to spend a *Shabbat* or Passover there, or give some Biblical or Talmudic or Hasidic lecture in some synagogue, or offer a course on literature and philosophy at some young and enterprising university. Why not admit it? They never have to beg; I accept invitations from Miami more readily than from other places.

The reason is that I have close friends there, one of them a childhood friend. We went to the same schools, we endured the same trials, until we were separated by war and lost touch. For many long years in Paris I knew nothing of what had become of him except that he lived in the United States and owned an ultra-Orthodox hotel.

Our reunion? It was in 1965. I had come to Miami for a weekend. Barely settled in my hotel, I began to feel ill. Could it be the horrible décor of my surroundings? I shook from fever, my head felt as if it would explode. How could I possibly deliver a lecture the next day? And where could I turn for help, since I knew no one?

Suddenly I recalled my friend the hotel owner — but how to find him? I riffled through the telephone book under "kosher hotels." Which one belonged to him? There were so many. I decided to dial at random, and in a stroke of luck I got him promptly on the line. I gave my name and he shouted, "What are you doing in a hotel for the idle rich?" I told him I was sick, that I needed a doctor. "Don't budge!" he said. "I know the personal physician of a great rebbe. I'll bring him right over."

I protested that I wasn't *that* sick, but fifteen minutes later they knocked at my door, the doctor performed a miracle, and so did my friend: he won me over to Miami.

I returned a few months later and stayed at his hotel, and now my family and I

The New York Times, Special Travel Section, October 9, 1983.

[53]

spend one winter week and a few days of spring there each year. My friend and I, isolated if not excluded from the present, often evoke the muffled world of our childhood, whose sounds and memories claw at us from far away, haunting us and driving us forward as well. We are back home, back in time, before the storm.

I have other friends there, too. One teaches at the university; another is a state senator; there are the parents of a girl who took my course in literature at Boston University. With them, we discuss modern art, the Côte d'Azur, Israel, and the Administration's Middle-Eastern policies.

But what about the other side of Miami? The rising violence? The fear? The crimes, assaults, racial riots? I am aware of all that, of course. Like everyone else, I am troubled, concerned. But my Miami friends are still there, and I still love to visit them.

Could I someday settle in Miami for good? Yes, without a doubt, if — if only Miami were surrounded by the shimmering crests of soaring mountains like those of my distant, innocent little city.

The Books: Genesis and Commentary

THE DEPORTATION

Night

In the beginning there was faith, a naive faith; and there was trust, a foolish trust; and there was an illusion, a terrible illusion.

We had faith in God, trust in man, and we were living an illusion. We made believe that a holy spark glowed in each one of us; that the image was mirrored in our eyes, and that it resided in our soul.

Alas, this was the source, if not the cause, of the misfortunes that befell us.

Opening of *Un di Velt Hot Geshvign*, 1956.

THE END AND THE BEGINNING

Night

After my father's death I stayed in Buchenwald for three more months — until the day of liberation, the eleventh of April, to be exact. I will not describe the last epoch of my camp life. It was not at all interesting, and certainly not a topic for literary writings. I simply became indifferent to everything and everyone.

They transferred me to the children's Block 66, where about six hundred children were quartered. I became one of them, unknown and forsaken. Two Sighet boys were my only friends: Irwin Forkash and Anshi Meisner. In the camp a lot of things were happening — people came and people disappeared — but nothing interested me.

Like a sleepwalker, I used to hang around the block day after day, and I dreamt only one dream: of eating. I was already an old man, combining the disaffection of *Kohelet* with the tragic reflections of Job. Famine ate my flesh and let my blood. I became a stone, a hard cold stone. For whom? For my father? My mother? For myself? My childish illusions? For my religious hopes? Maybe for all of them.

On April 5 the rhythm of history quickened, the terror-symphony was playing its last chords. We were coming close to the finale. About five o'clock in the afternoon, we stood in the middle of the block waiting for the SS to come and take the roll. He did not come. Such a thing had not happened since the construction of Buchenwald. We felt something was going to happen. Two hours later we knew. The camp commandant's order blared over the loudspeaker: All Jewish inmates to the roll call grounds. The end. Five minutes before twelve Hitler would fulfill his pledge. The American army was closing in. Buchenwald would be liberated. But would we live long enough to see the day of liberation?

The Jewish children of Block 66, I among them, started walking towards the roll call grounds. There was no way out. Gustav, the block supervisor, a Polish Jew, herded us with his stick. On the way, we met our camp-police who whispered to us: "Go back to the blocks. The Germans plan to shoot you. Go back to the blocks and don't move from there." So we ran back to the blocks and hid in boxes. Later we learned that the camp underground had decided not to forsake the Jewish inmates and to protect us from liquidation. That same evening we received papers identifying us as Christian children. We passed the night sleepless and afraid.

The following day the loudspeaker blared new orders: since all the Jews were

---

Final chapter of *Un di Velt Hot Geshvign*, 1956.

[58]

. hiding under Christian identities, a roll call would be held for all inmates. The camp commandant announced that the camp would be liquidated: each day ten blocks would be evacuated. From that day on they stopped giving us food. No bread, no coffee, no soup. The evacuation began. Thousands of inmates went out through the iron gate and died on their way. I did not even attempt to hide. I let myself get carried with the tide. I stood before the iron gate of the camp on the threshold of death innumerable times. But something always happened that brought us back to the camp. If I did not perish then, it must have been by some accident of Providence. Because of hunger, I even wanted to go to the gate where they distributed bread and marmalade.

By the tenth of April only about 20,000 people were left in the camp, a few hundred children, and the elite inmates. The Germans decided to evacuate all the inmates of Buchenwald by evening and blow up the camp.

As we stood on the vast roll call grounds in rows of five, waiting for the gate to open, suddenly an air raid alarm sounded. All gates were immediately shut. The air raid alarm lasted till evening. Since it was not normal procedure to evacuate inmates at night, they took us back to the blocks. The last transport was postponed till the following day, April eleventh. We were starving. For six days we had eaten nothing, nothing except grass and five or six old rotten potato peelings we had found on a garbage pile. At about ten o'clock the following day, the SS appeared in the small camp in front of Block 66. They began driving us, the last victims, to the gate.

Just then the underground opened fire against the SS. Armed men suddenly appeared in the camp. We heard the firing; grenades exploded. We children lay on the ground in our block and waited. We didn't believe we would be rescued, that we would at last be free. It was a short battle. At about twelve o'clock the shooting in the camp ended. The SS had fled and the underground took command of Buchenwald. At six o'clock in the evening the first American tank appeared. We were free.

Three days after liberation I fell terribly ill with food poisoning. I was taken to the hospital, and the doctors said I was lost. My condition deteriorated daily. For two weeks I hovered between life and death. One day, mustering all my strength, I managed to get up. I dragged myself over to the mirror that hung on the wall. I wanted to see myself. I had not looked in a mirror since leaving the ghetto. A skeleton gazed back at me, skin and bones. I saw a picture of myself after death. At this very moment the will to live awakened in me. Not knowing why, I raised my fist and broke the mirror, broke the image that dwelt there. I fainted. From that moment on my health improved. I stayed in bed a few more days, during which time I wrote the outline for *Night*.

But...

Now, ten years after Buchenwald, I see that the world forgets. Germany is a sovereign nation and its army has been resurrected from the dead. Ilse Koch, the mean, sadistic woman of Buchenwald, has children and is happy. War criminals walk around in the streets of Hamburg and Munich. The past is being wiped out, forgotten. Germans and anti-Semites say that the story of the six million martyrs is only a legend, and the naive world will probably believe them, if not today then tomorrow or the day after tomorrow.

I thought to myself: Perhaps it would be worthwhile to write a book from the notes I took in Buchenwald — not that I am so naive as to believe that this book will change the course of history or shock the conscience of mankind. A book doesn't have the power it used to have. Those who kept quiet yesterday will also keep quiet tomorrow.

Now ten years after Buchenwald, I often ask myself: Was it worth breaking the mirror? Was it worth it?

And the world was silent.

THE CALL TO LIFE

Night

To forget is to go mad, to die, to give up faith in language, in art, in man, in the past, in all that links man to his world, to his past, and to others. To write, therefore, is not to forget: it is to call people not only to remember but to affirm their faith in themselves and their future.

I wrote *Night* in 1955, ten years after the war ended. I waited ten years in order to be sure that what I wrote would be the truth.

I was afraid of words. Words had been degraded. Words had been betrayed. There had been a kind of aggression against the word itself during the war. And I was afraid of becoming an accomplice, retroactively. Ten years of silence led me to the belief that what I said perhaps did have some link to the event itself.

We called him Moshe the Beadle. I remember he was small, shy, intimidated — afraid of his own shadow, afraid of the image he gave of himself.

He was a beadle in a Hasidic synagogue where I would come to pray and study, and to weep at night over the destruction of the Temple.

In 1942 he was deported to Galicia, along with many Jews in our town who were called stateless. I was too young to understand what it meant to be deported. I only remember that one *Shabbat* the whole town accompanied him, his friends, and his family to the railway station, and we all brought food. All the food that we could gather we brought to him and to his friends.

They left. Several weeks later he came back, and we did not recognize him. He was not the same person. He had gone mad, literally mad; he would run in the streets, awaken people, and tell them, "I want you to know that what I have seen no human being is allowed to see or to experience. I want you to know that after we left Sighet we were deported to Galicia, to a forest, and there German soldiers and officers took men, women, and children and brought them to a mass grave and began shooting. And men and women and children, people that I know, people that I knew, people that I loved, people that liked me, are no longer alive."

He was telling tales, and we refused to believe. He was telling tales of horror, not tales of survival. And we refused to believe.

He gave us descriptions, he gave us names, facts, and figures. And we refused to believe.

One day he stopped talking. For two years he was silent — and in his silence

Adapted from *The Eternal Light*, May 24, 1970.

[61]

became my teacher — until the Germans occupied Sighet, and then he too disappeared, together with all the others.

Sometimes today when I write, I wonder whether it is not he who is writing in my place, whether the voice which I think is mine is really his. Perhaps it is his, the tales are his tales, and what he has seen I have seen, and now I try to make you see.

One year later, one year after we all left Sighet, we were in Auschwitz. Many people who had left with me were no longer alive. Moshe was no longer alive. My teachers, my friends were no longer alive. The only one who was still alive was my father.

What does a storyteller say to the people that haunt him today across ages and centuries, places and continents?

I hear the violin of my friend Juliek play today. I hear the voices of my friends today. And the voices of my friends and the voice of the violin become one. And I no longer know who I am.

Who am I? The hero of my tales? The voice of that hero? Who am I?

A SIMPLE DIALOGUE

The Gates of the Forest

The fourth chapter of *The Gates of the Forest* is about Brooklyn, the *Farbrengen*, and my idealized image of a Hasidic rebbe, the Lubavitcher Rebbe. I describe how we met, how I came to the first *Farbrengen*. I describe our first conversation, which lasted hours. At one point I asked him point blank, "Rebbe, how can you believe in *Hashem* after the *Khourban*?" He looked at me and said, "And how can you not believe after the *Khourban*?" Well, that was a turning point in my writing, that simple dialogue.

Excerpt from statement marking thirty years of Rebbe Menahem Schneerson's leadership of Lubavitch movement, New York, January 28, 1980.

THE SONG OF RUSSIAN JEWRY

The Jews of Silence

The Jews of Silence was misinterpreted and misunderstood. Many people believed that I spoke of persecutions and fear. Many people believed that I tried to transmit the suffering of the Jews in Russia.

It is true; I tried to do exactly that. I tried to describe the fear of the Jew in Kiev. I tried to describe the solitude of the Jew in Tashkent, in Tiflis, in Leningrad. I tried to describe the strange, joyful despair of the old Hasidim in Leningrad. But mainly I attempted to bring back a message of fervor or, as we call it, *hitlahavut*.

I tried to show that despite all persecutions and fear, despite fifty years of dictatorship, despite fifty years of anti-Jewish laws, despite fifty years of ignorance of anything Jewish, a Jew in Russia still has hope.

In spite of everything, the young Jew in Russia remains Jewish, wants to remain Jewish, and brings forth a song, a Jewish song: a song of faith in Jewish immortality. I tried to describe the fervor and the ecstasy of the young Jewish people, Communists or not, on *Simhat Torah* in Moscow. And if ever I shall try to claim some *zekhut*, some privilege, either in literature or in history, it will be because of the few lines I brought back, telling the world that the young Jews in Russia sing, although they do not know yet what their singing means.

Adapted from *The Eternal Light*, June 7, 1970.

THE TALE OF THE TALE

Legends of Our Time

In *The Town Beyond the Wall* I described the return before it took place.

Why did I go back? I do not really know. I cannot say — maybe because the element of return is so important in my life and in Judaism.

The concept of the Fall is not a part of the Jewish tradition; it is a Christian concept. The concept of the Return prevails in our tradition. We go back to the beginning, to *Bereshit*. We go back to the first light, the first truth. We go back to the source. There is no Fall, only a profound and moving nostalgia for that beginning. This longing for a link to the past, to the first longing, to the first vision, to the first desire, to the innocence of that desire, exists, I think, in all literature, but especially in the literature of my generation, a generation with a keen sense of loss — loss of the past, loss of faith, loss of trust.

I always had a strange feeling about my return. Yes, I did return to Sighet once; still, I do not believe it. I often have the feeling that the whole episode was part of a joke.

The hotel night clerk asked me my family name. I gave another name. Then he asked about my birthplace. I said: Sighet.

He looked up: "Sighet? What are you doing here then? Why do you come to the hotel?"

His question made me understand the ludicrous aspect of the tragedy, which is the tragedy of our generation. We came back to places that were ours and felt like strangers, aliens, and we still do.

I went back to the street, which was my street. Everything was there. I went back to the home that used to be the home of my parents, my home. It was there. I opened the gate and heard a strange little squeak, so familiar. I entered the courtyard. I went up on the porch. I looked into the rooms through the windows. They had not even bothered to change the furniture. I became afraid, afraid that the door might open and a little *yeshivah* boy with side curls resembling me would come out and ask me innocently, "Tell me, stranger, what are you doing here? What are you doing in my dreams and in my childhood?"

I was so afraid of being judged by that child, I was so afraid of shattering the dream and killing the child once again that I did not dare go in. I retreated and began running, running away from the street, from the town, from all the places that once were ours, away from the cemeteries. I ran so much that I reentered my own tale, and this is the tale of the tale itself.

Adapted from *The Eternal Light*, May 31, 1970.

[65]

MORDECAI SHOSHANI

Legends of Our Time

"The Wandering Jew," in *Legends of Our Time*, is a true story. This man was my teacher for three years. And whatever I know now I owe to him.

In *One Generation After* I give his real name, or at least the one that I thought was his real name, because he died last year in Uruguay, in Montevideo. And in *One Generation After* I speak of his death; I speak of manuscripts that I found afterwards and of the mystery surrounding even his afterlife.

But now, in this tale, he hasn't died yet. Will he ever?

He usually came in the morning and we stayed sometimes five hours, sometimes a whole day. And we learned everything. Whatever I learned in class at the Sorbonne, I learned first with him. Whatever I write now — the words are mine, the spirit is his. Whatever I try to communicate — the melody is his. And sometimes even the voice or, at least, the rhythm is his.

Three years he was my teacher, and then one day he disappeared because I became too personal. I simply wanted to know: What is your real name? Where do you really come from? Where are you going? Who are you?

He was so annoyed that he almost slapped my face. He left, and I did not see him again. For a couple of months I looked for him all over town, even in the hospitals, and even in prison. I could not find him.

Later I learned that he went to Israel. I also went to Israel. Somehow we were together in Israel in 1948, but we did not know about each other.

Then I learned that he was in Uruguay. I wrote him a letter saying I needed him to be my teacher again, that I was ready to get a few friends together and pay his way to New York. We would pay for everything, if only he would come and teach us.

And he answered me. He said, "I lost too many millions of dollars in New York. If you want to learn come to Uruguay. I'll pay you for the trip."

I have letters from him; I have memories of him. I have his voice in mind. Last year I received a letter in an indirect way. He died on a Friday afternoon while giving a course in the Talmud, a half hour before the *Shabbat*, and in his pocket they found a story I had written about him.

Adapted from *The Eternal Light*, February 21, 1971.

[66]

LETTER TO THE PUBLISHER

A Beggar in Jerusalem

I remember: I was preparing myself to work on a novel set in the nineteenth century. Then came the Six-Day War and I had to put everything aside. I went to Jerusalem because I had to go somewhere, I had to leave the present and bring it back to the past. You see, the man who came to Jerusalem then came as a beggar, a madman, not believing his eyes and ears, and, above all, his memory.

This tale aims to be all-encompassing, on all levels. It tries to show what cannot be shown (the Holocaust), to explain what is not to be explained (the weight of history on dreams and dreamers), to recapture an experience that cannot be relived.

What else can I say about my tale? What else is there to say? A novel, as you very well know, is not to be explained; it is to be read. If there is a secret in it, it must be communicated as such. And I hope the *Beggar* does.

If I were to qualify this tale, I would say perhaps: this is neither novel nor anti-novel, neither fiction nor autobiography, neither poem nor prose — it is all this together. It is an adventure of one madman who one night saw not the end of all things but their beginning.

Printed on book jacket, 1968.

THE MADMEN OF SIGHET

A Beggar in Jerusalem

This story is about madmen. I tell it because I like stories and because I like madmen. Besides, the story takes place in Sighet, the town where I was born — and that, won't you agree, is reason enough. To be truthful, I should say that I had thought there was nothing left for me in Sighet. But I was wrong. Banished once from its borders, I find my roots there are struck deeply still; the greater the distance I place between myself and Sighet, the more profoundly do I find myself entwined. I know this seems incomprehensible, but I shrink from comprehending it.

Twenty years after having left Sighet, I returned for a single day, for a solitary glance, without knowing exactly what I was looking for; I still don't know, but I fear to attain such knowledge. Perhaps I was drawn there by the child that I had been — the child I left behind as a kind of pledge, as a watchman. Until my return I had no way of knowing that madmen had got hold of that child, that, like Sighet itself, he had become their prisoner.

The fact that I now come back to Sighet again, though all unwillingly, may be taken as further evidence that I belong to a generation which is concerned more with the past than with the future. For us, that which will be has already been. The Messiah has been and gone, slipping fearfully away from the house in flames, and dispersing the night behind him. Now, starved for recollection, the ageless elders of the town stir their memory to relive one hour of their old nocturnal life, that hour when the hands of the clock point forever to midnight. In my own memory, a child awaits me, but I am afraid to follow him, for I know that of the two of us one has died. Yet I know, too, that he and he alone can lead me to his masters, to those men, sunk in gloomy bereavement, who sit at the crossroads, silent and invisible, judging the passerby.

Three years ago I wrote about my return to Sighet. With the exception of my encounter with the madmen — an omission at once unexplained and inexplicable — I told the story then in its entirety, and it seems to me that I did not forget any details. I described how unreal it was to me, wandering about in my old neighborhood; how I found my way into my childhood, to my home; how by the porch, in the courtyard, a dog howled as if to chase away returning spirits. I walked for

These seven paragraphs, a kind of prologue to the story of the madmen at the beginning of Chapter 2 of *A Beggar in Jerusalem*, were originally published in *Commentary* in May, 1968. They vary significantly from the initial paragraphs actually used in Chapter 2 of the 1970 American edition of the novel.

hours from street to street, from memory to memory; I wished someone would finally come to wake me, to ask me what it was I wanted to do, and with whom and for how long. No one recognized me, and I didn't recognize anyone.

As I wrote, I also recalled my surprise at not finding the old synagogue that used to stand in the narrow street close to the town square. In other years, that synagogue had caused the hearts of the superstitious, old and young alike, to quake in fear. They used to say then that after midnight the dead would gather in the synagogue to pray. But the synagogue was set aflame by the Germans; it became an unseen temple of fire, and so I missed it. Had it still been standing, it would have revived in me that fear for which I hungered, as a field at night hungers for dew.

Also I told about my impressions of the cemetery, which once in my childhood I had been forbidden to visit. Now its great black gate lay open before me. The watchmen had gone elsewhere to die; their grave lay somewhere in heaven, and their names were inscribed on the name of God.

Not a word did I leave out of my account, except for my visit with the three madmen, in the insane asylum. These madmen were the last survivors of a community that had disappeared, the only ones to have escaped deportation. Everywhere else the insane had been made to leave in the first convoys; it seems that the Germans, perhaps afraid of them more than of the others, took care to get rid of them first.

And even in Sighet, our free and independent madmen — like Moshe the Cantor, Shmukler the Prince, Lazar the Fat, along with some other God-intoxicated dreamers — were placed at the very head of the convoy, to serve as trailer-blazers for the rest of the condemned. But those who had been already institutionalized remained miraculously untouched. I decided to visit them. . .

ENCOUNTER WITH JERUSALEM

A Beggar in Jerusalem

On the surface, *A Beggar in Jerusalem* deals with the Six-Day War. But it deals with more than the war. I intended it to be a tale encompassing all my other tales. I wanted it to be the sum total of all my characters, of all the visions they had, of all the anxieties I had inherited from them. I wanted it to be a meeting point for all the tales I had heard from my masters and my friends, and they in turn from theirs.

I brought it to Jerusalem so that Jerusalem could become the framework, the scenery for the tale to unfold.

Why a beggar and why Jerusalem?

Jerusalem, because in my life — in the life of the Jewish child that still haunts me — Jerusalem played an important role even before I was there. I think I learned to pronounce the word Jerusalem — *Yerushalayim* — before I could pronounce the name of the town in which I was born.

The first time I came to Jerusalem, the Old City of Jerusalem, I felt I had never been there before, that I had not yet arrived there — but also that I had never left it.

Literature to me is nothing if not an encounter, and words are nothing if not bridges and links. Jerusalem is the place of encounter for all the generations that have molded mine. To be a Jew is to accept Jerusalem as the center of one's life. To be a Jewish writer is to tell the tale of that encounter and to accept all the tales that have preceded the one he tells.

Therefore, in *A Beggar in Jerusalem* all the characters from my previous novels, invented, imagined, or real, will be allowed to enter. But why a beggar? Because I like beggars. They belong to the landscape of my youth. Already in *Dawn*, my second book, I described the influences the beggars had on me, that they taught me how to differentiate between night and day, between silence and language, between purity and what passes for purity. The beggars: I remember them, I try to, and I hope I shall never forget them.

For some reason — it is very strange — the Jewish people has the extraordinary capacity to reconstruct its destiny and even its framework upon ruins. We have done this for two thousand years. The Jewish people has reconstructed its past in America and in Israel, even in a few parts of Western Europe. Once more we have *yeshivot*, with rabbis and students, even Hasidic rabbis and Hasidim. We even have mystics and mystical scholars. We have children and parents. But we do not have beggars, at least not beggars such as I knew in my childhood.

Adapted from *The Eternal Light*, June 14, 1970.

The beggars of my childhood are gone, completely gone. They have disappeared from the Jewish stage. They have vanished nameless, rootless, faceless, tombless. There are no more beggars.

On the other hand, we are all beggars. Therefore, I brought the beggars into my tale, and I made them follow me to Jerusalem. Let my tale be a roof over their heads. Let my tale be a kind of refuge for them, a haven. Let my tale be their tale.

In *A Beggar in Jerusalem* I describe the way they arrived. I describe what happened, and I try to describe what happened before.

There is a prince among my beggars. Why a prince? Because to the poor children in Eastern Europe every beggar was a prince in disguise. We saw the Messiah as a beggar. Every beggar might have been the Prophet Elijah. Every beggar represented to us a mystical kingdom brought to us through the power of words and silence and song and dream. We owed so much to these princes that sometimes we would simply make them speak on our behalf, and we would then become their characters. We would become their dreams.

But the culmination point of the book and of the meeting of the beggars is in Jerusalem on the day the Old City was liberated. I remember it clearly, and I have tried to describe it. It was a strange moment, vital for our history, and necessary, vibrant for the storyteller, Jewish or not.

I was there the day after the Old City was liberated. I saw so many people come and hug the Wall, kiss it, and cry that I felt the privilege of being alive during a historic or perhaps a trans-historic event. I felt that those Jews came to the Wall as beggars and as princes, that they belonged not only to our generation but to many centuries, that they had all helped our people win the war and survive — and helped keep the victory human, meaning pure of injustices, pure of vengeance. I had a fleeting sense of triumph that the victory had remained human and therefore Jewish.

I remember I was standing next to the Wall, and I felt: This is it, what I see now I see not only for myself but for many other people, the witness must assume his responsibility and speak. And I remember that I heard then the words I was to write later. What I did later was nothing but transcribe them. . . .

THE ADVENTURE OF JERUSALEM

A Beggar in Jerusalem

Recently, the United Nations held a debate on Jerusalem. It went on for days. Everybody opposed Israel, even America. I must say that I did not understand what they wanted of us. You would have thought that everything in the world is perfect — that there is no more poverty, that all the little wars and all the big wars have ended, and that the only thing disturbing the world's peace, necessitating a Security Council meeting, was Jerusalem. Why do we bother them so much? I think I know why.

Actually we are not the only ones who have a stake in Jerusalem. Christianity has its holy places in Jerusalem, and Islam as well. I understand why the Christians and the Moslems want Jerusalem so much. After all, one has a history of eighteen hundred years and the other of fourteen hundred years — and what is the difference between three thousand years and eighteen hundred years? Moreover, they have proven that they really love Jerusalem. Have they not waged wars to get Jerusalem? True, Christians love Jerusalem. True, Moslems love Jerusalem. Some died for Jerusalem. But some killed for Jerusalem. Christianity has armed itself eight times in eight bloody Crusades to get Jerusalem. So why shouldn't the Christians get it?

They should not get it because they armed themselves eight times in eight bloody Crusades to get it. The Jews loved Jerusalem. We cried for Jerusalem. Sometimes we died for Jerusalem. But we never killed for Jerusalem. And that is what makes our link to Jerusalem so specific and so beautiful.

It will be said that in 1967 we did kill. I say "we" advisedly, for whatever Israel did, Israel did in my name. Whatever any Jewish community does in the world it does in my name. To me that is the Jewish condition. However, in 1967 Israel did not want Jerusalem. Talk to anyone in Israel who knows, and he will tell you: the plans of 1967 did not include Jerusalem. The war was only being fought in the Sinai against Egypt, not against Jordan. Eshkol sent two letters to Hussein pleading with him not to enter the war. We did not want to kill for Jerusalem. I am always very moved by this refusal to kill, this refusal to join the hangman, this refusal to become an accomplice of violence and cruelty and inhumanity.

I wrote *A Beggar in Jerusalem* in 1967. I called it "A Beggar," first, because we were all beggars. We came to Jerusalem then as we came to the world — with open hands, pleading for one gesture of generosity or of consolation. The Jewish

Lecture, Temple Sinai, Hollywood, Florida, February 28, 1972.

people then were alone. The solitude of the Jewish people then had no parallel except for the Holocaust. And it had all the implications of the Holocaust. Once again men spoke openly of destroying a Jewish community. And once again everybody kept silent.

I used to sit in the United Nations listening to the Arab leaders openly promising, threatening: this is going to be the final war. I remember thinking the fight is reopening. It will be the same story as the Warsaw Ghetto. This time we will fight — but we will lose. And — who knows? — perhaps this is the end of the Jewish people. I thought the hell with it and with the entire world.

I remember I took a plane in New York the day after the war began. It was hard to get a seat on the plane because every young Jew then wanted to go to Israel. In Paris I switched from TWA to El Al and caught the last El Al plane going to Israel. As I came aboard and took the last seat near the door, the hostess, a very pretty, young Israeli girl, smiled and said, "I know who you are." Usually, when someone says she knows who I am, I blush with embarrassment. Once in Paris, while I was in a bookstore, someone came in asking for my book, and knowing that it had a picture on the back, I fled as though I were a thief. I was frightened she might see me. But now it was during the war, and she was pretty, and I was tired, so I didn't say anything. She came by every five minutes with cognac and coffee and fruit, and I thought these are the messianic days: if a Jewish writer, not a Jewish millionaire, gets such treatment on El Al, that means either the Messiah has come or he should come. And I enjoyed the whole affair.

At one point she came up to me and said, "You know, your book had such an effect on me. I read it and reread it." Usually, when someone says that, I simply say, "Which book?" — at which point the person is embarrassed. But I was not nasty in the airplane. So, when the stewardess said she had read my book, I said, "Thank you." And then again cognac. It was beautiful. But then she came and said, "You know, I must confess there is one passage in the first part of your book which I do not understand, and, please, I hope you will explain it to me. You see, Mr. Schwarz-Bart. . ."

Regaining my modesty I said, "I am terribly sorry, but I am not André Schwarz-Bart. I did not write *The Last of the Just.*" She said, "Come on." I said, "Please. I did not write *The Last of the Just!*" She said, "Really, I know everything about you. I know you are modest. I know you are shy and want to go *incognito.* All right. I won't tell anybody. But to me — ?"

So I said, "Listen, I know why you make that mistake. Number one, I am also a writer. Number two, I am also Jewish. Number three, I also write in French. Number four, we have the same themes — the Holocaust, Jewishness. Number five, we have the same publisher in Paris. Number six, we have the same publisher in New York. Number seven, we are very close friends. Number eight, there is even a physical resemblance, which even my wife admitted to when she met André Schwarz-Bart. Number nine, we resemble each other so much that either in New York or in Paris the publisher inadvertently published his picture on my book, or the other way around." So she said to me, "You know, Mr. Schwarz-Bart, you are my hero, and therefore I think I know everything about you. I have read everything about you. What I did not know is that you have a sense of humor."

So I gave up and went on enjoying the cognac and the coffee and the fruit. Five minutes before landing — we already had our seat belts fastened — she came back and she looked vicious. She said, "Listen, I don't know who you are." And I said, "At last — " "But one thing is clear. You are not André Schwarz-Bart." Very weakly I said, "Prove it." And she said, "Because André Schwarz-Bart is over there."

He sat three seats in front of me! I unfastened my seat belt and jumped up to embrace him. I said, "What are you doing here?" And he said, "What are you doing here?" We were so confused we almost became characters in our own novels.

Actually we had come to be witnesses. A Jew is a witness, not a bystander. A Jew is a participant as a witness. When you see an event, you must be part of it. And when something is being done on your behalf, in your name, you *must* become a participant or at least a witness, and a real witness is a participant. We came there with our hands outstretched like beggars, asking to be taken in, to be part of the experience, one of the greatest, most exuberant experiences that can be given to a Jew living today.

Both he and I knew that to be a Jew is to be aware that the great adventure of Judaism is one of the most stimulating and gratifying adventures that can be given to man. I myself cannot choose myself, naturally: I was born a Jew. But I can make that choice retroactively, and I make it every day, accepting the consequences. Otherwise the whole tale, as one non-Jew said, is nothing but a tale of fury told by a fool.

I called my novel *A Beggar in Jerusalem* for another reason. When the Nazis destroyed the *shtetl* they also destroyed the beggar. We called him the *bettler*, the *schnorer*. I remember those beggars, with their sticks and their bags on their shoulders, walking from town to town, telling stories. They were the real storytellers. What I learned from them, I did not learn at the Sorbonne. And because they were taken away from us, I decided to bring them back, to give them a haven in my tale.

So we were all beggars at the *Kotel Hamaaravi*, at the Wall. In the book I describe what happened in Jerusalem, what happened in Israel, and what happened in the entire Jewish world — how for one moment everything stood still and all Jewish history began marching . . . marching . . . running . . . running toward the Wall, toward the beginning, how every single Jew from the very beginning, from Abraham on, all of them, came to participate in that scene and be witnesses and actors on the spot, witnesses and actors in the adventure of Jerusalem.

LETTER TO JAMES H. SILBERMAN

One Generation After

Mr. James H. Silberman
Random House
New York, N.Y.

Dear Jim:

One Generation After — after the Holocaust — is my tenth volume. You asked me why I wrote it. Well, I wrote it — I think — in order to explain — to myself perhaps — why the others were written. You may say it is my way of taking stock.

And also of moving away from an area and an era that until now have been central to my entire work. In other words: this is my last book dealing directly with Auschwitz and its dark kingdom. From now on I shall write other things — or perhaps the same things in different disguises. Hasidic masters, mystical wanderers talking to each other or to themselves, children caught up in Messianic fire and perilous dreams: the Holocaust will remain present — present, say, by its very absence.

Why this decision? It has to do with certain strange guilt-feelings we, the storytellers of the recent past, carry inside us because of our writings.

Some of us are convinced we have committed a sin: we revealed secrets to the non-initiated. Others fear they have distorted their own truth and that the real tale has not been transmitted — and never will be. Where we sense mystery, the new generation sees banality. The event which marked us has become anecdote. Just listen to young radicals comparing Treblinka to Harlem, the Warsaw ghetto to Watts, and you will understand what I mean. Just read your daily paper. And compare it to yesterday's. Whoever said that words can change History?

Strange: had it not been for the survivors' overwhelming urge to one day communicate to outsiders what they were seeing and enduring, many would not have survived. What kept them alive was the conviction that the tale must be told, thus imposing a meaning upon suffering and agony which had none.

Their efforts have resulted in near-failure. Would you have thought twenty-five years ago that Jews will once again — so soon — be persecuted in Poland? That anti-Semitism will once again be respectable — if not fashionable — in so many quarters, liberal and otherwise? And would you have thought that, in the same

April 3, 1970. Letters from Elie Wiesel to James H. Silberman appear here in their original form.

period, the resigned or defiant victims of yesterday would astonish the world with their military achievements? And that in Russia, fifty years after the Communist revolution, young Jews by the thousands would suddenly emerge and claim kinship with their past and their people? Dangers, wonders, metamorphoses on all levels: that was the generation that was.

Of them I speak in the present book. Call it diary, collection of short stories, essays, dialogues, and quasi-polemic texts: As usual, my writings tend to defy qualification. Because they deal with themes and obsessions which, by their very essence, negate existing categories in history as well as in literature: whoever writes about Auschwitz — does *not* write about Auschwitz.

Together with other "witnesses," I thought I had captured some of the echoes and flames from *over there*. Today I wonder whether that was not an illusion after all. So, the things I have said in the past I say again — for the last time. The mosaic will close from within. With the gates shut, the Dialogues will not be reopened.

So, Jim, here is the book — another glance into the night, perhaps the last.

While I look back to the beginning, I make various stops and try to remember, or simply to reevaluate, certain thoughts and episodes of twenty-five years: the return to a Jewish-less Jewish town, the burial of a gift, my first attempts to bring life to words and weight to silence, my attitudes to complex problems such as Germany, Russia, and Israel's new image, my feelings towards modern-day radical rebels; it is a personal, non-objective viewpoint on both topical and timeless issues. Hence the mixture of styles and tones, accents and approaches; what joins them is Auschwitz. Auschwitz explains; yet Auschwitz will never be explained.

Imagine my beggar doubting whether his testimony was given or received at all, and you will see that this book is the tale of his doubts, which make him waver between despair and fervor. His arguments? In New Mexico, a local priest — highly intelligent and sincere — told him: "Know that we are all *bored* by books about the Holocaust." In France, a member of Parliament published an open plea to the Jews to "stop peddling their suffering." See, Jim? People are not ready to listen, let alone understand. Yesterday's silence is followed by today's forgetfulness. The Holocaust will forever symbolize failure. Then why bother? Let the past bury the present.

So let us turn the page. Naturally when you turn pages, you hear a sound, and that is the sound — a murmur, a quiet sigh — which I hope you will find in these pages.

Be well, as ever:
Elie Wiesel

LETTER TO JAMES H. SILBERMAN

Souls on Fire

Dear Jim:

Since both of us like traditions — at least those established by us and by mutual consent — I think I ought to tell you about my forthcoming volume before you talk about it to others. To break a tradition is more than a sin; it is a loss, a waste. So, listen.

First, may I repeat what I have told you — and what every other author probably tells you about *his* forthcoming book — that *Souls on Fire* is something special to me.

Not only because it is the result of four years of research, work, and public lectures; not only because the subject is at the same time topical and timeless; not only because the protagonists are — what our youngsters would call — beautiful men, but also because the book relates to my own childhood even more than my novels and my autobiographical narratives.

The world of Hasidism, Jim, is the world of my childhood, and perhaps of my innocence lost.

But — what *is* Hasidism? I talked about it in all of my ten books. *En passant.* I invoked some Masters and repeated some of their tales in order to illustrate some of my own writings; they came to my aid now, just as they did in my childhood. Whenever a passage in a novel needed intensity, depth, and some other dimension, I drew on my Hasidic experience; and suddenly the story turned into tale.

Now, for the first time, I have attempted to do the opposite: Hasidism became the main theme, with my other works only as settings.

Hasidism, thus, survived Hitler, although most of the Hasidim perished under him. The killers managed to exterminate the Hasidim (they were the first victims) but somehow proved powerless against the Hasidic idea. Anyone will tell you: Hasidism has become popular, especially among the youth, more than ever before.

Why?

Perhaps because Hasidism, the apotheosis of humanism in modern history, stresses the importance and the sacredness of man and what makes him human. In a society in which machines dominate the scene, it is only normal that young men and women, in their helplessness, are fascinated by those Masters who tell them

April 14, 1971.

[77]

that it should not be so, that the mystery of the universe is man, and that he is the key to that mystery.

There is also a more socio-philosophical reason to it: our times are, in more than one way, similar to those of Rabbi Israel Baal Shem Tov who had, at the beginning of the eighteenth century, somewhere in the Carpathian mountains, gathered dispersed sparks and turned them into fire through joy, fervor and song. He was the founder of the movement.

Just as then, our people had to start again building upon ruins and unite surviving individuals and decimated communities. Just as then, man is looking for something — or somebody — to hold on to, so as not to give in to despair. Just as then, reason has failed, and so has everything else — everybody else. Hasidism was founded — or dreamed? — after numerous deadly pogroms. As an antidote.

Who doesn't need such an antidote today? There are so many reasons to despair: you remember the past and your eyes die in the flames. You think of the future, and you lose any desire to bring another life into this mad and cursed world.

But here comes Hasidism and its message: although night surrounds you, it is up to man to lift himself up to the stars and sing about what you left and what you found. It is up to man to sing, though or because there is no reason to sing. It is difficult? So what. Because it is difficult you *must* do it. It is impossible to go on believing? Because it is so, you must do so. You see, Jim? Hasidism offers something — not an answer, nor a solution: perhaps a tale — to all our nihilists, anarchists, hippies, dropouts, radicals of all sorts who simply feel they cannot go on living in this world, doomed by its own guilt and ugly indifference.

Another reason: Hasidism stresses the element of beauty in Judaism, in the largest — and purest — sense of the word. It teaches us that Judaism is not only religion, not only philosophy, not only ethical principles, but also a work of art: it contains beauty. And you know as much as I do to what extent our society lacks beauty.

But — the most important aspect of Hasidism is the following: its teachings are transmitted not in abstract formulas, nor in rigid systems, but in tales — in legends.

And they are, believe the critic in me, Jim, they are of extraordinary beauty, even from the sheer literary point of view. They are short, concise, naive: you read them with a smile, with a sense of elevation.

And that is how I wrote them. That is how I rewrote them three times. Why three times? First — because, as you already know, I always do three drafts of each of my books. Second — because I simply enjoyed my writing them. Each time I discovered something new — something more subtle — in each tale, and even more so in each master.

For, as you will see, the volume — which includes some of my "Y" lectures — is a weird combination of portraits and legends. In other words: I offer a number of Hasidic masters as portraits shown through their tales. As a result: open any page — and you can read it. No need to *know* what preceded it and what followed it. Each tale stands on its own. Yet — all combined make up a man, a life; a destiny.

The portraits include the First Great Masters: from the Baal Shem to Rabbi Nahman. The transition chapters are made up of their companions and disciples. And — needless to say that I try to show not only their relevance to contemporary experiences, but also their effect on me and my own writing. To me, they are all alive; I hear their stories, and do my best to transmit them.

I must admit: mine is not the first attempt in this direction. Martin Buber has made it years ago. *Entre nous*: I do not like what he has done. He spoke as an outsider for outsiders, whereas — well, you know what I mean.

Anyway: in this — first — volume, I try to show who they were and what they tried to achieve. I tell of their adventures, their secrets, their trials — and of their strange powers, of their charisma too.

And all this, I feel I must insist on this, I try to show in their tales, which, after all, are a bridge between then and now, between what has been and what will never be — between the joy of then and the anxiety of today.

One last remark: why "Souls on fire"? Because theirs were on fire? Yes. But even more so because they possessed the rare ability of inspiring others and giving them more than excitement, more than hope, more than comfort; they gave their followers something that is lacking today: fervor.

Well, Jim: I hope, as in our past dialogues, I have managed to give you the feeling of what went into these tales — and a spark of whatever fire they contain.

In friendship, as ever —
Elie

THE BAAL SHEM TOV

Souls on Fire

Souls on Fire is a volume of tales, portraits, and memories. The "souls on fire" of my book are the souls that caught fire through the words and imagination of our people and its tradition. The souls on fire are, of course, the Hasidim and their masters. Why fire and why souls? Because I believe that a history of the Jewish people is actually the history of a soul. The mystery of the Jewish people is the mystery of that soul. And whatever happened to us in our generation, whatever happened to me, the teller of tales, is part of that mystery.

I have lived certain experiences. I try to recapture them. And the more I think about them, remember them, and try to transmit them, the more I believe that perhaps the Holocaust of European Jewry had nothing to do with geography, with military strategy between the Nazis and their enemies, or with sociology. It had to do with theology and philosophy, and, mainly, with the soul.

Whatever happened in Auschwitz happened in the soul. What happened in one soul contained more mystery than all the events in the world then. How did we live? How did we survive? How did others go to their death — in silence or in prayer? What were their memories? What made one person become a hangman, and what made the other become his victim?

All this is part of that tale: the tale of a Jewish soul, which is the tale of a human soul.

I called my book *Souls on Fire*. Naturally there is an explanation why I called it that. One, it has to do with fire. I am part of a generation that is obsessed with fire. As a child, I was very religious, full of dreams — dreams of fire, Messianic dreams of fire. Day after day I saw the Temple of Jerusalem being destroyed by fire.

Later, when I was fourteen, fifteen, I physically approached that fire. I saw Jacob's ladder, the ladder of fire, upon which a third of my people went up to heaven and did not come back. "Souls on Fire" are the souls of a people who disappeared, who vanished in fire — one million children! Three million Hasidim and their masters!

I begin with Rebbe Israel Baal Shem Tov, the founder of the Hasidic movement. He was a mysterious man, a man who adored mystery and, yet, whatever he said was clear, simple, and very beautiful. If he caught the imagination of so many Jewish communities — in a matter of twelve years he conquered almost all the

Adapted from *The Eternal Light*, February 20, 1972.

Jewish communities in Eastern Europe — it is because he believed in beauty, in simplicity, and in purity.

He did not boast of his erudition. He did not make demands that could not be met. He simply told tales and shared his songs with others. And people listened to his songs, repeated his tales, and became Hasidim and survived. Thanks to his songs and tales, they survived until two hundred years later, when those same Hasidim, the most generous, the most compassionate of people, were the first to go away.

I heard the tales I tell in *Souls on Fire* from my grandfather, Dodye Feig, a Hasid of the rebbe of Wizsnitz. My grandfather had a very strong influence on me. He taught me the first songs. He took me into the kingdom of Hasidism, where everything is simple and human, where nothing is an obstacle to man's association with God in His Creation.

A Hasid is a committed person, and someone who tells Hasidic tales must be committed to the ideals of humanity, to the ideals of brotherhood. The Hasidim were so close to each other, even in their quarrels, that none ever abandoned his neighbor or his friend; they were all part of the same destiny and they all constituted the beauty of that destiny.

Many stories are told about the Baal Shem. All of them are beautiful. They should be told and retold. The Baal Shem was known as a miracle maker, and many opponents to the Hasidic movement reproached the Baal Shem and the Hasidim for his miracle making, which was not to their taste. Miracles appeal not to logic, not to reason, but to something else — perhaps to some instinct. Why did he need to perform miracles?

I think the entire subject of miracles in Hasidism has been misunderstood. The Baal Shem performed miracles simply because the Jews then needed them. They needed to know that someone could accomplish miracles. In those days it was so hard for a Jew to survive, to remain Jewish, that simply to remain on the surface was a daily miracle. Each child not killed; each Jew not jailed; each man who could go on praying day after day to God: all were miracles. To believe in man, to believe in the future, and even to remember the past: all miracles. Therefore, the Baal Shem and his disciples were supposed to perform them, simply to show the Jews that things are possible — that the laws of man are not irrevocable, are not eternal. But whether he did perform miracles or not, that is for Hasidim to tell.

The Baal Shem died at sixty, his heart broken. He may have foreseen what was to happen to his Hasidim much later. He may have foreseen that a few generations later all who claimed kinship with him were to go away. In the kingdom of Hasidic legend, in many poems, the Baal Shem follows his disciples to the end of night. Some poems describe him in Auschwitz; other poems describe him in mass graves; still other poems describe him as the one who tries to console those who cannot be consoled. All these stories of the Baal Shem and his disciples define themselves in relation to the old master's long death.

Today Hasidism is reborn. Although three million Hasidim died in Poland, Hungary, Rumania, and Russia, Hasidism has undergone a new awakening, even in America. Hasidim live in America, but they belong to Lizensk, Mezeritch, or

Rizhin in Europe. There are no more Jews in Wizsnitz, but there are Wizsnitzer Hasidim on both sides of the ocean. The same is true for the other Hasidic branches or dynasties. Sighet and Satmar are no longer in Transylvania but wherever Satmarer and Sigheter Hasidim live and remember.

And then there are, of course, the tales of the Baal Shem Tov, those he told and those told by his disciples. Are we worthy of these tales and legends? It all depends. Are we still able to repeat these legends and tales without impairing their innocence and ours? It all depends.

LEVI YITZHAK OF BERDITCHEV

Souls on Fire

Levi Yitzhak of Berditchev was the protester par excellence. Levi Yitzhak of Berditchev means the Hasidic protest. He succeeded in showing that one can be a Jew — a believing Jew — and say no: no to the universe and no to its Creator, provided the protest is on behalf of man.

But there is a mystery about him. In legend, in tradition Levi Yitzhak was an extrovert, always surrounded by people. He loved children; he loved man; and everyone, except for the adversaries of the movement, adored him. When he prayed, it was a spectacle. When he sang, they all came to listen. Yet, Levi Yitzhak, at one point — for one year — went into a deep depression. And that year — the eclipse in his life — is passed over almost in silence in Hasidic literature.

We know he was born in Galicia in 1740. The date 1740 is important, because the eighteenth century in Europe was filled with wars, revolutions, and massacres. And while all these upheavals took place, in the very heart of Europe a small sect of Jews was persecuted and made to suffer by everyone, even by God. This small sect lived in its own small ghetto, in its own small kingdom, announcing a message of hope and beauty, singing the glory of man and his future, and serving as example of what man can and should do for himself and for others, and of what man can do even when opposed by God.

Every revolutionary movement provokes antagonism, and the Hasidic movement was no exception. Levi Yitzhak suffered most because he was great, attracted many disciples, and had a strange way of being a Jew and being a master. He was humble.

We try to follow his steps, his example: to protest but from within the human condition, from within the Jewish destiny, from within our history, and for man. I included the Berditchever Levi Yitzhak in *Souls on Fire* because his soul was on fire and because his image puts our own souls on fire.

Adapted from *The Eternal Light*, February 27, 1972.

[83]

BACK TO THE SOURCE

Souls on Fire

After I wrote *A Beggar in Jerusalem*, my ninth book, I told a few more tales in *One Generation After*, and with that tenth book I tried to return to the source, to my grandfather Dodye Feig, who was a Hasid of Wizsnitz. And I decided to tell his tales. Why? First, because they are beautiful. Second, because Hasidism has something to offer today, as Judaism does, to the young Jew, with its fervor, with its sensitivity to anything human, anything profound and authentic. But mainly because to me Hasidism is my childhood. All the stories that I tell are only stories of my childhood.

Literature is inspired by two themes: one's childhood or one's death. Christianity is obsessed with the theme of death. Judaism is obsessed with the theme of children. The *Yenuka* in the *Zohar* is a child. Moses was discovered as a child, as a crying baby, and that was the beginning of Jewish history. The Talmud is full of old masters going in the street and stopping children and saying, "Child, tell me, what am I to study today?" The Hasidic stories, though they belong to a generation gone, are full of beauty and fervor, and they really contain all the elements that I am trying to transmit in literature. The Hasidic masters were so exquisitely beautiful and touching and extraordinary that they made every man who came to see them a different person. It is said of anyone who came to see Rebbe Bunam of Pshiskhe that his soul caught on fire. And they all became souls on fire.

Adapted from lecture, Temple Sinai, Hollywood, Florida, February 28, 1972.

[84]

ISRAEL OF RIZHIN

Souls on Fire

The Rizhiner tried to establish something new in Hasidism. His concept of Hasidism is called *Malkhut Yisrael* — the royalty of Israel. He wanted to show that to be a Jew is also to be part of a legend of kingdom and royalty: that God is not only the God of Israel, but also the King of the world and the King of Israel, and that the Messiah, when the Messiah will come, will not only be the Redeemer, but also the King. Because each rebbe has something of the Messiah in him, and because each Jew has something of the rebbe in him, it is permitted to establish a kind of physical setting for this concept. He saw himself as the embodiment of that concept. The Rizhiner was a king.

And because he was a king, he was arrested. It is said that the czar of Russia took umbrage and had him put into a fortress prison in Kiev, where he spent almost two years in solitary confinement for being a "rebel."

The Rizhiner was great before his imprisonment and surely afterwards. People came especially to Sadigor after his imprisonment, after his escape from Russia. He became a martyr because martyrdom, as we know, is a sign of being chosen by God. The Rhiziner was chosen by God to suffer. And because he suffered, many things were forgiven — his palace, his glory, his luxury.

We still do not really know why he lived in luxury, why he liked riches so much. What we do know is that he was a great man. His way was to remind Jews of *Malkhut Yisrael*. To remind Jews and men everywhere that we are all princes, that it depends on man to become what he is.

Of course, he died before the Messiah became King. Of course, he died before seeing the great tragedy that was to befall his followers and his descendants one generation later.

Israel of Rizhin is the great dreamer of the Messiah, the man who waited his entire life for the tale of the Messiah to be enacted in reality and who must have known that it is not enough to call the Messiah — not even with fervor, not even in prayer, not even with consuming desire — to hasten redemption.

Adapted from *The Eternal Light*, March 5, 1972.

MENAHEM MENDEL OF KOTZK

Souls on Fire

I tried to paint the portrait of Menahem Mendel of Kotzk in *Souls on Fire*. His soul was among the most elevated and his fire was dark, frightening.

I must confess, I am profoundly touched by Mendel of Kotzk — because of his anguish, because of the depth of his anguish. This man is our contemporary more than all the others.

If he were alive today, I am convinced he would be the leader of our youth. He would be the leader of the hippies; he would be the leader of the rebels. He would be the leader of all those who today try to change man, because man needs to change.

Even then he tried, and in the beginning succeeded, until he too succumbed to despair and to a strange lucidity within that despair, and he lived twenty years of solitude and sadness.

He is the last master in my book. But in all the preceding chapters, in all the preceding portraits of the great masters, somehow we find at least one element of the same sadness. All of them, including the Baal Shem Tov, including the Berditchever and Elimelekh of Lizensk and the Seer of Lublin, all of them, at one point, gave in to despair.

Why? These masters — what were they?

They were friends, as well as teachers, to the Jews. Since most of the Jews then lived in solitude, especially in the small villages, they had nowhere to go, no one to turn to. When they came to the rebbe, he listened.

One of the great qualities of the Baal Shem was that he knew how to listen. When he listened to a hundred people, each had a feeling that he listened only to him. When he spoke to a thousand people, each had the feeling he spoke only to him.

The quality of listening is basic to Hasidism. So all these rebbes listened.

But what were they listening to? To miseries, only to miseries. When someone was happy he did not come to the rebbe. He came only when his wife was sick and he had no money to buy medicine, or if he was a father of twelve children and had no means of providing for them.

These rebbes listened to so many tales of horror and so many tales of sadness that naturally, at one point, they had to be contaminated by the sadness. And they

Adapted from *The Eternal Light*, March 12, 1972.

gave in to dark thoughts: "How much longer will it last?" And, "Why must all this suffering be part of human existence?"

But these masters all succeeded in overcoming their afflictions. They who were more desperate than their disciples and their followers succeeded in giving joy to those very followers and disciples.

When they were alone, many of these masters cried bitterly and fought madness, but when they had to help others, they helped them and gave them joy. One of them, the Seer of Lublin, even complained: "People come to me and go away relieved. Only I remain sad as before, sadder than before, because my fire is a fire that gives light but not warmth, anyway not to me."

The Rebbe of Kotzk was exceptional in Hasidism in that he did not surmount his despair. He remained desperate, in darkness for twenty years.

The Master of Kotzk is probably the greatest, most tragic, most colorful figure in Hasidism. His is a Hasidism of anger, a Hasidism of rebellion, a Hasidism of anxiety. No one can see it, even in print, without trembling.

The Kotzker Rebbe attracted men — the best, the youngest, the purest, the most fanatic ones of Hasidism in his time. They all left their masters, their parents, their wives and came to Kotzk. Kotzk became a center of Hasidic rebirth, of renaissance. It became an adventure, a laboratory for new ideas.

The rebbe was not only a master, he was a kind of older brother. Before he entered solitude he taught them that despair, too, can lead to absolute discoveries. He taught them what words mean and what silence can give to words or take away from them.

The Kotzker Rebbe, therefore, remains a giant in Hasidism. And if he were alive today, I think I would be his disciple. Indeed, I am his disciple.

And, in fact, he is here. He is here in his tales, in his parables. And his anguish is ours.

The Kotzker Rebbe and the Berditchever and the Rizhiner, they are all gone. Maybe the world did not deserve them. Maybe mankind did not deserve their tales and their songs. And maybe the Kotzker Rebbe foresaw these things. And maybe he withdrew into solitude because he did not want to be part of the indignity that was to befall mankind as much as the Jews.

LETTER TO JAMES H. SILBERMAN

The Oath

Dear Jim:

What would you say to a young stranger who wishes to die? What arguments would you use to restore his will to live? What ideas and ideals would you invoke to save him? Faced with just such a situation, my principal character — an old wanderer named Azriel — decides to tell him a story: his own. The very one he was not supposed to tell — the one he had pledged to keep to himself.

Outwardly, structurally, this is the central plot of *The Oath*, a 100,000 word novel — my longest — which Paul Flamand, my French publisher, describes as "the most poignant, despairing, and suspenseful book you have written."

But you want to know what it is about. Well, it is about Jews and their enemies, friendship and hate, bigotry and war, historians and their faith, testimony and silence — silence above all. Do you need to know more? All right, Jim. It is about conflicts and clashes between generations, societies, religions. About the dangers and the stupidities inherent in intolerance. About the tragic consequences of seemingly unimportant acts. Still not satisfied? All right, listen:

Somewhere in the Carpathian mountains there was a little town named Kolvillàg, a little town like all the others, a little town unlike the others. Don't look for it on any map or in any book: It exists only in the memory of its last survivor — Azriel — and in the *Pinkas*, the Book of Chronicles in his sole possession.

How did it vanish? and why? It all had to do with the disappearance of a teenager: Yancsi. Fanatics were quick to accuse the Jews of ritual murder. A blood-trial was in the making with the entire Jewish community as the target. So one man — Moshe: mystic, dreamer, madman — chose to take the guilt on himself. But his self-sacrifice was to be in vain. A pogrom broke out even before the trial. The Jewish quarter was besieged and burned — and along with it the entire town. The story ends in apocalyptical images: executioners and victims swallowed up together in the flames, becoming part of the same hallucination: scars on the same landscape. Only one youngster — Azriel — managed to escape. And save the Chronicles. . . And remain faithful to the oath. . .

You see, before the pogrom, the community had gathered to listen to Moshe's last address and exhortation. His plea was for silence. All those present were to

March 30, 1973.

take an oath: whoever would survive would never reveal the truth of the town's last trials and agonies.

Thus for decades and decades Azriel roamed around the earth searching for someone with the authority to release him from his vows. He sought out a Hasidic master who "knew how to listen" but forbade him to speak. He became a *Na-venadnik* (one of the most colorful and exciting characters of Eastern European Jewry), a wandering preacher, healer, and . . . Komintern agent. He visited famous capitals and God-forsaken hamlets, met all kinds of people and explored their destinies. Everywhere they would attempt to make him speak and reveal the content of the Book of Chronicles, which contained the life and the death of a town and a universe long forgotten.

Now, sixty years later, he will break his oath at last. To save a young student from suicide: man's loyalty to his dead may become his reason to go on living.

"Now that I have entrusted you with this story," Azriel tells the young man, "you no longer have the right to die."

You see, Jim? It is a simple story. It unfolds in two places — Kolvillàg and a big modern metropolis: New York? Paris? — in two eras — 1920 and the early seventies — and on many levels.

The cast of characters? Community leaders, officers, priests, Jews, merchants, beggars, revolutionaries, grave-diggers, saints, and . . . madmen (naturally). They all participate in the events, evolve within the same framework, inviting the reader to follow them on the same journey.

Of course, there are plots-within-plots, stories-within-stories, all building up to the climactic hallucinatory eruption of violence.

Azriel's visit to a community of cripples who see in him a miracle-maker. Childhood memories. Funny episodes, tragic incidents. A saint is tricked by people afraid of his powers. His wedding with the ugliest and unhappiest woman in town. His arrest. His torture at the hand of a sadist. The waiting for the pogrom. The fear. The resistance. The end.

Also: a variety of "historical" vignettes, excerpts from the Book, dating back many centuries, back to the Crusades.

Also: aphorisms, anecdotes, legends. Also: the extraordinarily intense scene of the oath-taking. . .

Well, Jim: this is only hors d'oeuvre. To make you thirsty. Marion will serve the wine.

As ever, your —
Elie

A KINGDOM OF FIRE

The Oath

Though they lived at the beginning of this century, the characters in *The Oath* are those I remember from my hometown, because the eyes of my memory, which are not always mine, cannot tear themselves away from those people, those mysterious messengers, and their tales where children were transfigured by ancient dreams, and the poor were less poor on *Shabbat*.

I remember them, I want to remember them and be worthy of them. Some worked twelve to fourteen hours a day, lived six persons in two cellar rooms, and hid their hunger beneath masks of piety and fright. Yet on *Shabbat* evening they all underwent a strange metamorphosis. It began Friday morning when the head of the household and his wife would get up earlier. He would go out, bring home a few pennies. She would remain to wash the floor. In the afternoon for the arrival of *Shabbat* the lodging would become a royal apartment. Everything would be clean, the table covered with a white cloth, the children washed. There would be bread and wine and sometimes meat. And all were happy. They had no complaints, no anger, no bitterness towards society and its leaders.

They had nothing and wanted nothing from others. Whatever they wanted, they wanted from themselves. Yet everybody was against them, punishing them, persecuting them. God himself was against them. But they did not mind, not on *Shabbat*.

What I really tried to do in *The Oath* is to bring back a fragment of that *Shabbat*. *The Oath* is a song of *Shabbat*, my song of *Shabbat*. It is a tragic song, because Kolvillàg is no longer here. There no longer is a Sighet, a Satmar and Lemberg, a Lublin, Bendin, and Warsaw; all these little kingdoms — where Jews became princes simply because of the word, because of the song — are no longer here.

All the characters in *The Oath* are desperate: Azriel because he is old and wants to die, the young man because he wants so much to leave this world and cannot.

But there is one difference. All my other books contain despair. If one has *Night* as a foundation, if *Night* is the yardstick to measure all other tales and words and memories, then one must live with despair, in despair. What else can one do? But while my other tales are desperate appeals to death, *The Oath* is a desperate appeal to life.

Ultimately, when Kolvillàg is destroyed, it is given to man to build up again, if not in the entire world, at least in one place, if not in one place, at least in one person, at least in one child. And then if that child picks up the story and turns it into a tale, and the tale contains its fire, then the fire will not be a destructive fire. It will be a tale of infinite beauty, enchantment, and reward.

Adapted from *The Eternal Light*, May 5, 1974.

[90]

LETTER TO JAMES H. SILBERMAN

Ani Maamin

Dear Jim:

Poem, parable, legend? *Ani Maamin* is all this — and more. It's a memory, a song — a *niggun*.

I used to sing it back home, in the early forties. For me it was an appeal to faith, to hope: even though the Messiah is late in coming — I believe that he *will* come . . . one day. Those who sang it, among Hasidim, on *Shabbat*, felt strong — invincible.

Then —

Then I heard it being sung inside the kingdom of madness by Jews who knew they were on the threshold of death. I did not understand then and do not understand now: what made them sing of their faith in redemption? How could they believe in the Messiah — over there? How could they go on waiting for him? They should have known better —

Perhaps the song had undergone a kind of metamorphosis — eventually expressing anger rather than hope: yes — the Messiah would be late in coming — too late — so what? As long as the victims were alive, they wished to prove that they were capable of singing their attachment to life.

Thus you see, Jim, I find it hard to talk about *Ani Maamin*. It deals with problems of faith — and I do not like discussing those. One's faith is a matter that concerns only oneself and God. And yet.

When you try to remember the Holocaust, you must inevitably confront the question: where was God? what did he know? what did he do? In other words: can one still believe in God? And conversely: can God still have faith in man? These considerations are at the center — at the core — of the poem — or, the tale, for it is also a tale — naturally. . .

It is the tale of Abraham, Isaac, and Jacob who — in those days and nights — came to speak to God of his people. They described to him what they saw down below. Their aim was to move God — to arouse his compassion. To bring him closer to his creation. To make him break his silence.

But God chose to remain silent. So they decided to leave heaven and go back to the victims below. Abraham withdrew not having seen God shed his first tear. Then Isaac withdrew not having seen God shed his second tear. Then Jacob withdrew and he too did not see God weeping.

September 25, 1973.

[91]

And while the trial was taking place, while the tale was being told, the chorus sang *Ani Maamin*: yes — we believe in God in spite of God, we believe in man in spite of man.

So — today, Jim, I can sing this melody again — one of the most poignant in our literature. My only wish is that it will carry my words.

> As ever —
> in friendship;
> Elie

QUESTION AND QUEST

Ani Maamin

Ani Maamin, which means "I believe," is a poem written on the theme of faith and on the theme of waiting — on the theme of waiting for the Messiah. It was written in French, but the theme is Jewish, the inspiration is Jewish, and the waiting is certainly Jewish.

The whole poem is a quest and a question asked by man of God. What differentiates Judaism from other traditions and other religions is that we alone are allowed, indeed commanded sometimes, to question God and His ways. From Adam to Moses, and Abraham to Job, from all our great sages down to the Hasidic master Levi Yitzhak of Berditchev: all question God. One may say no to God on behalf of His Creation, on behalf of one's people, one's community. If one uses God against man, or man against God, then one betrays both God and man. But one can speak to God, and one may question Him.

In those years anyone who did not question God was not a true believer. In those years anyone who saw what was being done to Jewish children, and did not make his entire life into an outcry, into a protest, was not a believer, was not human, could not be human. I believe God himself became a question mark then.

When I was a child, when the child in me entered that kingdom of night, what disturbed me most was God's silence. As a child I did not expect much of man, but I expected everything of God.

My only question then was: How can *God* be silent? And the question remains a question. Thirty years have passed and the more I think about it, and the more I live, and the more I meet myself in my own memories, the deeper the question becomes — and the deeper the mystery.

But, then, what is one to do? What is one to do at the end? When you experience all this suffering, all these questions, and all this despair, what is one to do today? Give in? Go under? No. If I were to come to that conclusion, it would be a defeat, and I am, with all my heart, against transmitting defeat to our younger generation, to our children.

I believe we are a part of these tales, of history. And Jewish history is dominated by faith as much as by despair. To be Jewish, I believe, does not mean to suffer, but to overcome suffering. It does not mean to enter exile, but to turn exile into a kingdom.

Adapted from *The Eternal Light*, May 12, 1974.

Therefore, at the end of this poem, the very end, the chorus expresses something of my belief, which is a belief against and in spite of everything.

I believe, I must believe in the coming of the Messiah. I believe that man's end is not in tragedy. I know that man suffers and that ultimately death is the victor. But as long as man is alive, he must claim victory with every breath and defeat the enemy. And as long as he says "*Ani Maamin*" he is the victor.

Remember, there were Jews who in the shadow of the flames, one moment before they were killed by the enemy, still shouted their faith in God and the Messiah. That is their victory — and someone else's defeat.

MY SONG OF SONGS

Zalmen, or The Madness of God

On Friday, on *Erev Shabbat*, Hasidim back home used to sing from the *Shir ha-Shirim* — *The Song of Songs*. *Zalmen* is my song of songs to the spirit of resistance, to the spirit of defiance, to the joy and to the celebration of Soviet Jewry and of Jewry at large, to the Jewish people.

Zalmen is a play of madness and solitude. It is a play about the 1950s. But it could and does happen today. Never before have we been so alone. Never before has there been such a need for Jewish unity, for Jewish solidarity, for Jewish celebration.

I believe the Jewish people is about to enter an era of danger, an era of abandonment. We who are a traumatized generation feel it almost physically, with our skin as well as with our soul. If there is a way out, it must be found from within the depths of our being, from within the depths of our past and our dreams.

Zalmen is a play about anger, and it is a play about hope. The anger should be ours, and the hope should be ours.

Above all, writing is an act of faith. Writing must be a work of friendship. In this play a spirit of friendship came into being from Alan Schneider to Joseph Wiseman to Richard Bauer. Something happened to all of us who participated in it. Some of the actors are not Jewish. Yet, when you see them, you will see that one can be not Jewish and still be Jewish.

The only answer to a world of madness is Jewish madness. The only answer to the reasons the world gives us to despair is to sing. My *Shir ha-Shirim* is a song against despair.

Statement, first performance, Arena Stage, Washington, D.C., May 8, 1974.

A TALE OF DEFIANCE

Zalmen, or The Madness of God

Zalmen, or The Madness of God: its name and its symbol is defiance. We believe in defiance. We Jews believe that no matter how strong the enemy, no matter how serious the danger, man is capable of defying both. Man should defy what tries to destroy him. If he does so with dignity and humanity, in the name of friendship, then the defiance may become redemption.

The play, therefore, is set in Russia, but it applies to people outside Russia as well. It could have happened anywhere or indeed it should have happened elsewhere.

This play is dedicated to the Russian Jews, to their courage, to their hope, and to the beauty with which they expressed both.

The play is a tale. Like most of my tales, it deals with certain of my obsessions. Literature is an accumulation of obsessions. And mine are madness, fear, silence, solidarity, or lack of solidarity. Of course it has a beginning, a middle, and an end, but not in that order. It ended even before it began. Zalmen is the madman, the old rabbi's madman, God's madman. He is mad with God, just as one is or can be drunk with God, as one can be in love with God, madly in love *with* God, or *against* God.

* * *

Zalmen, in my world, in my place, is the wisest of men; he knows the limits of our despair, he wants to deny them, to break them. To him madness is an answer to man's evil and to God's silence. One has to be mad, he says, to go on believing in justice, in history, in man's future.

One has to be mad to want to go on telling the tale to a world which refuses to listen. Still, silence is not the answer. What then is the answer? That is what Zalmen tries to find out.

The first act ends on an act of defiance, the supreme defiance of the rabbi — the victim turned hero, the victim turned rebel.

And yet, in spite of the anguish that fills our tales, in spite of the pain that dominates their heroes, Zalmen and his friends will not be defeated. The rabbi and his followers will not give in. In spite of their solitude, in spite of their hopelessness, they represent an appeal to hope, to friendship, to commitment. The old rabbi's gesture is not in vain. All the people around him, frightened in the first act, undergo a change in the second. They all become his friends and protectors. His gesture is not in vain because thousands of young Jews throughout the world responded. And they gave the answer to the rabbi, shouting: "You are not alone; we are with you. We, too, share in your defiance."

Adapted from *The Eternal Light*, March 9, 1975.

THE STORY OF *ZALMEN*

Zalmen, or The Madness of God

The story of how the play *Zalmen* came about deals with Jewish memory. I wrote the play during my second visit to Russia. It was *Yom Kippur* and I sat on the *bimah* and watched Rabbi Levin, the late chief rabbi of Moscow, who was a beautiful man but tired, weak. He was tall, with sad, sad eyes. I had sat with him the year before, day after day during the High Holy Days. I did not want to embarrass him or endanger him so I did not speak to him. He was afraid to speak to me, so we simply looked at one another. I saw a flicker of a smile in his eyes. It was his way of saying thank you. When he saw me again, I saw he was pleased and that was to me a source of reward.

Then on *Yom Kippur* in the evening, during *Kol Nidrei* — there were three thousand people in the synagogue — I had an idea. Ah, if only he had the strength to free himself and become mad, if only he would break out of his fear, if only he would suddenly stand up, interrupt the services, the reading of the Torah, as we are allowed to do in our tradition when a matter of justice is concerned. If only he had the courage to bang his fist on the table and say, "No, KGB! No, Mr. Kosygin! No, I want you to know the truth about my people! The truth is that we suffer. And the truth is that we want to be Jews and we can't!" I begged him with my eyes. If ever I regretted that I did not study hypnotism, it was that evening. I begged him, do it! But he was so tired, so old, so broken that nothing happened.

So I decided to correct this injustice: I would rearrange history, and in my play he *would* speak. I would write a play in which he would do what he did not do in life.

But you cannot simply write a play about a rabbi on stage alone. For this you do not need the theater; you go to the synagogue. You need other people. In order not to be accused of male chauvinism I felt I needed a woman. If I had taken an old woman I would have been criticized, so I decided to introduce a younger woman, not too young, because then it would be Broadway but not my play; it would be Vashti but not Esther. So I decided to give him a daughter. Since he has a daughter, why not give her a son? And since she has a son, why not make it dramatic? And I decided that the son Misha will be twelve and that at one point the grandfather will say, "Misha, you are twelve, so soon you will be a *Bar Mitzvah*." And the boy will say, "*Bar Mitzvah*? What is that?" And the grandfather will be so shaken by the realization that the last link will be destroyed that he will

Lecture, B'nai B'rith Hillel Foundation, Toronto, Canada, March 2, 1977.

[97]

become mad, and he will bang his fist on the table and tell the truth. Since she has a son, she deserves a husband, so I gave her a husband. Misha's father is a Communist. In the thirties communism appealed to our people tremendously and, when a Jew is a Communist, he out-Communists all the others.

The play was produced in Paris, in Washington, then on television. We decided to preview the television version for the United Jewish Appeal convention in New York in Carnegie Hall in December, 1974. It was Friday afternoon. I came to introduce the film, then I hurried home. I found on my desk a letter that made me shiver. It was written by a Hasid of Lubavitch: Dear Mr. Wiesel, the daughter of the late chief rabbi of Moscow is in New York, and she wants to see you.

I ran to the telephone to call her. But *Shabbat* in Brooklyn begins before everywhere else. It was too late. Immediately after *Shabbat*, the longest of my life, I phoned her and asked, "Can I see you?" She said, "Certainly. That's why I wrote to you." I said, "Come right now." She said, "No, tomorrow." I had a sleepless night.

The next day she came — a nice woman, a dentist from Kiev. Now she lives in Ashkelon. Her name is Rivke Rosenshein. I said, "Tell me, have you seen the film?" From time to time, everybody deserves a lesson of humility. She said, "What film?" I said, "Have you seen the play?" The play was produced in Israel, too. She said, "What play?" I said, "Don't you know I wrote a play about you and your father?" She said, "No." "Then why did you want to see me?" "Oh," she said, "I read your books in some *samizdat* in Russia and I know you love stories, so I decided I owe you a story." Had she not been a rabbi's daughter I would have kissed her. "Tell me the story." She said, "Listen. One day I received a telephone call from my father. He was sick, dying. I came, and my father said, 'Rivke, you must promise me to save your children. I want them to grow up Jewish. If they remain in Russia they will not be Jewish. Take them out.' That was his last wish. I decided to obey. But it wasn't so simple," she said. "You see, my husband is a Communist and he refused." I said, "A Communist! What happened?" She said, "Nothing. We began quarreling about it and finally we divorced." I said, "And?" She said, "Well, we have three children, two daughters and a son. The two daughters are now in Brooklyn, and they are getting married to Lubavitcher Hasidim." And I said, "And how about the son?" "Oh," she said, "the son. Unfortunately, he didn't want to let him go, so he is in Russia." I almost cried. I said, "How old is your son?" "Twelve."

When I created the part of Misha I did not know what to do with him at the end. Should I keep him, bring him back to his grandfather? No, too sweet. But my Jewish heart did not let me remove him from the grandfather and give him to the Communist party either. I didn't want to lose a child, another Jewish boy, so I opted for a compromise. Somehow, he is in the shadow, and you don't really know whether he is coming back to his grandfather. So I was very sad. Rivke Rosenshein remained in New York a couple of days. She saw the movie on television. Then she wrote me from Israel, saying, "I watched it and cried, and I simply said one thing all the time: 'That's exactly how it was, exactly how it was.'"

A few months later I received a telephone call from a rabbi. He must come and see me right away. What is it? He said, "I know you love stories. I have a story to tell you." "What is the story?" He said, "I'll tell you. Last week I was in Israel and I went to Masada. The military chaplain showed me thirty or thirty-five Jewish boys — war orphans who were there for their *Bar Mitzvah*. Suddenly he said, 'Do you see this boy? He is not a war orphan. He is a special boy. He is the grandson of the late chief rabbi of Moscow'."

At that point I wanted to shout with anger: If you are a Jewish writer you cannot write fiction! But who wants to write fiction, really? What we want to do is to transmit a tale that gives our life meaning and intensity.

MESSENGERS THROUGH TIME

Messengers of God

All figures in the Bible are messengers of God to man, and some are messengers of man to God. In *Messengers of God* I try to understand some of these messengers: What were their motivations? In what way was their message universal? I try to tell a story, the story of a pilgrimage. My role is that of disciple rather than teacher; I but transmit what I receive. I go back to the sources of my memory, to the legends that enriched my imagination, to meet the heroes that filled me with both wonder and anguish.

As a child I watched them live and disappear around me. I followed them on journeys into the distant past. Thus I escaped my little town and shared their adventures. I would weep with Abraham, dream with Jacob, and laugh with Joseph. The Bible was for me what literature is today for many others: a remedy against solitude.

Of course, people would tell me not to take Biblical tales too seriously. They were after all only tales, and they belonged to ancient history. I am glad I did not listen to their advice. Today, I know that a Jew is older than he seems to be. His memory does not begin with himself. It includes his people's collective experience from its very origins; the past survives forever.

According to Jewish tradition, the past is rarely very distant and never irrelevant. In fact, day after day, we witness ancient events unfolding in the present. Our Talmudic sages have always expressed themselves in the present tense. Somewhere disciples of Shammai and Hillel are still debating points of law. Somewhere Rabbi Akiba is still arguing with Rabbi Ishmael over interpretations of Scripture and the mystery of martyrdom. And somewhere, somehow, we listen in.

The Law was given only once. But we must be willing to receive it and transmit it every day.

The Biblical characters I have chosen to deal with are deeply related to contemporary life. And their stories *are* relevant to contemporary experiences.

Only today do we understand them. They were forefathers, not myths, and their singular destiny affects ours. We identify with them. They were neither saints nor idols. They were human beings with weaknesses and shortcomings, but thrust into a drama of cosmic magnitude. I feel as close to them as to any friend of mine.

There was a time when I studied these legends in Scripture and in Midrash to

Adapted from *The Eternal Light*, April 4, 1976.

[100]

satisfy some theological or philosophical quest. Today I read them for their beauty. They are literary gems, possibly even masterpieces. Content, style, rhythm: every story suggests a world of its own. The Midrash is to Scripture what imagination is to knowledge: an invitation to a feast of the mind. To read these parables is to participate in the feast. I use them to reconstruct ancient portraits with existing, though often unknown, material.

Nothing is more rewarding than to see a portrait as it emerges from words. In a way you may say that what I have tried to do is to take words and bring them back to life. Only the structure is mine and the tune — the *niggun*, as we say in Hasidic vocabulary. But is this not the role of tellers of tales everywhere? In the beginning was the word, and the word is the story of man told by man. And man is the story of God, told by God.

WHOSE MESSENGERS ARE WE?

Messengers of God

In Scripture and in Midrash, Jacob seems to be weak, pale, compared to his predecessors, to his father and grandfather. I tried to understand Jacob's character, so meek, yielding all the time, never resisting, never asserting himself. And yet, Jacob is beautiful; he becomes so *after* he has fought with the angel; *after* he has gotten a new name; *after* he has become a person in his own right.

What do we learn from our heroes, from our tales about them? We learn that man is both parable and the meaning of parable. We learn that behind words there is mystery, just as there is mystery in words.

We learn the art of waiting. While we are with Abraham, we are waiting for Isaac. And, when we are with Isaac, we are waiting for the angel. And, when we are with the angel, we are still waiting for the meaning of the encounter.

We are not ashamed of our past. Quite the contrary, just as it keeps us alive, we keep it alive. And in so doing, we claim kinship with Abraham and David, Isaac and Isaiah. We speak their language and share their concerns. Were it not for our common quest, why continue? Why not submit to hostile forces in history and put an end to our adventure *in* history?

But we do continue. And we do so because our acts commit more than our own person. We speak on behalf of a long line of princes and prophets. To silence their word in us is to betray them. And that we must never do.

We try to read in the past the meaning of the present. And we try to find in the past a hope for the future. Everything is in our past. Everything has been predicted in it. And our past is for us a command to humanize events.

An example: in the story of Jacob, strangely enough, Esau comes off better than Jacob. In most legends we feel more sympathy for Esau, much more than for Jacob. Jacob was a liar. He cheated his brother and his father. But Esau, what was he? He was a hunter. Well, better be a descendant of a liar than a descendant of someone who loves blood.

A great Hasidic rebbe, Rebbe Menahem Mendel of Kotzk said: When Esau discovered that he had fallen victim to Jacob's deceit, he uttered a cry that seemed to come from the deepest recesses of his heart. And in front of his petrified father he shed three tears. For these three tears Israel was to suffer the throes of exile. But, said the rebbe after a long sigh, there is a limit, God, there will have to be.

Adapted from *The Eternal Light*, April 25, 1976.

Over the centuries we have shed so many tears, enough to flood the heavens. There is a limit, Lord. There must be a limit.

In Jacob's vision of the future, he wept together with his persecuted descendants. And this was how he addressed God: In Your Book it is written that one may not slaughter an animal and her young on the same day. This law shall not be observed by the enemy. He will kill mothers and their children in each other's presence. I shall not ask You who will observe Your Law. I shall simply ask You to tell me who will study it.

Many tears have been shed, and we must collect and transmit them, but not only tears, and not only sadness. When we think of the past, we feel a certain comfort too. We find a certain consolation in it. True, the Temple was destroyed. True, there were victims then, and there are victims now. But we do remember. And as long as man remembers, he is human and he is alive.

The Talmud is the greatest oral history project that exists, because there is much truth in it and because there is much life in it. All that is shown is but a vision of the invisible: behind every word, every gesture of every man or woman, you can and must feel three thousand years of a people whose memory is yet to be equalled.

No, to turn away from that memory is not the answer. To forget is the wrong answer. To be without a past, I believe, is worse than to be without a future.

Therefore to assume one's past — to share in our collective memory — is a privilege. But the tales that my generation has to transmit will forever remain a mystery. The tales I would really like to tell cannot be told. So I tell them through the Biblical tales, the Hasidic tales, the Talmudic legends.

How do we tell the tale? We write not with words but against words. And in doing so we develop our own genre, our tone, our style, our language. We try then to transmit not experience but at least a certain secret of the experience untouched by words.

All the Biblical characters are in the most beautiful sense of the word God's messengers to His Creation. But, then, aren't we all? We are all emissaries, carrying messages from one to another, across many lands and many generations. We are all messengers, and some of us are the messengers' messengers.

What is man? A link. What is man? A messenger. From one world to another, from one era to another. Sometimes I wonder whether one generation ago the victims, so many of them, were not messengers, too. Could it be that they were sent up to heaven to influence God?

If so, they failed. They had to fail because they were sent against God. If they could not bring salvation, who can? If they could not humanize history, who can? Perhaps that was not what they wanted to achieve. Perhaps their death had no purpose. I don't know. All we can do is remember them. All we can do is remember their tale, remember some of their words and some of their songs, and silences.

If they carried the message, I do not know what it was. Nor by whom it was sent, and to whom. I am afraid to know.

But then perhaps it is more urgent to ask ourselves not whose messengers they were, but whose messengers we are. Let us remain with the question: Whose messengers are we?

THE JEW AND
THE HUMAN CONDITION

Messengers of God

We believe that whatever happened to us happened to everybody. We believe that Jewish tales affected mankind, and therefore we repeat them. We communicate them from person to person, from era to era, from people to people.

The irony of Job, the absurd fate of Adam, the silent anguish of Isaac: to evoke them is to show their topicality as well as their timelessness. Such is the fascinating mystery of Judaism. The more concrete the problem is, the more general it is. Tales that are linked to a specific era — the destruction of the Temple in Jerusalem, the march in the desert — have nourished us through centuries of exile. Such are the unfathomable depths of Judaism. Everything has been said, yet everything is still to be formulated again, discovered again, communicated again, explored again. Every period contains all periods. Every man was seen and comprehended by our first ancestor.

Moses, Job, Adam, Abraham, Isaac — all were responsible for all men. For each man resembles Adam in his solitude, Job in his suffering, and Abraham in his ultimate defiance.

What do all these characters have in common? Most of them, with the exception of Moses, perhaps, were not Jewish, not in the strict sense of the word. For the Law had not yet been given to Abraham or Isaac or Jacob. Yet their experience and their struggle are part of our conscience. In other words, though speaking of Jews, we illustrate the human condition. We never made a distinction between Jew and man. We reiterate our belief: that a Jew can be a man only through his Jewishness. Our legends aim to abolish the distance between one and the other.

To be a Jew is to put the accent on being, on the necessity of having faith in one's fate. Job, Moses, Abraham, and Isaac — no tale could therefore be more universal.

Moses is the Torah. Moses is the Bible. The Bible bears his name. Without him we would not be what we are, where we are. When you read about him, you realize that the greatness of the man was his humanity. He became Moses only when he was confronted with the suffering of his people. Until then he lived in a palace. As we remember, he was taken by Pharaoh's daughter into the palace, but he *became* Moses, he became the prophet, he became a conscience only when he realized that people can be brothers and yet cruel to one another.

Adapted from *The Eternal Light*, April 24, 1977.

First he saw an Egyptian who wanted to kill a Jew. So Moses killed the Egyptian. Then he saw that two Jews were quarreling with one another, and he realized that a Jew is not necessarily a saint, that a Jew is also human, and that a Jew can be human only when he faces the problems of his brothers and his fellow man.

A JEW TODAY AND ITS AUTHOR

A Jew Today

CROMIE One of the parts that I think moved me most in *A Jew Today* was the dialogue between "A Man and His Little Sister." I knew it was a dialogue between you and your little sister. That must have been a difficult thing to write.

WIESEL Of course it is difficult. Everything is difficult. I do this kind of writing occasionally — every five or six years. I have tried to invent a new genre. The problem with my generation is that we lived through certain experiences and we do not know how to write about them because there is no language. Language itself was killed or distorted or poisoned. So we have to invent something new, a new approach — to imbue it with a certain silence, a primary silence that is as expressive as language itself. In *One Generation After*, a book I wrote ten years ago, I invented dialogues with the dead, who are so present to all of us. We talk to them and they talk to us in clean, austere language. Not one word should be useless, not one comma out of place.

CROMIE You describe an incident which I am sure was taken from something you either saw or heard about in which a German officer is trying to get a Jew to denounce his Creator. It is unbelievably moving.

WIESEL That's a true story. It happened in a camp. The officer tried to convince one of the inmates to repudiate God. He said, "I will give you bread," and the man said no. He said, "Repudiate your God, curse your God, and I will give you happiness, joy." He said no. "I will give you life." He said no. So the officer shot him. And still the man went on saying no. He shot him with five bullets. In his agony the man kept on saying *Adoshem Hu Ha-Elokim*, the ancient call of our martyrs: "God is God. God alone is God." And then he died. The son told me the story. The son said, "You know, my father was not a believer." And I find it extraordinary.

CROMIE He was a hero but he wasn't a believer.

WIESEL He was a hero but not a believer. But he was a believer.

CROMIE He had to have been.

WIESEL Oh, he was, I think, a greater believer than many of us, because he affirmed not his belief in God but his power over the killer. The killer can kill, but the killer cannot kill ideas. He can kill people but not words; he can distort them but not kill them.

Adapted from television interview by Robert Cromie, *Book Beat*, December 16, 1978.

CROMIE You also have a letter "To a Young Palestinian Arab" in this book.

WIESEL I wrote it because I believe from time to time we must take stock and ask ourselves: "Where am I?" "What am I doing?" I believe the problem of our generation is that we know so many things, but we don't know where we are. I asked myself what my attitude is toward the Christian, for instance. As a child I knew absolutely nothing about Christianity except that Christians would beat me up twice a year. So I had to rethink my attitude toward Christianity.

And the same applies to a Palestinian Arab. After all, these people are suffering. What do I have to tell a Palestinian Arab? Not long ago I gave a lecture in a university, and a young man got up, very polite, very courteous, very sweet. He said, "Professor Wiesel, we read you, and I am not trying here to make any propaganda, but what do you have to tell me? I am a Palestinian. I was born in Haifa or in Jaffa, and because of Jews I am a refugee." If he had been nasty, I could have answered him, but he was so polite and so human that I wrote him a letter. And that is how the letter came about.

What I really try to say there is that I do feel responsible for his pain; I do feel responsible for his suffering. Everybody's suffering involves me, indicts me in a way. The suffering in Cambodia today indicts me. The Vietnamese suffering today indicts me. I accept indictment if I don't speak up. And this is true of the Palestinian too. If he suffers, and I do nothing about it, I feel responsible for him. But then I tell him, "I do not feel responsible for what you are doing with your suffering, because suffering confers no privileges. It all depends upon what you do with it. If you use it to create more suffering, then you betray it." And I say to him, "The PLO has used your suffering to kill Jews, from Maalot to Entebbe to Lod, from murder to murder, from massacre to massacre. They are betraying your suffering. And you did not speak up against them. Therefore what can I do? I cannot accept it." And he answered, by the way. He was a very beautiful young man. He said for the first time a human being spoke to him like a human being.

CROMIE You also have a kind of open letter about Biafra, which is one of the most powerful writings I have ever read.

WIESEL Who remembers Biafra? People have forgotten Biafra. There was genocide in Biafra, and I remember that when we tried to help them, nobody cared. What bothers me is the indifference of this generation. Do you know who cares? The survivors care. This is illogical. It is almost paradoxical. If you go beyond a certain threshold of pain, then you are desensitized; you are no longer sensitive to anyone else's pain because you suffered more than he did. In this case it is just the opposite. These men and women who suffered so much, who actually should not be sensitive to anyone else's problems any more, are more sensitive, and they are involved in everybody else's pain and agony and fighting. And Biafra involved me.

I remember I fought for Biafra, as I did for Bangladesh, as I am trying to do now for Cambodia. I think it is a scandal. That the United States government has not done anything to stop the massacre in Cambodia is something I cannot understand. And the UN of course has other things to do than think of Cambodia.

CROMIE What happened to the tribe in Paraguay?

WIESEL There is a tribe in Paraguay which is being exterminated. Nobody cares. And I am convinced that Mengele, who is in Paraguay, is helping the government.

CROMIE He is the concentration camp doctor who did the horrible experiments.

WIESEL He did the selections. He was called the Angel of Death. He was a doctor, and I remember him. He is the one who with his stick would send right, left, right, left hundreds and thousands of Jews, my Jews from Hungary.

CROMIE Is he known to be in Paraguay?

WIESEL Yes. He is in Paraguay. He is protected by President Stroessner. He has his own bodyguards, his own security people. He has money.

CROMIE You wrote about a Jew who betrayed his fellows and became an outcast among all the Jews after the war? Was this based on somebody real?

WIESEL Yes and no. It was partly true. There was a man in my neighborhood who was known as a traitor. He was known as an anti-Semite who converted. I also know that he became a penitent and went to Israel. I used that image as part of the experience. He joined the fascists in Rumania but he was never involved in the killing. There is no atonement for killing.

ENCOUNTER WITH CHRISTIANITY

A Jew Today

QUESTION What is the connection between silence and François Mauriac getting you to write?

WIESEL Art means conflict. Unless you have a conflict, art cannot be. In order to create, there must be a resistance to creation. In our tradition we are told that God had to consult with the angels before creating man. The angels were against it. That's why we are here not as angels but as human beings. If language and silence were not in conflict, language would not be poetic, literary, or truthful.

Mauriac was not instrumental in making me write. He was instrumental in making me publish my work. I would have written anyway. It was he who prevailed upon me to publish.

QUESTION What was the reason for the ten-year period of silence from 1945 to 1955?

WIESEL I come from a Hasidic background. When I was twelve, I was preparing for my *Bar Mitzvah*. And I had just started studying the forbidden subject, Kabbalah, with a teacher. In Kaballah there is one mode called *taanit hadibur*, which is the renunciation of language, to fast with language: I would not speak on *Shabbat*. From Friday evening to *Motzei Shabbat* I would drive my parents crazy. I wouldn't speak. They didn't know why, but I knew why. I was following a certain rule.

My work after the war involved asceticism. I wanted to make a comparative study between suffering and attitudes toward self-inflicted suffering in Judaism, Christianity, and Buddhism. That was my subject. So the vow of silence that I took from 1945 to 1955 was partly a result of that. I wanted to see what one can do with silence. In another way, I knew I wanted to find the right words — and not say just anything, because anything we would have said would have been all right, we had so much to say. But how do you maintain the sacred with words, in words? That was why I was silent.

QUESTION In your initial confrontation with Mauriac it seemed you felt the Catholics were overly involved with the dying or death of one Jew, with the exposure of that Jew and his suffering. And I felt there was a parallel between the

Question and answer session, Moriah Congregation, Deerfield, Illinois, March 27, 1982.

[109]

exposure of your suffering, your role as a witness, and Christ's as a witness for the Christians.

WIESEL That's what *they* believed, and I protested. My story with Mauriac has not been told altogether. What I wrote in *A Jew Today* was only one short chapter. I am preparing a book called *Disputations*. I use the word in the medieval sense — of disputations between Jews and Christians. It will be based on dialogues, conversations, and letters between the two of us for fifteen or eighteen years.

We separated at one point. I did not like his preface to *Night*. It was very generous of him to write it. Whatever success I had in France was really due to him. He meant it. He was sincere, he was an *ohev Yisrael* — a lover of the Jewish people. Of course, as a Catholic he had to see the book through his own viewpoint. Therefore there are some Christological overtones in the preface which I don't like. But it is his preface — not mine.

Then he wrote a book called *The Son of Man*. It was published in French, in English, in many languages — he was a great man. It is his personal biography of Jesus. He sent me the book, and when I opened it I was shocked. It was dedicated to me in a way which moved me to protest, because he dared to compare me to Christ, and that was a bit too much. He said, "This book I dedicate to Elie Wiesel, who was a crucified Jewish child who stands for many others." And then I had to say it. I said, "I accept your present. It is very nice of you, but the comparison with Jesus Christ is surely not applicable to me because of my background, because of my attitude, and because of my belief."

That is when we decided to start our disputations. And when they will be published, they will create some stir.

QUESTION Some Christians, such as Mauriac, are willing to listen. Is that all they can do? Is there any way they can and should be witness to what they have heard and bear the message back to their own community of Christians?

WIESEL They can. Just listening — that is already a lot. If they listen for the right reasons, with the right predisposition, it is important. I do believe in persuasion. If we could find Christians to listen to us — I mean *really* to listen to us — I still hope we have enough arguments, enough reasons, enough intelligence and sensitivity to convince them that they will never succeed in converting us. It's a lost cause; it's silly. We don't want to convert them. They shouldn't convert us. And we can still live in the same world, respecting one another. But I insist: respecting one another.

My background justifies a total suspicion. As a child, I wouldn't even come close to the church. I changed sidewalks. It wasn't because of me: it was because of them — because twice a year they would beat us up. Also we were afraid of being taken into the church by force. I would never go close to it.

Today I have changed my view. Today I do believe there is a possibility of coexistence between Judaism and Christianity, provided, again, it is built on that respect, that they will not do what their ancestors did. I do not say that the Christian of today is responsible or guilty for the Inquisition. No. We measure a person by whatever he is doing today.

QUESTION You suggest that the most the Jewish people can hope for is to have the Christian world listen. Is there a chance that the Moslem world will listen?

WIESEL I am a manic depressive. I am never in the middle. Either I am terribly depressed or I am terribly hopeful. When I am terribly depressed, I say not even the Jew will listen. When I am very hopeful, I say the whole world will listen.

We can teach the world the art of survival because we have survived, and therefore I think they look to us. I believe we should do everything, but as Jews. In working deeper on our Jewishness we will be helping others to work deeper on whatever they are, and together perhaps save this planet which for the first time in history is in danger.

QUESTION Because of the increase in intermarriage some rabbis are seeking conversions, particularly within the intermarried families. Should the Jewish people become proselytizers?

WIESEL No. I do not believe in proselytizing. It is something so alien to our tradition that I am amazed at the idea. We believe, and we should believe, that we have a mission, as others do. We emphasize the uniqueness of the Jewish suffering to teach others to believe that *every* suffering is unique. Every death is outrageous. It *is* a scandal to inflict suffering or to accept it. Everyone has a mission.

The mission of the Jewish people has been to humanize the world, never to convert or to proselytize.

Anyone who knows anything about Jewish thought, from the earliest writings, from the Talmud and the Midrash, will tell you that we have never sought to convert others. On the contrary, we have discouraged conversion, though once a stranger becomes Jewish we respect him. Only once did one of our kings, John Hyrcanus, try to force conversion, and, says the Talmud, we lived to regret it under Herod.

So to decide today to convert others — tell me, have we finished yet converting our own Jews?

THE STORY OF
THE TRIAL OF GOD

The Trial of God

The Trial of God has a story, as everything has a story. In 1944 I was still young, and I was "there." It so happened a great *rosh yeshivah* from Poland was my work companion. I never knew his name because nobody knew anyone's name. I do not even remember his face, because we all had the same face. All I remember is his voice. The very first day we began working together he said, "Listen, not to study is a sin, even here. Since we work together, at least let's study together." We had no books, no Talmud, nothing. But he knew everything by heart. I had learned a little Talmud before. So we began studying. I never stopped studying, not even there. One day he said, "Tonight don't go to your place. Stay with me." So I stayed next to him. I did not know why, but I soon found out. He and two colleagues — also great masters in Talmud, in Halakhah, in Jewish jurisprudence — had convened a rabbinic court of law to indict the Almighty. He wanted me to witness it, to be there, to see it. And I remember every word, I remember every phase of that trial. It lasted for several nights. Witnesses were summoned. Arguments were heard, always in a whisper, in order not to arouse suspicion and punishment from the others. The arguments? You know the arguments: why and why and why and how long and how long will it last. At the end, after due deliberation, the tribunal issued its verdict, and my teacher, my friend, was the one to pronounce it: Guilty. There was a silence then that probably permeated the entire camp and the entire world, a silence that could be compared only to *Mattan Torah* at Sinai, which the Talmud describes as a special silence. Then after a minute or an infinity of silence he shook himself, smiled sadly, and said, "And now let us pray *Maariv*."

I did not know what to do with that event for many years. I hinted at it in some of my books. But I knew it deserved a full treatment. But I did not know how. First I wrote a novel. I put it in my drawer. I wrote a play. I put it in my drawer. I wrote a cantata. Again into my drawer. You see, I have a very big drawer. Finally I understood what was wrong with it: I could not make literature out of it. I could not reduce it to drama. I had no right to make this event into theater. Then I had an idea. I would push it back in history — back to the Chmielnicki pogroms of 1648-49. And I turned it into a *Purim shpiel*. It became a farce.

What is the story? Three minstrels, three *Purim shpieler*, come to a city called

Adapted from lecture, Loyola University, Chicago, Illinois, April 12, 1980.

Shamgorod in the Ukraine. It is *Purim* eve, and they want to perform a play in order to get food and drink. The innkeeper says, "Are you crazy? Don't you know where you are? You are in Shamgorod. There was a pogrom here last year. Everyone was killed. I and my daughter are the only Jews here. And you want to perform here?" They insist on performing and finally he says, "All right. Under one condition — that I will give you the idea. The theme will be a *din torah* with God, a trial of God. I want you to indict God for what He has done to my family, to my community, to all these Jews." The hungry performers accept.

In the first act the decision is made to hold a trial. In the second act there is a problem: nobody wants to play the role of God's attorney. In the third act we have the trial itself.

LETTER TO JAMES H. SILBERMAN

The Testament

Dear Jim:

Of all my novels, this one is the hardest to define or describe. Richer and more complex than the others, it evolves around more than one theme, involves more than one destiny, and evokes more than one setting.

I began working on it in 1965, during my first visit to the USSR. I knew I would not meet Paltiel Kossover there: like the real-life Jewish poets and novelists, he was executed in 1952. But I had hoped to find out more about him — and them.

Remember? At the end of his life, Stalin's demented anti-Semitism led him to order the arrest and then the murder of the leading Jewish writers in Russia: Peretz Markish, David Bergelson, Der Nister — among many others — vanished without leaving a trace. Nothing is known of how they behaved in jail, what they told their interrogators, and how they confronted their executioner: he even deprived them of their death. Well, in a way, I wrote this novel in order to restore it to them.

This is the substance of the story, Jim. A novel of action and ideas, suspense and anguish, it reflects the dreams and the hopes of our century, marked by disenchantment and violence. Everything begins and ends with words: the same words. Except that the meaning is altered in the process. And suddenly yesterday's heroes receive their share of malediction, not promise.

Messianism and Communism, revolution and poetry, love and adventure, clandestine missions to Nazi Germany and prewar Palestine, pogroms and exiles, the Spanish War and front line duty on the Russian front: all these events find their "dénouement" in a solitary cell of the Soviet secret police, where silence becomes the most refined of tortures.

The characters? A man who is unable to laugh. (The novel actually opens with his line: "I have never laughed in my life") . . . A messianic wanderer who emerges wherever Jews are being persecuted . . . A shrewd prosecutor who traps his victim to write his confession . . . And, of course, Paltiel Kossover, the poet, who tries to explain to himself and to his judge, and to his son, how a religious, mystically inspired adolescent became an agent for the Communist revolution, and how he unmasked its false idols.

How my disillusioned hero recovered his faith, how the mute son managed to redeem his dead father's testament, how an anonymous court stenographer succeeded in outwitting the KGB — all this, and more, is part of the tale . . . which

April 15, 1980

[114]

ends on the eve of *Yom Kippur*, 1973. Which means the tale does not end there; it begins again.

Have I said enough or too much, Jim? Since this novel is so close to me, I am reluctant to speak about it. All I can do is to allow Paltiel Kossover to dream and sing, and remember, in my place.

As ever —
Elie

WORDS ARE THE LINK

The Testament

The hero in the Bible is usually the man of action, the man of faith, the man of commitment. In Hasidism the hero is always a man of compassion. We know of the hero and the anti-hero, and how the anti-hero becomes a hero. Paltiel Kossover comes from a land which has invented a new term. In Russia there is a third category: the non-hero. He is the worst. In the Russian encyclopedia, which is rewritten every year, last year's giant does not reappear, not even as a villain. He becomes a non-writer, a non-military man, a non-person. He simply disappears.

I became interested in Paltiel Kossover in 1965, when I went to Russia for the first time. I met people who had known the poets Stalin had killed in 1952. It was then that I began working on the book. I will tell you why.

I no longer see literature as an art of entertainment. For me literature must fulfill a certain mission in categories of history and justice. Literature is the art of correcting injustices. If there is nothing else I can do, I write a book. This is precisely the task of the witness today, of the modern storyteller, of the Jewish writer. We use words to try to alter the course of events, to save people from humiliation or death. Words have kept us alive for 2,000 years; even more miraculously, we have kept them alive for 2,000 years. This is the beauty of the Jewish tradition and the beauty of the link which binds our people to it. If Isaiah were to come to Jerusalem today and speak, he would be understood. He might even say the same things.

A professor in Jerusalem gave a course in the manuscripts of the Dead Sea Scrolls. At one point he said, "I feel here four lines are missing. I feel it. If I were the author of that chapter in Ben Sira, this is what I would write." And he invented the four lines. Many years later other manuscripts of the same Ben Sira were discovered. And those very four lines were there! They spoke 2,000 years ago, and now we hear the words. Nothing is lost in our memory. Nothing is lost in our history. Whatever we do leaves an imprint somewhere — on one person, on the ground, even on the sand. But once you write it, it stays. Sometimes it takes a few centuries to come back, but it stays.

In the Jewish tradition the individual must be linked to the community. Some have been consciously, others subconsciously. Leon Blum was the first Jew to become prime minister of France. Before he accepted the post he consulted the chief rabbi, asking him, "Do you think I should? Maybe it is bad for the Jews."

Adapted from lecture, Boston University, November 10, 1980.

[116]

Mendès-France, the second Jewish prime minister of France, has been at work on his genealogy since 1936. He wants to trace his Jewish ancestors to Portugal and Spain. He too wants to be linked to his people. That is the only way. I believe again and again that for a Jew the only way to attain universality is through his Judaism. I believe again and again that dialogue is possible, but it must be between two authentic groups, and not with one that would like to be the only authentic one. I believe more and more in the necessity, if not in the power, of words, and in the small daily miracles of bringing a few people together to listen to some words.

THE STORY OF *THE TESTAMENT*

The Testament

Every book I have written fits in with the others. That means there is a link. The body fits organically. Take away, let's say, *The Jews of Silence*, and I could not have written *The Testament*. Take away *A Beggar in Jerusalem*, and I could not have written my other novels. Every book belongs to that structure. Every novel, every story, every essay is part of my life. Each is part of the testimony I am trying to share and to communicate. And *The Testament*, which I began writing in 1965, is part of that structure too.

What is the book about? At the end of his life, which unfortunately was too long, Stalin went crazy, almost clinically crazy, and he gave orders in 1950, '51, '52, first to arrest and then to kill all the Jewish writers in Russia. The greatest poets — Peretz Markish, Itzik Fefer; the great novelists — like Der Nister and David Bergelson: they were all arrested and they vanished. The KGB in Russia — formerly the NKVD or the GPU — has a law, a rule that any document belonging to it can never leave its offices. The documents are stamped "To be conserved for eternity." There have been many defectors, but no documents have ever been brought from there. They remain locked away in the safes. As a result, we do not know what happened to the prisoners, what happened to the Jews who were killed under Stalin. From the moment they were arrested, they vanished, and we do not know how they behaved in jail, what their dreams were, how they spoke to the interrogators. We do not know how they were killed. We do not know anything.

And that troubled me, that pained me, because I believe we should never permit the executioner to deprive his victims of their death. He can kill them. After all, the executioner is stronger than the victim. But at least the death of a person belongs to the person. And here the executioner managed to deprive his victims of their deaths, since we do not know how they died. I decided to deprive the executioner of his victory and to restore their deaths to the victims.

The Testament is the story of a Jewish poet who to me is a combination of Peretz Markish, a poet I admire fervently, and Der Nister, a novelist I also admire fervently. I admire Markish because of his poetry and Der Nister because he was a Bratzlaver Hasid.

I took them as prototypes, and I wrote a story of a Jewish boy called Paltiel Kossover. Kossover is born in 1910 somewhere in Russia, and I describe the way he becomes a Communist. Only after the war did I find out that several of the *yeshivah* students in my little town were Communists. In the evening when every-

---

Lecture, Niles Township Jewish Congregation, Skokie, Illinois, December 7, 1980.

body had already left the *shul* or the *shtibel* to go home, they would stay there —
kaftan, *payes*, *yarmulkas* — open the holy books of Karl Marx and study them in
the way we would study Talmud. They would *shokl* the same way. It was not a
joke. One night in 1939, when the Russian army came near my town, only twenty
miles away from the border, all the Jewish Communist *yeshivah* students disappeared from Sighet. They had crossed the border to discover the fatherland of
communism. They were all arrested and sent to Siberia, where most of them died.

I could not understand what made a *yeshivah* student surrender to communism.
Why did Moscow become their new Jerusalem?

When you study both Judaism and communism, you see they have something in
common. In the beginning communism was a beautiful movement. It was
prophetic, promising fraternity, peace, and the universality of ideas and ideals.
There would be no more hunger, no more slaves, and no more exploiters. Jews
were attracted to the messianic quality of communism. But when you take God out
of the equation, something terrible is bound to happen. Instead of being what it
was supposed to be — a beautiful idea for man — communism became an atro-
cious experiment against man. I describe this in telling how Paltiel Kossover
becomes a Communist.

He leaves Russia, the pogroms; he goes to Berlin, to Paris, to the Civil War, and
then back to Russia, where he is jailed. And there I did not know what to do with
him. I knew he had to be in jail because that was the fate of the poets. But what did
he do while in jail? So I began inventing a kind of testament, which Paltiel
Kossover leaves behind. The interrogator, the judge who speaks to him, realizes
that Paltiel Kossover is a strong man, that he will not betray his people, that he will
not betray his friends. Since Kossover will not become an informer, his interrogator falls upon a brilliant idea. He says to him, "Listen, Tovarich Kossover,
you don't want to confess? It doesn't matter. But you are a writer. Write your life
story." And that does it. Where the human being resisted, the writer cannot. And,
when they give him pen and paper, he begins to write his story — the testament of
Paltiel Kossover.

Kossover sees his son Grisha for the last time when the boy is two years old.
The son survives. He goes to Israel and carries his father's testament to the free
world.

The Testament is actually a story of a repentance. It is the story of a despair that
turns into triumph. Written in prison, this testament frees others from prison.
Somehow, the testament does make its way out, and the story is told.

And that is the beauty of our Jewish memory: the story is always being told.
There is always someone to tell the story. There is always someone to say, "These
are the words, and this is the silence that separates the words, and it is *all* part of
your heritage." There is always someone — one boy, one girl, one father, one
mother, one person — who will say, "I shall become the source, I shall become
the link, and I shall give you my memories."

What does Paltiel Kossover understand at the end? As a Communist he wanted
to save mankind and thought he had to give up his Jewishness in order to do so. At
the end he understands that he was wrong. At the end — too late — he understands
that only as a Jew can he hope to save mankind.

ORIGINS OF *THE TESTAMENT*

The Testament

A few words about the genesis of *The Testament*.

In 1965 I went to Russia for the first time. In the years that followed I tried to find material, documents, anything about the Russian Jewish poets and novelists whom Stalin had killed. I have read their works. Peretz Markish is a powerful poet. Der Nister wrote a two-volume novel called *The Family Mashber*, which is a masterpiece of world literature. And there were others, many others. What astonished me about these intellectuals was that they were Communists, fervent Communists. They could have lived in the Western world, where they were glorified. Markish could have stayed in Poland, in France, or even in Palestine. He had visited Palestine. Bergelson, Fefer, Der Nister, Mikhoels: all could have lived outside, freely, creatively, beautifully. Yet they chose to heed the call of the Revolution.

They returned to Russia and stayed there. They believed in Stalin, and they believed in their cause. They believed in the ultimate victory of the Russian ideal. Yet they were killed by that ideal. They were killed by those who embodied that ideal, by those who ruled over Russia, by Stalin.

Why the faith, and why the hate? How is one to explain that so many Jews belonged to the Communist party in the beginning? How is one to explain that the Communist leaders, especially Stalin, hated them so much? Furthermore, I did not understand how we could go on living and not know more about the last days and last hours, the last minutes of these victims.

I began working on this subject in 1965. I read hundreds of documents and books, published and unpublished. I met hundreds of men and women who came out of Russia. Some of them had even been members of the KGB, and they knew more than the others.

Then I wrote this novel. In a way, Paltiel Kossover is the image of both Der Nister, the novelist, and Peretz Markish, the poet.

He, too, begins as a religious Jew. He, too, is caught by the Communists in their web. He, too, believes fervently that communism is the answer to all the sufferings in the world. And he, too, goes through all the upheavals, all the experiences that modern men, that modern intellectuals endured in the 1920s and 1930s in Germany and France, in the 1940s during the war, and in the 1950s, when he, like the others, was killed.

Adapted from *The Eternal Light*, May 10, 1981.

After my novel appeared, a young man came to see me in Paris. He is a professor at the University of Geneva. And he introduced himself. "My name," he said, "is Shimon Markish." I was startled. He said, "Yes, I am the son of Peretz Markish. Now, tell me, how do you know so much about my father?"

Well, I didn't, but now I do. When I wrote about Paltiel Kossover, I tried to admire, to love, to rehabilitate and redeem all the writers murdered by Stalin, all those who believed in the power of words, in the power of humanity.

PALTIEL KOSSOVER'S SEARCH

The Testament

Paltiel Kossover was searching for a cause, for a meaning, for memories, for redemption. He was searching for the redemption of man. He wanted to save mankind. But that was the aim of every Jewish child in Eastern Europe, whether he wanted it or not. He drank it from the air, from the water, from the leaves and the trees. There was something so powerful in the suffering of these men and women and children that they wanted to stop not only their own suffering but all suffering. They wanted to bring the Messiah.

Adapted from *The Eternal Light*, May 17, 1981.

THE MARK

The Testament

How did Paltiel Kossover become a Communist? How does anyone become a Communist? Not because one reads certain books but because one meets certain people. Whatever happens in our lives is always influenced by our friends, by a chance encounter. I can go one way, or I can go another. And because, for no reason at all, I go to the right rather than to the left, my life has changed. Often I wonder what would have happened if I had gone to the left. What would have happened if I had met one person and not another? Every encounter leaves a mark. Every person leaves a mark. Every story leaves a mark.

Adapted from *The Eternal Light*, May 17, 1981.

THE WATCHMAN AND THE POET

The Testament

Viktor Zupanev becomes a very important character in Paltiel Kossover's life and destiny. The watchman and the poet. Why? Because this book is not only the story of Paltiel Kossover, it is also the story of Viktor Zupanev, just as it is the story of Grisha Kossover, just as it is the story of any man jailed, imprisoned, tortured, and mutilated, in Russia or in any other dictatorship.

We may even say that this is the story of laughter. In the beginning Zupanev cannot laugh. At the end he laughs. Why does he laugh? Because the story that was meant to be stifled, that was meant to be dead comes to life elsewhere — in Jerusalem. What a laughter! What a victory!

The element of laughter plays an important role in all my tales. There is something about laughter that makes man more human or less. It all depends on what we do with it. When someone is sad, and he laughs, then there is strength in him. When someone is sad, and I laugh, then I am less human than before. So it all depends on what we do with our capacity, our ability, to laugh when confronted by tragedy.

Often, in my novels, I make people laugh. Although the tragedy around them is tremendous, all-powerful, they laugh. That is their victory. I did not know the origin of my obsession with laughter until I began working on my Hasidic books and found myself coming back again and again to the great master, the great storyteller, Rabbi Nahman of Bratzlav. Rabbi Nahman is also enchanted with people who laugh. Laughter plays a role in every one of his tales. For Nahman of Bratzlav there is always a place in the world where all the laughter concentrates, where laughter redeems the world or brings it to its senses.

When I think of Paltiel Kossover, I feel he has all the right to join his friend, his unknown friend, Viktor Zupanev, and laugh at the world, but not only at the world: with the world and for the world.

Adapted from *The Eternal Light*, May 17, 1981.

AGAINST GOD AND MAN

The Testament

Communism started out as a movement of compassion, fraternity, and humanity. But it lost its humanity, and it became one of the most vicious, one of the bloodiest, one of the cruelest experiments in history — because it began by denying God entry into history. And the next step was to deny man the right to be in history, freely, independently as a sovereign human being.

Adapted from *The Eternal Light*, May 31, 1981.

Open Letters

AN OPEN LETTER TO PARENTS EVERYWHERE

Last Wednesday, while your kids were in school having fun, Israeli kids were in school being slaughtered.

You say it's a horror. An outrage. An unspeakable tragedy.

And this is the greatest tragedy.

Only a generation ago, the world stood by silent while one million Jewish children were massacred in Europe.

Everyone knew about it. They turned away and forgot.

Will the world continue to be silent while ruthless murderers kill Jewish children in Israel?

As survivors of the Holocaust, we appeal to men and women of conscience everywhere to cry out against Arab assassins and their planned wave of terror.

Those who give shelter to killers are killers themselves.

Those who give money and weapons to assassins are assassins themselves.

Those who try to invent political or ideological excuses for their unspeakable crimes are their accomplices, as are those in the United Nations who do not condemn, unequivocally, their policy of murder.

The UN Security Council must bear responsibility for the tragic killings at Maalot because of their refusal to condemn the Arab killings at Kiryat Shemonah, and all earlier massacres.

Now — this time — we must succeed in shaking mankind's indifference.

How much sorrow and shame can one generation endure?

Will we again turn away and forget?

Full page advertisement, *The New York Times*, May 20, 1974 (also signed by Josef Rosensaft).

[129]

AN OPEN LETTER TO PRESIDENT GISCARD d'ESTAING OF FRANCE

Dear Mr. President:

It is because of my love for France and my respect for its people that I feel compelled to express to you my sadness and my indignation — shared by many other Americans — over your handling of the Abu Daoud affair.

Although born in Eastern Europe, I owe France more than I owe my own native land. I owe France my secular education, my language, and my career as a writer.

Liberated from Buchenwald, it was in France that I found compassion and humanity. It was in France that I found generosity and friendship. It was in France that I discovered the other side, the brighter side, of mankind.

I was proud of France.

France, to me, represented humanity's highest values in a sterile and cynical society. It evoked Rousseau and Bergson, Proust and Zola, Camus and Mauriac. It symbolized an inspiring quest for justice and brotherhood. In France, I thought, the word humanism does not make people laugh.

Yes, I was proud of France.

France, the birthplace of revolutions against tyranny. France, the ally of our American independence. France, the herald of human rights. France, haven for the persecuted. France and its freedom fighters. France and its Resistance. France and its response to Dreyfus.

No nation had so much prestige. No culture was so readily accepted. No example as universally extolled.

And now, Mr. President?

Now, what has become of France?

Its moral leadership is gone, and its luster tarnished in the eyes of men of conscience. In fact, few countries have lost so much prestige so quickly. What has become of France?

It has betrayed its own traditions.

France has become as cynical as the rest of the world.

Why did your government free Abu Daoud?

And why so hastily?

He lied under oath about his false identity.

Why wasn't he held until Germany or Israel could offer evidence of his crime?

Why was he allowed to leave Paris in the comfort of a first class airline seat, when eleven Israeli athletes left Munich in coffins?

Full page advertisement, *The New York Times*, January 20, 1977.

[130]

Your prime minister claims that the courts were not politically motivated. Does anyone believe him in your country?

Not in mine.

In my country we believe that France quite simply, and quite shockingly, yielded to killers' blackmail, oil merchants' bribery, and the chance to sell some fighter planes. And in doing that, France deliberately humiliated the victims' widows and orphans and insulted the memory of their dead.

Are you surprised the world responded with dismay and outrage?

Your own people rose to speak out against you.

Because while you have visited Auschwitz, you have forgotten its lesson.

But then, in truth, one should have expected nothing else from France today. In recent years the signs have multiplied.

Offensive statements. Sneering remarks. Sudden policy reversals. Strange alliances. Broken promises. One-sided embargoes. The Cherbourg affair. The Mirage sale. French governments have rarely missed an opportunity to demonstrate their hostility to Israel and the Jewish people.

For ideological reasons?

Much worse: purely for money.

Yes, Mr. President, I used to be proud of France and what it stood for.

I no longer am.

A RESPONSE TO A LETTER
FROM THE FALASHAS

Dear Friends:

Recently, many of us have received numerous letters from you or about you. Most of us are moved, deeply moved by your plight and by your plea for help. If only I knew what course to follow, what action to recommend. Unfortunately I do not. Frankly, if Israel and the Jewish Agency have failed to respond, they must have reasons. Are they valid? For us too?

Your criticism of the Israeli government disturbs me. No one will ever convince me that Israel could be or would be insensitive to a situation where Jewish lives are involved. And yet, and yet.

I am shattered by your reports; I trust your sincerity. Something must be done — and soon. By whom? By world Jewry first of all. When Jews in distress ask to be saved, we must respond.

Would it be impossible for great Jewish organizations to work out a rescue plan in cooperation with the Israeli government and the Jewish Agency? Let us hope not. Together we may achieve results. And save lives.

Present Tense, Summer, 1979.

TO A JEWISH FRIEND IN FRANCE

Swastikas on walls. . .
Elderly Jews beaten in broad
daylight. . . Machine guns
firing at Jewish nurseries, at Houses
of Study and Worship. . .
A synagogue bombed on holiday eve. . .
Painted slogans:
"Kike, your hour has come. . ."

My friend:

I feel your pain and I share your anger. The explosion at the synagogue on Rue Copernic has been heard throughout the United States. Those who murdered innocent people on *Simhat Torah*, in Paris, attacked us all.

For the first time since Auschwitz and Treblinka, Nazi murderers set out to kill Jews — only because they were Jews.

You have been told by the French people that "We are all Jews." And we are grateful to them for this act of solidarity. Nevertheless, numb with outrage and horror, we must ask: Why? How could this happen? Perhaps we are being told something by events, something we have been afraid to understand.

When the cynical rhetoric of the United Nations, day after day, tells us that "Zionism is racism" . . . When Israel's right to exist is continually challenged. . . . When nearly a hundred books have been published in a dozen languages calling the massacre and burning of six million Jews "a lie" and "a hoax" . . . Then perhaps these "new" Nazis may feel they are following a trend — that they have some claim, however twisted, to legitimacy.

Is it not time for people of good conscience, everywhere, to recognize the face beneath the mask? To recognize that even passive assent to intellectual racism leads the way to open anti-Semitism and murder? How else explain the resurgence of organized Nazism all over the world? You have your Nazis and, apparently, we — all of us — have ours. But these disciples of Hitler must be denied even the semblance of support. They must be denied the dignity of dialogue. They must be cast out from civilized society. In attacking you, my Jewish friend in France, the killers have issued a warning to all of us.

As Pastor Martin Niemoller, the German theologian, said: "*First the Nazis went after the Jews, but I was not a Jew, so I did not object. Then they went after the Catholics, but I was not a Catholic, so I did not object. Then they went after*

Full page advertisement, *The New York Times*, October 16, 1980.

[133]

the trade unionists, but I was not a trade unionist, so I did not object. Then they came after me, and there was no one left to object."

Perhaps the killers think we have forgotten our history. I write this letter to assure you — and them — that we have forgotten nothing.

TO OUR FALASHA BROTHERS AND SISTERS

First we refused to recognize you as brothers and sisters. Then we were reluctant to allow you to come and join us and become part of our communities. Then we chose to remain deaf to your plight. It took years for your outcry to reach our hearts. Have we changed in the process? Has our attitude changed? Has our commitment deepened? Only you may answer these questions.

As for myself, I know that we have not done enough. We could do more; we must do more.

Some of you are in danger; only we are concerned. Only we could help. Not to respond to your pleas would diminish us in your eyes, and in our own as well.

Elie Wiesel

Release (A Report from American Association for Ethiopian Jews), Summer, 1984. Letter dated June 13, 1984.

Jewish History and World History

THE TALE OF ARAB JEWRY

If we do not speak of the Jews in Arab countries, we are committing a sin. Even more desperate, even more in danger than the Jews in Russia are the Jews in Arab countries.

No Jewish gathering anywhere should take place today without remembering those forgotten Jews, so abandoned by their own people. We do not even think about them. Why? Because there are only 10,000 — as though numbers matter. In the absolute sense of the word one Jew is as important as one million Jews. The moment you start thinking that the individual Jew anywhere is expendable you have already denied your commitment to try to defend your people.

If at all one can invoke the Holocaust period as a comparison, it cannot be applied to Soviet Jewry but only to Arab Jewry. I do it not with a light heart, because I never make these comparisons. I have always said — I still do — that the Holocaust is a unique event, like the *Mattan Torah*, like the giving of the Torah, never to be repeated again. The only echo of the Holocaust I find today is in Arab countries. We have unimpeachable reports of what is happening there.

In Egypt Jewish men have been in concentration camps since 1967. Their families are starving. They have no one to support them. In most cases, supreme irony, the camps are guarded by former SS men. In Iraq eleven Jews were hanged one night, and the populace of Baghdad was requested to come and rejoice under the gallows. And the populace came and danced under the gallows. In Syria, again, Jews are in jail. They have committed no crime. They are mainly old people. They don't even have what they have in Russia — young people to rebel, to sing, and to defy the regime. These are old, broken Jews. They are in jail, and they are being tortured in medieval manner. The Red Cross published a report a couple of years ago on how these Jews are being mistreated and tortured in Syrian jails. I have spoken to one of these Jews in Israel. The Syrian jailers send hungry dogs into solitary cells where they tear the prisoners' flesh. I hate propaganda. But this is true, and we must not hide it. These Jews are in jail or in camps. Those who are not, who are "free," live in ghetto conditions. Their bank accounts are closed. They have no jobs, either in government or in private industry. They are under curfew regulations; they cannot leave their homes from six or seven in the evening until the next morning. They have no right to use the telephone. They have no right to communicate with their relatives abroad. What can these Arab governments want with them? No one asks these governments to let them go to Israel.

Adapted from lecture, Congregation Shaarey Zedek, Southfield, Michigan, February, 1971.

An emergency conference took place in Paris a month ago. It had no echo. Arthur Goldberg, Professor Isidor Rabi, who won the Nobel Prize, and Bayard Rustin came from America. Presidents of parliament and other very important personalities took part in it. Twenty-six countries were represented. The delegates were not even received by the French government. Did the newspapers cover the conference? No. Is there one single government that tries to do something about these poor Jews? No. Somehow we have forgotten them. The remorse and regret these poor Jews must now feel for not having left their countries when there was time to leave must make them the unhappiest Jews on earth today.

I do not know what we can do for them. I am becoming very skeptical in general, very pessimistic where Jews are concerned. But at least let us remember them. Maybe one day some Jew in Syria, in Iraq, in Egypt will find out that a few Jews here and there in America met and were told their tale.

THE IMPENETRABLE SHIELD

Of course I find the UN resolution equating Zionism with racism despicable. In terms of propaganda I could not care less what they are saying. One has to be stupid to believe that we are racist. No tradition in the history of culture is as generous as the Jewish tradition.

Really, what can the UN do to a people whose memory and whose suffering is the most ancient in the world. What can the world do to us that it has not done already?

In a strange way we are stronger than ever. Wounded, terribly wounded, we are scarred, profoundly scarred — but stronger than ever. Physically, we are in danger, vincible, but metaphysically, we are invincible.

Of course, the Arabs can always buy the Communist advisers' help. But in terms of history — not of geography, not of economics, not even of politics — but in history we have power. I really believe what they are doing in the UN is more dangerous than we realize, because they try to deprive us of that power. Everything they have done to us they accuse us of having done.

When the enemy tries to corrupt language and distort history, when he comes and says that we, the victims, are racists, that means he deprives us of our memory. He deprives us of our specific past and he removes us, or he tries to remove us, from our place, which is so painfully unique with regard to the Holocaust.

For the last thirty years we were shielded by the Holocaust. Now our enemies have realized how strong a shield it was, and they would like to destroy it. And that we shall not let happen. Ever. Why? Not only because we owe it to those who died. We owe it to ourselves and to the living.

Adapted from address, 75th Anniversary Celebration of Jewish Federation of St. Louis, February 22, 1976.

[141]

IT ENDS WITH OTHERS

Two Muslim groups fight one another, and they take Jewish hostages! It is like the Jewish joke of the two princes who meet during the Middle Ages in Poland and quarrel. One says to the other, "If you will beat my Jew, I will beat your Jew." Why should they beat Jews at all? True, the Hanafi episode is only an episode. But in Jewish history there are no anecdotes, there are no episodes — there are only events. The smallest anecdote becomes a segment in history. And the smallest episode becomes an event. It attains the intensity of an event.

In this little episode we have the substance of Jewish destiny — with its fears, its hopes, its helplessness, its absurdity. It was absurd. The victims were helpless. Because a few madmen, mad with violence, were there with guns, the poor Jews at B'nai B'rith headquarters could not do anything. And they lived through traumatic events. What was worse, we could not do anything. We were helpless. What could we have done: except be aware, and we were aware; except empathize, and we did empathize; except not to sleep at night, and we didn't sleep at night? But what did it do to those Jews there?

We heard the stories from Washington, what they did to the people there. They took one girl and made her kneel and read the Koran aloud. This reminded me of what happened one generation ago when an SS officer came into a *shul* on *Shabbat* in a ghetto, stopped the service, and said to the rabbi, "You are not going to read your Torah, but you are going to read *Mein Kampf*." There is no parallel between *Mein Kampf* and the Koran. The Koran is a holy book, which I revere, which we should all revere. The parallel is not the books but that one group imposed its will upon the vision and the soul of another group.

They were cruel not only to Jews. Most of the hostages were not Jewish. Most of the hostages were black people who worked for B'nai B'rith. And the Hanafi group was more cruel to the black people than to the Jews. What does it mean? It means that those who hate Jews hate everybody. Those who are cruel to one group of people are cruel to all groups of people. They begin with Jews. Again the theme of beginning. We are always those with whom they begin and begin again. But it ends with others.

Adapted from lecture, Congregation Shaarey Zedek, Southfield, Michigan, March 20, 1977.

MANKIND IS THE TARGET

Violence, brutality, and terror are part of the modern world. Kidnaping, hijacking, political assassination — bizarre, unholy ties exist between Palestinian murderers and German nihilists, between Japanese anarchists and Latin American militants. At first when Jews were singled out as principal targets, most so-called civilized nations said nothing, did nothing. But now everyone has become a possible victim. Once again we have learned, therefore, that as a result of what took place one generation ago Jewish history and world history are now one and inseparable. What happens to the one affects the other. True, once upon a time Jews were destroyed as Jews, and it appeared a simple matter: killers on one side, victims on the other. Only in the process mankind too was assaulted, wounded, murdered.

This was not known then, but we know it now: Any attack on the Jewish people today may lead to the end of the world.

Adapted from lecture, 92nd Street YMHA, New York, November 3, 1977.

THE VICTIMS OF INJUSTICE
MUST BE CARED FOR

Homeless, helpless, voiceless — these anonymous uprooted men and women who are unwanted everywhere and know it; these emaciated, forlorn children who, behind barbed wire, can barely walk or even breathe; those enormous eyes mute with terror and devoured by hunger — are they still alive?

You see them, the boat people, on TV and on front pages everywhere, and you cannot help asking yourself whether in the meantime they have not fallen victim to malnutrition, disease, or quite simply: despair. Or whether, while governments begin to make plans about what to do with them, they have already been thrown back to the sea, the jungle, or into the prisons of their native lands.

Hundreds of them perish every day, according to eyewitnesses. Thousands will be dead before the United Nations conference on their plight convenes in Geneva on July 20.

Why so late? Why the delay? With so many innocent lives at stake, why wasn't this meeting organized earlier? What does it take to make the UN leadership realize that such an emergency warrants greater haste?

These are but some of the questions that must disturb every decent person concerned with the scandal and tragedy of the boat people. There are others as well.

President Carter and six other Western leaders happened to be in Asia two weeks ago. I wish they could have made a point of visiting one or more of the refugee camps in Thailand and Malaysia, simply to show these latest victims of our society that we care about their fate, that we are aware of their ordeal and are touched by their anguish. Such a visit surely would have had a moral impact. It might even have influenced certain officials to act more humanely toward these refugees before and after they became refugees.

What about Pope John Paul II? Why hasn't he gone there to help and console, to see and to be seen? He who went to Auschwitz surely understands the importance of his presence — for a day, an hour — in the midst of these starving, dependent human beings.

Of course, I will be the last to make analogies about what happened in the 1930s and now. We ought not to use Holocaust terminology for other tragedies.

And yet, how can we witness the conditions of today's boat people *without* remembering those who, one generation ago, were not given shelter anywhere and whose misery and death were met with organized complacency?

How can we watch them, wounded and frightened children, *without* thinking at

Los Angeles Times, Opinion, July 8, 1979.

the same time about other children, of another generation, who were disowned by an allegedly civilized world?

Granted, the tragedies are different in essence and scope — but the universality of man's indifference remains the same.

In the meantime, victims continue to suffer as they have now for some forty years, first under the French, then the Americans, then the Chinese, the Khmer Rouge, and finally the Vietnamese — their own brothers.

Well, soon there will be an international conference in Geneva. Speeches will be made; resolutions will be adopted. Let us hope that it will not be another version of the infamous 1938 Evian Conference, which resulted in Hitler's vindication when the Western powers refused to take action on behalf of the persecuted. In its wake, the German propaganda machine lost no time pointing out that no one wanted the European Jews.

If we remember the Evian Conference, the Geneva meeting will bring forth opposite messages; it will announce to the world at large that victims of injustice and oppression must be cared for — and will be.

The Geneva conference will bring results *because* the Evian meeting brought none. Today's boat people will find a haven because the passengers of the *St. Louis* found none. Today's victims are not forsaken because the Jews of the 1930s were. If the fate of the boat people does inspire a vast movement of solidarity and compassion throughout the Western world, it is because the life and death of another people, only some forty years ago, were met by society's indifference.

There exists a link between yesterday and today; and we, the witnesses, are the link. Hence, our tendency to weigh and judge all events against the background of what preceded them, and perhaps paved the way for them.

This must be why we survivors of the Holocaust are so deeply — so personally — involved in the tragedy that unfolds in Asia now. More than others we know, yes, we know that we must save these new victims from death or rejection and despair: not to do so would mean to betray them — and those who were betrayed before them.

THIS IS HISTORY

There are those who say the world would listen to us more closely if we would universalize our experience by linking it to the five million non-Jews who also were murdered. I am absolutely against this position.

I believe that the uniqueness of the experience is such that the only way for us to honor it is to remember it in its uniqueness. The implications are general, the lessons are universal, but the event is Jewish. No other people was ontologically threatened. Only the Jewish people — and to a certain extent, but only to a certain extent, the Gypsies — was exposed to a death sentence only because of *being* Jewish, meaning to be was a crime. Only the Jews. Those who speak about the 11,000,000 do not know what they are talking about. The figure 11,000,000 is nonsensical. Either it is 30,000,000 civilians, or it is 6,000,000 Jews.

At one of our ceremonies President Carter spoke of 11,000,000. I asked him, "Where did you get that figure?" He said, "From other Jews." Then I felt I had to explain to him, and I said, "Mr. President, it is true that not all victims were Jews, but all Jews were victims. Always remember that." And then I said, "I am not saying there were no Gentiles in the camps. There were — and some of them very good human beings: resistance fighters, some priests, some Communists. There were decent human beings, but they were in the minority." And, in fact, the majority of the others there were enemies of the Jews. When a Jew finally survived the selection and entered Auschwitz or Treblinka or Buchenwald, his agony did not stop. He had to face all the anti-Semites from the other minorities. A Jew was beaten up much more by Ukrainians in the camp than by Germans; he rarely saw the Germans. They were in their towers with the machine guns. "And you want me," I asked the president, "to honor their memory together with that of a million Jewish children and Hasidim and rabbis and grandparents? How can you?"

I think anyone who does this is doing a total disservice to Jewish history. It is a betrayal of Jewish history to make comparisons. I am not against honoring victims of nazism during the Second World War. I am for it. I am ready to do whatever I can to honor their memory, because they deserve it. But they were not victims of the Holocaust. Only the Jews. What can we do? This is history. And we have no right to change it now. Once you start watering it down, again we are lost. You cannot. I reject such universalization. I believe the Jewish tragedy was a Jewish and human tragedy in its substance, with universal lessons and consequences.

Statement, Niles Township Jewish Congregation, Skokie, Illinois, December 7, 1980.

President's Commission on the Holocaust

A QUEST FOR MEMORY
AND JUSTICE

We have gathered here in this hall echoing with history — the Declaration of Independence has been hanging on these walls for generations — to try to find the proper ways to remember what it meant to live and to die in the era of darkness.

It is with a deep sense of duty, privilege, and humility that I have accepted to serve as chairman of this uniquely distinguished group of civic, religious, and political leaders.

Some of you, I know, are worthier than I, and most of you are surely more experienced in this kind of endeavor. With your help and cooperation, I hope we shall fulfill our task.

The problems facing us may seem insurmountable. We are supposed to remember and move others to remember. But how does one remember individually and collectively an event that was intended to erase memory?

By its scope and incommensurable magnitude, by its sheer weight of numbers, by its mystery and silence, the Holocaust defies anything the human being can conceive of or aspire to.

All the documents, all the testimony, all the eyewitness accounts, all the history books notwithstanding, we know that we have not yet begun to tell the tale.

How does one reconcile the purely Jewish aspects of the tragedy with its inevitable universal connotations?

True, all Jews are victims; but not all victims were Jewish. How are they to be remembered? Specifically? Collectively? Individually? Personally? Through monuments? Education? Special liturgy? Ceremonies of remembrance?

We lack a reference point. We do not know what to do because of the uniqueness of the event. We cannot even go back into history and learn that this is what people used to do to commemorate such events, because there was no such event.

Also, whatever our purposes will be — and I hope they will be lofty and daring — we must remember at least this: that we must think boldly. Let the scope and magnitude of our endeavor not frighten us.

Whatever we do, let it strike the imagination of people everywhere, of all faiths, of all creeds, of all nationalities, of all nations, and perhaps of all centuries.

Let people know that our generation — probably the last that still has something to remember — does indeed remember. For whatever happened yesterday is already history, but is it history alone?

Opening statement, President's Commission on the Holocaust, Washington, D.C., February 15, 1979.

The men and women whose memory we try to evoke — their shadow weighs upon the present. And this opens again for our consideration another question: Can we hear of the desperate and despairing boat people and not recall in our minds the homeless, wandering refugees of the Holocaust era? Or can we remember the statute-of-limitations debate in Germany and not see it in its timeless context of crimes and horrors never to be forgotten, never to be equalled?

We around this table represent a noble quest for memory and justice. We are all committed to truth. And though we come from different horizons, we shall respect one another's beliefs.

The Holocaust was possible because the enemy — the enemy of the Jewish people and of mankind, and it is always the same enemy — succeeded in dividing, in separating, in splitting the human society: nation against nation, Christian against Jew, young against old.

Well, we must not submit to such temptation now. We around this table must see to it that the memory of the Holocaust draws us all closer together.

Therefore, the survivors in our midst will have to bear with us if, due to the technicality of some of our proceedings, some of us will seem — I insist, "seem" — insensitive to their memories.

And the non-survivors in our midst will have to bear with us if at times, due to the personal interpretation some words have to us, we may seem too sensitive.

We are all entering this project together with a sense of history. This moment is solemn because it is linked to history and because it tries to turn history into a moral endeavor.

Forgive me for introducing into this session a note of melancholy. While we are grateful to President Carter and his advisers for being so deeply concerned with the Holocaust now, I cannot but wonder what would have happened had the president of the United States then, and his advisers then, demonstrated the same concern.

If a presidential commission had been appointed in 1942 or 1943 to prevent the Holocaust, how many victims — Jews and non-Jews — would have been saved?

Well, they were forgotten while they were alive. They are dead now. Let us at least remember them and include their memory in our own.

We have gathered here because we remember, and we hope to move others to remember as well.

So, we have this unique occasion, and this unique group of people — scholars and statesmen, rabbis and priests, social activists and writers, Jews and Christians, believers and secularists. We are here not to indulge in politics, nor to dwell in other people's pain; we are here to maintain alive the memory of that pain which transcended the accepted categories of national, religious, and ethnic groups.

Not to do so, my friends, would deprive us of the right to preach sermons and teach classes and represent people in Congress, to write novels and create books of all types.

In other words, not to do so would deprive us of the right to speak on behalf of universal conscience, for conscience cannot but be universal.

For some of us, this moment is both solemn and poignant. As we were being sworn-in at the White House, the survivors in our midst — you have seen them — had tears, both visible and invisible, in their eyes.

There was something — something in the atmosphere. We have been entrusted with an awesome legacy, and we are being judged by invisible friends, brothers, teachers, parents, and they are all dead. And they all had but one wish: to be remembered.

As we begin our proceedings, we hear the *Kaddish* of a community somewhere in the Ukraine, a community that did not live long enough to complete the prayer.

We hear the whispers of thousands of human beings, walking in nocturnal processions toward flames, wondering whether the Messiah had come, a strange Messiah, the anti-Messiah.

We hear the battle orders of ghetto fighters. We hear the mute laments of abandoned children. We hear "Bergen-Belsen." We hear "Treblinka." And we hear "Chelmno." And we are seized by "Majdanek."

We shiver because of Auschwitz, and we burn because of Auschwitz. Unless we hear all these sounds and voices, my friends, we must not speak.

Unless we remember in good faith and in sincerity in the very depths of our being, we must not speak.

But speak we must.

For our generation is a privileged one. Children condemned never to grow old . . . old men doomed never to die . . . a solitude engulfing an entire people . . . a guilt tormenting all humanity . . . a despair that found a face but not a name . . . a memory cursed, yet refusing to pass on its curse and hate. . . an attempt to understand, perhaps even to forgive: that is our generation.

And therefore, my friends on the Commission and on the Board of Advisors, I hope it is with this sense of purpose and in this framework of flames that are still burning in our memories that our proceedings will begin.

THE HOLOCAUST: BEGINNING OR END?

Mr. President, Mr. Vice President, Mr. Speaker, Leaders and Members of the House and the Senate, Distinguished Guests:

Allow me to tell you a story.

Once upon a time, far away, somewhere in the Carpathian Mountains, there lived a small boy, a Jewish boy, whose dreams were filled with God, prayer, and song.

Then one day, he and his family, and all the Jews of his town were rounded up and exiled to a dark and evil kingdom. They arrived there at midnight. Then came the first separation, the first selection.

As the boy stood with his father, wondering whether his mother and sisters would come back, an inmate came to tell them the truth: this road led to the final destination of the Jewish people. The truth was there: in the fire, the ashes. The truth was in death. And the young boy refused to believe him. It had to be a lie, a nightmare perhaps, this could not be happening, not here, not now, not in the heart of civilized Europe, not in the middle of the twentieth century. "Father," said the boy, "if this were true, the world would not be silent. . . ." "Perhaps the world does not know," said the father. And father and son walked on, part of an eerie nocturnal procession, toward mysterious flames of darkness.

Thirty-five years later — almost to the day — the same Jewish boy stands before you with a deep sense of privilege, to remind our contemporaries that in those times of anguish and destruction, only one people — the Jewish people — was totally, inexplicably abandoned — only one people was simply, cynically handed over to its executioners.

And we, the few survivors, were left behind to bear witness and tell the tale.

But before doing so, allow me, on behalf of your Commission on the Holocaust and its Advisory Board, to thank you, Mr. President, for summoning our nation — and all nations — to keep its memory alive.

We also wish to express our profound gratitude to all the distinguished guests and national leaders for being here today at this unprecedented assembly, responding to this call for remembrance. No other country, and its government, besides Israel, has issued or heeded such a call, but then Israel is a case apart. Israel's commitment to memory is as old as its history itself.

Address, National Civic Holocaust Commemoration Ceremony, Capitol Rotunda, Washington, D.C., April 24, 1979.

Of my first night in the camp, which was the last for most of my friends, my family, my relatives, my teachers, I wrote:

> Never shall I forget that night, the first night in camp, which has turned my life into one long night, seven times cursed and seven times sealed. Never shall I forget that smoke. Never shall I forget the little faces of the children whose bodies I saw turned into wreaths of smoke beneath a silent blue sky.
> Never shall I forget those flames which consumed my faith forever.
> Never shall I forget that nocturnal silence which deprived me, for all eternity, of the desire to live. Never shall I forget those moments which murdered my God and my soul and turned my dreams to dust. Never shall I forget these things, even if I am condemned to live as long as God himself. Never.

But Mr. President and friends — what does one do with such memories of fire — with so many fragments of despair? How does one live in a world which witnessed the murder of one million children and remained world?

Those of us who were there are haunted by those whose lives were turned into ashes, by those whose cemetery was the sky.

Terror-stricken families hiding in ghetto cellars. Children running with priceless treasures: a potato or two, a crumb of bread. Endless lines of quiet men and women on their way to mass graves, reciting the *Kaddish*, the prayer for the dead, over themselves. Teachers and their pupils, mothers and their infants, rabbis and their followers, rich and poor, learned and illiterate, princes and beggars — all pushed inexorably toward death. "Father," says a young boy, "is it painful to die? Must I die?" "Think of something else," answers the father. "Think of tomorrow."

Treblinka and Ponar, Auschwitz and Babi Yar, Majdanek and Belzec: What happened? Did Creation go mad? Did God cover his face? Did the Creator turn against His Creation? Did the God of Israel turn against the people of Israel? The question everyone asked upon arrival inside the gates was: What does it all mean? Was there a design, a secret pattern?

We didn't know, we still don't. How can anyone explain evil of such magnitude? How can anyone comprehend so much pain and anguish? One cannot conceive of Auschwitz with or without God. But what about man? Who can understand the calculated deprivation of the killers? The indifference of the onlookers? When Jews did have a possibility of leaving Europe, how many countries were there ready to accept them?

What was the Holocaust: an end or a beginning? Prefiguration or culmination? Was it the final convulsion of demonic forces in history? A paroxysm of centuries-old bigotry and hatred? Or, on the contrary, a momentous warning of things to come?

Turning point or watershed, it produced a mutation on a cosmic scale, affecting all possible areas of human endeavor. After Auschwitz, the human condition is no longer the same. After Treblinka, nothing will ever be the same. The event has altered man's perception and changed his relationship to God, to his fellow man, and to himself. The unthinkable has become real. After Belsen, everything seems possible.

Admittedly, I belong to a traumatized generation; hence I speak of my people, the Jewish people. But when I, as a Jew, evoke the tragic destiny of Jewish victims, I honor the memory of all the victims. When one group is persecuted, mankind is affected. Still, for the sake of truth, we must remember that only the Jewish people's extermination was an end in itself. Jewish victims, stripped of their identity and of their death, were disowned by the whole world. They were condemned not for what they did or said but for who they were: sons and daughters of a people whose suffering is the most ancient in recorded history.

Every occupied nation, every underground movement received help from London, Washington, or Moscow. Not the Jews: they were the loneliest victims of the most inhuman of wars. A single airdrop, a single rescue mission would have proved to them, and to the enemy, that they were not forgotten. But, Mr. President and friends, the truth is that they were forgotten.

The evidence is before us: the world knew and kept silent. The documents that you, Mr. President, handed to the chairman of your Commission on the Holocaust testify to that effect. Actually, pictures of Auschwitz and Birkenau had reached the free world much earlier. Still, when the Hungarian Jews began arriving there, feeding the flames with ten to twelve thousand persons a day, nothing was done to stop or delay the process. Not one bomb was dropped on the railway tracks to the death factories. Had there been a similar joint session of Congress then, things would have been different for many Jews.

And yet, and yet when the nightmare lifted, there was no hate in the hearts of those who survived — only sadness and, paradoxically, hope. For some reason they were convinced that out of grief and so much suffering a powerful message of compassion and justice would be heard and received. They were convinced that the Messiah would come and redeem the world. They were convinced that, after Auschwitz, people would no longer yield to fanaticism, nations would no longer wage war, and racism, anti-Semitism, and class humiliation would be banned forever, shamed forever.

Little did we know that in our lifetime we would witness more wars, new racial hostilities, and an awakening of nazism on all five continents. Little did we know that in our lifetime books would appear in many languages offering so-called "proof" that the Holocaust never occurred, that our parents, our friends did not die there. Little did we know that Jewish children would again be murdered, in cold blood, by killers in Israel.

The survivors advocated hope, not despair. Their testimony contains neither rancor nor bitterness. They knew too well that hate is self-debasing and vengeance self-defeating. Instead of choosing nihilism and anarchy, they chose to opt for man. Instead of setting cities on fire, they enriched them. Many went to rebuild an ancient dream *of* Israel *in* Israel; they all chose to remain human in an inhuman society, to fight for human rights everywhere, against poverty everywhere and discrimination, for humankind, always.

For we have learned certain lessons. We have learned not to be neutral in times of crisis, for neutrality always helps the aggressor, never the victim. We have learned that silence is never the answer. We have learned that the opposite of love is not hatred, but indifference. What is memory if not a response to and against indifference?

So let us remember for their sake and ours: memory may perhaps be our only answer, our only hope to save the world from the ultimate punishment, a nuclear holocaust.

Let us remember the heroes of Warsaw, the martyrs of Treblinka, the children of Auschwitz. They fought alone, they suffered alone, they lived alone, but they did not die alone, for something in all of us died with them.

AGAINST EXTRAPOLATION

The universality of the Holocaust lies in its uniqueness. If I speak as a Jew about Jews, of course I speak about others as well. If I were to stop speaking about Jews, I would betray both the others and my own people. I simply do not believe in denials. If I speak of my people, I speak of all people. . . . We simply have to do what we must do: remember. Once you remember, you remember everybody. Memory is not something that shrinks but something that enriches. You go deeper and deeper and deeper, and you find new layers.

Truly, I must tell you when I hear certain extrapolations, I am worried. For instance, we used to speak, when we spoke — we didn't dare speak too much — about six million Jews. Then some friends, some people, began reminding us, "True, but after all there were others as well." It is true; there were others as well. So they said, "Eleven million, six of whom are Jews." If this goes on, the next step will be eleven, including six, and, in a couple of years, they won't even speak of the six. They will speak only of eleven million. You see the progression: six million plus five, then eleven including six, and then only eleven.

If I were to tell you that I have an answer how to solve, how to combine these terms, I would lie. I do not know how. For the moment I am weak. My heart is not that large. It can barely include the figure six million.

Statement, meeting of President's Commission on the Holocaust, Washington, D.C., April 24, 1979.

[156]

TO DEEPEN MEMORY

Ultimately, the secret of the Holocaust lies not in figures, not in facts, but in the story. Cain and Abel perhaps were not brothers but one person, one person who tried to kill himself by killing the other.

What do we believe in then? We believe that when we speak of the six million Jews who were killed, we speak of all the others who were also killed. In speaking about the Jewish Holocaust, we transcend it. In speaking of the Holocaust, we address ourselves to the universality of the Holocaust, but under the condition that we never forget the Holocaust. Only in remembering the six million can we ever remember all those who died outside. We never deny that they died; we never forget their death.

Unfortunately, the more Jewish the victims that we remember, the more universal the memory. Memory, as you know, can be diluted or memory can be deepened. I believe in deepening our memory and, the deeper we go, the more faithful the exploration. But then the fire that we have seen will be seen by others as well.

So I urge you and I plead with you to accept what we have already accepted and to remember what we all actually believe. Let us not divide ourselves when we speak of the Holocaust. The Holocaust was a result of division. The killers tried to divide the Jews from the non-Jews, the old from the young, the healthy from the sick. Because of the division, the Holocaust was possible.

I believe that the Holocaust must unite, not divide. I believe the Holocaust therefore should be faced, to the extent that we can face it, with humility and with a sense of extraordinary privilege that we can bear witness.

Statement, meeting of President's Commission on the Holocaust, Washington, D.C., June 7, 1979.

PLEA FOR THE BOAT PEOPLE

We who live with the memory of the Holocaust, we who judge all things by its shadow and in its light are particularly distressed by the specter of silence and apathy which greets the fate of the "boat people." We are outraged at the sight of people set adrift with no country willing to welcome them ashore. We are horrified at the imposition of quotas which exclude women and children in the full knowledge that such a policy of exclusion can be a sentence of death. We know that such failure to act will take its moral toll on those who stand on the sidelines as well as a physical toll on the victims.

Therefore, as chairman of the President's Commission on the Holocaust, and on behalf of the Commission, I implore all countries to open their borders and to extend rights of refuge and asylum to the boat people. We call upon the nations of the world to coordinate their activities and to extend themselves with humanitarian generosity so that we may not once again be divided into a world of perpetrators, victims, and bystanders.

We know that the president of the United States, in the spirit of this Administration's commitment to human rights and human dignity, will do all within his power to alleviate this situation and assume a leadership role in resolving this problem. We hope that this nation will grasp this clear opportunity to learn from the history of the Holocaust not to err again.

Now is the time for this country and for the world to take decisive action to save the boat people. Now, before it is too late.

Statement, *Congressional Record-Senate*, June 27, 1979.

FOR THE SAKE OF HISTORY
AND JUSTICE

Mister Justice Minister, Ladies and Gentlemen, Colleagues:

When I read in the program that you would graciously be receiving the members of our President's Commission on the Holocaust, I was both pleased and surprised. But as I thought about it, I realized how appropriate it is for us to have such a meeting in Poland. After all, whatever happened a generation ago to my people, the Jewish people, and through them to other peoples as well, has as much to do with justice as with history. One generation ago, the German regime, which was supposed to be based on culture, abused justice and turned it around, adopted illegal laws, proclaiming them as just, and in the name of justice killed millions upon millions of men, women, and children. When Jewish fathers and mothers were forced to witness the hunger, the misery, the shame, and the death of their children, justice was denigrated and assaulted.

Some weeks ago, I served as a member of the American delegation to the Conference on the Boat People in Geneva. The chairman of our delegation, Vice President Mondale, spoke like a poet; he was so effective and so convincing that he was the only one among the sixty or so delegates to be applauded. Why? Because he used the event with which we are dealing as the basis and texture of his speech. He spoke of the tragedy today in the light of the greatest of all tragedies of the past, the Holocaust. He compared the situation of the Vietnamese boat people to that of the refugees as discussed at the Evian Conference in 1938, when tens of thousands of Jewish people might have been saved but were not, when homeless Jews might have been allowed to go on living but were denied that right. Therefore, punishment came — to the victims as well as the so-called victors.

What is happening once again today has as much to do with justice as did the Holocaust itself. I am referring to the movement now taking place in more than one country and in more than one language which has one sole aim: to deny the historic event of the Holocaust. Some ninety-five books already exist in a dozen languages, written by former Nazis and Nazi sympathizers, each of them negating Oswiecim, Majdanek, and Treblinka. On behalf of our delegation, which is made up of both non-Jewish and Jewish members, I submit to you that this is a most vicious injustice, and it is taking place in your lifetime and mine. After having killed the victims, the killers are now denying them their deaths. Mister Minister of Justice, could there be any greater injustice?

Address to the Main Commission for the Investigation of Hitlerite Crimes in Poland; Warsaw, Poland, July 30, 1979.

[159]

We have come to you, Mister Minister, with open hearts and with open wounds. This journey is not an easy one; some of us were inmates of Oswiecim, Majdanek, and the Warsaw Ghetto; some of us were born and once lived in Bedzin, Sosnowiec, and Warsaw. To return to these places is exceedingly difficult. And yet, we have come because we feel we have no choice. It is our mission and our task to bear witness for the sake of those who perished and for those who, by chance, are still alive, however mutilated and wounded in body and spirit, but who are determined not to let the truth be distorted or forgotten.

Mister Minister, we have just arrived and are eager to see and learn as much as possible. But since you have been so kind as to meet with us, I must tell you in all honesty that for many years — in the United States, where I reside and serve as chairman of the President's Commission, and in France, where I spend a considerable amount of time and in whose language I write all my books, and from all over the world — I have been receiving reports to the effect that the Jewishness of the Jewish victims is being ignored in many lands, including this one. I hope those reports are wrong. Mister Minister, the three million Polish Jews who died along with the three million Jews from other countries, all six million of them dying only because they were Jews, is one of the reasons we have come here. They died not because they were human beings or Poles, but for the sole reason that they were Jews. Not to give them, after their deaths, the identity they tried to fulfill and sustain with all their souls while they were alive is something that pains us deeply. It would, therefore, be an act of justice to remember them as they were, as human beings and as Jews. For the more Jewish the Jew, the more universal the Jew; the more unique the Jewish experience of the Holocaust, the more universal that experience. We have no intention to exclude; we include and lament all victims.

Let me say again, Mister Minister, how privileged we feel to have been invited to meet with you. Our Commission was established by the president of the United States, not only as an act of history for the sake of history, but as an act of justice for the sake of justice. And to whom should we talk about justice if not to the Minister of Justice of this land?

My friends and I have come from very far and are deeply appreciative of the opportunity to discuss this matter with you. All I can express now is our hope, my own as well as theirs, that after our adjournment here appropriate members of both our delegation and your staff will meet to establish the framework for the continuity of our relationship. We are grateful for your gift of the photographs we have not seen before and for documents about our parents and co-religionists to which we have not hitherto had access. We have in our midst Professor Raul Hilberg, one of the foremost historians of the Holocaust, who will know how to deal with these documents.

As I said before, I hope you will agree to establish these working procedures with us in the very near future, perhaps even tomorrow; Professor Hilberg and two additional delegates whom we shall appoint should meet with your people for that purpose. On behalf of the president of the United States, I wish to express the appreciation of the American people as well as the Jewish people for whatever can be achieved.

THE FOCUS IS MEMORY

Dear Mr. President:

It is with a deep sense of privilege that I submit to you, in accordance with your request, the report of your Commission on the Holocaust. Never before have its members, individually and collectively, given so much of themselves to a task that is both awesome and forbidding, a task which required reaching far back into the past as well as taking a hard look into the future.

Our central focus was memory — our own and that of the victims during a time of unprecedented evil and suffering. That was the Holocaust, an era we must remember not only because of the dead; it is too late for them. Not only because of the survivors; it may even be late for them. Our remembering is an act of generosity, aimed at saving men and women from apathy to evil, if not from evil itself.

We wish, through the work of this Commission, to reach and transform as many human beings as possible. We hope to share our conviction that when war and genocide unleash hatred against any one people or peoples, all are ultimately engulfed in the fire.

With this conviction and mindful of your mandate, Mr. President, we have explored during the past several months of our existence the various ways and means of remembering — and of moving others to remember — the Holocaust and its victims, an event that was intended to erase memory.

Our first question may sound rhetorical: Why remember, why remember at all? Is not human nature opposed to keeping alive memories that hurt and disturb? The more cruel the wound, the greater the effort to cover it, to hide it beneath other wounds, other scars. Why then cling to unbearable memories that may forever rob us of our sleep? Why not forget, turn the page, and proclaim: Let it remain buried beneath the dark nightmares of our subconscious. Why not spare our children the weight of our collective burden and allow them to start their lives free of nocturnal obsessions and complexes, free of Auschwitz and its shadows?

These questions, Mr. President, would not perhaps be devoid of merit if it were possible to extirpate the Holocaust from history and make believe we can forget. But it is not possible, and we cannot. Like it or not, the event must and will dominate future events. Its centrality in the creative endeavors of our contemporaries remains undisputed. Philosophers and social scientists, psychologists and moralists, theologians and artists: all have termed it a watershed in the annals of mankind. What was comprehensible before Treblinka is comprehensible no

Letter to President Jimmy Carter, September 27, 1979.

longer. After Treblinka, man's ability to cope with his condition was shattered; he was pushed to his limits and beyond. Whatever has happened since must therefore be judged in the light of Treblinka. Forgetfulness is no solution.

Treblinka and Auschwitz, Majdanek and Belzec, Buchenwald and Ponar, these and other capitals of the Holocaust kingdom must therefore be remembered, and for several reasons.

First, we cannot grant the killers a posthumous victory. Not only did they humiliate and assassinate their victims, they wanted also to destroy their memory. They killed them twice, reducing them to ashes and then denying their deed. Not to remember the dead now would mean to become accomplices to their murderers.

Second, we cannot deny the victims the fulfillment of their last wish, their *idée fixe* to bear witness. What the merchant from Saloniki, the child from Lodz, the rabbi from Radzimin, the carpenter from Warsaw, and the scribe from Vilna had in common was the passion, the compulsion to tell the tale — or to enable someone else to do so. Every ghetto had its historians, every death camp its chroniclers. Young and old, learned and unlearned, everybody kept diaries, wrote journals, composed poems and prayers. They wanted to remember and to be remembered. They wanted to defeat the enemy's conspiracy of silence, to communicate a spark of the fire that nearly consumed their generation, and, above all, to serve as warning to future generations. Instead of looking with contempt upon mankind that betrayed them, the victims dreamed of redeeming it with their own charred souls. Instead of despairing of man and his possible salvation, they put their faith in him. Defying all logic, all reason, they opted for humanity and chose to try, by means of their testimony, to save it from indifference that might result in the ultimate catastrophe, the nuclear one.

Third, we must remember for our own sake, for the sake of our own humanity. Indifference to the victims would result, inevitably, in indifference to ourselves, an indifference that would ultimately no longer be sin but, in the words of our Commissioner Bayard Rustin, "a terrifying curse" and its own punishment.

The most vital lesson to be drawn from the Holocaust era is that Auschwitz was possible because the enemy of the Jewish people and of mankind — and it is always the same enemy — succeeded in dividing, in separating, in splitting human society, nation against nation, Christian against Jew, young against old. And not enough people cared. In Germany and other occupied countries, most spectators chose not to interfere with the killers; in other lands, too, many persons chose to remain neutral. As a result, the killers killed, the victims died, and the world remained world.

Still, the killers could not be sure. In the beginning they made one move and waited. Only when there was no reaction did they make another move and still another. From racial laws to medieval decrees, from illegal expulsions to the establishment of ghettos and then to the invention of death camps, the killers carried out their plans only when they realized that the outside world simply did not care about the Jewish victims. Soon after, they decided they could do the same thing, with equal impunity, to other peoples as well. As always, they began with Jews. As always, they did not stop with Jews alone.

Granted that we must remember, Mr. President, the next question your Commission had to examine was whom are we to remember? It is vital that the American people come to understand the distinctive reality of the Holocaust: millions of innocent civilians were tragically killed by the Nazis. They must be remembered. However, there exists a moral imperative for special emphasis on the six million Jews. While not all victims were Jews, *all* Jews were victims, destined for annihilation solely because they were born Jewish. They were doomed not because of something they had done or proclaimed or acquired but because of who they were: sons and daughters of the Jewish people. As such they were sentenced to death collectively and individually as part of an official and "legal" plan unprecedented in the annals of history.

During our journey to Eastern Europe — a full description of which is attached (Appendix B) — the Commission observed that while Jews are sometimes mentioned on public monuments in Poland, they were not referred to in Russia at all. In Kiev's Babi Yar, for instance, where nearly 80,000 Jews were murdered in September, 1941, the word Jew is totally absent from the memorial inscriptions.

Our Commission believes that because they were the principal target of Hitler's Final Solution, we must remember the six million Jews and, through them and beyond them, but never without them, rescue from oblivion all the men, women, and children, Jewish and non-Jewish, who perished in those years in the forests and camps of the kingdom of night.

The universality of the Holocaust lies in its uniqueness: the event is essentially Jewish, yet its interpretation is universal. It involved even distant nations and persons who lived far away from Birkenau's flames or who were born afterward.

Our own country was also involved, Mr. President. The valiant American nation fought Hitler and fascism and paid for its bravery and idealism with the lives of hundreds and thousands of its sons; their sacrifices shall not be forgotten. And yet, and yet, away from the battlefield, the judgment of history will be harsh. Sadly but realistically, our great government was not without blemish. One cannot but wonder what might have happened had the then American president and his advisers demonstrated concern and compassion by appointing in 1942 or 1943 a President's Commission to prevent the Holocaust. How many victims, Jews and non-Jews, could have been saved had we changed our immigration laws, opened our gates more widely, protested more forcefully. We did not. Why not? This aspect of the event must and will be explored thoroughly and honestly within the Commission's framework. The decision to face the issue constitutes an act of moral courage worthy of our nation.

The question of how to remember makes up the bulk of the Commission's report. Memorial, museum, education, research, commemoration, action to prevent a recurrence: these are our areas of concern. I hope that these recommendations will be acceptable to you, Mr. President, reflecting as they do the joint thinking of the members of the Commission and its advisers over a period of seven months.

During that time, we held meetings and hearings and studied known and hitherto undisclosed material. Our hope was to reach a consensus among our diverse membership, which includes academicians and civic leaders, Christians and Jews, native Americans, and survivors from the death camps who found a welcome and a refuge here and who now, as American citizens, enjoy the privileges of our democracy.

Special attention was paid to the opinions, views, and feelings of the survivors, men and women who know the problems from the inside and who ask for nothing more than the opportunity to show their gratitude. "Our adopted country was kind to us," says Commissioner Sigmund Strochlitz, "and we wish to repay in some way by helping to build a strong and human society based on equality and justice for all." Their willingness to share their knowledge, their pain, their anguish, even their agony, is motivated solely by their conviction that their survival was for a purpose. A survivor sees himself or herself as a messenger and guardian of secrets entrusted by the dead. A survivor fears he or she may be the last to remember, the last to warn, the last to tell the tale that cannot be told, the tale that must be told in its totality, before it is too late, before the last witness leaves the stage and takes his awesome testimony back to the dead.

In the hope that you will enable this testimony to be brought to the attention of the American people and the world, I submit the attached report to you, Mr. President.

> Respectfully yours,
> Elie Wiesel
> Chairman
> President's Commission on the Holocaust

PRESENTATION OF THE REPORT OF THE PRESIDENT'S COMMISSION ON THE HOLOCAUST TO THE PRESIDENT OF THE UNITED STATES

Mr. President, Ambassador Evron, Distinguished Members of the Senate and House, Ladies and Gentlemen:

Thirty-eight years ago on September 27, 1941, during the *Aseret Yemei Teshuvah*, what we call in our tradition the Days of Repentance, thousands of Jewish men, women, and children were led through the sunny and peaceful streets of Kiev to be slaughtered at a place called Babi Yar. For ten days — from *Rosh Hashanah*, the Jewish New Year, until *Yom Kippur*, the Day of Atonement — the massacre continued. The procession seemed endless. The killers killed, the victims tumbled into ditches, and Creation somehow remained unchanged and undisturbed.

What took place in Kiev, Mr. President, was repeated elsewhere in hundreds and hundreds of towns and villages in the Ukraine, Lithuania, Byelorussia, Poland. All over Eastern Europe the process of destruction went on and on and on. Entire communities perished overnight. Families disappeared. Ancient dynasties whose lineage could be traced back to King David and Moses were swept away with the winds of ashes. And God himself must have covered His face in pain and anguish. Were they but a spasm of history? A tear in the ocean? An experiment of eternity in death?

In the course of our study, Mr. President, we tried to capture some of their silent outcries. We asked them for guidance. We returned to some of the sites where they perished. And all those who were there came away changed.

Mr. President, we were struck first by the beauty of the surroundings: the hills around Treblinka, the skies over Birkenau, the silence in Auschwitz. The killers had chosen the most beautiful sites and the most poetic words for their most hideous crimes.

We were struck by the proximity to cities and villages. Treblinka, Mr. President, is a two-hour bus or train ride from Warsaw. Babi Yar is part of Kiev. Buchenwald is near Weimar. Auschwitz is close to Cracow. Ten thousand human

Statement presenting the Report of the President's Commission on the Holocaust to President Jimmy Carter, the Rose Garden, the White House, Washington, D.C., September 27, 1979.

beings were being murdered and burned every day; and, nearby, life went on as usual.

How was all this possible? We do not have the answer, Mr. President. Perhaps there is none. Any given answer must be the wrong answer. But the members of your Commission believe, Mr. President, that we must seek an answer, and this will not be easy. Unprecedented and unparalleled in magnitude, the event of Auschwitz and Belsen is still surmounted by a wall of fire which no outsider can penetrate. All one can do is come close to the gate.

Some are living gates, the survivors. They alone know what happened. And they are ready and willing to share their knowledge; they know that they survived only to tell the tale, only to bear witness.

The words of the dead, too, are gates. Documents, poems, messages, diaries, letters, prayers, meditations; through them one can feel something of what they felt as they were waiting for the Angel of Death, for the Messiah.

I confess, Mr. President, that I belong to a traumatized generation and a traumatized people.

As a Jew, I was — and am — distressed by the tragic fate of the Jewish people; after all, they alone were destined to be totally annihilated; they alone were totally alone.

However, as a Jew I also came to realize that although all Jews were victims, not all victims were Jews.

But this is perhaps the first lesson we may draw from the event, Mr. President, that although Jews were the first to be killed, they were not the only ones; others followed. The murder of one group inevitably provokes more murder.

We must also learn from what happened that words must be taken seriously. The time lapse between the anti-Semitic slogans in Berlin and the death industry in Treblinka was only ten years.

We must take seriously all those who threaten other people today and all those who threaten the Jewish people today. From words to deed, the distance is not great.

We must also learn the dangers of indifference and neutrality. In times of evil, indifference to evil is evil. Neutrality always helps the killer, not the victim.

And we must learn the importance of stressing the moral dimension of all human endeavors. We have seen that scientists, scholars, physicians, politicians, and artists murder children and still enjoy the cadence of a poem, the beauty of the painting. Culture without morality can easily push mankind to darkness, not redemption.

Yes, Mr. President, there are urgent lessons to be learned from this awesome event. And yet, and yet. We, the members of your Commission and their advisers, are aware of our limitations. We have acquired some knowledge, but what are we to do with that knowledge? What are we to do with the whispers of men and women going to their graves? With the wisdom of ghetto children who knew more about life and death than the oldest of my teachers? What are we to do with the sounds of the dead, the mute dreams of the living? What are we to do with them?

We must share them, and we understood this most intensely when we visited

Poland, Soviet Russia, and Israel. Birkenau arouses man's most secret anguish. Jerusalem symbolizes our most fervent hope, and, therefore, we are attached to Jerusalem in such love and admiration. We must share whatever we receive with conviction and dedication, if mankind is to survive.

Thus, Mr. President, it is with a profound sense of privilege and hope that on behalf of the President's Commission on the Holocaust and its Advisory Board I present to you its report. And for your own historic initiative, Mr. President, it is submitted to you with infinite gratitude.

SECTION 19

United States Holocaust Memorial Council

MAN'S RIGHT TO BE REMEMBERED

In the shadow of the burning shadows that inhabited Auschwitz, Treblinka, Babi Yar, we must affirm man's right and man's need to be measured in terms of human suffering and human compassion, and we must affirm man's right to be remembered. . . .

In an age tainted by violence, we must teach this generation and those that follow the origins and consequences of violence. In a society of distrust, skepticism, and moral anguish, we must tell our contemporaries that whatever the answer it must grow out of human compassion and reflect man's basic quest for justice. The Holocaust was possible because the law was violated by the state itself and its principles distorted by its leaders. From the Holocaust we have learned that we are responsible for one another. We are responsible for the past and for the future as well.

For some of us this is the most solemn and awesome day in many months and, perhaps, in our lives. We are going to delve once more into the darkest recesses of our memory, only to confront a vanished universe surrounded by flames and penetrated by silence.

The living and the dead are locked together — young and old, princes and madmen, sages and wanderers, beggars and dreamers. On this day we shall close our eyes and we shall see them — an eerie procession which, slowly, meditatingly, walks toward angels of death carried on wings of night into night. We see them now as you see us. We are the link between you and them. And for allowing us to be that link we thank all those who have made this the project of their lives. We must realize the immensity of our task.

We, here, represent a broad spectrum of the American people. There are in our midst illustrious academicians and businessmen, artists and statesmen, Christians and Jews, survivors and non-survivors. But all share a passion for truth, a commitment to memory, a dedication to justice.

Let us hope that we shall do our work in harmony, that we shall learn from one another and help one another overcome obstacles and fears that are inherent in the project itself. In spite of our various origins and vocations, let us form a cohesive group bent on bringing back to life, in words and images, in memory — in memories alone — a desperate world filled with multitudes of courageous victims, their last hopes and their despair. Our task will not be an easy one for, whatever we do,

Statement, meeting of U.S. Holocaust Memorial Council, Washington, D.C., May 28, 1980.

[171]

we involve burning memories. We must show the world at large that we are capable of transcending petty divergencies, that we are capable of absolute quest for justice. We must remind the world that one generation ago, six million men, women, and children — all Jews — were forsaken, betrayed, massacred. As a Jew who belongs to a tormented and traumatized generation, I do not view the memory of the Jewish victims as a forum to exclude the others. I have said it before, I shall say it again: Although all Jews were victims, not all victims were Jews. And the other way around — not all victims were Jews, but all Jews were victims.

As Jews, we therefore shall remember the others as well. Our friends who perished because they gave us shelter must be remembered. And the resistance fighters from all over occupied Europe must be remembered and will be. And we shall remember them all with gratitude. No people is, or has been, so grateful as the Jewish people. But to mix all the victims together is unfair and unjust. There was something unique — uniquely Jewish — about the Holocaust. The event was Jewish, yet the implications are universal.

To our non-Jewish colleagues here, I therefore address my humble plea: try to understand our sensitivity as we shall try to understand yours.

SETTING PRECEDENT
FOR HISTORY

As for the general work and the general ambition for the group, some of us believe that the event that we are dealing with is unique and, therefore, deserves a different and special approach. We are not a government agency like many others; therefore we can emulate no one. We lack records; there are none. What is clear and efficient for other commissions and councils may very well not be right for our Council. Not only do we deal with the most sensitive and burning issue in our lives, we are also setting a precedent for history. I am convinced, as you are, that future generations will want to learn how we, we who have accepted the privilege of remembering and sharing it, have dealt with our memories. They will want to know how we, contemporaries of the victims, and the survivors, dealt with their legacy and their awesome vision. Therefore, the decision has been made to record all our efforts as faithfully as possible. All our statements, our letters, our suggestions, our aspirations: all await the judgment of our children's children.

Yes, I am thinking far ahead. The present is of importance to us but less so than the future. When the survivors are gone, that anguish must remain. I am saying this, first, because I believe in it, and also because I want this Council to understand why the pace of its work is feverish, but not crude; passionate, but careful. I know that some of you wish things to move faster; so do I. But as a French philosopher advised us, "In some cases it is wiser to run slower."

Some of us have devoted our lives to memory. With every word, with every move here and elsewhere we have placed thirty-five years of work, of hope, of pain, of testimony in the balance. And whatever we possess, whatever we are, is to be judged and justified now by what we do here, by what we say here and elsewhere. Therefore, I see in our work an expression of nobility and a call to nobility, and I must say that each time we meet I feel profoundly rewarded. I know of no other group, within the academic community or any other professional community, where people collaborate, cooperate, with such friendship, with such understanding, with such a human compassion for one another. We represent many areas. We come from many landscapes, and we carry many different memories. I have yet to hear an angry outburst or one word of disrespect in response to another's opinion, and for this we should all be grateful. But it is not surprising. Whoever touches this subject is purified by it, is changed by it. Whoever enters it, in a way, is humanized by it.

Statement, meeting of U.S. Holocaust Memorial Council, New York, December 10, 1980.

REMARKS ON ANTI-SEMITISM
AND ON THE REVISIONISTS

Number one: the proposed Conference on Anti-Semitism. I wish I had another name for it. But when people speak of anti-Semitism, do you really think they think of the Arabs? They think of Jews. When they speak of anti-Semitism, it is clear that they mean Jews. That is one thing that belongs to the victim. We know who the anti-Semite is. Arabs have never suffered from anti-Semitism; nobody else has. Only Jews have. I am not ashamed of anti-Semitism. They should be ashamed. Why should I be ashamed?

Number two: the denial of the Holocaust. It is a very serious problem. As some of you may know, I was probably the first to alert the American Jewish community to that danger. In the beginning there were only a few articles and two or three books, and nobody listened. Then I said, "You know, there are already ten books." Somewhat later I said, "There are already twenty-four books." Year after year the number has increased. The problem has finally caught up with us. I must say that I feel impure when I touch these books. I don't know what to do. Debate them? I would not dignify them with a debate. I would not dignify them with a dialogue. I would not speak to a Nazi even if the Nazi were to be as eloquent as Goebbels. I would not. And I would not speak to a person who has written a book denying the Holocaust. I did not speak to a person who wrote a preface to such a book. There are certain limits to my tolerance, and this is probably the limit.

On the other hand, what should be done with them? To ignore them? I do not know how. We cannot. The best thing to do is what we are doing: to write more books, to speak about the Holocaust in more authentic voice, and to commit ourselves with more passion to our task. The only way to eliminate bad literature is to write good literature, as Terrence Des Pres would say. And the only way to put those revisionists to shame is to work for history and with history.

Statement, meeting of U.S. Holocaust Memorial Council, New York, December 10, 1980.

REMEMBERING THE HOLOCAUST

About sadness later; first some words of gratitude. We thank you, Mr. President, for joining us and for participating in this solemn assembly of remembrance. Your presence here today, Mr. President, so soon after the senseless attack upon your person, is a tribute to your understanding and concern for human values and is especially meaningful to us. We all know that your being here, Mr. President, is not a ceremonial gesture but an expression of your sense of history and your dream of a future with hope and dignity for the American nation and for all mankind.

So we thank you, Mr. President, and we thank our Father in Heaven for having spared you. And now with your permission, Mr. President, I would like to share with you some lines by a young Jewish poet, a young boy in Theresienstadt named Mottele. He wrote a poem that reflects more than his own moods, more than his own fate:

> From tomorrow on, I shall be sad.
> From tomorrow on.
> Today I will be gay.
> What is the use of sadness,
> Tell me that.
> Because these evil winds begin to blow?
> Why should I grieve for tomorrow, today?
> Tomorrow may be so good,
> So sunny.
> Tomorrow the sun may shine for us again.
> We shall no longer need to be sad.
> From tomorrow on I shall be sad.
> From tomorrow on. Not today. No,
> Today I will be glad.
> And every day,
> No matter how bitter it be,
> I will say: From tomorrow on,
> I shall be sad,
> Not today.

Mr. President, how does one commemorate the million Motteles and Shloimeles and Leahles and Soreles? How does one commemorate six million victims, all descendants of Abraham and Isaac and Jacob? What words does one use? What metaphors does one invoke to describe the brutal and unprecedented extinctions of a world — thousands and thousands of flourishing Jewish communities survived

Address, Remembrance Day observance, the White House, April 30, 1981.

the fury of the Crusades, the hatred of pogroms, the afflictions of wars and the misery, the shame, the despair of religious and social oppressions only to be swept away by the Holocaust? In all their chronicles and testaments, memoirs and prayers, litanies and poems, the victims stressed one single theme over and over again — remember, remember the horror, remember. Bear witness. And that is their legacy to us, the living.

Of course, there may be some who will ask, "Why remember at all? Why not allow the dead to bury the dead? Is it not in man's nature to push aside memories that hurt and disturb?" The more cruel the wound, the greater the effort to cover it. The more horrifying the nightmare, the more powerful the desire to exorcise it. Why then would anyone choose to cling to unbearable recollections of emaciated corpses or violations of every human law? Maybe we have not yet learned to cope with the events, intellectually, socially, philosophically, theologically. Perhaps we never will. The more we know, the less we understand. All we can do is remember. But how does one remember? How does one remember and communicate an event filled with so much fear and darkness and mystery that it negates language and imagination? Auschwitz, Mr. President, history marks it with the burning seal. Our century, Mr. President, may well be remembered not only for the monuments it erected, or for the astonishing technological advances it made, but most of all for Treblinka and Majdanek, Belsen and Ponar, Auschwitz and Buchenwald. How is one to explain what happened? It could have been stopped or at least slowed down at various stages. One word, one statement, one move — it was not stopped. Why not?

I am a teacher, Mr. President. And my students, young, fervent, compassionate American students, often express their puzzlement in my classroom — why the complacency? Why the tacit acquiescence? Why weren't the Hungarian Jews, for example, warned about their fate? When they arrived in Auschwitz at midnight they mistook it for a peaceful village. Why weren't the railways to Birkenau bombed by either the Allies or the Russians? And the Russians were so close.

The calculated viciousness of the executioner, the helplessness of the doomed, the passivity of the bystander — all these lie beyond our comprehension — the killers' fascination with death, the victims' with hope, the survivors' with testimony. A new vocabulary needs to be invented to describe the event. Can you imagine the silence preceding a selection in a death count? The fear of a man who suddenly understands that he is the last of his family — the last of the line? Imagine? No, no one can imagine that kingdom. Only those who were there know what it meant to be there. Theirs was the kingdom that will forever remain forbidden and forbidding.

And yet, and yet, we must tell the tale, we must bear witness. Not to do so would mean to render meaningless the years and the lives that we, those of us who survived, received as a gift, as an offering to be shared and redeemed.

We must tell the tale, Mr. President, and we want to tell it not to divide people but, on the contrary, to bring them together; not to inflict more suffering but, on the contrary, to diminish it; not to humiliate anyone but, on the contrary, to teach others to humiliate no one. This is why we bear witness, Mr. President and friends, not for the sake of the dead. It is too late for the dead. Not even for our own sake. It may be too late for us as well.

We speak for mankind. The universality of the Jewish tragedy lies in its uniqueness. Only the memory of what was done to the Jewish people and through it to others can save the world from indifference to the ultimate dangers that threaten its very existence.

Mr. President, that the survivors have not lost their sanity, their faith in God or in man, that they decided to build on ruins in Israel or in the United States of America, that they decided to choose generosity instead of anger, hope instead of despair, is a mystery even to us. They had every reason to give up on life and its promise. They did not. Still, at times, Mr. President, they are overcome by doubt and fear. The world has not learned its lesson. Anti-Semitic groups spring up more and more, and some shamelessly, viciously, deny that the Holocaust ever occurred. In our lifetime fascist groups increase their memberships and parade in the streets. Intolerance, bigotry, fanaticism, mass executions in some places, mass starvation in others, religious wars, quasi-medieval upheavals, and, of course, ultimately, the nuclear menace and our indifference to it. What is to be done?

Though Jewish, profoundly Jewish in nature, the Holocaust has universal implications, and I believe, we believe that the memory of what was done may shield us in the future.

Naturally, other nations were persecuted and even decimated by the Nazis and their allies and their collaborators, and we honor their memory. But the Jewish people represented a different target. For the first time in history being became a crime. Jews were destined for annihilation not because of what they said or proclaimed or did or possessed or created or destroyed, but because of who they were.

Is that why we survivors, we Jews, we human beings, are so concerned? And is that why we are so attached to a land where so many survivors have found a haven, pride, refuge, and hope? Please understand us, Mr. President. We believe that the subject of the Holocaust must remain separate from politics, but if we plead so passionately for Israel's right not only to be secure but also to feel secure, it is because of Israel's nightmares, which are also our nightmares.

Israel is threatened by a holy war, which means total war, which means total annihilation. Mr. President, some may say that these are words, words — yes, words. But we are a generation traumatized by experience. We take words seriously. The very idea of another Jewish catastrophe anywhere in our lifetime is quite simply unbearable to us.

Israel must never feel abandoned. Israel must never feel alone. Israel must never feel expendable, Mr. President. We plead with you because it is the dream of our dreams. It is perhaps the pain of our pain but the hope of our hopes. It is an ancient nation of 4,000 years that should not be judged in categories of one day or one incident. Only in its totality can we understand and perceive and love Israel.

We must believe so because there were times, forty years ago, when Jewish communities felt abandoned and betrayed. In 1943 on April 16, the gallant young commander-in-chief of the Warsaw Ghetto Uprising, Mordechai Anielewicz, wrote to a friend: "We are fighting. We shall not surrender. But as our last days are approaching, remember that we have been betrayed." That is what he felt. That is what we all felt. They were betrayed then. To forget them now would mean to betray them again, and we must not allow this to happen.

In the Jewish tradition, Mr. President, when a person dies we appoint him or her as our emissary in heaven to intercede on our behalf. Could it be that they, the six million Jews, were messengers? But then, then, Mr. President and friends, whose messengers are we?

TO THE LIBERATORS
OF THE CAMPS

Liberators of the Camps:

On behalf of my friends, the survivors of the ghettos and death camps, and on behalf of the entire Council, I bid you a heartfelt welcome.

You were the first free men to discover our world of terror. You will never forget what you have seen, just as we shall never forget the anguish, horror, outrage, and deep compassion expressed by your every look and gesture.

Did you know, could you imagine, what your coming meant to us? Life, of course, but something more: the dawn of hope, the beginning of a belief that waiting is not always in vain and that, despite the loneliness of the survivors and despite the dead lying under the ashes, human solidarity is still possible.

Assuredly, for six million Jews and for their comrades who resisted and were massacred by the common enemy, you came too late, but in our eyes you soldiers and officers of the Allied forces personified mankind's noblest qualities, the need for freedom, and, even more, the thirst for liberation.

You were living proof that, despite the attempts by the Nazis to dominate man by making him inhuman, despite the efforts by Hitler's Germany to govern through fear and terror and to serve Death by making Death its servant, sovereign nations were able to unite in the same struggle, inspired by the same ideals, to fulfill the same promise.

We told you then, and we repeat it today as we welcome you among us: Thank you, thank you a thousand times, for fighting for the honor of mankind.

Letter to International Liberators Conference, U.S. Department of State, Washington, D.C., October 26-29, 1981.

MEETING AGAIN

As chairman of the United States Holocaust Memorial Council, it is my privilege to welcome you and thank you for having accepted our invitation to join us as we undertake a unique pilgrimage into history and its darkest, convulsive nightmare.

Thirty-six-and-seven years ago, we experienced, together, a moment of destiny without parallel — never to be measured — never to be repeated, a moment that stood on the other side of time, on the other side of existence.

When we first met, at the threshold of a universe struck by malediction, we spoke different languages, we were strangers to one another, we might as well have descended from different planets. And yet — a link was created between us, a bond was established. We became not only comrades, not only brothers; we became each other's witnesses.

I remember — I shall always remember the day I was liberated: April 11, 1945. Buchenwald. The terrifying silence terminated by abrupt yelling. The first American soldiers. Their faces ashen. Their eyes — I shall never forget their eyes, your eyes. You looked and looked, you could not move your gaze away from us; it was as though you sought to alter reality with your eyes. They reflected astonishment, bewilderment, endless pain, and anger — yes, anger above all. Rarely have I seen such anger, such rage — contained, mute, yet ready to burst with frustration, humiliation, and utter helplessness. Then you broke down. You wept. You wept and wept uncontrollably, unashamedly; you were our children then, for we, the twelve-year-old, the sixteen-year-old boys in Buchenwald and Theresienstadt and Mauthausen, knew so much more than you about life and death. You wept; we could not. We had no more tears left; we had nothing left. In a way we were dead, and we knew it. What did we feel? Only sadness.

And gratitude. Ultimately, it was gratitude that brought us back to normalcy and to society. Do you remember, friends? In Lublin and Dachau, Stuthoff and Nordhausen, Ravensbruck and Majdanek and Belsen and Auschwitz you were surrounded by sick and wounded and hungry wretches, barely alive, pathetic in their futile attempts to touch you, to smile at you, to reassure you, to console you, and most of all to carry you in triumph on their frail shoulders; you were heroes, our idols. Tell me, friends, have you ever felt such love, such admiration?

One thing we did not do: we did not try to *explain*; explanations were neither needed nor possible. Liberators and survivors looked at one another, and, what each of us experienced then, we shall try to recapture together, now, at this reunion, which to me represents a miracle in itself.

Welcoming address, International Liberators Conference, U.S. Department of State, Washington, D.C., October 26, 1981.

At this point, allow me to say a few words about the Council.

Created by the president of the United States and enacted into law by the unanimous act of both the House of Representatives and the Senate of the United States, our Council is essentially non-political. It has not been used and shall not be used by any Administration for any other purpose than to make our citizens — and people everywhere — aware of the unspeakable crimes perpetrated systematically, and officially, against the Jewish people and humanity.

Our activities are manifold in nature and in scope. The International Relations Committee, which coordinated this conference, is but one of the committees functioning within the Council.

Another committee is in charge of gathering pertinent archives; another is preparing educational programs for elementary and secondary schools and universities. There is a committee to prepare the annual Remembrance Day ceremonies, another to plan the museum, and yet another is engaged in raising funds to finance all these activities. What we all have in common is an obsession: not to betray the dead we left behind or who left us behind. They were killed once; they must not be killed again through forgetfulness.

This conference has its own history. Moscow, 1979. Members of a presidential delegation met with certain high-ranking Red Army officers. One of them in particular meant much to us: General Petrenko had liberated Auschwitz. It was an extraordinary encounter. We exchanged stories. He told us of the preparations to break through the German lines, and I told him of the last day in camp, the last roll call, the last night, the last consultations among inmates, friends, fathers and sons; what should one do? hide? where? The Red Army was so near, so near. We prayed, I told General Petrenko. We prayed for you and your men, and no believer ever prayed to his or her God with more fervor.

And so — while General Petrenko and I were telling each other tales of courage and despair, I suddenly had the idea of bringing together liberators from *all* the Allied forces: to listen to you and to thank you and — why not admit it? — to solicit your help. *Our* testimony is being disputed by morally deranged Nazis and Nazi-lovers; your voices may silence them. You were the first men to discover the abyss, just as we were its last inhabitants. What we symbolized to one another then was so special that it remained part of our very being.

Well — here you are, friends from so many nations, reunited with those who owe you their lives, just as you owe them the flame that scorched your memories.

On that most memorable day, the day of our liberation — whether it took place in 1944 or in 1945, in Poland or in Germany — you incarnated for us humanity's noblest yearning — to be free.

For us, you represented hope. True, six million Jews have been annihilated, millions of brave men and women massacred by the Nazis and their collaborators, but we are duty-bound to remember always that to confront the Fascist criminal conquests, gigantic armies, transcending geo-political and ideological borders, were raised on five continents, and they went to war on behalf of humankind. The fact that millions of soldiers wearing different uniforms united to fight together, be victorious together, and, alas, die together seemed to justify man's faith in his own humanity — in spite of the enemy. We thought of the killers and we were ready to give up on man; but then we remembered those who resisted them — on open battlefields as well as in the underground movements in France, Norway, Holland, Denmark, and the USSR — and we reconciled ourselves to the human condition. We were — can you believe it? — naive enough to think that we who had witnessed, for a while, the domination of evil would prevent it from surfacing again. On the very ruins of civilization, we aspired to erect new sanctuaries for our children, where life would be sanctified and not denigrated, compassion practiced, not ridiculed.

It would have been so easy to allow ourselves to slide into melancholy and resignation. We chose differently; we chose to become spokesmen for man's quest for generosity and his need and capacity to turn his — or her — suffering into something productive, something creative.

We had hoped then that out of so much torment and grief and mourning a new message would be handed down to future generations — a warning against the inherent perils of discrimination, fanaticism, poverty, deprivation, ignorance, oppression, humiliation and injustice, and war — the ultimate injustice, the ultimate humiliation. We were naive, and perhaps we still are.

Together, we express unspeakable human suffering, suffering without name or precedent. Let us invoke it in order to spare suffering to others. Together we have the right and the duty to launch an appeal to which no one can remain deaf: an appeal against hate, against the degradation of man, against violence, and against forgetfulness.

We have seen what no one will see: the human condition insulted and diminished. We have seen what fanaticism can lead to: cruelty, imprisonment, and murder on a national scale — on a planetary scale.

We have seen the metamorphosis of history, and it is incumbent upon us to testify to it. When one people is doomed to death, all the others are threatened. When one group is insulted, all humanity is menaced. Hitler's plans to annihilate the Jewish people and to decimate the Slavic peoples carried in them the germ of a total end: one murdered the Jews, and it was humanity that was assassinated.

You, friend liberators, you stopped the process. Be proud of it, be thanked for it.

If we unite our memories and our wills, as we once did, everything becomes possible. Forgetfulness leads to indifference and indifference to complicity — therefore to dishonor.

Friends, I address you as brothers: the ties which unite us are powerful and lasting; we form a community without parallel. It diminishes day by day. Which of us will be the last messenger? We cannot *not* formulate our judgment of past and present events. Our honor depends on it. And, yes, we are against prisons, against dictatorship, against fear, against outrage, nuclear or otherwise. We incarnate living, vibrant proof that it is possible for men to unite in order to affirm the right to live and to dream in peace.

I am perhaps naive, but I believe with all my heart that if we speak strongly enough, death will not triumph.

To paraphrase Nietzsche, we looked deep into the abyss — and the abyss looked back at us. No one comes close to the kingdom of night and goes away unconcerned. We told the tale — or, at least, we tried. We resisted all temptations to isolate ourselves and be silent. Instead we chose to affirm our desperate faith in testimony. We forced ourselves to speak — however inadequately, however poorly. We may have used the wrong words — but then there are no words to describe the ineffable. We spoke in spite of language, in spite of the limits that exist between what *we* say and outsiders *hear*. We spoke and . . . explosions in Paris, bombs in Antwerp, murderous attacks in Vienna. Is it conceivable that nazism could dare come back into the open so soon, while we are still alive, while we are still here to denounce its poisonous nature as illustrated in Treblinka?

Again we must admit our naiveté. We thought we had vanquished what Brecht called the beast, but no: it is still showing its claws. At best, what a gathering such as this could do is to shame the beast into hiding. If we here succeed — and I hope and pray that we shall — in rising above politics, above the usual recriminations between East and West, above simplistic propaganda, and simply tell the world what both liberators and liberated have seen, then something may happen; the world may choose to pay more attention to what hangs as a threat to its very future.

If we succeed — and I hope and pray that we shall — in putting aside what divides us — and what divides us is superficial — if we dedicate ourselves not only to the memory of those who have suffered but to the future of those who are suffering today, we shall be serving notice on mankind that we shall never allow this earth to be made into a prison again, that we shall never allow war to be considered as a solution to any problem — for war *is* the problem. If we succeed, then our encounter will be recorded as yet another of our common victories.

If we do not raise our voice against war — who will? We speak with the authority of men and women who have seen war; we know what it is. We have seen the burnt villages, the devastated cities, the deserted homes, we still see the demented mothers whose children are being massacred before their eyes, we still follow the endless nocturnal processions to the flames rising up to the seventh heaven — if not higher. . . .

We are gathered here to testify — together. Our tale is a tale of solitude and fear and anonymous death — but also of compassion, generosity, bravery, and solidarity. You the liberators and we the survivors — together we represent a commitment to memory whose intensity will remain. In its name we shall continue to voice our concerns and our hopes, not for our own sake, but for the sake of humankind. Its very survival may depend on its ability and willingness to listen.

And to remember.

WHY WE TEACH

We are profoundly moved by your presence and by your statement, Mr. President. We have not forgotten, nor shall we forget, your words from last year.

As you know, the ceremony itself is simple, sober, and penetrated with prayer, symbolism, and the desperate need for faith. Much remains unsaid. Such is the nature of this particular tragedy. It defies communication. There are simply no words to describe what happened, Mr. President. People cannot understand now. How could human beings inflict so much pain and fear and death upon other human beings? At what point did the killer set into motion his own dehumanizing process? What happened to the killer as a person when he tortured old sages, old Talmudic scholars, and mutilated their young disciples? We remember the victims with incommensurate sadness and the killers with infinite fear.

The war has been over for thirty-seven years, Mr. President, but we are still fighting the enemy. You spoke last year so movingly, condemning those who denied that six million Jews had, indeed, been killed in the death camps. But, Mr. President, they didn't hear you, nor do they hear us. They continued their vicious, ugly, morally-demented propaganda. In our country their work is being done by right-wing fascists. But in Europe, in France, it is being done by extreme left-wing intellectuals. They all join in this insane need to deny what we went through.

Mr. President, what does it all mean? What do they say? That I am a liar? That we invented our suffering? What do they want us to do? To show our wounds? We don't like it, Mr. President. We don't like to speak of our agony. Our work is not an exercise in morbidity, Mr. President. We are trying to teach something. We are trying to teach the vulnerability of culture when it is not imbued with morality. We are trying to teach the world that what was done to one people, to the Jewish people, has actually affected humanity. As you have said, the dangers in the future are planetary. They are huge. They are fearsome. How can we save the world, Mr. President, if not with our tales?

We must do it for the sake of our children. Mr. President, for a Jew who went through the war, to bring a child into this world was a very great act of faith, for we had all the reasons in the world to give up — to give up on man, on humankind, to give up on civilization, to give up on everything, to stop, as in Talmudic times when at least one attempt was made to stop. But we did not, Mr. President. We decided to wager on man and God. Therefore the survivors are the most generous, the most compassionate people you can imagine. They are always in the front

Statement, Remembrance Day observance, the White House, April 20, 1982.

lines, fighting against every injustice, for every just cause. They are always there to fight for humanity when humanity is in danger.

Your words about Israel touched us very deeply, because we are concerned about Israel. And we are concerned about those who are in jail in Poland, and those who are in the camps in Russia, and the Jews in Ethiopia, and all the dissidents and all the victims. We are terribly concerned. We would like to help, and that is why we are teaching.

There is an urgency, Mr. President, on the Council which works under your authority. Men and women from all walks of life — Christians and Jews, scholars and rabbis, people of industry and of letters — we are working with a profound sense of urgency. Time is running out. It reminds me of the ghettos when everybody was writing, when everybody was becoming a historian writing for the future. Now, too, we are teaching more. We are challenging more. We are exploring that period more because we believe it is late. It is very late.

One chronicler — Chaim Kaplan, a religious Jew in Warsaw — wrote: "If my life ends what will happen to my diary?" His life ended. His diary remained. But if our teaching ends and if we forget, Mr. President, what will happen to our lives? And what will happen to humanity? Humanity will perish in shame and in guilt for having permitted such a unique event in history to be forgotten.

But we do believe it is possible to remember, it is possible to pray, it is possible to study, and it is possible to live for man and with man. The proof is our children. Therefore, Mr. President, today the six candles that symbolize those six million Jews shall be lit by our children and their parents. The first is a young boy named Elisha.

THE TEMPLE OF FIRE

As a child I loved a particular story in the Talmud, a story of an invisible temple. First I learned it, then I repeated it, and later I taught it. It is the story of the Third Temple, an indestructible temple erected in heaven, a temple of fire, built with fire. It would be a temple forever. Never would evil penetrate it. Never would death vanquish it.

This vision has accompanied me since we began work together in 1979. Since then I have always feared that because of bureaucracy, because of meetings, budgets, telephones, and other prosaic matters, because of the nature of things, somehow this vision of the temple, suspended between heaven and earth, somehow living between the heart and the soul, occupying a space between one world and another, between one word and the silence that precedes it or follows it — that this vision might disappear.

I do not want this to happen. I could not and would not go on working for a project of this magnitude, of this sacred dimension, if it were just another project. To me it is the most urgent project for our generation, not only because of the victims, but because of all of us, because of our children, because of future generations, because of mankind, even because of God in Heaven who needs our lesson and perhaps our testimony.

I am sure that this is the feeling that has moved all the members of the Council to serve it, as it is the spirit that has moved all those associated with our effort — the special advisers to the chairman, the children of survivors, and friends.

We feel we are doing something out of the ordinary, something which future generations will study and want to understand when they ask: How did people act under duress? What did they do afterwards? What did they do with the lessons they carried within themselves? What did they do with the pain of others?

Ours is a special group, one that has no equivalent, no parallel even in the rich and human fabric of American society. We are Christians and Jews, men and women, young and less young — all with experience, all educated by suffering, all open to the ideas of others, as long as the ideas are for the sake of humankind, not against it. Among us are professors and students — but, then, we are all students — businessmen, lawyers, teachers, rabbis, men in the labor movement, cantors, scholars, philanthropists. No segment of our society has been omitted.

If we did not know that up there between heaven and earth there is a temple in fire which nobody can destroy and which we have to rebuild, we would not do

Statement, meeting of U.S. Holocaust Memorial Council, Kennedy Center, Washington, D.C., December 2, 1982.

what we are doing, nor should we do what we are doing. It is this temple that we are trying to bring down in Washington and give it meaning, so that children and their parents and their teachers and their friends from all creeds, all colors, all trades, all spheres, and all persuasions will know that, in fact, there is only one temple, although the gates into it are many and all alike.

WHAT WILL REMAIN

When Leningrad was freed from the German siege, every citizen — every man, woman, and child — received a medal, the medal of liberation. Why? Because all had suffered — and come through. I believe that we who have remained faithful to the principles of humanity, Jew and non-Jew, also deserve medals.

But we do not want medals. What we want is to give and to share, for we believe that this century, to our shame and our regret, will be remembered not by the monuments it has built but by the camps it erected. It will not even be remembered by the space we conquered, but by the barbed wire we drew from community to community in order to divide people of different creeds, religions, ages, families. This is what will remain as a reminder and a warning for future generations.

But for now it is up to us to think about our time with shame or sadness. We think of the killers, and we feel terribly ashamed, because they, too, were human beings. We think of the victims and we feel sadness. They, too, were human beings. The victim was more human in his humanity than the killer was in his.

I do not know what will remain of our world. But I do know that what will remain of our meeting is an exalting feeling of commitment to purpose. One day our words will be read and they will sound as offerings from a very privileged generation. For ours is a privileged generation — privileged because we have seen so much, known so much, and remembered so much.

We have undertaken a unique, impossible task. It will always be impossible to communicate the silence of even one child, the tears of one mother, the fear of one father, the solitude of one family, the anguish of one ghetto waiting for the Angel of Death to pass. It will always be impossible, but because it is impossible we shall try and we shall do it.

Statement, meeting of U.S. Holocaust Memorial Council, Kennedy Center, Washington, D.C., December 2, 1982.

THANK YOU, THE AMERICAN PEOPLE

It is a great day and a great event. Both will be remembered by future generations. We shall write about this event with words of gratitude. No one is as capable of gratitude as we survivors. Instead of anger, we have chosen compassion. Instead of hate, we have chosen sensitivity. When the war ended — it is hard to believe, but it is true — the words on our lips were mainly "Thank you." When the first American soldiers arrived in Buchenwald, we rushed to them, we embraced them, we kissed them: they were princes from a faraway land, bearers of a message perhaps filled with redemption. And since then we continue to say "Thank you." Thank you, therefore, members of the Congress and the Senate, President and Vice President. Thank you, the American people, for having given us this museum.

In building this museum, we feel we accomplish a mission the victims have assigned us to collect memories and tears, fragments of fire and sorrow, words of despair and defiance, and names. Above all, names. It would take more than a lifetime simply to recite all the names of the victims. It would take more than one people, it would take more than one generation to bring back the names the killers have destroyed. So we shall house names in our museum . . . in all languages — in Ladino and in Greek and in French, in English and Russian and Polish, in Ukrainian and Lithuanian and Hungarian and Yiddish — because the killers wanted to destroy Jews from all the countries speaking all these languages.

Then we shall bring words into the museum, words we have found under the ashes in Auschwitz and Treblinka. My friends, there were chroniclers and historians in the camps. Even in Buchenwald and Treblinka, laboratories for total extermination, there were historians. Therefore it is our duty to take their message, keep it, study it, cherish it.

But there will be questions, too, that we shall have to include in our memory and program. Granted, the American army, the Allied armies liberated many camps, and we shall remember them forever. But why did they come so late? I have to teach my children and students and tell them that we should have faith, and I do teach them to have faith. But what can I answer them when they ask me, "Why wasn't one military plan changed to liberate the camps one day earlier? Why didn't the Allied forces bomb the railways going to Auschwitz?" Ask us, and we will tell you that in those days ten thousand people died daily, and if the

Statement, Museum Transfer Ceremony, U.S. Capitol, April 13, 1983.

[189]

railways had been bombed, at least ten thousand people would have lived one day longer.

Friends, survivors, and friends of our friends, we pledge to you to remain faithful. We shall tell the story, although the entire story cannot be told. We shall give fragments, sparks of the fire, although nobody will ever tell the full story.

The story we tell is Jewish, therefore universal. For as Kafka said, "When a Jew is beaten, mankind falls to the ground." When Israel is threatened, democracy is threatened. We pledge to tell as much as we can: the brutality of the killers; the cynicism of the bystanders; the heroism of the lonely ghetto fighter in Warsaw, Bialystok, and Vilna; the defiant stand of the partisans; the fate of the pious; the silence of the children; and the pain, the intense pain, of the mother who was forced to watch her children being murdered. We shall speak of our allies, we shall speak also of our Righteous Gentiles, we shall speak of our friends. And I swear in the name of all that is sacred to me and to us that we shall try to avoid cheapening the experience. I swear to avoid cheap slogans, simplistic conclusions, and vulgar spectacles. The subject commands us to preserve its awesome purity.

An ancient legend tells us that the Prophet Elijah roams the world collecting stories of human suffering and Jewish suffering and that one day when the Messiah will come, he will take all these stories, turn them into a book, and hand it to the Messiah. I know one place the Prophet Elijah will have to visit for a very long time: this museum, our museum.

PROTEST AGAINST IRAN

The world has heard disturbing news — members of the Bahai religious group in Iran have been imprisoned and executed because of their religious beliefs. Professing the Bahai faith in Iran is enough to be imprisoned and killed. Once again, religious hatred has taken a terrible toll.

We must protest this outrage with all our power. We hail the fact that President Reagan and other governmental authorities have raised their voices in protest — so far, to no avail.

I am particularly troubled that echoes of the Nazi cruelties are again being heard in our world. It is especially distressing that this occurs in a land ruled by representatives of one of the world's great religions — Islam. Believers in the God of all men should spread compassion, not persecution; understanding, not hate.

All governments and private citizens should not stand idly by while people are executed for religious beliefs. Perhaps the Human Rights Commission of the United Nations should look into this matter, and perhaps an international conference should be called to deal with the question.

We all vowed after the Nazi outrages — Never Again! Now is the time to act on that vow.

Statement, news release of U.S. Holocaust Memorial Council, Washington, D.C., July 7, 1983.

WE MUST REMEMBER

For some of us this is the most solemn and awesome day of the year. We delve into the darkest recesses of our memory to confront and evoke a vanished universe surrounded by flames and penetrated by silence. The living and the dead are locked together as they are during *Kol Nidrei* services. Young and old, pious and secular, princes and madmen, sages and wanderers, beggars and dreamers: on this day we close our eyes and we see them — an eerie procession which slowly, meditatingly, walks toward angels of death carried on wings of night into night. We see them as you see us. We are the link between you and them.

Therefore, we thank you, members of the House and the Senate, and Mr. Vice President, for allowing us to be that link. We thank you, the people of the United States, for creating a framework in which we can share visions and memories that defy language and comprehension.

Symbolically, our commemoration takes place in this august hall of legislation and commitment to law, to truth, and to humanity. From this room we teach the world that laws must be human, that they must serve humanity and not destroy it, that they are given to human beings to perfect life and not to profane it. We survivors have known the inhumanity of laws that became corrupt. Here with your deeds and our words we shall shield our laws for the future.

And so once more, as we have done since 1979, on this Day of Remembrance we gather from all the corners of exile to tell tales — tales of fire, tales of despair, tales of defiance — tales that we must tell lest we be crushed by our memories. In remembering them, in remembering the victims in the ghettos, camps, and prisons, we become aware of man's singular vulnerability but also of his stunning ability to transcend it.

We remember the killers and we lose our faith in humanity. But then we remember the victims and, though scarred, our faith is restored — it must be. The Jewish victims never became executioners, they never victimized others, they remained Jewish to the end, human to the end. That they could speak of God, to God, inside ghettos and death camps, inside gas chambers, that they could say *Shema Yisrael, Adoshem Elokenu, Adoshem Ehad* — God is God and God is One and God is the Lord of Creation — that they could say those words there on the threshold of death and oblivion must restore our faith in humankind. We think of the victims and we learn that despair is not the solution. Despair is the question. And that is why we gather year after year: to fight our despair.

Address, Remembrance Day observance, Capitol Rotunda, Washington, D.C., April 30, 1984.

As a son of the Jewish people, as a citizen proud to be a member of the American people, I live with the memory of the victims — of Jewish children and their parents. It has been our task, it remains our task, to maintain that memory alive. We remember not because we seek vengeance; we do not believe in vengeance. We only seek justice. We do not aim to hurt, only to sensitize. By retelling our tales we seek to make our contemporaries aware of what happens to human beings when they live in an inhuman society surrounded and penetrated by indifference on the one hand and evil on the other.

Nothing should be compared to the Holocaust, but everything must be related to it. Because of what we endured then we must try to help victims everywhere today: the Bahais who are being murdered by the dictatorship in Iran; the Miskitos on the border of Nicaragua; the boat people who are still seeking refuge; the Cambodian refugees; and the prisoners, so many of them, in Communist jails. Because we remember what has been done to our people we must plead at every opportunity, in this House and in all other houses, for Anatoly Shcharansky, Iosif Begun, Vladimir Slepak, and all the dissidents and prisoners who are in jail waiting for someone to shake humankind's indifference. If they were to lose faith in us, we should be damned.

It is because we remember the solitude of Jews in those times that we feel so linked to and so proud of the State of Israel today. We survivors, our friends, and allies are grateful to Israel and its people simply for existing, for inspiring us to keep faith in a certain form of humanity and tradition.

While we remember the victims we also remember those who tried to help us: the Raoul Wallenbergs and the Oskar Schindlers. They were so few, so alone. It breaks our heart to think of their solitude, of their sacrifice. Memory is not exclusive. Memory is inclusive. Because we remember the singular aspect of the tragedy we remember its universality.

We must also think of tomorrow as though it were part of our memory. The world unleashed madness forty years ago, and that madness still dominates the mind and spirit of all too many countries. There are many danger signals: racism, anti-Semitism, bigotry, fanaticism. We fear what humankind can do to itself. Therefore, we tell the story.

The Talmud tells us that when God gave the Law to the people of Israel he lifted Mount Sinai over the heads of the Jewish people and said: "If you accept the Law, you shall live. If not, you shall die." And so we accepted the Law.

Today I feel that God has lifted above our heads a mountain of fire, and it is as though God were saying to us: If you obey the Law — if you remember that we are all children of one father, if you remember that whatever happens to one people must affect all other people, if you remember that stupid cruelty is absurd and grotesque and that it is not by hurting others that one can redeem oneself — if you remember, you shall live and if not —. But we must remember.

SECTION 20

Explorations and Explanations

You see, I still, in the presence of life (or what you deny to be such), have reactions — as many as possible — and the book I have sent you is a proof of them. It's, I suppose, because I am that queer monster, the artist, an obstinate finality, an inexhaustible sensibility. Hence the reactions — appearances, memories, many things, go on playing upon it with consequences that I note and 'enjoy' (grim word!) noting. It all takes doing — and I *do*. I believe I shall do yet again — it is still an act of life.
— Henry James, in a letter to
Henry Adams, March 21, 1914

THE KEY TO THE MYSTERY

FLENDER What questions do you wish your interviewers had sometimes asked but didn't?

WIESEL The same questions that I am trying to ask myself. I won't tell you what they are. In general, all my work is a question mark. My work does not contain one single answer. It is always questions, questions I always try to deepen. These questions have to do with the content, with the soul of writing. I still believe that writing has a soul and that a writer is a prophet. The questions I try to put in my books are always the same, from my first book, *Night*, to my latest book, *Entre Deux Soleils*, my tenth book. They deal with life and death and solitude. What does man do to break out of his own self and attain a kind of presence in the world? Why does one write, if it is not to break out of this solitude?

FLENDER Your answer is by writing.

WIESEL No. I have no answers. I merely share my questions with others. I put the reader into my own circle. I open my mind and say, "Please come in." And what does he find? He finds questions. But the sharing itself of the questions can become a possibility of a direction, if not of an answer.

FLENDER You still study the Talmud.

WIESEL Yes, I still do. The Talmud has sustained me until now. . . . The Talmud to me is more than an accumulation of knowledge. It is more than a way of life. It is an opening to Judaism through the aesthetic dimension. It shows the aesthetics of Judaism, that Judaism is not only a philosophy, not only a set of ethical codes, but a thing of beauty. I study the Talmud to find the beauty in Judaism.

FLENDER You divide your time pretty much among New York, Paris, and Israel. Do you have any preference?

WIESEL It depends for what. New York is the best place to work because the isolation in New York is better than anywhere else. Paris is good because it is beautiful and because you cannot work in Paris even if you try. As for Israel, it responds to a need. I need to be there. Whenever I need to feel gratitude, I go to Israel. My feeling for the people of Israel, or for the Jewish people, which is to me the same thing, is a feeling of gratitude.

FLENDER You equate Israel with the Jewish people. Then one cannot be against the State of Israel and not be an anti-Semite. Do you agree?

WIESEL Wholeheartedly. If you are against Israel today you are *ipso facto* anti-

---

Adapted from Harold Flender, *Women's American ORT Reporter*, March/April, 1970.

Jewish. And if you are a Jew and against Israel, you are a renegade. You cannot have it both ways. The Jewish kids in the New Left, so-called intellectuals, who join El Fatah or support El Fatah, knowing that this would destroy Israel, must be proclaimed openly and publicly renegades of the Jewish people. Let them do what they want. But they should not be part of the Jewish people. They are not. Because the Jewish people today could not survive physically or spiritually if it were not for Israel.

FLENDER   You have been living in New York now for quite a few years. You have an excellent command of English, but you write your books in French.

WIESEL   My English is not really that good. I write my books in French because that is the language I acquired immediately after the war, as a protest. I know Hungarian, but I hated it and made a physical effort to forget it, to eradicate it from my brain. I never knew German well, and the little that I did know I didn't like. Yiddish for me was always connected with my studies of Talmud and so forth. So there I was without a working knowledge of any language. I chose French as a refuge, and whatever I read later in literature and philosophy was in French. I really do not know English as well as I should. Perhaps it is because subconsciously I am trying not to hurt my French. That is why I do not write in English.

FLENDER   The climax of *A Beggar in Jerusalem* is the Six-Day War. Since all of your books are, obviously, at least in part, autobiographical, I wonder, did you participate in the Six-Day War like the character David in your book?

WIESEL   I did not participate because I have never been a soldier in my life, and I do not even know how to handle a rifle. You said all of my books are autobiographical. Actually, only one is, *Night*. The others are not. I was never a terrorist, like the central character in *Dawn*. *The Accident* is partly autobiographical, but the others are fiction. I would say, however, that the mood of all of my books is autobiographical. As for *A Beggar in Jerusalem*, I did go to Israel during the Six-Day War. As soon as it broke out, I did everything I could to get there as soon as possible, and I arrived while the fighting was still on. I did not fight, but I think if they had needed me, and if I had been a soldier, I would have probably joined the army.

FLENDER   I'd like to congratulate you on your recent marriage.

WIESEL   It is not so recent. I have been married since last Passover.

FLENDER   You once told me that you would never get married, and you would certainly never bring children into this world. Have you become a little more optimistic over the years towards the world?

WIESEL   No. I have become more optimistic towards the Jews, but not towards the world. I think Jews have certain secrets of survival which we are trying to share with others. As for the world, I am very pessimistic, and the same questions I had remain. The same doubts that I had have almost become certainties. In 1960, when we met, we could somehow foresee 1970, we could speak about it. Now, in 1970, I cannot foresee 1980. There is a block in between, a wall in between, maybe the end. Something will happen, I am sure. I think I know why. Nineteen seventy marks the end of one generation after the Holocaust, our generation. This, by the way, is the theme of my new book which is coming out in Paris now, *Entre Deux Soleils*, and with which I depart from the Holocaust theme. I will not write about the Holocaust again. It is now 1970 and nothing has changed, and I have a very bitter feeling about it. I feel that we have failed, all of us.

FLENDER Silence is a key theme in all of your books.

WIESEL It is an obsession. My obsession, my universe, the universe of silence. I think we have tried to transmit, to communicate certain words of that era, but not the silence of that era, not the solitude of that era. Nothing. . . . To me, it is all very simple. The Jew is the key to all mysteries, because he is a mystery himself. Whatever happens to the world first happens to the Jew. We are the forerunners. Twenty-five years ago, there was an attempt to kill all the Jews. The world was indifferent. Now the world is trying to kill itself, and it is indifferent to itself. Paradoxically, the Jew can save it, by telling, by warning. This is what we have been trying to do for twenty-five years. It has not worked and I am very pessimistic.

FLENDER Do you think silence might have been more effective?

WIESEL Absolutely. Except I do not think the world could have sustained it. The world would have gone mad.

FLENDER Like silence, madness seems to be a recurrent theme in all of your books.

WIESEL Yes, but it is not a clinical madness. It's a mystical, literary madness. Every writer is a madman. One must be mad to imagine certain things.

FLENDER Are you worried about the change in America's political position towards Israel?

WIESEL Israel is today the cornerstone, the backbone of Jewish existence everywhere. Should America abandon Israel, it would be a tragedy for Israel. Should Israel, by some means, end in tragedy, it would be the end of the human race. I do not know how to justify or to explain this statement militarily. I only know philosophically that for the first time man's fate and the Jewish fate have converged. That means it is impossible today to try another Holocaust without committing the collective suicide of the whole world. If the world will again try to kill the Jew, it will mean the end of the world. I cannot foresee the end of the Jew today, either as a witness or as a messenger or simply as a being, without distinguishing his life from the life of man.

FLENDER Are there any contemporary writers you like?

WIESEL I like André Schwarz-Bart, who is a close friend. I like Bellow and Malamud, and Piotr Rawicz in France. Mainly, I like the works of my friends. The only cult I really worship and believe in is friendship.

FLENDER How about Philip Roth?

WIESEL I liked *Goodbye, Columbus,* but I do not understand his novels well. I have read *Portnoy's Complaint*, of course, but it describes a milieu which isn't mine. His obsessions are not mine. I do not understand why people were so outraged on one hand, and why people were so taken by him on the other hand. It's not my universe, but he's a very gifted craftsman, and I'm sure he has his own *Weltanschauung*.

FLENDER And Nabokov?

WIESEL Nabokov is different. He is a great writer. We have at least one thing in common: he, too, writes not in his own language.

FLENDER Do you do any writing these days besides books? Any journalism?

WIESEL No. For the past two or three years I have been on-and-off on a leave of absence as a journalist, because writing books takes most of my time. Then there are my lectures. I give very few, but they, too, take time. Each lecture requires two months of preparation and research. These lectures will eventually constitute a volume, but they still take a lot of my time and energy. At the end of a lecture I am so tired that I do not even recognize my friends.

FLENDER I found *A Beggar in Jerusalem* the most cheerful of your works. Can it be taken as a signal of works of a more positive nature to come?

WIESEL All my books are positive. They are not sad books, except for *Night*. *The Jews of Silence*, for example, is not a book about anger but of exaltation. It is a book of victory. And the same is true of my new book. What is *A Beggar in Jerusalem*? It is about the conquest of Jerusalem, victory in Jerusalem, the victory of the spirit of imagination, immortality.

A WRITER'S FEARS

AGMON Let me put a very personal question to you: Why do you not settle in Israel?

WIESEL All sorts of people ask me that question but I have no answer. If I wanted to, I guess I could invent an alibi, I could make up excuses, concoct pretexts. For instance, I might claim that in America I can do more useful work than in Israel. What would I be doing in Israel? Would I work as a journalist for the Hebrew daily *Yediot Aharonot*, for which I have served as foreign correspondent the past twenty years? There was some talk of my entering the Israel diplomatic service. Then what? I suppose they would send me abroad again. The truth is I do not know, except that I am not yet mentally prepared to live in a world which is the negation of my previous world. For Israel and the Holocaust are two worlds which negate one another.

In Paris, in 1948, I tried to enlist as a foreign volunteer in the Israel Army — that was during the War of Independence. All my friends and I knew we had to fight. But I was turned down on medical grounds. So I made it to Israel as a correspondent for a French newspaper. It was the only way I could get there. I stayed for some months and returned to Paris. Since then I have visited Israel nearly every year. When something happens there, I show up.

Malraux would call this a *situation fausse* — a false situation, a lie. People take me for an Israeli. I speak Hebrew. I move in Israeli circles. I identify with Israel in public. When I appear on television in France, I am presented as an Israeli. I feel I would be betraying something if I said: "No, gentlemen, I am not an Israeli." I do not live in Israel. Why not? I do not know.

AGMON How about other lovers of Israel who stay away from Israel? How do you account for their attitude?

WIESEL I don't. Everyone has his own personal reasons. I have only one remark to make to those who, like myself, don't migrate. "You don't want to? You're a free agent! But neither you nor I can boast of a clear conscience. Let's not fool ourselves."

AGMON Personal consideration aside, would you draw from your own and other people's reluctance to settle in Israel the conclusion that Zionism and the Jewish State do not constitute the absolute answer to the Jewish problem?

WIESEL That is a matter for philosophers of history. I am not a historical philosopher; I am merely a writer of stories. But why do you raise the Jewish *problem*? Judaism is no problem. Only those who hate Israel use this expression.

Adapted from Yaacov Agmon, *Israel Mágazine*, April, 1970.

[201]

Is a man a problem? A man is a situation, a man is life. Judaism is something living, not a problem. And we are gravely mistaken if we think or try to persuade others to think that Israel is the answer to the Jewish problem. There is no Jewish problem.

AGMON Let me put it this way — Is Israel the answer to certain problems facing the Jewish people, such as the problem of anti-Semitism?

WIESEL Yaakov, you are looking for answers. I do not believe in the existence of answers. I believe only in questions. As a people we Jews always have been and will always remain a question mark to the world at large. You are well versed in Hasidic lore. You may be familiar with the beautiful saying of Rabbi Nahman of Bratzlav: "In a certain place, at a certain time, a man asked a question. Later, elsewhere, another man asked a second question, which without his knowing it constituted the answer to the first question." We ask many questions and the very asking is the nearest we can get to the answer. But I do not believe in real answers.

AGMON You believe that the Jew holds the key to solving universal problems.

WIESEL The non-Jewish world today is interested in Judaism because it identifies with us. For two thousand years we have lived on the brink of extinction yet stayed alive. Today, from the existentialist point of view, the entire world lives on the brink of extinction. It is enough that one man in Washington, or tomorrow in Cairo, presses a button, and the entire human race disappears. So people come to us and say: "You have proved yourselves masters at staying alive. You have the key. Show us how to survive."

Much of what is happening in the non-Jewish world is linked with the Holocaust. The student revolt is linked with the Holocaust. LSD, the escape from reality, is linked with the Holocaust. The heresy of the students is prompted by the Holocaust, by the awareness that what happened to the Jews may before long happen to all mankind. Every Jewish boy has an uncle or a cousin or a grandfather who was wiped out. I am sure that this is the most important event in the history of Judaism, even more important than the rebirth of Israel. And the non-Jews, often without realizing it, use Holocaust terms of reference. What is the chief subject of discussion in New York today? The black ghetto. What words do blacks bandy about? Genocide, mass murder. They aren't Jews!

But here a tragic paradox has arisen. The people who take their inspiration from us do not thank us but attack us. We find ourselves in a very dangerous situation. We are again the scapegoat on all sides. There are streets where it is dangerous for a man to walk, especially if he is a Jew. I read in the paper yesterday that the blacks beat up a rabbi and burned a synagogue. And you know the things that the blacks are saying on the television, on the radio, in the papers.

It is terrible. I am really afraid. On the other hand, what is to be done? We helped the blacks; we always helped them. Should we stop helping them? This is a very tough problem. We have problems that the blacks do not have. We have problems that the Irish do not have. I do not know if this means that we are different today from what we were a hundred years ago. I think, on the contrary, that this is the fine thing about Jewish history. It is not important from what point you set out; you always reach the same center. No matter what period you examine, you will always find the same basic truth, the same perils, the same hopes, God and man, the messianic belief. Today, we live no differently, from the absolute point of view, than we did five hundred years ago. We are no safer now than we were then. There is a danger, a very acute danger, that the Jews will again be blamed for the past, for everything that is wrong in the world, for all the suffering in the world. I can easily imagine the white Christians saying in a crisis what the blacks are already saying: "It's the fault of the Jews!"

On the political plane, the accusations against us are liable to be related to Israel. What if tomorrow the current president, or in a few years' time the next one, declares: "We could bridge the gap between ourselves and Russia, or China, if it were not for Israel — Israel is the stumbling block"? Jews will be seen as a menace to world peace. You can hear State Department officials complaining that Israel undermined good US-Arab relations. More and more they may hold us responsible for all the evil in the world. That is what frightens me.

GOLDA AT 75

WIESEL Madame Prime Minister, I have been asked truly the most terrifying question in my life: Have I ever doubted the continuity of Israel? Did I ever believe that at one point the history of the Jewish people would come to an end?

It was hard for me to answer. Did you ever have any doubts?

MEIR No. No, I did not. There was never a doubt that the Jewish people would go on. And there was never a question of its connection with the Land of Israel.

The fact is that for any Jewish child brought up in Eastern Europe there was no day in which there was no Jewishness, no connection with the Jewish people. We were always the objects of discrimination, of pogroms. The first thing I remember in my life was the preparation of a pogrom in Kiev. The pogrom was against Jews — it was against *me*.

So there was the consciousness that I was Jewish, and different from all the other children in the yard. There was no pogrom against them. Their fathers were not nailing boards to the door — only my father.

Two things went together: this consciousness that we are different and not wanted, being hurt — and the fact of our not giving in. Because the next thing I remember — one of the first memories of my life — is of my older sister joining a movement of self-defense against pogroms.

WIESEL During the night — during the Holocaust — I remember the very first time I saw those trains unloading. I thought that perhaps this is the end not only of the Jewish people but of man.

MEIR That's different. I have never conceived of a world without Jews. Even during what you call the night, the Hitler period, with the sorrow and the fear, there was immediate action taken. I remember we then met in the Histadrut, and we thought, "What can we do, first of all, to let them know that we know and we're doing something about it. And second, we need to do something."

I remember distinctly we decided somebody should go to Ankara and try from there all kinds of ways that didn't make much sense. We finally sent parachutists down to them. There was no such thing as giving in to sorrow or to tragedy or to danger. The immediate reaction was: "This is the situation. It looks terrible, it looks hopeless, but something must be done immediately."

WIESEL Did you believe the first reports?

MEIR We believed them immediately. I remember when we first got the reports about the gas chambers, about the soap from the fat of Jewish bodies, and so

Adapted from *Hadassah Magazine*, January, 1973.

on, there was a big demonstration in Tel Aviv. The next day I had to see a British official — in connection with my work in the Histadrut — a very fine person. And we began talking about this big demonstration.

He looked at me, and he said: "Tell me, do you really believe it?" He remembered the atrocity propaganda from the First World War. But to us it wasn't atrocity propaganda. We believed it.

WIESEL That's very strange because I did not. I remember when I came there, and I was in it, it took me many, many days to believe it.

MEIR You were a child. We took Hitler seriously from the very beginning. In 1933, when he came into power, I happened to be in the United States, and a very large demonstration of Jews was organized — because we took it seriously.

But this is something that Jews have learned throughout their history, that when a man or a group makes it their program to kill Jews, no matter how outlandish it sounds, we believe it. But, even then, there were some Jews in the United States that didn't believe it, but most of them did. There was a very large demonstration in New York in '33.

WIESEL I still do not believe it happened.

MEIR We still are a Jewish people. With one-third gone, but we are still here, we are still alive. One of the factors that has saved the Jewish people is that throughout history we were not allowed to forget. For instance, when we sit at the *Seder* at *Pesah* and read the *Haggadah*, one sentence is so significant: that every Jew must see himself as though he were among those that went out from Egypt and was liberated.

WIESEL You once told me something very profound. You said you do not feel guilty for what you did not do during the Holocaust. But then you said, you feel guilty because you were not there. What do you mean by that?

MEIR Well, I do not know whether one can explain it — but we were more or less safe, although there was a time when Rommel's army was practically on our doorstep. We didn't run away. It isn't as though we were there and ran away. But there's a feeling that, at a time of such tragedy, one should have been part of it — it is as though you were not where you should have been. I can only give you one more example, which also is pretty terrible.

We have wars — to my sorrow — and I meet fathers and mothers who have lost their sons. At a certain point I feel a little guilty that such a tragedy did not happen to me. But there's such an abyss between parents who lost their sons and those who did not, that one who is among the fortunate feels indebted to the unfortunate ones, as though he is to blame for something. Which doesn't make sense, of course. I'm not at fault, but still there is an indebtedness.

WIESEL Did you go back to Kiev?

MEIR No, I never did because when I came to Moscow in 1948 (as Israel's ambassador to the USSR), one needed a special permit to travel to Kiev. And I thought, we'll get settled first, and I'll go later. But then, after our first elections, I was recalled to join the Cabinet. I'm sorry I didn't go to Kiev, not that I have clear recollections of it — I left Kiev when I was five.

WIESEL Do you remember it?

MEIR Practically not. I remember Pinsk, the city that we came to after Kiev, because I left Pinsk for the US when I was eight. I remember my grandfather's home, facing the church. During the First World War, Jewish men, forty of them, were lined up near the wall of the church and shot. So, whenever I think of it, I think of these men. Many from Pinsk are here in Israel, for instance, our minister of agriculture. It just happened that he was not among those forty.

I do not say that I have no happy memories, but I think everyone in my generation who was brought up in Eastern Europe has some recollection of tragedy and of sadness.

WIESEL When I'm in Jerusalem, I think of Sighet, my little town. In Sighet we met an old man, a very beautiful man. He is a *shoihet*, a ritual slaughterer. I asked why he didn't come to Israel. His children are here; he has three sons and they are tank commanders in the army. And he told us something very moving. He said, "Israel is for my children, but not for me." And then he said, "Maybe I am not worthy to be in Israel."

MEIR Everybody is worthy. Everybody that wants to come is worthy.

WIESEL Do you think that I am worthy?

MEIR You know, for many years I have thought that this is where you should be. I am sure you will come eventually. Everybody that wants to be here and chooses Israel is worthy to be here. They do not have to be angels, none of us is an angel. Israel is for Jews as they are.

WIESEL Do you think that I would be as moved every time I come to Jerusalem, if I lived here?

MEIR I do not believe that Jerusalem should be a place where one comes occasionally to be moved. Jerusalem is a real place, with everything that it has in it, and everything that it will be. When you live here, it does not become less exciting and less important. Jerusalem is not a thing of the past.

You know, when I first went to Africa, to the liberated countries, I was asked again and again, "You come from Jerusalem?" I said, "Yes."

"You mean there *is* a Jerusalem? But Jerusalem is in heaven. You mean there are streets, houses, people living there?" I said, "Yes." Jerusalem is not in heaven, it is here. What is heavenly about the city is that it's here — still here. It has houses, it has men, it has women, it has children, it has culture, it has work, it has problems. We are living in the present, although we are conscious of the past. We are building a future for it. We cannot make it something that is holy, to be viewed only from afar.

WIESEL When did you first come to Jerusalem?

MEIR Well, we arrived in the country in July, 1921. About two weeks we were in Tel Aviv and got settled, and then we came to Jerusalem. Jerusalem, naturally, was not what it is today, but we did not go to the new Jerusalem first. We went directly to the Old City, to the Wailing Wall.

Although I knew what the Wall was, and what it represented, I cannot honestly say that on my way to the Wailing Wall I was very emotional. I suppose I pictured it more or less as a monument. Until I got there. Then everything changed. And then everything made sense. I had heard, of course, that men and women — old people primarily — put little pieces of paper with wishes on them in the cracks of the Wall. I cannot say that it made much sense to me.

WIESEL Did you do it?

MEIR I did. Suddenly it made sense. To me this was the symbol of our struggle, of having been driven out of this country. But the Wall had remained there as a fortress of guarantee that the land will be there when the Jews return.

To me it is everything, almost something alive. And if it's not alive, then you talk to it, you have contact with it.

WIESEL What did you write on the first slip of paper you inserted in the Wall?

MEIR I wrote that this country should be rebuilt. And the next time I put in a piece of paper was two days after Jerusalem was liberated in 1967. Jerusalem was liberated on a Wednesday and I came early Friday morning. There was still sniping in the streets. I knew that the parachutists who were fighting for Jerusalem had many, many casualties, mainly because the Jordanians had their guns on the roofs of churches, and our men were under strict orders to preserve the holy places.

So it was a face-to-face struggle, and they lost many men. Civilians were not yet allowed into the city, but I was leaving that same morning for New York, and the general in charge went with me to the Wall.

It was not as it is today. You remember it — there was that little alley, and you had to go through yards and so on. And then I saw again something at the Wall that was almost beyond description.

There was a table, and on it were Uzi submachine guns. Four or five parachutists, with prayer shawls over their uniforms, were praying at the Wall. That's how I found them.

Every once in a while another one would come running in. This was their first chance to get to the Wall, and these heroes wept like babies.

For many of them, it was the first time that they had been near the Wailing Wall, because they were born after the Old City came under Jordanian rule. Here were these men who were strong and determined, and victorious — but when they met up with the Wall they broke down.

And then, it was so natural — I took a piece of paper. This time I wrote *shalom* and put it in the Wall.

WIESEL And then a young man came up to you.

MEIR And one of them — he wept near the Wall as though he would leave his heart there. And he turned around, still with his machine gun, and saw me. I'm not sure that he knew who I was. At any rate, I did not know him, certainly. Suddenly he walked up to me, put his head on my shoulder, and really wept like a baby. And I thought, with all his heroism, and with all this, at this

moment he felt he needed a mother's shoulder to cry on. I also cried a little
bit, I must admit.

WIESEL Madame Prime Minister, when you were in Moscow as Israel's first
ambassador to the Soviet Union — and you happened to be chosen by destiny
or by Jewish history to see those thousands of eyes that later haunted me, and
still do — did you ever think that one day you would see the Jews of Russia in
Israel?

MEIR Those were the days of the honeymoon between us and the Soviet Union.
They had voted for us in the United Nations and made great speeches: why
Jews should have a state of their own, and so on. But we had no idea what we
would meet as far as Jews were concerned. We had had no contact with them
since the Revolution.

I said to the men on my staff: "Look, bring prayer shawls if you have
them. If not, get some of the books that I brought for services. And the first
Saturday after we have presented our credentials, we will go to the synagogue."

We went, and there were a hundred, maybe a hundred and fifty, old Jews
there. That was in August. Then came the High Holy Days.

A few days before *Rosh Hashanah*, Ilya Ehrenburg wrote a big article in
Pravda, saying that if not for Stalin there would not be a Jewish State, and so
on, and so on. "But let there be no mistake," he said, "the State of Israel has
nothing to do with the Jews in the Soviet Union. In the Soviet Union there is
no Jewish problem, and they do not need the State of Israel. Israel is for Jews
in capitalistic countries, where there is anti-Semitism. Besides, there is no
such thing as a Jewish people — that's ridiculous. It's as though one said that
everybody that had red hair belongs to one people."

The Jews in Moscow read this just before the holidays, and they understood. They read between the lines. It was a warning to keep away from us.

As we came up the main street to that narrow street going to the
synagogue, we stood still. The street was packed, an ocean of people. And
one Jew came up to my counsellor, Namir, and said to him: "This is the
answer of Moscow Jewry to Ehrenburg's article."

And when I came out, and stood in this ocean of men and women — some
in Red Army uniforms — I knew that the Soviet Union had not succeeded in
breaking the spirit of the Jews.

What I feared was that they would find some other solution, and I reported
that to my colleagues when I came back. Either they will let them come here,
or they will do something terrible, brutal, cruel. If Stalin had lived, I think it
would have been the brutal solution. I had a nightmare that one morning I'd
get up and read in the paper that tens of thousands of Moscow Jews had volunteered to go to Birobidjan! That to me was a nightmare.

But I knew that Russia, with all its power, had failed. Jews remained Jews.

WIESEL Madame Prime Minister, are you happy?

MEIR Of course.

WIESEL I mean, happy with what's happening to our people?

MEIR Look, despite all that's happened, here we are, in the twenty-fifth year of a state that is independent and free, with over two and a half million Jews. There are countries where Jews have suffered, mainly the Arab countries, and we've brought practically all their Jews here.

I saw the Jews come in from Yemen, or from the Atlas Mountains of Morocco, and I see them now, the generation that was born here. Yemenite children came with their eyes — those big, black, beautiful eyes — full of fear. They were so undernourished that children of four could not stand up. And you see them now, tall and strong and free and fearless.

They've become good farmers, excellent farmers. They work in the factories, and they go to school, and they're in the universities, and they are teachers, and they're excellent soldiers when it's necessary to fight. And it's the same with Jews from Morocco and Jews from Libya — from the caves of Libya they came to us.

Of course, there are problems, and there are worries. And there are still wars, and that is the worst of all. Imagine what we could have done if we did not have to fight wars. But how can one not be happy when he has lived to see this?

WIESEL How do you manage to go on and on and on, aware that the Arabs do not want peace, and still speak about reconquering Jerusalem? What is your secret?

MEIR Look, I cannot say with certainty that the war is over. We hope so, but that depends upon them.

I am convinced, absolutely, that if there is another war, we will win again. The heartbreaking thing is, it means more people dead, not only on our side, but on the other side. I don't believe that an Egyptian mother cares less for her son than a Jewish mother cares for hers. Jewish mothers had their hearts broken, but they knew what their sons were fighting for. They were fighting for our life, for our very existence. What are the Egyptian sons fighting for? To destroy us.

Because it is so cruel, so senseless, and so hopeless to aspire to "throw us into the sea," it must stop. We are doing everything we can: it is a most terrible thing to send men to war.

But despite this tragedy of wars and fighting and so on, everything is growing. Everything is growing.

BEYOND SURVIVAL

RUDOLF When asked where your home was, you once replied, "Jerusalem when I am not there." Is this the writer speaking or the Jew, or since Edmond Jabès once identified the experience of writing with the experience of being a Jew, perhaps both at the same time?

WIESEL I do not believe in making distinctions. What I do, I do as a whole. I am a writer and a Jew. I am a Jewish writer and I am a writer. When I say "I," I express a certain totality. Jerusalem is my writing. Throughout my life I wrote about Jerusalem even when I was not there, but the question is, had I been in Jerusalem, would I have written about it? I do not know.

RUDOLF Is it true or significant that today Jewish experience and Jewish existence are translated by writers such as Jakob Lind, Jabès, yourself, and not by the traditional sources of wisdom, the rabbis?

WIESEL I think the rabbinic institution is important. For many centuries it performed its function. Today, I know many rabbis in all quarters, but I do not know enough "rebbes." I prefer "rebbes" to rabbis; I prefer masters to rabbis; I prefer teachers. That means I prefer people who give something of themselves rather than perform a function which is bestowed upon them, or for which they are hired. This is their vocation. But I hate generalizations. I know some rabbis who are good, who are honest. I know some rebbes who are fakes.

HEIMLER You and I were in the same camps, were deported about the same time, and wrote about it at the same time. When you wrote *Night* I wrote *Night of the Mist*. You keep writing about this subject; I write about other things. Why can't you get away from this subject, or don't you want to get away from it?

WIESEL You suggest that I wrote about the war. My fear is I think I did not. The more I wrote about it, the less I wrote about it. The more the years passed, the more I feared the real experience, which we tried at one point to capture, was not communicated. . . . Perhaps we should have kept silent and let silence speak and silence kill — kill in the sense of put an end, change and mystically transform reality. . . . I wrote only one book which had a direct connection with the experience, and that was *Night*. This very first book was an understatement. I knew very well that the real things were not in the book. I went around them. I described a child. I did not describe the Holocaust. I described a child *in* the Holocaust. I did not say what made the child become

Adapted from *European Judaism*, Winter, 1971/72. Discussion participants: Elie Wiesel, Eugene Heimler, Anthony Rudolf, Michael Goulston.

[210]

an old man in one night. In those days a ten-year-old boy and a sixty-year-old man looked alike, felt alike, walked alike, lived alike, and died alike. There was a certan "levelling." How could one write about it, when the very object and the very subject of the writing was so fluid? The child in *Night* is too old to write about children. That has been the source of my doubt for so long. Therefore in my subsequent books I touched upon the war theme lightly, indirectly.

RUDOLF It has been said that those who survived the Holocaust, who went through the camps, survived with a sense of guilt. Is it so?

WIESEL I feel guilt. Simply for being alive and knowing that because I am alive others are dead. There had to be a certain mathematical logic to what happened. When Heimler and I were in Buchenwald, the SS took roughly ten thousand out each day. I happened to be, let's say, ten thousand and fifty, but if I had been within the ten thousand someone else might have survived. On a very, very deep level I feel guilty because I was alive then and I am alive now. There is a certain betrayal. No matter what, we feel that betrayal. Is it more horrifying that we alone feel guilty? Those who committed the crimes do not feel guilty. Those who were neutral do not feel guilty. Those who were passive do not feel guilty. But we feel guilty for being here.

GOULSTON Do you find it necessary to continue writing?

WIESEL I would rather not, really. There is no compulsion in me. I would prefer to become, let's say, a Hasid rather than a rebbe. If I could find a good master from whom I could learn I would be happier. I am still looking for a master. If I am writing, it is because — it is arrogant — I do not find too many things to read.

RUDOLF The rebbe in *The Gates of the Forest* at the end says, "Auschwitz proved nothing had changed." In *Legends of Our Time*, you say, "The world incinerated its own heart at Auschwitz." What is the connection or distinction between morality, theology, and politics in the light of those two remarks?

WIESEL From a theological point of view, let me tell you a story from the Talmud. It is about either Rabbi Yohanan ben Zakkai or Rabbi Eleazar. When his son died, his disciples came to console him, and they said, "You know, Rabbi, when Adam's son Abel died, even he was consoled. Why aren't you consoled?" So he said, "My friends, don't you think I am sad enough with my own tragedy? Why do you add the tragedy of Adam too?" So they said, "Remember Aaron the high priest? When his sons died even he was consoled." And he said, "Don't you think I am sad enough with what happened to me? Why do you add the sorrow of Aaron?" And so on and so on. What does that mean? That pain is cumulative. One does *not* negate the other but adds to it. This is the answer I gave to the Lubavitcher Rebbe (because he is the rebbe in *The Gates of the Forest*) when he tried to tell me that the first *Khourban* of the Temple two thousand years ago already posed the problem of Auschwitz. I said, "But these two tragedies add to each other, making the problem more and more serious and more more difficult to cope with.

GOULSTON Although your persona is that of a soft-spoken Hasidic teacher, your

written words possess a certain hardness, a certain harshness, an almost puni-
tive quality.

WIESEL I do not attack anybody. I make people aware of their guilty conscience.
But then I believe that the first task of the Jew and of the writer is to make
people aware of their conscience. We have been the guilty conscience of the
nations for two thousand years. We have survived because of the guilty conscience of others! I do not attack others. Actually, I pity them, especially the
kids today. Therefore they come to me.

My readers are young kids. Eighty per cent of them are young French people who come to my lectures — Hippies and Yippies. I feel sorry for them
because they did not carry the burden of events they did not personally experience. The same goes, at a different level, for the adults who were in
Sweden, in Switzerland, in America but did nothing. I tell them, you were
alive then, you could have had a *crise de conscience* and your life might have
changed. But you did not.

THE LESSON OF AUSCHWITZ

REYNOLDS You say that when you open the newspapers today, you have the feeling that nothing has changed in thirty years. What does that do to you, Mr. Wiesel? How can you read the papers?

WIESEL I make an almost existential decision every day — because there is nothing to be done, I must do something. Because the tale cannot be told, I must tell it. Because I cannot believe in man or in God, I must make other people understand that there are certain things to believe in. So I create things out of nothingness.

Albert Camus said, "In a universe of misfortune, one must create happiness." This is what I am trying to do — to create a meaning in a universe that has no meaning.

REYNOLDS When you say that you try to create happiness, are you in fact trying to locate it or to let us know that it still exists somehow or other?

WIESEL I try to point to a direction and to name it. Naming things is very important in Judaism. I cannot create it. No one can.

REYNOLDS Were you confident thirty years ago that if you could survive and tell everybody what had taken place, the world would be so chastened and shocked that we would stop?

WIESEL Oh, yes. I remember my feelings in 1945. I remember them very well. On the one hand, I knew that I would never experience true joy again. Never. On the other hand, I knew that because of that fact others will.

REYNOLDS Do you feel that people today do not want to read your books?

WIESEL Young people want to read them more than their parents, who feel guilty.

REYNOLDS Why is that?

WIESEL I think young people want to understand what is happening to them. At the same time, they literally feel they lost something by being born too late — that, with all the misfortunes and curses attached to that period, there was something very great. The Holocaust had a mystical magnitude. What happened thirty years ago was so great that not even God can understand and comprehend it. And, in a way, it is a privilege to have endured those experiences. Young people today would like to relate to those experiences and to that Event, with a capital E. Did you go to Jerusalem when Eichmann was tried?

REYNOLDS No.

WIESEL I did. I remember when Eichmann came to Sighet, my hometown. One Saturday in 1944, two Germans, one of them Eichmann, came into town with

Adapted from Frank Reynolds, American Broadcasting Co., Inc., *Directions*, ABC-TV, June 25, 1972.

50 Hungarian gendarmes. And these 52 persons deported the 15,000 Jews of Sighet. I remember Eichmann at the railway station, with a melancholy smile on his face. The job was done.

Therefore, I went to Jerusalem for the trial. I wanted to see whether he had two eyes, whether he could smile, whether he dreamed, whether he could speak. I hoped to see Cain's mark on his forehead. After all, if a man kills and kills and kills so much, it must leave an impression on his body, on his face, in his look. Nothing at all.

One day during the trial, I asked a wise, old Yemenite woman, "Would you like to come to the trial?" She said, "No." I said, "I can get you a ticket." She said, "No, thank you." I asked, "Aren't you interested?" She said, "Yes, but I read the newspapers." And I said, "Why don't you want to see him? Are you afraid to see him? He is defenseless. He is in a glass cage." And the wise woman said, "No, I am afraid that he will see me." She did not want his eye to focus on her. She did not want to have anything in common with that man. Then I understood that perhaps during the Holocaust the cosmic eye was focused on mankind, taking in everybody, making us all guilty.

REYNOLDS Did you feel guilt when you looked at Eichmann in the dock in Jerusalem?

WIESEL No, I felt like laughing.

REYNOLDS You did, really?

WIESEL Yes, laughing with a metaphysical laughter. I had doubted often whether history — Jewish history — had a sense of justice. But suddenly I realized that it had a sense of humor. The Eichmann who once was God, who repudiated all laws of men, suddenly now sat in a glass cage trying to explain paragraph after paragraph, invoking all kinds of laws. Something was metaphysically wrong and right at the same time. In that courtroom I, a survivor of his crimes, felt guilty. That is another reason I felt like laughing.

REYNOLDS What was your feeling toward Eichmann as you watched him in the dock?

WIESEL Intense curiosity, from beginning to end. I tried to read my life on his face. I tried to see in what way my destiny was linked to his.

REYNOLDS As you looked at him, did you not think of that day, years before, at the railroad station?

WIESEL Yes, I did. And I came to a strange conclusion. When I saw him at the railroad station, he was in uniform. He was the God, yet he did not inspire fear. When I saw him in the glass cage, somehow I was afraid. I realized that evil does not have to be expressed in action in order to be evil or powerful.

REYNOLDS Can it happen again?

WIESEL It happened in Biafra, Burundi, and Bangladesh. But I don't think it will happen again to Jews. I think probably, for the first time in two or three thousand years, Jewish history and universal history are identical — to destroy Jewish history is to destroy human history. This is probably the only lesson that we learned from Auschwitz.

GIVING AND RECEIVING

KRESH What is the Hasidic concept of giving?

WIESEL In Judaism the one who gives does not feel superior, and the one who receives does not feel humiliated. Remember — the word *tzedakah* does not really mean philanthropy. It means justice. The one who gives to the one who has not is regarded as accomplishing an act of justice in the metaphysical sense. Of course, in my hometown, in that tiny universe of Sighet in Transylvania where I was born in 1928, giving on the scale that Americans do today to the United Jewish Appeal was inconceivable. Yet, even so, the one who gave and the one who received never knew each other. There was a secret fund, and the giver always remained anonymous.

It is much like that today, isn't it, even though the scale is immense! The newcomer in Israel from the Soviet Union who benefits from a gift halfway round the world by a prosperous contributor in Detroit does not know the identity of his benefactor. I find this beautiful.

KRESH There were old Hasidic traditions of giving — of carrying out the precept of *tzedakah*.

WIESEL There were certain rituals, as before *Pesah*, when both poor and rich were expected to make contributions to a special Passover fund. Poor as well as rich — for no matter how poor you were, there was always some Jew still poorer. Of course, there was the giving of *shalachmones* at *Purim* time, too; and, again, no one boasted of his generosity. It was expected — part of being a member of the community and sharing one's good fortune with others less fortunate. You must remember that the Hasidic movement was a poor movement. In each congregation there was a rich man or perhaps two who helped keep the rest of us alive.

KRESH In your mind, how does the generosity of the Hasidim you remember compare with the huge fund-raising efforts of the United Jewish Appeal in America today?

WIESEL I recently spoke to four thousand women of the New York UJA Women's Division. Those women could have been playing cards or spending their time at a museum or the theater or just wasting it; instead they were taking part in this effort to better the lives of other Jews so far away.

KRESH Have attitudes toward fund-raising changed?

WIESEL The older generation loved to listen to speeches, to be harangued, to be stirred emotionally. Today the younger generation wants to learn. They want

Adapted from interview by Paul Kresh, *UJA World*, 1972.

[215]

information. They want to know *why*. They are concerned with the welfare of their fellow Jews more than ever — and with the welfare of the world in general. I am convinced from my meetings with young people that the Jews today have a universal mission greater than ever before — to help the world save itself. I believe Israel can become an example to other nations.

A SMALL MEASURE OF VICTORY

INTERVIEWER What made you choose France as a home after the Holocaust?

WIESEL I did not choose France. Buchenwald was liberated on April 11, 1945. When the Americans came in, 20,000 of us remained out of about 80,000. The American soldiers were so kind, so innocent — so foolishly innocent. They gave us fatty foods when we had not eaten such food for many months, and not at all for several days. Some 5,000 died. I myself fell sick; I described it in *Night*. For ten days I was very ill. Only after I recovered did I learn that there were 400 of us children in Buchenwald. None of us knew what to do. We did not want to go home. I knew that my father had died, and I was convinced that my mother and my little sister had died also. I was not certain about the fate of my two older sisters. Had I known that they were still alive, I would have gone back home. But I did not know. For two or three weeks I went through lists of survivors, but was unable to find their names. So I decided not to go home. And when the authorities asked: "Where do you want to go?" I said, "Anywhere. Perhaps Palestine." It was the only place I could think of. But they said, "No, you can't go to Palestine; the English won't let you." Then they asked me about Belgium. Belgium? I didn't even know where it was. France? Why did we go to France? De Gaulle heard about us. He heard about 400 Jewish children in Buchenwald who did not know where to go. As prime minister, president, and provisional governor, he rerouted a train to take us to France. When we crossed the border, a French police officer approached us and asked who among us wanted to become a French citizen; whoever did should raise his hand. Not understanding French, I did not raise my hand. Those who did became citizens immediately, even though they, too, did not understand French.

That is how I came to France and why I remained there as a stateless person. I remained stateless until I came to America in 1956 because France does not grant citizenship easily and, moreover, the French were angry at me for not having accepted it back in 1945. Ironically, when in 1964 or so I received an award from the French Academy for my first four books, I received at the same time a letter from de Gaulle congratulating me and reminding me that he had been the one who had brought me to France and had opened the gates of French letters to me.

I lived in France on and off, until 1956. I traveled all over the world. I went

Adapted from interview by Gene Koppel and Henry Kaufmann, University of Arizona, Tucson, Arizona, April 25, 1973.

to India for a few months. There I studied in an ashram; I studied the Vedas. I was preparing a dissertation, a comparative study on asceticism — Jewish, Buddhist, and Christian. I lived in Israel from 1948 to 1949. Then I came to the United States as a correspondent for an Israeli newspaper. Every night I used to send a cable to the paper. Three months after I arrived, as I was coming back from the cable office one night, a taxi hit me. That is the story of *The Accident*. I spent a year in a wheel chair with forty-eight fractures (even today I cannot walk more than five minutes).

In the meantime my one-year visa had expired and I had to renew it. I went to the immigration office with my request. They said, "With pleasure, since you are a UN correspondent. But first you need a new travel document — it too has expired. Since you are stateless, it was valid only for one year." So in my wheel chair and with my crutches I went to see the French consul who told me that such a document could be renewed only in France. To my question: "How can I? I am on crutches," he replied: "Sorry." So I went back to the immigration officials who said that they would like to give me a visa — but on what? Back to the consul I went. I think I made the trip back and forth a dozen times. Finally, the American immigration officer told me there was only one way out of this predicament. "Why don't you become a United States citizen?" I had never thought of it. "How does one go about it?" And they said, "We'll help you." And that is how I became, with gratitude, an American citizen.

INTERVIEWER To return to France for a moment — how do you explain the turnaround towards Israel of the de Gaulle and Pompidou governments?

WIESEL De Gaulle was a strange character. I owe him much. As I have already explained, he was the one who brought me to France; he was the one who, you could almost say, gave me my tools, gave me my language, the French language. Yet in 1967 I broke with de Gaulle as I broke with many people who then abandoned Israel. De Gaulle was behaving like an anti-Semite; I said it on French television. Of course, much of the respect, the esteem, and the gratitude I had for him were lost at that time.

How is one to explain it? There probably were many political or geopolitical considerations. Israel is a small country, and France wanted to become a major power; and one way to become a major power in de Gaulle's view was to abandon Israel and look for markets where neither Russia nor America had a controlling influence: the Arab countries.

But that is really too easy an explanation. I think there is a more profound one. De Gaulle was well-disposed toward Germany; his best friend was Adenauer. He immediately — or almost immediately — made peace with Germany when he came to power. He was even friendly toward Russia. Whom did he hate? The British; he opposed their entry into the Common Market. He hated America, and he hated the Jews. Why? He owed nothing to Germany or to Russia. But he did owe almost everything to the British, who had taken him in and given him grandeur and status. He owed a great deal to America and much to the Jews. You see, most of those who helped him in the beginning were Jews. This surprised de Gaulle. He said, "I expected to see the France of the churches, and instead I see the France of the synagogues."

So he wanted to free himself of these three obligations. And how does one free oneself? By becoming an enemy. Pompidou, too, is perhaps responding to similar needs. He worked for the Rothschilds. Now he wants to show that, not only is he a good disciple and successor of de Gaulle, but that he doesn't owe anything to any Rothschild. There are probably other reasons, but I am not familiar with them.

INTERVIEWER You have touched now upon the three countries that you know best: France, Israel, and the United States. What is your impression of present Jewish life in these countries? How do you think the future will shape up for the Jews living in them?

WIESEL I think something is happening today to Jewish communities all over the world. Jews everywhere go through the same periods of anguish and hope. Jews everywhere react the same way to certain events, meaning there is a certain revolution within Jewish history, and this revolution affects everybody. So that today the Jews in France, and America, and Russia (of which I also have a little knowledge) respond to the same challenges, to the same appeals, in the same manner. What is happening here happens in France. What is happening in France happens in Israel, and in Russia, meaning, the situations tend to be extreme. Never have young Jews been as alienated as they are now: the New Left, Jesus Freaks, and other freaks. At the same time, never have young Jews been as dedicated as they are now. In the middle there is a tremendous mass, an amorphous mass of Jews waiting for a call, waiting for some stimulating call for beauty, truth, sincerity, and commitment. And I am afraid for this large mass in the middle.

INTERVIEWER What really is the hope for these Jewish masses waiting to be galvanized, to be brought together? Throughout all of your own books you show the agony of trying to put together some kind of a world picture, some kind of a religion, some kind of a view of God and man that can give hope for one to go on. In your book *The Accident* I'm still not quite sure when the artist walks out, if the ashes that he leaves behind are the last word, or if the hope that he tries to leave behind is the last word. Now, how can there possibly be any hope for any great vision that will seize the Jewish masses when for both yourself and for so many others everything is still in fragments?

WIESEL In *The Accident*, when the painter leaves my principal character, he leaves him not with hope but with ashes. This is a dialectical approach, which I believe must be ours. On the one hand, there is total despair; on the other, what does one do with one's despair? I have no answer to that. What I try to do is to bring both extremes into focus — to demonstrate that because there is no hope we must invent it. I do not think I succeed all the time. Still I know I am following a tradition, the Jewish tradition. I always think about it when I think of the first man in our tradition, Adam. Adam had two children, two sons; the whole world was inhabited by only a few people. So Adam, the father, sees how one son kills the other, dividing mankind into executioners and victims, in the absolute sense of the word. Cain is the absolute executioner, Abel the absolute victim. And Adam is the father. I would think that, after having seen what he saw, Adam would have given up his belief in man, that he would have stopped having children. Yet he did have another son, a third son.

The same is true of Abraham. Abraham had Isaac. Isaac should have gone mad. He saw what God does to man. He wants man to become either murderer or victim, Abraham or Isaac. He saw his father almost turn murderer. Isaac should have stopped the adventure right there; he should not have married, should not have had children. But he did. And Jacob saw what Esau did to him and what he did to Esau, and what his father went through. Jacob too had children. This is the human condition. When you live on the edge of the mountain, you see the abyss, but you also see very far. And so, because never in human history have people had more reasons to despair, and to give up on man, and God, and themselves, hope now is stronger than ever before. It is irrational; it is absurd, of course. But it may be a way of achieving a certain victory. Not absolute victory. A small measure of victory.

That does not answer, of course, the question that you are asking about the masses. Once upon a time when I was a child, I had high hopes. I come from a religious family, from a mystical background. I was convinced that every Jewish child must either bring the Messiah or become the Messiah. But I am much more modest now. I do not think one can save mankind. I try to save a few people, one child here, one man there, one student here. What I try to achieve is a daily miracle, the small wonder of giving a human being a reason to take one step forward in his life, perhaps in mine.

INTERVIEWER I would like to move now from the problem of the spiritual future of the Jewish people to the question of their continued physical existence. When Nathan Glazer was here last year, he spoke of what he discerned as a new movement (perhaps "motivation" would be a better word) among American Jews, which he called "survivalism." In other words, the main emphasis now is on the sheer survival of the Jewish people. And this has resulted in a change. It used to be that the Jews existed to serve their religion, to serve God. But now it is the opposite: the Jewish religion is there to serve the Jewish people, to hold them together. Would you like to comment on this view?

WIESEL I have discerned the same phenomenon; survival has become the key word. But then I understand why. The Jewish people has been in danger of extinction in our generation; so survival is a categorical imperative. Yet, I am not that concerned, strange as it may sound. For I do not believe that our survival is now in danger. I do not believe that the Jewish people now in this generation, and perhaps for generations to come, is in danger of extinction again. I do not think there can be another Holocaust.

INTERVIEWER Not in Israel?

WIESEL Nowhere.

INTERVIEWER You don't think there is a possibility that the United States will experience great uprisings of violent anti-Semitism?

WIESEL No. There may be anti-Semitism, but no Holocaust. Why? One reason is that the Holocaust was so immense, so incredible, that it was a unique event. There can be no other event like it. Number two, the Holocaust saves Jews now. That is a horrible thing to say, but because of the memory of the Holocaust some things cannot happen again. Three, and this is the most frightening of all reasons: for the first time in history, perhaps, or at least for the first time in the last two thousand years, Jewish history and world history coincide. Whatever happens to the Jewish people will ultimately happen to the world. Should the world try to kill the Jews today, it would kill itself. Another Holocaust would be a universal holocaust. Should mankind try again to destroy the Jewish people, it will be a total conflagration. So I am even more pessimistic than the others. Survival is no longer the key word for the Jewish people alone, but for all mankind. . . .

INTERVIEWER Mr. Wiesel, you said before that you have no fears (unless it occurs in a universal holocaust) that the Jewish people will be wiped out. But isn't there another kind of threat — the disappearance of the Jewish people through assimilation and indifference?

WIESEL Yes, I believe assimilation does pose a danger. Naturally, I try to fight it. I do not know how, but I try — my books, my teaching, my stories. But, I must say, whenever I meet assimilated or alienated Jews, I feel a kind of pity for them. They miss so much. They take of their Jewishness only the burdens, but none of the privileges. They are wasting so much of the resources at their disposal. Great men outside of our tradition, outside of our people, would have given everything to be in touch with these resources. Camus regretted that he wasn't Jewish. Mauriac was full of envy. Kazantzakis almost *became* Jewish. And here you have born Jews who simply give it up. I feel so sorry for them. They don't even know that during the war the Jews who were most miserable were those who were either assimilated or converted.

INTERVIEWER Why was that?

WIESEL Because from their point of view they suffered for nothing. They were not even Jewish, and they suffered. In the Warsaw Ghetto there was a church for converted Jews, and yet they were treated just like all the other Jews. They did not understand why. They were not Jews, but the enemy decided they *were* Jews. The same thing happened with the assimilated Jews in Paris and in Hungary. When the chips were down, they were treated just like Jews. The religious Jew, at least, could say to himself: "Well, I have to suffer. I'm Jewish." But the others couldn't even do that.

INTERVIEWER In Germany it was even worse.

WIESEL Yes, it was worse.

INTERVIEWER When Hitler came, many of them committed suicide.

WIESEL In Vienna, there was mass suicide. They didn't understand what was happening. It was beyond them.

INTERVIEWER In the actual Jewish community around us there are many Jews
who can find no "soul," no genuine Jewish life, nothing to relate to. I
believe that this is the plight of many intelligent American Jews today.

WIESEL This I know. How many times I face these questions from young people
who come to tell me, "You speak of *Shabbat*, but where can I find it?" I love
Shabbat. I miss *Shabbat*, because in my *shtetl Shabbat* was so important. So
I try to describe what *Shabbat* was like, and some young people ask: "Well,
why don't *I* have such a *Shabbat*?" I don't know what to answer. Criticize
their parents . . . how can I? I speak of the beauty of the Jewish tradition
because I believe in it. And they say, "What's so beautiful about it?" Sometimes I speak with American Jewish writers from big cities, whose description of the Jew is not very flattering. They say things like: "You see, the
difference between you and us is that you have something to remember. We
don't. What was *Shabbat* for us? Nothing. Our parents were Socialists.
When we came home Friday evening from school and from the shop there
were no prayers, no candles, nothing. It was just another day, another difficult day." Well, I don't know what to answer. I could simply say that Jewish
leaders are at fault. It's so easy and so true. They are at fault.

INTERVIEWER What do you think about the very strained relations between the
American black community and the American Jewish community?

WIESEL I feel sorry for the blacks. There is one thing they should learn from us
and that is gratitude. No people in the world knows gratitude as we do; we are
forever grateful. Someone not Jewish does something good for us: he
becomes a prince in our eyes. Jews have done some good things for the black
community, and I would expect the blacks to respond with gratitude, not with
abuse. That does not mean that I think we should now turn against the blacks.
I would say that young Jews should be concerned with all racial inequalities
and try to correct them. But I certainly would not help the militant, extremist,
anti-Jewish blacks. I have no sympathy for them.

INTERVIEWER What modern theologians, either Jewish or non-Jewish, do you
find helpful or influential in your efforts to put together some kind of coher-
ent hope for the future?

WIESEL I don't like the word "theologian." I find it disturbing. What is a
theologian, really? Someone who knows things about God. But who knows
what God is? I'm still trying to speak *to* Him. How can we speak *of* Him?
Still, there are certain people who have this title whom I respect very much.
Camus, although he was agnostic, spoke to theologians as a theologian.
Sartre, who is an atheist, has written some very beautiful things that could be
part of theology. And, on the other hand, we have Heschel and Buber and
Scholem — mainly Scholem, the great scholar of mysticism. But my influences really were much more removed. I am still studying Talmud with Professor Saul Lieberman in New York. Whatever I know comes from such
sources; whatever I try to give I have taken from them. The Midrash, Geonic
literature, Hasidic literature — their authors were "theologians."

INTERVIEWER Then from others who have gotten so much modern attention (men such as Reinhold Niebuhr and Paul Tillich) with their efforts to find new concepts of God, you personally haven't found anything very relevant?

WIESEL No, I personally have not. I have read some of what they have written, and I am impressed by their quest. Maybe it sounds arrogant, but as a Jew with my Jewish background, whatever I discover about my own problems (let alone the approach to the problems), I must derive from within my own tradition. I can appreciate what others are saying, but in order for me to transform knowledge into my own consciousness, which is the purpose of literature, I go back to my own sources. . . . After the war I studied philosophy in France, convinced that I would find some answers in philosophy; those I found did not work. They were not applicable to my questions.

INTERVIEWER Why not?

WIESEL Because by their very nature these questions have no answers. To these questions I had to ask (that any child of my age could have asked), there were no answers — not even in our literature, not even in the Talmud. The writers try, but they are inadequate. Therefore I read Victor Hugo and Dostoyevsky and Kafka — I read them because I live in the twentieth century, and I want to know, I want to feel, I want to love what they are giving me, and I do. But still, when their writing undergoes a metamorphosis inside me, it inevitably comes out as a fragment of a Talmudic legend or a tale; it must have the same *niggun*, the same voice.

INTERVIEWER You are not a rabbi, but still your basic point of view is a religious one. Your definition of a Jew, I think, must include the religious dimension — if I understand you correctly.

WIESEL Yes, but I wouldn't say in what way: mystic, Reform, Orthodox, or whatever. I do not want to divide the Jews; I think Jews should be united. I will help any endeavor that leads toward that unity. He who divides Jews is wrong.

INTERVIEWER Then would you give me a definition of the way you feel toward the Jewish *people*, a definition that would include its relationship to an unknown God, in which the individual Jew —

WIESEL I'm terribly sorry. I really never speak about God. I have enough trouble speaking of myself — I cannot speak about God.

INTERVIEWER When you speak of the Talmud, aren't you really speaking about God?

WIESEL Yes, but I do not say it. Here you are, trying again to lead me into theological exploration. When people talk about God, they become enemies. Everyone thinks his is the closest relationship to God. If men do not talk about God, they have a better chance to speak to each other and perhaps even to feel closer to Him. God does not want to be talked about. He wants to be listened to, to be heard. He talks and He listens but not when people speak about Him to others. When I speak about God, my only listener should be God.

INTERVIEWER Your latest book, *Souls on Fire*, deals with the development of the

Hasidic movement. In your younger years you were close to the Wizsnitzer Rebbe. Do you still have a rebbe of your own?

WIESEL Of course, I wish I had. The Wizsnitzer Rebbe died two years ago, and now I have different rebbes, more than one. I am still a Hasid. That means I still believe in what I believed as a child. I still love to sing and to tell stories. I still love whatever characterized the Hasidic movement in its early stages — a longing fervor, passion, and compassion, doing things together with other people. The Hasidic movement was a movement of friendship. That is why it has always had such a strong appeal to me.

INTERVIEWER Is it still that way now?

WIESEL Well, you know in Judaism we believe that there is usually regression from generation to generation. Abraham was better than we, and David was stronger and more beautiful than we, and so forth. The Hasidim today cannot be compared to the early Hasidim two hundred years ago, or even to the Hasidim I knew in my youth. That goes for the rebbes as well. But in a world so dehumanized, so ugly, and so drained, it is refreshing to find young people who still believe and older people who still inspire that belief.

INTERVIEWER Then you would disagree with the critics who say present-day Hasidim have become hardened and dispirited?

WIESEL I don't think that the criticism of Hasidism today is that it is suffering from a hardening of the spirit. The criticism is that it is phony.

INTERVIEWER That is an even harsher criticism.

WIESEL Much harsher. Once, to be a Hasid was not as easy as it is now. It was a way of life. Today you go and sing a few Hasidic songs and you are a Hasid. Well, it's not really that simple. That is not the way to be a Hasid. It is only a beginning. If you go on to study Hasidism and accept Hasidic principles, then you become a Hasid.

I don't think the critics are right, by the way. I think that there are phony people everywhere, just as there are authentic people everywhere.

INTERVIEWER Let me ask you a depressing question. I have read several writers lately (some of them are Christian) who say they are afraid that anti-Semitism has penetrated into the very heart of Christianity. Do you think this is true?

WIESEL Unfortunately, it is true. If you study the history of Christianity, you will find that it is full of anti-Semitism. More than that — there would have been no Auschwitz if the way had not been prepared by Christian theology. Among the first to dehumanize the Jew was the Christian. He turned the Jew into a goat. From the very first sketch, the illustrations showed that the Jew belongs to Satan, not to God. In Christian theology the Jewish people belonged to "Satan's Synagogue." Therefore the Jew did not have the rights of a human being. He was not a member of the human species, of the human family. In the Middle Ages, a Christian who killed a Jew was held accountable only for having deprived a prince of the money he might have gotten from the Jew. Yes, absolutely, there is anti-Semitism in the Church. And the person who understood it best was Pope John XXIII. He understood that he had to change the course and the outlook of the Church, not because he wanted to help the Jews — that too was true — but because he wanted to help the Church. He understood that anti-Semitism was a disease which afflicted the Church, and he felt that the time had come to redirect and reroute the Church's destiny by curing the disease.

INTERVIEWER The young State of Israel hopefully will be one of the foremost Jewish cultural centers in the world. But, so far, not too much literature has come out of Israel. Why do you think this is so, and when do you think it will change?

WIESEL If I knew, I would be a prophet, and prophets, as you know, do not fare too well in our tradition. But I think I do have some understanding of it. You see, whatever happens in Jewish history at one point becomes mysticism. The moment you touch a certain aspect of Jewish history, you push it to the extreme and you enter mysticism, which means that you do not know what is happening. What has happened in Israel is so great, so overwhelming that it cannot be explained or expressed yet. That is why we still have no great novel about the Israeli experience. The subject is simply too overpowering; no one can imprison it in words or in a literary structure. It will take a few years, maybe a few generations. We can wait.

INTERVIEWER What fiction writers have been most important in shaping you as a craftsman, as a novelist? Who has inspired you?

WIESEL First, the Jewish masters, the Talmud. I try to write in a Talmudic vein. My legends are Talmudic legends, I hope, or Hasidic legends. In secular literature: Dostoyevsky and Kafka. My life can be divided into a pre-Dostoyevsky period and a post-Dostoyevsky period, a pre-Kafka period and a post-Kafka period. . . . I learned much from Kafka: how a writer can get at one kind of truth by creating yet another kind. From Kafka, one learns to write; from Dostoyevsky, one learns to write novels.

And there have been others. Camus. And then — very much, Mauriac and Malraux. Mainly these writers.

INTERVIEWER As someone greatly influenced by Hasidic traditions and legends, you keep emphasizing your role as a storyteller, as a teller of tales. Isaac Bashevis Singer, too, thinks of himself as a storyteller. He believes that one of the things wrong with modern novelists and poets is that they think of themselves too much as commentators, as saviors of the world who try to impose their personal "messages" on their art from the outside rather than let their story take form from within. Do you agree with Singer?

WIESEL I don't like to give literary comments. I do not speak about stories, I tell stories. Stories have their own message, and stories have their own *raison d'être*. You do not really invent stories. You can invent a novel but not a story. You think you invented it, but you didn't. You have received it, and I am honest enough to admit that whatever I have, I have received. Whatever I give belongs to who knows how many generations of Jewish scholars and dreamers and poets. I have received the words, and in combining them I am simply fulfilling the function of a messenger, which is to me as important as that of a storyteller. In fact, the storyteller is important only as a messenger; I am communicating what I have received; I am passing it on, perhaps because in my experience I have seen so many messages lost with their messengers. The greatest tragedy of all, though, is when the messenger is deprived of his message, when he waits but does not receive the message he must pass on.

INTERVIEWER Some of your critics have said that the blurring of conventional distinctions between fact and fiction, observation and invention, gives your books a peculiar strength, and others see it as a source of weakness. I think of a particularly powerful part of *A Beggar in Jerusalem*, where a group of Eastern European Jews are being shot and the Nazis are letting them line up by families; the scene is devastating in its realism. One man refuses to die, and the reader does not really know what is happening. Is this man, who is being shot again and again, living on in fact or in spirit? How do you view your critics' perplexity over this blending of fact and fiction?

WIESEL What did I try to show in that scene in *A Beggar in Jerusalem*? Precisely that because we live in extreme situations, fact and fiction matter less than the tale of their combination. At one point I did not believe that what was happening to me really happened. When I was inside that experience, I did not believe that I was I and that the killers were killing.

But in that particular passage what I try to show is much more than that. I try to show that a Jew cannot die. Even if he wants to die, he cannot. And this is both the privilege and the tragedy of the Jew. A privilege because it makes him into a witness. And a tragedy because he *cannot* die. I used that image because for many years I wondered why the Jewish people did not commit suicide. After all, others have done it. Why didn't the Jews turn to God and say, "Enough. We are partners in the same history. We are Your people. We had a covenant. It's either-or. If You prefer to have a world without Jews, have it Your way." And there were times when they could have done it. In the eighteenth century there were less than a million Jews in the entire world. In the times of the pogroms, the Crusades — they could have gone under. Why didn't they? Because the Jew cannot die.

THE SILENCE BETWEEN
QUESTION AND ANSWER

HURWITZ Why is it wrong to suppose a question has an answer?

WIESEL The question is what is important. An answer satisfies; a question dissatisfies. What is the question — thirst. What is the answer — water. What would you prefer, a thirsty man or a man who had plenty of water? I prefer always a thirsty man, someone who is walking, searching, who is looking forward. If we can advance, if we can step forward, it is because of the questions, not because of the answers. The answers have been used to divide people; questions unite.

HURWITZ What are the questions themselves?

WIESEL Why. The questions are the same questions you should ask yourself. Why did the event happen? Why there and not here? Why you and not me? Why? One question leads to another. That is what we call literature, culture.

HURWITZ What do you think of the current state of Jewish leadership?

WIESEL We have no moral authority or leadership, and this affects all of us. Much of our spiritual leadership still derives from Eastern Europe and those few survivors who came over before or after World War II. In another generation we will not have them, and then our Judaism will be even emptier than now. I foresee a serious spiritual crisis in this country. But of the Jew I am always optimistic.

HURWITZ Don't you think people, especially young people, are more sensitive to Israel than to the Holocaust?

WIESEL Someone who is sensitive to Jewish events is sensitive to all Jewish events. As an event, the Holocaust is certainly greater than the creation of Israel, which could have come earlier, later. But the magnitude of the Holocaust, measured in tears, is unmatched in history.

HURWITZ It is difficult not to hate the Germans.

WIESEL You must transpose the hate into something creative. As a writer you transpose hate into something you write, a novel. You express what you feel, and the hate becomes something else. But do not hate.

Adapted from Donald Hurwitz, *Together*, March, 1974.

QUESTIONS AND ANSWERS: AT THE UNIVERSITY OF OREGON, 1975

STUDENT What do you think would have been Jesus Christ's response to the Holocaust?

WIESEL I am convinced that had Jesus Christ lived during the Holocaust, he would not have done anything about it because he would have been a victim. And who knows? I wonder whether deep down the killers did not try to kill Jesus by killing the Jews.

STUDENT What compelled you to write *Dawn*, which places the Jew on the other side of the gun?

WIESEL *Dawn* is my first novel. It is about a Jewish terrorist in Palestine who has to kill an English hostage. *Night* was a memoir, totally autobiographical in nature. *Dawn* is fiction. I have never killed anybody in my life. I never held a gun in my hand. Why did I write *Dawn*? Because *Night* to me was the foundation, a new beginning, and I had to start exploring different options. If night is everywhere, what *can* we do? Maybe political action — call it war, call it executions. So I explored it until I found out within myself that it is not an answer. Killing is never an answer.

STUDENT If Israel collapses, how safe are American Jews in the United States?

WIESEL I don't believe Israel can collapse. I simply cannot imagine it. I refuse to imagine any such outrage. I don't want even to think in these terms — should France collapse. We are human beings, and I cannot anticipate any peoples' death. It's a sin. It is inhuman to think of them as though they were already dead. I can tell you only one thing: I am not a soldier and I am not a fighter, but when Israel is in danger, I leave my family and I leave my son and I go to Israel. Call it what you may, I don't think I could survive it.

STUDENT In your lecture on Job you speak of divine injustice and the idea that absurdity is the most efficient weapon. Can you comment further on these ideas?

WIESEL What I try to do is to relate the past to the present. I try to show Job as a contemporary hero or victim.

The problem of God's inaction in history, to me, has been more baffling, more puzzling, more tormenting than man's action in history. When I was a child and I discovered what was going on, somehow I could accept man. I

University of Oregon, Eugene, Oregon, April 10, 1975.

was not really that surprised by man's action. But coming from a religious background, I could not understand God's silence. I still do not.

My disputation with God still goes on. To me it was an injustice on a theological scale, on a universal scale. God was silent, and therefore His silence was unjust.

But then, what is one to do with it? To give in? To say, "Since You are unjust, I may be unjust too. After all, I am created in Your image"? That can be a solution. Some people have chosen it. I believe that it is the wrong solution. I believe that man's power lies precisely in his rejection of that solution. When man says to God, "Even when You are unjust, I will show You that I am just. I take Your injustice, which makes me suffer, and I will share it as an offering with friends, known or unknown," there is a certain beauty, an absurd beauty. Why should man be more just than God? But if you can do something against what is trying to crush you, something possibly good, then you redeem more than yourself.

STUDENT Would you say that the purpose behind God's injustice is to give us the opportunity to redeem ourselves?

WIESEL Well, I am sure that believers would say that. Believers usually say that God punished you for your good, for my good. But I find it hard to accept. But then what am I to do with my not accepting it? I cannot stop, I should not stop. If I were to stop, then it is easy, it is finished, there is no more problem. But I do not believe that life is worth living if there are no problems. So I try to lift it up and to give it a larger context and, again, to take even cruelty, and to transcend that cruelty. That is the purpose. But, of course, again you could say that's God's purpose. I will tell you: If He were to say it, I would accept it. I do not accept it when men say it in His name.

STUDENT There is a shift in your writings from *Night* to the *Ani Maamin*. In *Ani Maamin* God comes down and is with His people. That seems to be a different view, a different understanding of God's relationship in history to His Creation.

WIESEL There is, not a change, but —. Let me give you a graphic example. I try to write following the example of a very great Hasidic storyteller, Rebbe Nahman of Bratzlav. He is really my teacher. He lived some two hundred years ago and had direct influence on Kafka. Some of Kafka's stories sound almost plagiarized from Rebbe Nahman, who writes in concentric circles. I try to write the same way. That means the "thematique" — as the structuralists today would say — the basic themes, or as Malraux would say, the basic obsessions, remain the same: always injustice, always God, always death, always man's dialectical impossibility to understand and not to understand what is happening to him. Always the same. And basically it is: "How do I live with God, and how can I live without Him?"

In *Night* I had to voice my protest. I say that anyone who was a believer and did not protest was not a true believer. To give validity to his belief he had first to shout his disbelief in his disbelief. The other way, too: anyone who was a disbeliever had to shout his disbelief in his disbelief. Something had to happen. The experience was so great, so total. The fire was burning. You had to do something, you had to shout, you had to change. In *Night*, because I came from a *yeshivah*, I came from God. I was very pious, and instead of going to a *yeshivah* and becoming a rabbi, I came there. I had to say to God what I thought about God.

But then again, I could not stop there. So in all of my other books I tried a concentric circle approach, exploring other themes, some related directly, some unrelated, but still the same themes: of protest, of testing faith, of testing the absence of faith, of testing the necessity to go on living, of testing the necessity of maintaining some values.

In *Ani Maamin* I tested the absence of faith, just as in *Night* I tested faith. In *Ani Maamin*, which means "I believe," I tested belief. In *Night* I did the opposite. But God was present to me, both in *Night* and in *Ani Maamin*. But present as what? As a stranger? As the enemy? As a friend? Is God a friend to His Creation? The question remains a question. And I really have no answer.

I must warn you against further questioning in this line: I really cannot answer you. Whether I believe or not, whether I practice or not — these are personal feelings, and they are so personal that I hesitate to answer because I would not want to lie to you.

STUDENT How did you manage to tell your story, and how does one go about telling one's story?

WIESEL I am not sure that I have told the story. I am trying. All that I do is still try. How one goes about it? It took me ten years before I felt I was almost ready to do it. I wrote my first book, *Night*, in Yiddish, as a tribute to the language which was mine, the language of my childhood, the language of those communities that were killed. I began writing it in 1955. I felt I needed ten years to collect words and the silence in them.

It was not easy; it still is not easy, because I believe writing today implies a special obligation. Once people wrote to entertain or to make money. They still do. Our kind of writing is more than that. We have only one measurement, one yardstick. It is the fire that one cannot cease to see. If the fire that we saw thirty years ago is not there, I do not write. If it is there, I am afraid to write. And somewhere between this fear and this hope, some words come, and they take hold of me, and they write themselves. Sometimes I read them, too.

STUDENT You say that through his Jewishness, through his particularity the Jew moves toward universality. This seems to me to be quite contrary to the way we in modern, Western culure have been taught to think. We seem to be cut off from our roots, from our history. Through telling your own story you also talk about storytelling. And I see in what you are doing the possibility of regrounding our minds in our own history and achieving some kind of affirmation. Do you have any advice for someone who wishes to learn what his own story is and to tell it?

WIESEL Yes, I do write in order to understand as much as I write in order to be understood. I write to explore my own self as much as I write in order to help you explore yourself. I believe that basically, and ontologically, there is only one person in the world. That is the beauty, really, of our teaching: there is only one person. That means the "I" in me and the "I" in you is the same "I." Between our deepest zones there is a bridge.

The bridge can be a literary one, it can be a theological one, although I am afraid of these words. I am afraid of the word "theology." It's such a sensitive word that in Hebrew we do not have a term for it. Somehow "theology" has never taken root in our religion. It can even be a political one, in the best sense of the word, if it is action, affirmation.

But I do believe that if I make demands on myself, it will help you make demands on yourself. In Judaism — and this is one of the differences between Christianity and Judaism, really — in Judaism we believe that in order to change the world I have to change myself. In Christianity, some of the Christian theologians say that in order to change the world, they have to change you. Christians want to change me in order to change the world. We believe every person must work on himself, and if he succeeds, with enough sincerity in doing so, everybody benefits from it.

So in my writing I try to go as deep down as I can in my zone, and I am convinced that if I go deep enough, I will find you. And somehow you will be there.

Naturally, I am Jewish, and therefore my frame of reference is Jewish. But to me Judaism is not a gate to be closed. It is just the opposite: a gate to be opened, an opening. When I speak of my own Jewishness, I hope it helps the Christian realize the richness, the intensity of his Christianity; and the same with the Buddhist and his Buddhism. Because of my past, I have my own problems. I can either reject it or I can assume it. Since I do not believe in rejection, I try to assume it. And since I am a writer, I try to assume it in my writing.

Now, if you are also a writer, you can do exactly the same thing, although the events are not the same events. It is really a matter of tone, of the voice. You know, literature is not words but a voice, a melody. If you have the melody, your book is there. If you do not have the melody, you may have ten books but not literature. If I know how to find my voice, you can find yours. I have found it in my own way.

Nobody can tell you how to write. I do not believe in creative writing schools. I believe in creative reading, not in creative writing. How can you teach someone how to write if he is not a writer already?

STUDENT Mr. Wiesel, in several of your books you dwell quite heavily and favorably on the madman. Wasn't Hitler a madman too?

WIESEL I am in love with madmen. I say it honestly. I have always been. I did not know how much. I owe it again to Rebbe Nahman who, I found out, was also obsessed with madness. After the war, I even spent two years studying psychiatry because I was so interested in madness.

Of course, there is a difference. There is a difference, first of all, between clinical madness and mystical madness. Clinical madness is destructive, or self-destructive. Mystical madness is redeeming. The difference between a mystical madman and a clinical madman is that a clinical madman isolates himself and others, while a mystical one wants to bring the Messiah. What is the ultimate aim of mysticism? To bring the Messiah. To make evil disappear and bring people together. So, obviously I am in love with the mystical madman.

But then, what you said about Hitler is true. He, too, was a madman. He was a clinical madman but not only a clinical madman. There was something more than that. There was something of evil, the evil madman there, which was almost mystical, the antinomian madman. I am not interested in him, because I am not interested in the killers yet. I am only interested in the victim. In all my books I try to understand the victim more than the killer. I simply cannot bring myself to take a German or a Polish killer into a character of my book. Maybe I do not dare say "I" in his place. Maybe one day, if I finish my exploration of the victim, with whom I identify, or at least I try, I will come to the killer too.

STUDENT I disagree with you on the distinction you made between Christianity and Judaism. I believe that Christianity means transforming yourself, to repent and be saved. But I can agree with you, maybe, that most Christians go about not repenting themselves but exhorting other people to repent. I can identify with you in *Night* as the victim, and I can empathize with you. But when it comes to *Dawn*, as the executioner, I cannot. How can the person who has gone through the hell of the Holocaust exist with these two extremities of polarity and connect them too?

WIESEL For the first question: If Christians accept your definition of Christianity, then I accept it too. But I have the feeling that throughout history Christianity did not listen to your definition of Christianity or mine. The Inquisition, the Crusades, the pogroms were not really a movement of self-repentance; they were a movement towards obliging others to repent. So if you tell me this is not Christian, then I accept it too.

As for *Dawn*, you know, in every book there is a secret. And very few people really get the secret. It is a kind of game, but it is more than that. The writer puts in one line in every book, and that line is the clue to the next one. And sometimes, I hope, one person will find it. I wrote *Dawn* because of one sentence. It comes almost at the end. When Elisha, the hero, killed the major, I myself killed Elisha: meaning, when he killed the enemy, the British enemy, he killed himself. I wanted to prove that whoever kills, kills himself. So I am against killing, just as I am against being killed. And in all my books I have tried to prove that point, at least to make more understandable what killing does not only to the victim but to all those who live in the same time with the victim and the killer.

STUDENT What or who is the Messiah to you?

WIESEL Again, this is something so personal. I do not have an answer yet. I only know what he is not. The Messiah is not someone who divides people, who preaches hate, who creates death. When I was a child, I lived so much with the Messiah, and for him, that I knew. Now all I know is how I felt when I was a child, but no more.

STUDENT After reading *Night* I experienced it as a nightmare. You experienced it in reality. For me that nightmare quality fades in my life during the day. Does the nightmare that was a reality to you ever completely fade in your everyday life? How do you balance that degree of horror with your everyday life?

WIESEL With great humility I would advise you to read my other books. I am trying to deal with this problem in my other books. Between *Night* and "Job" there are fourteen books. And in them I try to deal with these demands and with these impossibilities that some persons today feel in their everyday life.

STUDENT Can you give us an idea of your conception of God?

WIESEL Kafka said something very beautiful. He said, "Man cannot speak of God. Man at best can speak to God." And I love Kafka much too much to disagree with him.

STUDENT You say one should never become indifferent to suffering. You yourself have never been indifferent in your relationship with God. Disregarding Him has never become a possibility with you. You view it as a crime to be indifferent.

WIESEL Yes, I would say that. I really believe that the sickness is indifference. There is nothing worse than indifference: indifference to God or to man, to life, to suffering, or to happiness or unhappiness. If I were to give you one word that encompasses all the evils in life, it would be "indifference." I try hard to break the indifference within me and around me.

STUDENT Was your intense relationship with God, even though it was turned into a very negative one for many years, one reason why you could continue to affirm life?

WIESEL I did not always affirm life. At one point I entertained the idea of suicide in a book, but not only in a book. I had to explore the possibility that maybe life is not worth living. But even then, suicide would not be an act of indifference; it would be a protest against indifference.

INNER GEOGRAPHY AND OUTER

MODERATOR When *Souls on Fire* was reviewed in *The New York Times*, the reviewer said, "The judgment has been offered before; Elie Wiesel is one of the great writers of this generation, and with the publication of this book, that judgment is underscored." We just have to accept that judgment, and you have to carry your fame as best you can. . . ."

WIESEL There is a beautiful Hasidic story about a great rebbe called Menahem Mendel of Vitebsk, one of the founders of the movement, a companion of the Besht. One day he decided he would go to Israel, to Palestine, to the Holy Land. And, of course, what do they organize for him? Parties, receptions, dinners. Even then. And what do they do at dinners? They make speeches. And what do they do with speeches? They praised the rebbe, the guest of honor. They praised him and they praised him. At one point, his turn came, and he said, "My dear friends, one day I will need you. One day when I shall present myself before the Celestial Tribunal, I will need character witnesses, so I will call upon you and you will say how great I am; and I will call upon you, and you will say how saintly I am; and I will call upon you, and you will say how erudite I am; and I will go on calling upon all of you. But then, at one point, the president of the tribunal will say to me, 'Menahem Mendel, we have heard many things about what people thought of you, but what did *you* think of yourself?'" And then he said, "I shall have to be quiet."

I don't read the reviews. I made it a point when I began writing not to read many reviews. Once you give in to that weakness, you are so vulnerable that you will be stopped, you will be paralyzed. So I don't hear, I don't listen. Those whose judgment I respect are almost invisible people, or sometimes dead people. I write for them, and I hear them. So when *The Times* says whatever it says, it's nice, nothing more.

QUESTION What are your reactions to the status and the problems of the American Jewish community right now?

WIESEL I would lie if I told you I know the American scene: I do not. I have written fourteen books, and I think only one is set in America, and even that one is only half set in America. I do not know America well. Sometimes, when I go around lecturing, I feel that I am at the same motel, going from one airport to another, speaking to the same audiences. In general, I feel that the American Jewish community is just like any other Jewish community. The bad are the worst; the good are the best. And in the middle there is a

Staten Island Community College, New York, April 28, 1975.

pendulum, a living mass: from time to time it swings toward the good, and other times it swings toward the bad.

MODERATOR Of the typical year of your life now, do you spend half of it in this country?

WIESEL Even more. I spend eight months at least, because I teach eight months a year.

MODERATOR Was your child born here?

WIESEL Oh, yes.

MODERATOR And you maintain a residence here?

WIESEL Certainly. I pay taxes.

MODERATOR You say you do not really know America, but do you feel being here as long as you have has had any particular impact on you? Does it influence the way you think you are?

WIESEL I really would have to go through five years of analysis to know to what extent America is influencing me. One thing I know: I did not influence America, which is bad.

MODERATOR When you spend time in France or in some other country, do you feel the same way about your experience there as you do about your American experiences now?

WIESEL There are two days that I love every year: the day I leave New York and the day I return to New York. I live in New York. I would love to live in other places. I am still looking for a small, prestigious university which would invite me to come and stay in a small village —and which would ask me not to teach.

MODERATOR Are you saying that the American part of your life has not interwoven with the Jewish base of your meaning to change anything?

WIESEL You know, we all have our inner geography. My inner geography is not an American geography. It is a very strange, faraway geography. These are places that are no longer here or anywhere. Sometimes I say to myself that they exist only in me, that when I go, they will go. To be the last person to remember a place, to be the last witness, to have witnessed a certain experience, and to have seen certain houses and certain schools, and heard certain teachers, and accompanied certain disciples: this is my geography.

But here I give, I try to share, which is of course my *raison d'être* for today; it is my justification. I feel I do better here than in many other places. Today I do better here than in France, although I write in French. The spiritual geography of France has changed; I do not feel at ease there anymore. I think they have become so anti Israeli that I cannot stand it, and almost anti-Semitic. So how can a Jew, such as I am, live in France? I cannot. I used to go three times a year. I used to give lectures at the Sorbonne. Maybe I am wrong, maybe I should go and fight. But I am a weak person, I do not have the physical strength to fight an entire country.

But the real roots are not here, and therefore I try to bring them here. I try to make America less America.

MODERATOR If one wanted to explore the inner geography, what would be the coastlines and the islands, and the marshes and the mountains?

WIESEL It would be names, faces, eyes, voices. Names, not really landscapes. Names. You know, we have lost so many names. I wish I could issue a law to the entire Jewish people that when they have a child, all parents should give a second name to that child. We have lost too many. When you write, they are there. And if they are not there, you do not write. Even if I write about other things — the Bible, Talmud, Hasidism — they must be there.

MODERATOR About the names and the people — do the events through which you recall them make any difference?

WIESEL When I close my eyes, I see better. There is a difference between the Talmud and the *Zohar*. When we study Talmud, the key phrase is "Come and listen," which is very beautiful because the Talmudic method was the Platonic method. "Come and listen. Come and join." In the *Zohar,* what you say is "Come and see." I try to say to the reader, "Come and see." The imagery that I try to transmit is a visual imagery — of fire, of night, of singing people, dancing people, revolting against all odds, for something they alone see.

QUESTION Currently there seems to be an increased interest in mysticism and Hasidism. What role do you think mysticism plays for a modern Jew?

WIESEL It depends if it is phony or not. Unfortunately, in our generation phony things appear authentic. It is so easy to imitate mysticism. It is not easy to imitate Talmud. It is not easy to imitate a good poem. But the less you understand a mystical poem, the more mystical you think it is. Somebody once asked me "What is Hasidism?" And since I do not like such questions, I said that Hasidism is a branch of mysticism. What is mysticism? Well, I heard a good definition. My teacher now, Saul Lieberman, is a great Talmudist, probably the greatest of the last ten generations. My troubles with him, in the beginning, were due to the fact that he came from Lithuania and was a Misnaged, an opponent of Hasidism, and I come from the Hasidic milieu and love Hasidism. So there was a little antagonism between us in the beginning. Now I think he understands better that not every Hasid is as horrible as he remembers.

Gershom Scholem is the greatest scholar of mysticism that we have. He almost invented the scholarship of mysticism. And he taught in Jerusalem. One day Scholem came to lecture at the Jewish Theological Seminary, and Lieberman, the dean, had to introduce him. But Lieberman does not like mysticism; he is a rationalist. Well, this is the way he introduced him. He said, "Ladies and gentlemen, you all know who Gershom Scholem is. If you don't, you should." Then he said, "Professor Scholem is professor of mysticism. What is mysticism? Nonsense." You can imagine Scholem changing colors. You can imagine the reaction in the room, and the elite was there. Lieberman, who has a tremendous sense of suspense and a sense of humor as well, waited for the shock to disappear, and then he said, "But you see, ladies and gentlemen, nonsense is nonsense. But a history of nonsense is scholarship."

MODERATOR What makes mysticism authentic?

WIESEL The trouble with mysticism and the blessing of mysticism is that you cannot really talk about it, not in public. Fortunately, the Talmud forbids us to talk about mysticism in the presence of more than three people.

In truth, really, I am against anything phony, not only phony mysticism; I am also against phony rationalism, against easy answers. Nothing is easy. Life is not easy. If you want to acquire anything, it should not be easy; you must work for it, you must go deep down, you must pay for it. You must pay for it with your time, with your energy, sometimes with your life — I mean with your everyday life, with your passion.

QUESTION But isn't there something phony in being a scholar and a rationalist of mysticism? Scholarship requires rational, systematic pursuit, and isn't that by definition the opposite of mysticism?

WIESEL No, because, again, I think the opposite of mysticism is not scholarship but phoniness, superficiality. Our tradition stresses the necessity to study Talmud, which is rationalism, *before* having the *right* to study mysticism. Maimonides, I think, said mysticism was not to be studied before the age of thirty. And the expression is very beautiful: "Not until he filled his belly with Talmud and the legislative, codifying words."

QUESTION I have read your books — not all — and I do not see in them any message of Jewish belief in redemption. I have thought, who needs another Jeremiah to write a new set of Lamentations? Why can't we have a new set of Isaiah to give us some hope?

WIESEL I disagree. First of all, I like Jeremiah, but I prefer Isaiah. I hope you believe me that it is almost an ideal for every Jewish child to be able one day to stand up and say to his people, "Be consoled, my people." I have done it a few times. I was privileged, not because I wanted it.

First, my message about Soviet Jewry is a message of hope, of extraordinary hope. Second, my message about Israel is a message of hope and faith. I have far fewer illusions now about man than before. But my faith in *Netzah Yisrael*, in the eternity of the Jewish people — take it the way you want it, mystically or historically — is profound. And I have written a novel about Jerusalem. It is a tale of hope.

A HIGH POINT IN HISTORY

MORTON With immense pleasure and honor, with great gratitude and humility I welcome, on behalf of the bishop of New York and my brethren of the Chapter of the Cathedral Church, Elie Wiesel as a colleague of this cathedral. And in token of our brotherhood I install you, Sir, in this seat. . . . Perhaps we can begin our dialogue very personally. I reread the other day your book *Night*, which was your story as a little boy in the concentration camps. For you, very personally, *then* how was hope experienced?

WIESEL Well, one generation ago we were convinced that hope meant the end of that experience. Unfortunately, today I am not sure it ended. I am glad you mentioned that I'm here as a Jew, and totally as a Jew, meaning I represent more than my own person. As a Jew, I think it is my duty to tell you that we feel more and more threatened. Our people once again is faced with solitude. One generation ago miraculous forces in our own past and in our own soul enabled us to overcome all the temptations not to speak to Christians any more. Today, should our people be once more left alone, I am convinced there will be historical and metaphysical consequences. If I plead for my people — and I plead for my people everywhere — I think that these words should be said: We are terribly, terribly worried. We are worried because somehow there is a sense of history that moves me to pessimistic conclusions.

MORTON Is not the Hasidic notion of God's presence in everything the only means of hope for us now as you speak of nothing but pessimism?

WIESEL God is everywhere; otherwise God would be nowhere, meaning: God of course is present in evil. And that is what makes our problem so tragic. But it is one thing to say God is *in* evil; it is another to say that God *is* evil; and it is still another to say that *evil* is God. We accept the first, but not the second or the third.

MORTON What guidelines do you follow as a political animal, as a citizen, and ultimately as a person of faith?

WIESEL I beg to differ. I am not a political person. I know absolutely nothing about politics.

MORTON Okay, in Hannah Arendt's sense, God rest her soul, of being a person who lives in the city.

WIESEL I am part of the community. And as such I have my obligations, and I

Dialogue with Dean Morton at Cathedral Church of St. John the Divine, New York, December 7, 1975.

[238]

think I share its anguish and its hopes. What I try to do is to say that despair is not an answer. Despair is a question, maybe *the* question. What I try to do as a Jew is to make Judaism into an opening, to share it with as many people as possible, and yet to permit everyone to remain what he or she is. If the Jew is a better Jew, I think the Christian will be a better Christian. I believe that Christians should give up their centuries-old hope of converting the Jews. And I think that Jews should simply try to be as they want to be, as we all want to be, better Jews, to assume our history, our destiny, and be as genuine, as authentic as we can. In a practical way, what I try to do is to teach my students, and I hope my son, that suffering is not an answer; it is not even an instrument. Suffering does not lead to saintliness. The human beings that we are should fight suffering. And if we suffer, we should not transmit it. We may transmit the message, but not the suffering itself. Well, these precepts are simple enough in words, but not in deeds.

MORTON Do we teach our students and our sons that through suffering, although it is not sent by God, we can come to a closer knowledge, a more intimate presence of the Lord? Or do we simply say that suffering and non-suffering are in a sense equal, not perhaps in intensity, but that one does not have an edge on the other in terms of a means through which the Lord is revealed to us? Do you see suffering essentially as neutral?

WIESEL Of course not. I am the son of a people whose suffering is the most ancient in the world. We know what suffering means. And yet we do not speak about it that often. We are afraid of magnifying it and therefore strengthening it. What do we do? Suffering in others moves us to action and to compassion. We turn our suffering into literature. We are simply bent on the idea that we are not alone, that man is not alone. We are responsible for the world, we are responsible for one another, without distinctions and without frontiers. We all give what we have, and we give what we are. In order to give I must be. And if the world has to learn something from our experience, it is precisely this: that I must *be*. And it is precisely that *being* that one generation ago was taken from us, at least there was an attempt to take it away from us, and from you. The Christian world I think could not survive the Jewish people. We are now one. Today the destiny of the Jewish people and the destiny of the world are the same. And if I am pessimistic, it is first of all because of the forces that are allied and aligned against us. But when the enemy strikes the Jewish people, he means to hurt mankind.

MORTON Because we are one — because God is one, we are one — we Christians know of our Jewish brothers' and sisters' escalating fear of the political alignments. What are the concrete actions, which include, of course, prayer, that we can take? The concrete actions certainly must be political but must be much more. I ask you, in conclusion, my brother, to share with those of us who are not Jewish ways in which we can support you by sharing, ways that do not disrespect your integrity — the history of the Christian Church is so full of helping someone else in order to catch him. How can we who are not

Jews express our solidarity with you in ways that are more than political and ways that underscore our common hope?

WIESEL A week or two ago, after the resolution equating Zionism and racism was passed in the UN, my wife and I received a letter from France, from a monastery. Some nuns and priests simply signed a letter saying to us that they are with us, that's all. And we were very moved by that. Simple words, a simple gesture sometimes suffices. What I think everybody should do today is tell us that we are not alone, and tell us each in his or her own way, in his and her own words. Whether it is by writing petitions, or calling the senator, the congressman, I do not know; these are really political actions. But I would like to place it on a moral level and in a historical context. I think everyone today, men and women of conscience and good faith, should tell the Jewish people: "You are not alone, and we are ready to fight to enable you not only to live but to live as Jews." That would be a high point in history and in the history of the relationship between the Jewish people and the Christian world.

MORTON You have helped me see hope. Thank you very much.

BEING AN AMERICAN

I feel very close to this country, and I am grateful to it. For the first time in my life I have a passport.

I remember that in 1942 Hungary enacted a law ordering the deportation of all alien Jews to Galicia. I remember seeing them leave. I also remember that my father and my grandfather spent months and months and a lot of money to find some proof of our Hungarian citizenship. I know that my ancestors lived there four centuries, five centuries, but we had no papers, no proof.

Finally we got the papers, and I would not part with them even on *Shabbat*. We were very religious, and on *Shabbat* religious Jews are forbidden to carry anything, so we had to bring our problem to our rabbis and ask, "What should we do with the citizenship papers? Can we carry them or not?" It was not easy to find a solution. Finally we found a compromise: we carried them under our hats.

Then in 1944 something happened that, for me, marked the beginning of the end. I lost faith in citizenship, in papers, in nations, in governments. It was on a Saturday, and some three thousand Jews were in the courtyard of the synagogue, standing in line, their papers in their pockets. At the entrance stood two Hungarian officers checking papers, I thought. When my turn came, they simply took my citizenship papers — my picture, my name — and tore them to pieces. Hungary gave me up without even knowing who I was. And that happened to my entire people.

So I can feel only gratitude to this country, which offered me citizenship.

Interview statement, Horace M. Kallen Memorial Symposium on "What does being an American mean to you in this bicentennial year?" Staten Island Community College, Staten Island, New York, February 18, 1976.

OUT OF THE NIGHT

REICHEK Madmen appear in almost all your novels. Why?

WIESEL I believe that reality disappointed us so much that I seek something in another reality. What is the other reality? Madness. I believe that anyone who was in the camps came out deranged. There is the basis of madness in every person who survived. When you have seen what they have seen, how can you not keep some madness? To remain normal would in itself be mad.

REICHEK Why has anti-Semitism been such a durable force in history?

WIESEL We always disturb people. I would even say we represent the artistic form in history, the conscience of history. Imagine Abraham or Moses coming out of a society full of murder and saying, "Do not kill" and "There is only one God." So from the very beginning, there was something in Jewish history that set us in opposition to the others. We were the forerunners. We said no.

  Then we became objects of hate because we did not yield. Man and mankind wanted to destroy the Jew, and the Jew refused to be destroyed. The Jew wanted to improve man and mankind. Man and mankind refused to be improved. Inevitably this aroused resentment between us, particularly in strongly Christian environments. It was either/or. Either Christ was the Messiah, and we were wrong and had to be punished. Or he was not. And how could the Christians accept the idea that he was not? So they *had* to persecute us in order to be able to believe that Christ was the Messiah. The end, of course, came one generation ago.

  For twenty-five or thirty years, the Holocaust shielded us. It wasn't nice to be anti-Semitic because automatically the person who hated us was in the same class with Hitler. But when you distort the past, when you devaluate the experience and cheapen it, the shield becomes useless. That is why today Christians no longer feel guilty. And today it has already become very easy for a person to come out and say, "I'm against Israel." To me that means, "I am against three million Jews in Israel."

REICHEK What do you mean by the "devaluation" and "cheapening" of the Holocaust?

WIESEL There is so much vulgarity on the subject. The subject is being betrayed.

REICHEK But if we are to remember what happened, how do we teach or learn about the Holocaust and escape the trap of "vulgarization"?

WIESEL I do not know. It used to be a sacred topic. It must be seen as a special event, meaning a special event which requires a special style, a special

Adapted from Morton A. Reichek, *Present Tense*, Spring, 1976.

approach, a special level, a special sensitivity, a special tone of voice. When we speak of anything related to the subject, a certain trembling goes through us. It must not become simply a subject among other subjects.

REICHEK Is this why you say you write and speak *around* the Holocaust and not *about* it?

WIESEL I say certain things not to say other things. I write a page and the absence of the Holocaust in it is so strong that the absence becomes a presence. My books are about the impossibility to write about the Holocaust, the non-communicability of the Holocaust. Something happened during the Holocaust, and we do not know what . . . we never will know what. We cannot even talk about it. . . .

REICHEK Why have you not settled in Israel?

WIESEL I do not have a clear reason. There must be many elements in my decision. I belong more to the Diaspora, the segment of our people that is still not redeemed, that is still in pain. I am sure it must have to do with the guilt felt by every survivor. There is something wrong with us. Logically, we should not have survived. I do not deserve redemption yet. I am not worthy. I am still waiting. I was more taken by the torment than by the triumph.

There must have been more practical reasons, too. It was easier to get a job as a foreign correspondent outside of Israel. But that was not the main reason.

REICHEK What is the purpose behind your writing?

WIESEL You know, for men of my generation, that event should be the yardstick. And once you have this as a yardstick, you do not want to invent. But we try to invent a meaning to events that had none. And we try to reinvent situations and to recreate, to bring back towns that were destroyed. We build on ruins.

REICHEK How do you reconcile the existence of a divine force with evil and suffering?

WIESEL . . . In *Night* I wanted to show the end, the finality of the event. Everything came to an end — man, history, literature, religion, God. There was nothing left. And yet we begin again with *Night*. Only where do we go from there? Since then, I have explored all kinds of options. To tell you that I have now found a religion, that I believe — no. I am still searching. I am still exploring. I am still protesting.

QUESTIONS AND ANSWERS:
AT WILLAMETTE UNIVERSITY,
1977

STUDENT Have you ever found it necessary to deny the existence of God?

WIESEL No. My upbringing is such that I am involved with God — I have been — totally. To deny His existence — there is no problem. The problem begins *if* He exists and *when* He exists. It would really be so much easier if He had done us a great service and ceased to exist. But He is not ready to do it. And do you now what? I am not ready to let Him do it. The problem really is when God is God. Let's not define now what God is, because that's not the problem, and, again, these are personal considerations and commitments. But God *is* God, and man is not human. What do we do then?

STUDENT Would you speak a bit about the Messiah?

WIESEL I speak of nothing else. I have written a poem, book about it, *Ani Maamin*, It is based on a poem we are supposed to repeat day after day, a poem codified by Maimonides: *"Ani maamin beviat ha-Mashiah* — I believe in the coming of the Messiah," *"v'af al pi sheyitmahmeah* — and although he is late in coming," *"ahakeh lo bekhol yom sheyavo* — I shall wait for him every day." There is something about the Messiah in every one of my tales: in every one of my beggars, my teachers, my wise men, my princes.

And I am still waiting. I have often wondered why Maimonides used the future tense, always the future. I think he did it because he knew that the Messiah would be very late in coming.

Well, he *is* very late in coming. So we are waiting. But the waiting is what makes the Jewish tradition as beautiful and as intense as it is. We are still waiting.

STUDENT How is anti-Semitism manifested today among leftist West German students?

WIESEL It is very much latent. Anti-Semitism among left-wing students in Western Europe is very strong, although they call it anti-Zionism. Names don't matter. What matters is that they are against Jews. I am offended when it comes in Germany. I would expect the young German students, left or right, to wait one generation before giving lessons to anyone, especially to Jews. But these are passing moods, I hope, for Germany.

STUDENT Are you able to define the God you worship?

Willamette University, Salem, Oregon, March 10, 1977.

WIESEL   I never was, and I don't think I am now because, really, my relationship to God is such a personal one. It has always been. I don't talk about God. . . . My work is drunk with God, even if I don't say it — especially when I don't say it. The way I relate to God, present or absent, is not something I care to articulate, for the moment you put these things into words you divide people, and I would like to bring people together.

STUDENT   To be pro-Israel but anti-Zionist — does that make any sense to you?

WIESEL   Not to me — no. To me Israel and Zion, after all, are synonymous. Zion means Jerusalem. And Jerusalem means Israel. When you start dividing, when you start splitting entities apart, it's always for the wrong reasons. It's always to find an alibi, to get permission to oppose one of these entities. When you say, for instance, "Oh, I love Israel but —," you must say the "but": "but I don't like Zion." "I love humanity but — I hate people."

   I think Jewish history is an entity: the history of Israel. Call it the land of Israel, the people of Israel, the law of Israel — but Israel exists in all of these fragments. They are indivisible. Whenever divisions were attempted, they were bad for the Jewish people. Our enemies always meant all of us, not just a part. They meant a religious concept, a historic entity, a national collective conscience — all that we are.

QUESTIONS AND ANSWERS: AT BRANDEIS-BARDIN, 1978

PRAGER You had twice in your life airline tickets for planes that subsequently crashed. Is that correct?

WIESEL Correct.

PRAGER Do you read anything providential into such accidents? Does God have a specific role for Elie Wiesel?

WIESEL Of course it's a frightening affair. You know that had you made a plane you would have been killed. But then I belong to a generation which no longer fears death. In a very strange way we have become immortal.

PRAGER In *Night* there is a very powerful episode wherein a child is hanged, and you write that you see God hanging in place of the child. What did you mean then when you wrote it, and how would you interpret that story today?

WIESEL What I meant there is very simple. I felt that the Covenant was broken. I had to tell God of my anger. I still do so. I rarely speak about God. It is something so personal and it belongs so much to the very inner landscape of my life and my childhood. And yet He is very much present in all my books. But the presence of God is accompanied by a protest, and I hope that as long as I live I shall somehow be able to formulate, to articulate, that protest. But from within and not from without.

What I meant there was protest. We had to say to God, "*Ribono Shel Olam*, I, Levi Yitzhak, son of Sarah, from Berditchev, I want You for a *din torah*! I have the right to call You to judgment. I have the right as a human being, I have the duty as a Jew to tell You that something is wrong in Your Creation." So that was, of course, the epitome of protest. Even when I wrote it, I was very careful. I was afraid of commentaries. What I said is that when I saw the child hanging, I heard a voice saying. Well, whose voice was it? I did not say it was mine. And what if it was God's voice saying? So I left it ambiguous on purpose. I like clarity except when it comes to certain very dangerous topics.

PRAGER Elie, do you *daven*? Do you pray?

WIESEL This is one of those dangerous questions I do not answer. I will tell you why. It is too easy to answer yes or no, whatever I would say would be a lie. If I were to say I do not *daven*, it would be a lie. If I were to say I do, that, too, would be a lie. And there is so much lying in the world, why should I add to it? What do I mean? I do not *daven* today the way I used to *daven* when I was

Brandeis-Bardin Institute, Simi Valley, California, January 22, 1978.

a child — that was the real *davening*. Now it is more difficult, maybe because I understand the words better. Now there are certain prayers I say only with great resistance. I cannot say *Ahavah Rabbah Ahavtanu* — that God loved us very much. How long can I go on fighting and quarreling with Him? So I say them, but I do not say them.

PRAGER I would like to know if you say another prayer: "And because of our sins we were exiled, we've been punished." Do you find that in any way applicable to the Holocaust?

WIESEL Absolutely not. I think that to say it is blasphemy. I have problems with sin and punishment. I do not believe that the just are rewarded. But I do believe that the wicked are punished. Maybe not directly. A does something bad to B, and then C does something bad to A without knowing why. The wicked are punished. Sometimes it takes longer. Well, we have time.

TELUSHKIN Do you believe in an afterlife?

WIESEL I believe that as long as we are alive we are immortal. I believe that one minute before I die I am still immortal.

TELUSHKIN In an interview with Harry James Cargas you said, "If I am optimistic it is because I believe that we, as Jews, can still save mankind." Cargas did not ask you how. How?

WIESEL By being. By remaining alive and by telling our story. I believe that only we can save mankind, first of all by telling mankind what it did, and therefore what it can still do to itself, not only to me or to my people.

Now, why am I an optimist as a Jew? Logically, sociologically, philosophically, historically, mathematically, we should have left the arena of history not once but a thousand times. And yet here we are. So how can I not be an optimist? There are always conflicts between history and Jewish history, and whenever there was a conflict — and the only conflict in my eyes is a moral conflict — we came out rather well. That means we never accepted the rules of the enemy. We never submitted to his way of life or death. We never accepted his law. We maintained ours.

If the Torah is so beautiful, and it is; if the prophets were so great, and they are; it is not only because they were great but also because we keep them alive. The fact that we repeat today a prayer composed 3,000 years ago gives that prayer another dimension. Let me give you a classic example. If you go to the Louvre in Paris or the Prado in Spain or the Hermitage in Leningrad, certain pictures, certain Rembrandts or Goyas, are not only great and profound because Goya and Rembrandt painted them but also because all of the thousands of people who saw these paintings left something of their eyes in the paintings. That is true of literature as well. A book that is being read gets something from the reader. That is the mystical quality of art, of literature, and of history.

So when I think that Jewish history could have ended with Abraham or with Isaac or with Jacob or with Joseph or with Hezekiah or with any period, and somehow it did not, that makes me smile. When I read Jewish history I smile, I always smile.

TELUSHKIN Do you feel it crucial that *Yom Hashoah*, Holocaust Remembrance
  Day, become an acknowledged part of the Jewish calendar? Do you think
  that within the coming decades it will become a fully observed Jewish holiday?

WIESEL I hope so. But I believe in books more than in buildings and other things.
  I have in my possession at least ten manuscripts written by survivors. I cannot publish them. And I believe this is an imperative! These people survived,
  believe me, only to bear witness. They did not want to go on living. They did
  not want to live in a society that denied them, that betrayed them. For them to
  live was a sacrifice. It was an act of faith the world did not deserve. But if still
  they went on living, it is simply to bear witness. They had no other purpose.
  And their testimony is not received! What greater punishment can be imagined? I have tried without success to interest some Jews in organizing a fund
  to publish these books. Well, I'm sorry if I let out my anger.

PRAGER You have anger about another subject, perhaps the most sensitive: the
  behavior of American Jewry during the Holocaust.

WIESEL I keep a kind of diary, which I call the Black Diary, and in it I collect
  evidence that must be collected — evidence about our own failures. I say
  "us." When I speak of Jews, it is always "we"; therefore, when I speak of
  the failures of the American Jew, I say "we" failed, not "they" failed or
  "you" failed. And in this Black Diary I collect facts and statements. I am not
  publishing it. I will tell you why: I do not want our enemies to get that joy. If I
  were to tell them what *we* failed to do, they would be pleased, much too
  pleased. So I keep the evidence because it is our duty, but it will not be published for a hundred years.

TELUSHKIN Did you know that in 1943 a revolt had taken place in the Warsaw
  Ghetto?

WIESEL Yes. The Hungarian press reported two lines about the ghetto rebellion.
  When we read about it, it was *Erev Pesah*, and I remember my mother
  asking, "Why did they do it? Why were they so foolish? Why couldn't they
  wait peacefully for the end of the war?" We thought that Jews could live
  peacefully while waiting for the war to end.

  Nobody in my town knew about the Holocaust. Had we known, I can
  swear to you in front of a *Sefer Torah* that many fewer Jews would have
  become victims. We didn't know. Imagine! Three months before
  Normandy, the Hungarian Jews came to Auschwitz and did not know what
  the name meant. In America everybody knew, in Sweden everybody knew,
  the pope knew, Roosevelt knew, Churchill knew, Weizmann knew, Ben-
  Gurion knew, everybody knew but the victims.

PRAGER Goebbels wrote in his diaries during the war that in his heart he really
  believed that Roosevelt and Churchill wanted the Jews dead because he could
  not understand why they did nothing to stop the death factories. Do you
  believe that?

WIESEL That Goebbels believed it? Absolutely.

PRAGER Do you believe what Goebbels believed?

WIESEL I hesitate, because this sentence is so strong. You know, my disillusion-
ment with Roosevelt is rather strong. We believed that he was a protector of
the Jewish people. Only later did I find out how much he knew and how little
he did. But still it would be unfair to say that he wanted the Jews to be killed.

PRAGER Maybe it is not even an issue of people wanting to see the Jews dead, or
of Roosevelt's indifference. Perhaps people do not care if anybody dies.

WIESEL I do not know. I read every single document and every single book on the
subject. I try to understand, but I do not. A friend of mine was a high official
in the American government. He was an adviser to five presidents. He is now
a professor in a great university, an old man, and I asked him once, "What
did you know during the war?" he said, "Everything." I said, "What do you
mean?" He said, "Well, we had the intelligence reports beginning in 1942,
about everything." "And what did you do?" He said, "Nothing." I said,
"Why didn't you?" And then he told me, "Well, I simply didn't." I went on
asking, pressing, "Why didn't you?" He said, "Well, we believed" — and
that was a terrible thing to say — "that if the Jewish leadership did not ask me
to do something that meant it must have its reasons." And he told me something which I am now revealing for the first time. A group of high Jewish
officials in Washington would meet every month to discuss current affairs,
and although they knew everything, they never discussed the question of
European Jewry. In 1943 after much institutional quarreling the American
Jewish Conference was convened to discuss the situation of European Jewry.
When you read the proceedings of that conference, you want to bury your
head in shame.

PRAGER Suppose an alienated young Jew comes over to you and says, "Mr.
Wiesel, I want reasons, not ideals, not dreams, not theology. I want reasons
why I should be a Jew and not assimilate and be like everybody else." What
would you say to him?

WIESEL I would try to teach him that by denying his people he denies mankind.
One cannot universalize a condition by denying the soul of that condition.
Victor Hugo was the greatest French writer, but the more French he was, the
more universal he was. The more German Goethe was, the more universal he
was. The more English Shakespeare was, the more universal he was. Only
among us do some believe that to become more universal we must become
less Jewish. This is a Jewish phenomenon — or rather an anti-Jewish phenomenon. I would tell him: First of all, you will not succeed. The enemy will
make you Jewish.

More important, you have no idea what you are giving up. If you were to
study and to live the Jewish experience first and then decide to leave, then it
is your decision. But you should not do it out of ignorance. First let me teach
you what you as an artist, as an industrialist, as a physician can do as a Jew.

And if I were to fail, I would probably have sleepless nights. But I must tell
you, there is no greater reward than to see young Jews become more Jewish
and therefore more human.

PRAGER What lessons can we learn from the good actions of people during the

Holocaust as, for example, the Danes and other righteous Christians? Do they "prove" anything?

WIESEL Absolutely, they prove it could be done. Let me give you an example. When the Yad Vashem in Israel proposed the idea of looking for Righteous Gentiles, one of their reasons was to show young Israelis that not all Gentiles are guilty. It was Ben-Gurion's idea to teach our children that some people were good too. But when they began looking for names, it was a catastrophe. In ten years they could not find even one thousand in all of Europe! I think by now they have located about eleven hundred.

It is an indictment of all those who did not help. If the French — and you know I used to love France — if the French had done what the Danish did, there would have been no massive deportation of Jews from France. But the French police collaborated with the Germans.

Take another example. Germany is proud of its own resistance movement, those who participated in the July 20 attempt to assassinate Hitler. But when you read the documents now, you realize that the main motivation for their act was not moral but pragmatic. They did not want to get rid of Hitler because of his crimes against the Jews and other people but because of his military failures.

TELUSHKIN Do you agree today with the conclusion you wrote to *Dawn*, where the hero, after great deliberation, murders the British soldier?

WIESEL I did not agree with it then, and I don't agree with it now. *Dawn* was fiction. I wrote it, first of all, because I wanted to explore the other side: What does it mean to kill?

But mainly I wrote it against killing. I wrote that book against political violence. Very few people noticed, but the end of *Dawn* is not really a murder but a suicide. When Elisha, my hero, kills the major, he says, "I killed Elisha." The identification is such that there is something going on between the murderer and the victim. He killed himself, and that is why the next book, *The Accident*, is about suicide.

Dawn came out first in France, when I was already living in New York. One day I received a telephone call from an Israeli officer whom I knew: he must come and see me. I said all right. When he arrived he was almost drunk. He began pacing my room and said, "I read your book. What do you know about this kind of murder?" I said, "I don't. I imagined it." And he began shouting, "You had absolutely no idea about it. I was involved in such a killing! This is not what happens. We do not have these philosophical conversations!" Well, my hero was a philosopher.

PRAGER What values do you want to pass on to your child?

WIESEL First, a sense of the importance of memory. At the same time, a sense of beauty. I know how to fight injustice, but I do not know how to fight ugliness, vulgarity. I also want him to have a sense of kinship with his Jewish contemporaries. I feel good among Jews. I have friends who are not Jews, and very close friends, but as a community when things happen, good or bad, I like to be among Jews. When I fear history is preparing one of its upheavals, I want to be with my people: a war, with my people; a triumph, with my people; a disaster, with my people. So I try to instill these values in my child, in our children.

What does it all really lead to? It leads to a very simple formulation of what I believe Judaism to be: taking responsibility for someone else. A Jew is not only responsible for himself; he is responsible for all of us and for all of those who lived before us.

TELUSHKIN In *Legends of Our Time*, you tell about your encounter with the Prophet Elijah. He tried to warn you and your family of the impending danger but no one believed him. Nor did you realize that he was Elijah until years later. If Elijah came to you or any of us today, would he be recognized? Would his message be heeded? What do you think his message would be?

WIESEL First, it is a poetic image, of course. I saw then in every wanderer the Prophet Elijah, as I see him now. It is a beautiful tradition — the Thirty-six Just Men remain hidden and always poor, always anonymous, so that when you meet a poor stranger, a beggar, he may be one of the Just or the Prophet Elijah.

Number two, I used that image to explain why we did not believe him. We did not believe him because he was a wandering beggar. Had he been the prophet, maybe we still would not have believed him. But had the warning come from important Jewish leaders, we would have believed them. If Elijah were to come today, I think he would speak not of the coming of the Messiah but of the necessities of today. He would ask for small gestures.

TELUSHKIN Do you perceive any specific enemy of the Jews in the United States?

WIESEL I am much more afraid of the people who are indifferent to the Nazis than of the Nazis themselves. Those who let Butz get away with it, they frighten me. I am terribly disturbed by the Butz thing.

PRAGER Butz is a professor at Northwestern who wrote *The Hoax of the Twentieth Century*.

WIESEL There are sixty-five books now trying to prove that the Holocaust is nothing but an invention, that Jews did not die, that Jews did not suffer. Why is it terrible? Not only because of the implications toward our people. But can you imagine the insensitivity of these people to forget the crime? They are saying these things while we are still alive. What can be more vicious than to deprive the victim of his suffering? For a year I went around working out ideas to counteract this propaganda. Apparently, writing was not enough. So I came up with the idea to organize an international convention of concentration camp survivors. Let us be together one week, and we will create an event. Well, I began checking. Do you know how many survivors there are in the world? In 1945 we would meet at weddings. A year later we would meet at circumcisions. Then came the *Bar Mitzvahs* and the weddings of our children. Now we meet at funerals. Today, in the whole world, less than sixty thousand survivors remain, and every day at least one of us dies.

So this kind of stupid, vicious theory is being propagated while we are still here. And the people do not protest! I went to Northwestern to protest, and the president of the university told me, "What can we do to Butz? He has tenure." I said, "Why didn't the faculty at least sign a declaration of moral condemnation?" They did, and out of twelve hundred members of the faculty only four hundred signed it. This is what hurts me. This is the enemy.

QUESTIONS AND ANSWERS: AT WASHINGTON UNIVERSITY, 1978

STUDENT You say madness caused the Holocaust and that madness is also an avenue in defining the truth. Can you explain your concept of madness?

WIESEL Madness has many possibilities, many definitions, many layers. There is clinical madness, which is destructive. There is political madness, which is criminal, and there is mystical madness. I am for mystical madness, a madness that has only one obsession — redemption, only one concern — one's fellow man. A mystic is alone because he wants to be closer to other people. A mystic denies himself many joys of existence because he wants to give it meaning. A mystic thinks of the Messiah and nothing else, not for himself but for everyone. One has to be mad, totally mad, to believe in such concepts — that we can redeem words, people; that we can save mankind; that we can help one another today. But I am for that madness.

STUDENT Why did some people survive in the camps while others did not? It could not have been only luck.

WIESEL Only luck. Do not believe anything else. It was our luck. Maybe there were some special cases. But I speak of the average Jew who was in the camp. Only luck. Physical strength, no — the strong lost their lives as easily as the others. Children — they were too weak even to survive.

On April 5, when they began to evacuate my camp, 80,000 inmates remained. And every day they would select 10,000 and kill them outside the gates. Somehow I was always among those left behind. It was luck, nothing else. I could easily have been among the others, which adds to the shame. We did not do anything. We simply let destiny choose. And destiny chose blindly — blindly, for no reason at all. Among those executed were people who surely were better than many of us, worthier than many of us, stronger, wiser.

STUDENT But according to Victor Frankl, it seems that some people had a kind of will to live and found a way to survive, and others lost it and died.

WIESEL Do not believe that. It was true of Victor Frankl. He makes a theory, as Bettelheim makes other theories. Theories. The truth is beyond theories. I like Victor Frankl's writing. I respect him very much. But his claim simply is not true. I can give you examples in the hundreds that refute his every word.

Washington University, St. Louis, Missouri, February 1, 1978.

[253]

Does it mean that he is right or I am right? Not at all. It goes beyond that. It goes beyond the examples, beyond that framework. There were so many religious people who wanted to live because they wanted to go on maintaining the faith, and they were killed. If anyone was motivated, it was a chronicler who wanted to survive and tell the tale. Most of them were killed. If Frankl is right, why didn't they survive? He is also right. Everybody is right. And wrong.

THE GREAT ADVENTURE

ABRAHAMSON One of your friends, one of the finest writers of our time, asked, "Can one be a saint without God?" Can one be a Jew without God?

WIESEL You refer to Camus, of course. Camus asked in his novel *The Plague*, "Can one be a saint without God?" I will tell you. The cards being what they are, I think a Jew can be Jewish with God and a Jew can be Jewish against God, but he cannot be Jewish without God. And believe it or not, this is what God wanted. He put us in a strange situation. Rabbi Israel of Rizhin once said, "If the atheist were to know that his denial of God is also willed by God, he would get an apoplexy." There is nothing we can do about it. God's name is in Jewish history. *El* — God — is in Israel. Even when you say no to God somehow you affirm Him. However, to be totally without God, outside God, would be to be outside the Jewish community, outside Jewish history. And therefore one cannot be Jewish.

ABRAHAMSON But many Israelis proclaim themselves atheists, yet they are in Israel, and I assume they are without God.

WIESEL That is what *they* think. It depends what the terms of reference are. Of course my definition is different. A Jew is someone who ties, who links his or her destiny to the Jewish people. Period. That is a Jew. I do not enter religious affairs. Whether a Jew observes religion or not, that is for God to say, not for me. I have never spoken about religious affiliations. I have never said that a Jew must come to a synagogue in order to be Jewish. Neither have I said the opposite. Because it leads to divisions. The Orthodox will say only an Orthodox synagogue, and even the Orthodox already have two kinds of services — with women or without. I do not enter into their disputes. A Jew must be a member of his or her community. For me that is enough.

But you asked whether, in my view, a Jew can be *Jewish* without God. That is something else. In Israel everyone is part of the Jewish community. No matter what, you cannot visualize the Jewish community without somehow taking into account the element of God in Jewish history. After all, Jewish history has been the history of the Jewish religion at least for three thousand years; you cannot remove it.

But when you speak of the atheists in Israel, they are not saying, "We are without God." They are saying, "We are against God." To be against God is perfect. There are times when one should be against God, provided one does

Interview by Irving Abrahamson at Congregation Am Shalom, Glencoe, Illinois, April 16, 1978.

so on the basis of knowledge. First, study, and if after studying you say, "OK, I do not accept You and Your ways, Master of the Universe," good for you. But those who come and say the same words out of ignorance, not only are they not Jewish, they are not even human.

ABRAHAMSON Some people fear assimilation threatens our very survival. What should we do? What can we do?

WIESEL You say there is assimilation. If there is, first of all, it is our fault. I am ready to assume the blame. That means we have not managed to teach our youngsters that to be Jewish for a Jew is the greatest adventure there is. For a Jew no other challenge is more uplifting, more enriching. For a Jew there is no other possibility of self-fulfillment, in ecstasy and anguish at the same time, than in Judaism. For a Jew who is an artist, a doctor, a physician, a lawyer, Judaism can become an added dimension, always the extra dimension. It can nourish and feed our heart, our inspiration, our humanity. There is so much, so much that Judaism can offer every one of us.

If some are ready to give it up, it means we have not been able to communicate our enthusiasm. But then I feel sorry for them, because they are giving up a treasure, an immense treasure. What is there to do? Teach. Teach. Teach. That is why we are teachers. Even writers are teachers. When we speak of teaching, the problem is how do you teach values in a world that does not want values? How do you teach beauty in a world that is surrounded by vulgarity? Well, I do not know how, but we must try. And I think we are trying.

ABRAHAMSON How do you teach an adult Jew to be Jewish?

WIESEL The same way I teach young people. There is something beautiful in teaching. Nothing is as uplifting to me as seeing some of my students grow, develop, ask the right questions. As a child, when I came home from *heder* and then from *yeshivah*, I was never asked, "Did you give a good answer?" My parents always asked, "Did you ask a good question today?" This is Judaism: to ask good questions. And, you know, questions do not change through the ages. Only answers change. Let me tell you a story. It is actually a Zen Buddhist story, but I attribute it to Hasidism.

Once upon a time a Hasid decided he had to know the meaning of truth. So he went looking in all kinds of schools. Nobody knew the meaning of truth. Finally somebody told him, "There is a rebbe in Kotzk who knows everything. He knows the meaning of truth. Go to Kotzk." So our Hasid said goodbye to his friends, kissed his children, and began walking to Kotzk. After many months of wandering, he finally arrived in Kotzk. He asked a Hasid in the street, "Where is the rebbe's house?" He showed him. He came there. It was full of Hasidim. He asked, "Can I see the rebbe?" They laughed at him. Why did they laugh? Because the rebbe was known for his solitude. For twenty years he was alone. "You just came and you want to see him?" He said, "Yes. I have an important question to ask. I must see him." He could not get in.

But he was clever. He decided not to move from the anteroom and waited there until everybody was asleep. Then he opened the door and entered the rebbe's study. The rebbe looked up and demanded, "What do you want?" The Hasid said, "Rebbe, I came from very far. I have a very important question to ask." "What is the question?" "Rebbe, what is truth?" The rebbe looked at him and slapped his face. The Hasid began to cry. He said, "Rebbe, why did you slap my face? I am serious. I am sincere. I really want to know what is truth?" The rebbe again looked at him and again slapped his face. Then he opened the door and pushed the Hasid out. Our Hasid was very unhappy, you can imagine.

He left the rebbe's home and began walking. Then he saw an inn. He entered, sat at a table, and ordered a glass of wine, but he could not drink. He cried and cried. Suddenly an old Hasid came in. He said, "Brother, why do you cry?" "Leave me alone." "Brother, why do you cry?" So he explained: "I came to see the rebbe. I asked him a question, and he slapped my face twice." "Twice, do you say?" "Yes, twice." The old Hasid began pacing up and down, up and down, thinking, thinking. "Twice. You said twice." And suddenly he smiled. He stopped at the table and said, "You know, my dear friend, we in Kotzk have always believed that our rebbe is very wise. I did not know he was that wise!" Hearing that, our Hasid almost slapped *his* face. "Where is the wisdom in slapping my face?" He said, "Oh, you do not understand. If the rebbe slapped your face the first time, it was because he wanted to teach you something very important." "What is it?" "He wanted to teach you the importance of questions. If you have a question, idiot, why do you need an answer? Questions are better than answers. That is why he slapped your face the first time. But he slapped your face a second time because he wanted to teach you something even more important. He wanted to teach you that actually there is never any relationship between any question and any answer." So now you know.

ABRAHAMSON But how do we convince adults to pursue the great adventure in Jewishness? We cannot slap all their faces.

WIESEL We cannot. These Jews end up being slapped, not by a rabbi, but by the enemy. It is inevitable. Those Jews who think they can live on the outside will learn that there always comes a time when the enemy teaches them that they are Jews. Therefore why not learn about it beforehand?

You see, Jewish history is fascinating because whenever you enter through any gate, you reach mystery in the best sense of the word. You open a window and you are dazzled by something that goes beyond us. Well, this is what we are trying to do   in writing, in teaching, as rabbis, as professors, as writers. We are trying to take the Jew, adult or young, and say, "Please come with me." It is always a journey. In the Talmud we say, "A Jew is someone who walks," a wanderer. We are always on a journey. Well, if not, I do not know what to do. If the Holocaust and the State of Israel and the Russian immigration, if these major events did not shake up some Jews, what do you think will?

ABRAHAMSON Throughout his history the Jew has demonstrated a certain belief in the power of reason to counteract the irrational. He has had less than complete success. What does the Jew of reason do in such an unreasonable world as ours seems to be?

WIESEL Well, we go on. In one of my novels I oppose a madman to my hero. My hero knows that if he remains with that madman, he too will become mad, so he tries to cure the madman in order to save his own sanity. And this is the quintessence of Jewish destiny. I really believe that our ambitions are universal, and so is our scope of activity — that we try to save the world in order to survive in it, sometimes with reason, sometimes with a mystical appeal. But then Judaism is all. Judaism is mysticism. Judaism is rationalism. Judaism is beyond paradoxes. So in a world of insanity we try to preach sanity. In a world of senseless, absurd hate we try to show the consequences of that hate. Into a world doomed by mediocrity we from time to time introduce flashes of originality — Moses, Rabbi Akiba, Einstein, and Freud. We manage somehow to shake history.

ABRAHAMSON You have spoken on literature as testimony. Is not all literature in some sense testimony? If so, what distinguishes literature from history? And what is the function of the imagination if you believe literature is a documentary record?

WIESEL Literature is testimony in our times, to our age, to our generation. Therefore all the components of that literature are part of testimony. But that is not new. That has been the Jewish attitude toward literature. In the Bible God says, "You are My witnesses." The Midrash goes on to say, "If you are not My witnesses, I am not God." A powerful thing to say. We are witnesses. So we are witnesses in whatever we are doing. Even with our imagination, of course, we should serve as witnesses. However, because of the sensitivity of the subject, because of the delicacy of the undertaking, we must be very careful. What imagination does is important. Is it a way to supplement? or to replace? If it is to replace, it is wrong. If it is to supplement, it can be useful.

ABRAHAMSON It has been said, "Where there is no vision the people perish." Many feel that the Jews are an endangered species. What is to be done? Where shall we get the vision?

WIESEL I do not agree with the concept. I do not think we Jews are worse off than non-Jews today. I think the crisis of civilization today is a universal one. Furthermore, it is worse outside. We are always speaking about the Jewish community — our crisis. Do you have any idea what is going on in the Church? They have worse problems than we do, and for good reason. They must struggle with the question: How come the killers were Christians? We must wrestle with the question: How come the victims were Jews? Therefore you have a crisis in the Church, both Protestant and Catholic.

I believe we have vision. Ours is the ancient prophetic vision that one day people will not need wars to solve their conflicts. If you tell me we have forgotten Isaiah and Jeremiah, then we have a problem.

IN SPITE OF EVERYTHING

REYNOLDS Father Hesburgh, in your foreword to Mr. Wiesel's book *Four Hasidic Masters* you spoke of the "vital center that embraces contraries." What does that mean?

FATHER HESBURGH I think it means that God is the vital center that embraces contraries, because contraries are not as contrary as they may seem. Take Judaism and Christianity as two religious traditions. You cannot possibly understand Christianity without understanding Judaism. Jesus Christ was a Jew, his mother was a Jew, his apostles were Jews. The whole culture in which Christianity burst on the world was Jewish. The whole language is that. Somehow if we would get back to our spiritual center, if we would transcend a kind of deep-set secularism, you would be amazed how close Jews and Muslims and Christians would be, because we are all, if you will, sons of Abraham. We all worship the God of Abraham, Isaac, and Jacob. We are all religions of the Book, if you will, the word of God impinging on human history. That is a vital center. It is the most vital center I know, and it is that which draws us together, and it does not draw us together by homogenizing us. But it draws us together in being what we are, and yet relating whatever contrariness we find around that common center which is the God we worship.

REYNOLDS In your foreword you also spoke of the "ability to perceive union without losing necessary distinctions." Well, now why in 1978 are the distinctions still necessary?

WIESEL I must go back to what Father Hesburgh said earlier. It is true that a Christian today must know Judaism; for the Christian to be Christian he must know Judaism. It was not necessary for a Jew in my time to know Christianity. In my little town I did not even know that the Jews and Christians believe in the same God. I thought that Christians only believed in Jesus. Why? Because Jews and Christians in my town lived in separate worlds. I never saw a church; if I saw a priest, I ran away — for good reasons. You know, we had our experiences.

REYNOLDS You ran away?

WIESEL I ran away because our priests were not Father Hesburghs. Twice a year, on Easter and on Christmas, I was beaten by my Christian school friends.

Now I believe that there is a possibility to establish a true and honest com-

Adapted from Frank Reynolds, American Broadcasting Co.,Inc. *Directions*, ABC-TV Network, June 18, 1978.

munication. And I emphasize true and honest, meaning I tell the truth. I say what I remember, and I'm sure this is what Father Hesburgh does too. But I say so in order for me to remain what I am. That means I want to remain Jewish, authentically Jewish, totally Jewish, and I believe that if I am Jewish, a Christian who speaks with me will become a better Christian.

REYNOLDS Father Hesburgh, Mr. Wiesel has told us of his early recollections of Christians. What are your early recollections of Jews?

FATHER HESBURGH I think probably like those of many people who grew up as I did in a rather closed society. As Elie knew mostly Jews, I knew mostly Catholics. I went to a parochial school in Syracuse, New York. And I think I thought of Jews as being somewhat different, which of course they are and should be. But you did not always think of someone being different in those days as being a good thing. It was generally thought of as being a bad thing: They are not like us. Why can't everybody be like us?

And that reminds me of a wonderful Midrash I heard once. It says, if I am what I am because you are what you are, then you are not you and I am not I. And what it really means, I think, is that we have to be ourselves to understand each other. We have to be ourselves to have what Elie said earlier, an honest and sincere dialogue.

REYNOLDS You are both men of very strong faith. Father Hesburgh, how do you deal with your Christian faith, sitting alongside Elie Wiesel . . . a survivor of the Holocaust?

FATHER HESBURGH Well, I deal with it, I guess, in saying that I have tried to live it in my life and to realize that at the very core of it is not only the glory of God but the dignity of man, and that anyone who works against that dignity in any way is doing a blasphemous thing. That is why a good part of my life has been given to trying to defend human rights. Of course, the Holocaust is the ultimate of blasphemies, the murder of so many innocent people, in a so-called political cause. While that horror is there and one should not forget it — it ought to be an educative horror even for those who had no part in it — at the same time I think we must look ahead. I am sure Elie would agree with me in this, from what I understand of him and his writings, that we have to look ahead so that we do not create another holocaust. We are creating one right now. We can blow up the world seven times over. And we are adding to the power to do that. That is another blasphemy. And do not say it cannot happen. You know Murphy's Law: What can happen will. I hope, I pray to God this does not.

But, in a smaller concern, I am happy to be sitting here with Elie Wiesel, because I think we understand each other, because we're honest with each other. We realize that we represent two great traditions that are religious and spiritual at their core. I do not think we could get into an argument about religion *per se,* because I understand that Elie is Jewish, and he wants to be Jewish, and I am Christian, and I want to be a Christian; and he understands and respects that, and I understand and respect what he is. It is important, though, that we understand each other. And once we have done that, then I think we have to stand together a little more than we have in the past, stand together for peace and stand together for justice.

We had a meeting in Portugal last November of a group called the Inter-Religious Colloquium for Peace and Justice. It was made up mainly of Jews, Muslims, and Christians. The Jews were both American and Israeli, the Muslims were from throughout the Middle East, as far away as Iran, and the Christians were mainly American with a few Europeans. We were Protestant Christians, Orthodox Christians, Anglican Christians, and Catholic Christians. We were together as distinct religious groups. We prayed together every morning taking turns praying, and what surprised us all was how similarly our prayers ran, how much we suffered for the same cause of injustice in the world, how much we wanted to eradicate it, and how much we thirsted for peace. But we came at that strongly out of our own traditions, and we came at it together. And at the end of a week's conversation in this matter, it was just incredible how much we felt like brothers. We were beginning to call each other "brother," which is a kind of Muslim custom.

REYNOLDS Now, Mr. Wiesel, you have heard Father Hesburgh's statement just now. He is a realist, but he is also an optimist. Are you?

WIESEL I am less optimistic than Father Hesburgh. I will tell you why — for the same reasons, by the way. Something happened one generation ago, and I am afraid that the world has not been punished yet. And I am afraid of the punishment, and I do not want that punishment — a nuclear holocaust. And yet, I know that the story has not been concluded, it is still going on. There are so many tragedies in this world: you have, in Zaire, savagery; in Cambodia, a new genocide; in Bangladesh, Muslims are being persecuted.

Simply there are too many things going on, and I believe that all of them are connected somehow to what happened one generation ago. It was done then, and therefore the gates opened. And evil was unleashed. The only way for us to prevent a nuclear holocaust is to remember the Holocaust: that is why we try, all of us, to remember it, and to remember it in its purity, in its authenticity, with all the pain that goes with it. To say that we will succeed, I am not sure.

REYNOLDS May I say to you, hearing you, you make me optimistic. I think you make Father Hesburgh optimistic too. This is a question I have no right to ask, but having gone through everything that you have endured, why do you still have faith?

WIESEL Faith in what? Faith in whom?

REYNOLDS Faith in God.

WIESEL I rarely speak about my faith in God, because it is something so personal, and whatever I would say, really, would not be the truth.

REYNOLDS Faith in man.

WIESEL Even less. In God — I know how to deal now with my faith in God. Even then, today I do not believe the way I believed when I was a child. Faith in man, I have faith in man. . . . The only thing for me to do is to have faith in man and faith in God. If not, then we are all lost. So I have faith *in spite of* everything. I have faith because if I were to lose faith, and I know why, what could I teach my students? I try to teach them something. I have a son. I try to teach him. Today to have children in this world and to be a teacher in this world are tremendous responsibilities. Why do you speak, and why do I write, and why do you teach? All for the same reason: we try to save mankind. It is very pretentious. But to live today is a very pretentious undertaking. . . .

REYNOLDS Did you detect any difference in the questioning that you received here from the students at Notre Dame than elsewhere around the country?

WIESEL No, students are students, and I have great faith in students. I love the young people today. Theirs is a religious quest. They want the truth. And in Notre Dame, of course, the emphasis is on religion. They want to know what you ask: How can I go on having faith? But then I give my questions to the students. I give them my anguish. But if you share your anguish, it is already an answer. You tell the students that there were reasons not to believe. At one point, only the believers refused to believe. At one point, one had to believe in God, and very firmly, in order to say no to God. And whoever did not say no to God was not a believer. So you try teaching that even this is part of my tradition, this is the beauty of the Jewish tradition: I can say no to God, I can quarrel with Him, I can argue with Him, and I do argue with Him. As for man, of course this is a problem. . . . Forgive me, but I must be honest with you. Those who killed were Christians.

FATHER HESBURGH That is right.

WIESEL As a Jew it is not my problem. As a human being it is.

FATHER HESBURGH Not good Christians.

WIESEL That is what I want to hear.

FATHER HESBURGH Yes.

WIESEL I want Christians to tell me again and again — for their sake.

FATHER HESBURGH Yes.

WIESEL It's not for mine. That they were not good Christians.

FATHER HESBURGH No.

WIESEL But the fact is that those who killed were Christians. Hitler was never excommunicated. Himmler was convinced that he was acting as a good Christian when he was killing Jews. Of course, you condemned them and that's why we are close.

FATHER HESBURGH Yes.

WIESEL What is my problem? My problem is that we as Jews live in a general society, and we have to save that society. I try to save it as a Jew, together with you.

FATHER HESBURGH Yes.

REYNOLDS Well, can it be saved? You acting as a Jew? Father Hesburgh acting as a Christian?

WIESEL I would turn the question around. It can be saved *only* if I act as a Jew. And *only* if he acts as a Christian.

REYNOLDS I hesitate even to say this, Father Hesburgh, but the differences are important, but not all-important.

FATHER HESBURGH Yes, they are not terribly important because we are all back at our roots at the moment, and the Jewish tradition comes as a covenant with a mission from God. That covenant, that mission is still there.

REYNOLDS You spoke of both Jew and Christian waiting?

FATHER HESBURGH That is right. We are waiting for the Second Coming.

REYNOLDS And the Jews?

FATHER HESBURGH And they are waiting for the Messiah. We are both in an attitude of waiting. But I must say that we both bring something terribly important to the world today. You said something that, believe it or not, I said an hour ago, giving a talk at another part of this campus. I was talking to a group of priests, and I said we are called to nothing less than to save the world. And that is, indeed, a very pretentious thing to have to do, to save the world, given the state of the world today. You, now, an hour later, say exactly the same thing from your tradition. And I say, let us do it together. Let us stand together for justice. Let us stand together for the dignity of that beautiful thing called humanity that God created and that you and I represent in different ways but represent loving Him and serving Him in humanity.

WIESEL We try.

REYNOLDS What did you learn here at Notre Dame, Mr. Wiesel?

WIESEL That I can speak to Christians.

REYNOLDS Was that the first time?

WIESEL Oh, I had spoken to Christians before, but here I discovered an environment so Christian that the words I said and the words they heard were the same.

WRITER SUMS UP HIS MESSAGE: LIFE IS DESTRUCTIBLE, MORE EVIL THAN GOOD

AGES Are you afraid of the influence you have on your audiences?

WIESEL If the enemy could not corrupt me, then my own success cannot. I am afraid of the success in my approach to my subject. Logically, whatever I say should not be accepted. If I have to say things that are so terrible, people should resist my message. And when I feel that resistance I am reassured.

AGES What aspect of your message do you think your audiences should resist?

WIESEL The message is that life is destructible and filled with more evil than good. My books are pessimistic. Even in my works showing that good is possible, the fact remains that we are dealing with an evil world. My works dealing with religious themes include positive elements: man can affirm himself against God. But it is still against God.

AGES President Carter has apppointed you to head a commission to establish a Holocaust monument.

WIESEL In May, 1978, when relations between Israel and America were strained, Carter needed a morale builder. The idea was to connect Israel's thirtieth anniversary with a permanent Holocaust memorial.

I was lecturing on the West Coast during this period and did not hear anything about the idea until the summer, when I was in Israel. I began receiving telephone calls asking me to head the project. At first I resisted. I do not want to be a political figure. I do not want to be manipulated. And I do not believe in monuments. Jews do not believe in monuments.

My conditions were met. We want to focus the memorial on educational ideas. I would like, for example, that ten chairs in Jewish studies be established at American universities, that one hundred fellowships be made available for establishing educational curricula, and that a joint session of Congress be held each year to commemorate the Holocaust.

AGES Did you discuss the idea with Carter personally?

WIESEL No, I went to the White House but the president was involved with the Camp David negotiations at the time and my contact was with Stuart Eisenstadt, a good man and a good Jew, a very close presidential adviser. I realize, of course, there will be problems. How does one deal with such an instrument? Other minorities will complain: Why only the Jews and not us?

Adapted from Arnold Ages, *The Canadian Jewish News*, January 18, 1979.

As to finances, I would like to raise $100 million by popular subscription, like the system which was used to finance the Kennedy Center in Washington.

AGES How were your fears of possible political manipulation eased?

WIESEL I have already spoken up against the Carter Administration. At a UJA meeting two weeks ago I said clearly that what Carter is doing now is pro-Egyptian. They know that if they try in any way to pressure me I would simply quit.

AGES Should American Jews be as outspoken as they have been with regard to the Administration's pressuring of Israel?

WIESEL Silence is never the answer when it comes to engagement.

BEFORE THE END OF HISTORY —
AND AFTER

REMSBERG On whose behalf do you speak?

WIESEL One person, one, not more. I think nobody has the right to say he speaks on behalf of six million Jews. Nobody can speak for them because the image itself conjures up such an amount of madness and fire and silence that all we can do is bow our head and pray, if we are capable of prayer. I speak on behalf of one person — of a child that used to be me and is no longer me. I wonder what that child would have become had I not gone through certain events. So I speak on behalf of that child, and I always hope that that child one day will dominate my life once more.

REMSBERG Are you trying to start again where that child had those horrifying experiences that you have illuminated for the world?

WIESEL No. Before that. When I was a child, the world was simple. God was good. Evil was evil.

My first contact with reality was when my entire town, a Jewish town — it was the most Jewish of the Jewish towns — was transported into the kingdom of night. Suddenly I realized that the world of the Talmud is not the only world. So I would like somehow to stop history before history ended. That means I would like still to find that religious boy, believing in God and believing in man, believing in history and believing in words and believing in friendship. And believing, period. I would like to find that boy again.

REMSBERG *The Testament,* your new book, takes the reader inside the feelings and events surrounding the incredible period in Russian history when so many Jewish intellectuals were simply annihilated.

WIESEL I thought the war ended in '45. And then we found out that it didn't, not for some people. These poets, these novelists, these philosophers, these thinkers, these scholars, these artists were killed *after* the Holocaust. I don't compare. I believe the Holocaust is *sui generis:* there is no tragedy like it. Therefore Stalin was not like Hitler. He was a different kind of tyrant. We should not compare anyone to Hitler. But suddenly I discovered there was a tragedy in Russia when Stalin in his madness, in his frenzy of madness, decided to kill the Jewish intellect, the Jewish soul, and he had all these people arrested. I worked on this novel for fifteen years — to find the documentation, the facts. But at the same time — it's a very strange thing —

Adapted from Bonnie Remsberg, *Some of My Best Friends*, television interview, Chicago, Illinois, June 28, 1981.

[266]

in the writing the book took on a hopeful note. I wanted to transmit some fragment of the despair of our people, and I realized at the end that it's just the opposite. It is the most hopeful, the most triumphant of my imagined tales. The story of this poet *is* being known, though the KGB thought it would never be known. The son of the poet *does* reach Jerusalem, and the confession of the poet is being shared by our people and, hopefully, by other people as well. The executioner is defeated at the end.

REMSBERG The theme of muteness is important to *The Testament*.

WIESEL Every writer has only a few themes. They are obsessions, and there is no literature without obsessions. Silence is one of my obsessions. Why? Whenever you will talk about our history, you will see that silence is a dominant element in it. In our generation I think of the silence of the world. Here you have a people that day after day lost its children and its sages and its princes and its beggars, and yet the world remained silent. Even God remained silent. So the silence to me is a mystification or a mystery. In this book, too, silence is a mode — meaning we are all silent, no matter what we do. We are mute. I try to talk, but deep down I know that I am mute. That means I stop before I use words, and if I use words, it is not to change silence but to complete it.

REMSBERG Who was God to you in those early, innocent, quiet, peaceful years of childhood?

WIESEL At one point he was my grandfather.

REMSBERG Literally? He looked like —

WIESEL Almost literally. Not what he looked like — but I saw God's presence, God's spirit, on his face. Then he was my teacher, my rebbe. Whenever I saw a person I liked — and I liked most people, I admired most old men especially, because they were teachers — I felt God's presence. The problem was that during the war I looked at faces and I asked myself, "Which face reflects His?"

REMSBERG And?

WIESEL And I am still asking that question. In all of my books at one point I always try to protest and say, "After all, we are Your children. We are associates. We try to be partners in one story. What are You doing? What are You allowing to be done?" What I try to show is that this is part of our tradition — that we may say no to God.

REMSBERG Is God part of your life now? Do you still have your image, your vision, your relationship with Him?

WIESEL Oh, if I study a lot. I study the Talmud every day, so how can you not feel, if not the presence, at least the urge to feel the presence?

REMSBURG What did you hope to accomplish in *The Testament*?

WIESEL Among other things I wanted to show the meaning of communism. The problem with communism was that it became an experiment of sacrificing living people for the sake of an abstraction. That is something one does not do. You do not take a living human being and sacrifice him today for the sake of another human being who will be born tomorrow. The end does *not* justify the means. When it comes to human life, every person is an end, not a means.

REMSBERG In addition to your books, what legacy would you like to leave behind you?

WIESEL A few words, really. When some words are being used, I would like them to be surrounded with a certain silence. One of them would be *night*. Once upon a time there was night. On the other hand, when we speak about Jerusalem we should smile. And then I would like that whenever we celebrate *Simhat Torah*, the holiday of the Law, we should think of the outpouring of ecstasy and exuberance and joy in Soviet Russia, when they began the real adventure. And then I would also like the poor Paltiel Kossovers to be remembered. Except for *Night* I prefer *The Testament* to all the others I have written.

MY FATHER'S *TALLIS*

BERKOWITZ What are the challenges of being a father today? In what way does one transmit our 4,000-year-old heritage? What do you tell your son Elisha about the world we live in at this moment?

WIESEL I am not telling Elisha, he is telling me. I try to tell him what my father told me except in a different language. But today children are freer, they feel much more independent than we did. When I was his age I would never speak to my father unless I was spoken to. Well, Elisha speaks, and when he does not, I ask him to. I love to listen to him.

The challenges of a Jewish father are the challenges of a generation. We have to transmit so much, and the vehicles at our disposal are not always adequate. We never know whether the words we use and others hear convey the same meaning — how much more so when it is your son. I try to teach by example. I would never ask my son to do something I did not do when I was his age. Of course, I talk to him about the Jewish people, but then he *reads* about the Jewish people. I tell him stories, and he loves the stories. I am writing a book of Jewish children's tales called "Tales for Elisha by His Father."

Beyond that, we take Elisha wherever we go. When I was Elisha's age, the farthest distance I traveled from home was to a village where my grandfather lived, probably an hour away. However, when Elisha was two months old he was already with us in Jerusalem. We took him to Russia, to Poland, to Argentina, to South Africa. We travel from one Jewish community to the other, and he comes with us.

BERKOWITZ In our tradition, memory plays a critical role. What is your earliest memory?

WIESEL My first visit to *heder*. As you know, in those years a father would take his son and wrap him in his *tallis* and bring him to *heder*. I still feel that *tallis* on me when I study. It is a dramatic moment. Here is your father bringing you to a strange world; you are with other children you have never known, with an angry *melamed*. Every *melamed* then used to act angry. This is the image I have carried with me all these years.

BERKOWITZ Many important teachers have influenced you. I would like to ask you about three of them and the impact they have had on your life. First, Dodye Feig.

WIESEL Dodye Feig was my grandfather. He was a Hasid, and he taught me how

Adapted from *The Jewish Week-American Examiner*, week of June 14, 1981.

[269]

to sing. He was more than a teacher. My teacher would frighten me; my grandfather never frightened me. Indeed, when I was frightened, I would run to him. I would run away from home to go to him. He would take me with him to the rebbe. My father was an emancipated Jew, very religious, but emancipated. He did not believe in Hasidism. But my grandfather did, so I went with him to the rebbe on *Shabbat*, on *Yom Tovim*. I remember my grandfather on *Rosh Hashanah* and *Yom Kippur*. I would be covered by his *tallis*, and I was part of him. His impact on me is the impact of a song, of a melody. To this day, I sing his songs.

BERKOWITZ Mordecai Shoshani.

WIESEL Mordecai Shoshani is a different story. I have written two chapters about him, and one day I would like to write more. For him knowledge was a destructive rather than a constructive thing. What do I mean by that? Later I found out that this is a Zen Buddhist principle. In order to impart knowledge you must break the cycle, and Shoshani, for the three years he was my teacher, broke every notion that I had about reality, about hate, about everything. He created a distance between the world and its meaning that was certainly destructive, although later on I realized that it was important for my formation and education.

BERKOWITZ Professor Saul Lieberman.

WIESEL Whatever I know, I owe to him. If I have a teacher, it is he.

BERKOWITZ Not very long ago, in a distinguished American magazine, an article written by a Christian entitled "The Holocaust: Are Christians Responsible?" made the assertion that in reality Christians are not responsible for the Holocaust, that to say so is to distort the truth and use them as a scapegoat. First, says this article, Christians did help Jews. Second, to assert Christian responsibility for the Holocaust is to engender guilt, thereby causing resentment and undermining greater interfaith understanding, cooperation, and tolerance. What do you see as the Christian responsibility for and towards the Holocaust? How do you react to this kind of article? Is it part of a larger trend?

WIESEL To begin with the last question, it is certainly part of a larger trend. I think the world would like to forget the Holocaust, and since it cannot forget it, it is trying to dilute it, to cheapen it, to trivialize it, to water it down. If everybody was a victim, then it means there was no victim. I did not read the article, but I know the argument. We were in Poland on an official visit last year and every person we met, from the prime minister down, tried to convince us that the Poles did nothing during the war but try to save Jews. At an official ceremony they told us that they too were victims, and I told them yes, you too were victims, but there is one difference — victims of the Nazis, but we were victims not only of the Nazis but of the victims. We were your victims as well.

Can they deny the fact that those who did the killing were Christians? They may say they were bad Christians. I hope they will say so. But they were Christians, and those they killed were Jewish. I am not saying that only Jews were killed, although I believe that only Jews were victims of the Holocaust. There were other victims of Nazi atrocities, but those who did the killing were Christians. I am not saying that all Christians were killers; on the contrary, there were many good Christians. First of all, there were the Allied armies, and they deserve our gratitude for what they did to defeat Hitler. Inside Poland, inside Hungary were a few Righteous Gentiles. But those who killed *did* come from Christian backgrounds. And now they are trying to rewrite history.

BERKOWITZ On many occasions you have called yourself a *galut* Jew. In 1948, a new era in Jewish history began, and yet the Diaspora remains. What does this mean to you? And in a broader sense, what do you see as the content of the Diaspora-Israel relationship, given the reality that the bulk of Diaspora Jews — at least at the moment — are not going on *aliyah*?

WIESEL Rabbi, I see myself as a Jew of the Diaspora, with all my love, which is total, for Israel; and with all my commitment, which is total, for Israel. But still I am here. This is something strange. If anyone had told me in Sighet when I was a child that I should be alive to witness the renaissance of Jewish sovereignty, of the State of Israel, I would not have believed it. But if anyone had told me that I should witness the renaissance of Israel and not live in Israel, I would surely not have believed him. And yet I am not in Israel. You know, the Israelis today are resentful with regard to the Jews of the Diaspora. "What are you doing there?" they say. "We need you. Come." Yet we are not going. I don't know the reasons. They are too complicated, much too complex. I have no answer. I admit the validity of the question, but then I also believe that the question is part of the Jewish history, part of Jewish existence. If you study the Talmud, you know that only when Elijah the Prophet comes will all questions be resolved. So this one too will have to wait for the coming of the Messiah.

BERKOWITZ How do you think you have changed in the past thirty years — if at all?

WIESEL I am still the same person I was thirty years ago and forty years ago; I am still a child going to *heder*, afraid of the *melamed*, waiting for a *tallis* to cover me and give me some warmth. I am trying to deepen what I have been. I do not want to change.

SECTION 21

Quotes
and Comments

Be careful. Should you omit or add one single word, you
may destroy the world.
— Rabbi Ishmael to Rabbi Meir,
the scribe

AUTOBIOGRAPHICAL

What I remember from those times is not murder but the other side of murder, the other side of cruelty. When I think of that period, strangely I feel no pain. Sometimes I feel remorse. But mainly I feel gratitude for having lived through such a great and profound mystery.

When I think of those years, I am still baffled and bewildered. How could so few do so much to so many? How did the victims remain human during and after the experience?

And, when I think of them, I cannot but feel privileged and full of gratitude, because there is a certain lesson involved — that generosity survives cruelty, that man survives the murdered.

February 28, 1971 (78)

I don't know what it was, but something happened that will affect generations to come — and our generation is privileged to have known it.

There are privileged moments when you live faster or more intensely, when you find yourself at the core of an event and everything is there.

October 16, 1971 (46)

As a child I dreamed of mankind and bringing the Messiah; I don't believe in a world redemption anymore. I'm satisfied with small daily blessings and with helping one person, if I can.

October 30, 1971 (18)

Hasidism was the environment of my early days, and in spite of everything I still feel closest to it.

October 30, 1971 (18)

I describe a *Farbrengen* in *The Gates of the Forest*. I describe a kind of *mesibah* — a Hasidic *shtibel*. The physical setting is Lubavitch; the content is Wizsnitz. I always come back to Wizsnitz. Wizsnitz is my rebbe. Wizsnitz is my place, my fidelity. My patriotism, call it, is Wizsnitz. I tried to describe one of my encounters with the Wizsnitzer Rebbe in one of my books. He is a beautiful man, very, very beautiful. He is not a *talmid hakham*. He is not such a scholar, but he sings beautifully, and he adores beautiful women. That is why I am a Wizsnitzer Hasid.

[275]

I left him for the last time in 1944. Just a month before the Germans came into our town I went for *Shabbat Shirah* to Grossvardein, where he stayed. And I will never forget him. He was still young-old. Twenty years later I came to B'nai Brak to see him. He had not changed much — a beautiful beard, a *shtreimel* — . But I had changed.

November 13, 1971 (81)

Something in me died during the Holocaust. Perhaps it was the divine part.

December 6, 1971 (15)

I remember *Purim* in my hometown, when my grandfather was still alive. What did we do on *Purim* evening? We became *Purim shpieler* — the children became comedians. We *yeshivah bokherim* became actors. I must admit it now, to my shame, or to my pride, for I have never done it since: we went from door to door and we became fund-raisers. We went from door to door getting money from the rich and we gave it to the poor. Meanwhile we played — what could we have played? I had never read a play in my life — we played Joseph and his brothers, or the *Akedah*, and we tried to make fun. But in a nice way. What else did we do on *Purim*? We went to the rebbe to listen to his *droshe*, to his sermon, to his lecture. But the lecture on *Purim* was a different lecture, because the *Purim* Torah is actually a caricature of Torah. The rebbe would come and make fun of his own teachings.

February 28, 1972 (75)

Jerusalem and Israel are not answers but questions. I confess that when I think about it, I do not feel at ease. Some of my Israeli friends are even angry with me. "You speak so beautifully about Jerusalem," they say; "why don't you live there?" I once tried to explain my position to Golda Meir, and I asked her, "You know, when I come to Jerusalem I am always moved by Jerusalem. Do you think I would be as moved by Jerusalem if I were to live in Jerusalem?" And she said, "I don't want you to be moved; I want you to live in Jerusalem."

Yes, it was typical of Golda, but despite all my admiration for her, it was the wrong answer. I want too much: I want to live there *and* to be moved by it. Naturally, one can. But I am not worthy of it yet. In the meantime I live here, though I do not feel good about it.

December 14, 1972 (80)

My son's first name is Shlomo. It was my father's name. His middle name, Elisha, means "God is salvation."

We believe in names so much. I was the only son. I cannot break the chain. It is impossible that 3,500 years should end with me, so I took these 3,500 years and put them on the shoulders of this little child. It took me some time to realize the outrageous courage that it takes to have a child today.

January 31, 1973 (13)

I used to go to the synagogue every Sabbath and listen to the *maggidim*. They were wandering storytellers who used to go from one village to another. They were the link between villages, the witnesses from one culture to another.

January 31, 1973 (13)

When Elisha was born I felt very sorry for him. I felt sorry for him coming into this ugly, difficult, horrible world. Now I still feel sympathy, but naturally the urge is much stronger than before to try to do what we can to make it a little better. Because he is here, we try.

January 31, 1973 (13)

How dare anyone speak in the name of the victims? There were so many Bundists among the six million and so many Communists and so many atheists and so many secularists. I do not know what they wanted. I only know one thing — that they are no longer here to speak. And I cannot speak on their behalf. I can hardly speak on my own behalf. I have only tried to speak on behalf of the child that used to resemble me.

March 22, 1973 (57)

Until three years ago I worshiped with a Hasidic group near my home. But they were poor and had to sell their building. Ninety percent of their members were survivors of the Holocaust. Now it is hard to find a synagogue close to my heart, especially in New York.

June 20, 1973 (28)

Why don't I live in Israel if I feel so strongly about it? I can't. I'm too private a person.

October 31, 1973 (99)

A Jew like me has to be in Israel in times of destiny.

October 31, 1973 (99)

I have few friends because of the intensity needed to be a friend. For this reason I live a solitary life.

March, 1974 (19)

After the war I had a true existential choice: to become an anarchist, on the theory that society was not worth the effort, or to make a leap of faith and confidence, although I had every reason to hate the world. I spent a year of silence in Paris, and I decided what I wanted to do — still want to do — is understand what happened.

I know people who spent five and six years in prison camp. What did they learn? The Germans taught them that only strength survives, that morality doesn't count. Why shouldn't those people who escaped, bitter and familyless, have destroyed the world in their turn? We had a right to accuse the whole world. But a peculiar thing happened. Instead of accusing others, we accused ourselves. Why me and not another?

May 7, 1974 (36)

I have always been very serious. As a boy, when I went out with a girl, I would talk to her about Kant and generally never see her again. The truth was so important to me.

May 7, 1974 (36)

When I was young I believed fervently in the coming of the Messiah. I believed that every child could be one or help to become one. Today I am less ambitious. To save the life of one child, one person, is enough.

June 11, 1974 (12)

I love Hasidism. I was brought up a Hasid. I still am a Hasid. Someone asked me recently, "What is a Hasid?" And I told him, "If a Jew stops believing in God, often he goes away from Judaism, and he is no longer a Jew. If a Hasid stops believing in God, he is still a Hasid."

February 18, 1975 (68)

How did I survive the period after the Holocaust? This is a very important question. In every single book of mine I try to deal with this question.

March 17, 1976 (38)

I began by writing commentaries for the Bible on the only typewriter in Sighet . . . . My dream was to get a typewriter for myself.

March 17, 1976 (38)

What motivates me to write? Time. I feel that I do not have enough time. As a survivor, I must justify myself. I must redeem certain events, bring back some faces from the darkness. There are stories to tell.

October 9, 1976 (29)

What I do believe we should do is to put everything against the background of the Holocaust. I know that whatever I do in my life must be justified against that background. Whatever I do, whatever I write, and whatever I say is always measured by that yardstick.

March 20, 1977 (52)

I realized if I was going to be a writer I would have to get out of journalism. I realized I could live my whole life as a journalist and not use more than 1,000 words. When you're a journalist, it's all the same story, you just change the names around. If you took the whole *New York Times* and put it in a computer and boiled it down, you'd find 1,000 words.

March 16, 1979 (98)

I'm not scared personally of anything that could happen to me.

March 16, 1979 (98)

My little boy is getting a very religious background. I want him to be what I used to be. Then let him have his doubts, let him have his questions. He will decide.

March 16, 1979 (98)

If I have to book a plane flight, my secretary or my wife does it for me. Officials scare me.

March 16, 1979 (98)

I saw it all again. Not as it is now. As it was then.

I saw the huts, and the furnaces, and the chimney. I remembered my family, my friends. I stood at the very place where they were taken away from me. I was standing there, in the camp as it is now, reading the services. And then I saw it the way it was. Somehow, without the people, it is even more eerie now than it was then.

August 15, 1979 (97)

I came here [to Thailand's border with Cambodia] because nobody came when I was there [in the concentration camps]. One thing that is worse for the victim than hunger, fear, torture, even humiliation, is the feeling of abandonment, the feeling that nobody cares, the feeling that you don't count. I have absolutely no right not to be here. Perhaps we cannot change the world, but I do not want the world to change me.

February 7, 1980 (23)

The World Gathering of Jewish Holocaust Survivors will be a unique event in our lives. Only by remembering what happened under the Nazi oppression can we be expected to remind and advise others how to prevent another such catastrophe. Only by remembering what happened to us can others be assured it will not happen to them.

March 7, 1980 (21)

I have learned to appreciate the daily miracles: again *Hanukkah*, a small boy, one little lamp of oil is enough, if it is there. I have learned to appreciate that if I have one friend I don't need more. I have learned to appreciate that if I have one suit I don't need more. If one person understands what I am trying to give and is ready to receive I don't need more. So a few will remain, and we shall go on shouting and protesting. Maybe someone will hear.

December 7, 1980 (88)

I believe in celebration. It is so strange, because we live in tragic times, in turbulent times. Every fiber of my being wants to celebrate. I want to celebrate the Jewish people.

December 7, 1980 (88)

After the war, I became more tolerant of people. Before, I didn't know any non-Jews. . . . My fear of the other was a wall. Without the war, I would never have questioned any of my beliefs. I wouldn't have been involved in action. The event made me realize the urgency of personal commitment.

April 7, 1981 (22)

There is no difference between the fighters and the martyrs. All were fighters; all were martyrs. But the young fighters of the ghettos took Jewish history in their own hands and taught us a new lesson. And here, at this gathering, we will teach this lesson, not only to our children, but to the children of the world.

July 3, 1981 (16)

I would like something of what I've seen to be perpetuated. There are certain things I have seen that nobody else has. So I must speak, even if I don't want to. But I do not think anybody has the right to speak for the dead. They speak for themselves. If we do not hear them, it is because we are not sensitive enough.

October 13, 1982 (14)

THE CREATIVE ACT: AUTHOR

The important thing is not to lie, not to become a comedian, not to give a performance, not to be too silent or too talkative, but to have a blank page and fill this in with the right things.

December 10, 1968 (10)

I knew I would write. Writing meant to bear witness. To bear witness, to testify, was the obsession of every Jew during the war.

December 10, 1968 (10)

One Generation After attempts to show that our literature has failed: What we wanted to tell we couldn't — the facts were too strong, and people didn't want to listen.

If they had listened, would we have Biafra and Vietnam and the massacre at Songmy?

I have a feeling of impotence. I see images on TV of Biafra children and of Songmy, and what am I doing? Putting one word after another: "He came. He said. . . ."

What can an individual do? We speak, we reassure our conscience, but basically we can do nothing. That's one reason intellectuals have been fascinated by power, by people who can make decisions. If I hesitate for hours about what word to use — blue? azure? — how could I not hesitate for weeks about whether to send people to their life or their death?

February 10, 1970 (42)

I had a psychosomatic experience while writing *A Beggar in Jerusalem*: I lost my voice. Everything had to go into the book.

February 12, 1970 (41)

I find no bitterness in me — perhaps because I deal with words. One thing we learned even before the experience of the Holocaust is that bitterness is an enemy of art, just as anger can bring art and give it some meaning.

December 5, 1971 (66)

Literature is an act of faith, because any writer who gives you his book is convinced that at least for two hours, more or less, you are seeing the same things he has seen. I must believe that the words I give you are the words you listen to and carry away in you. Literature is more than an act of faith towards man; it is an act of faith in literature itself.

December 5, 1971 (66)

We do not create. We re-create.

January 31, 1973 (13)

. . . in our view, no act is gratuitous, be it literary or artistic; it requires justification in its relationship with the shattering mystery of the Holocaust. For the survivor everything is mystery. And everything is grace. . . . For better or worse, everything sends him back to the past. He remembers and shares that memory.

May 4, 1973 (82)

I tried murder, madness, suicide. I tried by writing them.

December 2, 1973 (3)

The first writing is always a voice for myself. The rewrite is for others.

December 2, 1973 (3)

I must go on shouting and recording the events of our extraordinary times. Our children will never forgive us if we forget one event that will shape and foretell the destiny of man.

December 21, 1973 (5)

In 1945 I came to Paris. I knew no French. I was an exile. And I speak not only for myself. Every Jew in Europe was almost invincible. Everyone spoke the pages of so many tales that he had the feeling he could shake up history. He could bring the Messiah. At last he could tell the tale.

February 15, 1974 (25)

I write every day a certain number of hours. Discipline is very important. No artist knows where his inspiration comes from. Perhaps mine comes from my past — the discipline of past experience.

February 15, 1974 (25)

Writing is the only thing I know how to do, if at all. I have no other profession. If I would be deprived of this medium, I would be totally lost.

March, 1974 (19)

I love the theater too much to enrich it with plays that are not absolutely good. I do not see myself as a playwright. My play *Zalmen, or The Madness of God* may be good, but then that is an accident. My role is that of a witness.

May 7, 1974 (36)

What most Jews wanted over there during the era of night was not so much to live — there was nothing much to live for — but to survive, simply because they knew they must survive and tell the tale. That is what they all had in common, to do the utmost to enable one messenger, one witness, to transmit one spark of the flame, one outcry of the tale, one tear of one heart.

December 15, 1974 (26)

One thing is clear: that as long as one survivor is alive, his tale will continue to be told, even though it may not be heard. For better or for worse, he has become the tale. As for me, I am still searching for it.

March 2, 1975 (89)

I am not a political person. I understand nothing in politics. My attempt is an ethical attempt, a literary attempt. I try to have a historic consciousness, not a political one. Therefore, whatever I say must be judged in this light.

April 10, 1975 (84)

In my books I speak about Jews, about Jewish problems, Jewish themes, Jewish obsessions. Why do I do it? Because I am Jewish. Jewishness to me is not a wall. We do not erect walls. On the contrary, Jewishness to me is an opening, it is an offering. To me it is really a bridge and a link. In order to give I must have. But, even more, in order to give I must be. A Jew who is not Jewish is bad for Jews and bad for the others. But a Jew who is Jewish is good for Jews and good for the others.

November 23, 1975 (64)

I am a writer. I testify in writing. Other survivors testify by other means. By speaking. By bringing children into the world. By occupying places in the community. By helping others. Or simply by taking notes.

I tell stories. . . . I try to defeat the executioner with words. Art is . . . a protest against the executioner.

March 17, 1976 (38)

To tell stories: that is all I try to do. Sometimes they are Hasidic stories. I love Hasidic stories. Sometimes they are modern stories. But they are all the same. They are simply modern stories that two hundred years ago were told as Hasidic stories. Five hundred years ago they were told as medieval stories by our ancestors in Spain. Two thousand years ago they were called Talmudic stories. It is always the same story. Our imagination is simply in one direction. We try to see what we have been, and we try to remember. That is all. If we could remember far enough, then maybe the present would have more relevance to our own lives. What we try to do, therefore, is to remember far enough.

March 30, 1976 (72)

No one can create. We are too weak. But I can try to re-create. And in re-creating I use my memory. But my memory is not only my own. It is all a matter of how far you think back, and I would like to think back as far as possible. And when I do, suddenly Abraham, Isaac, and Jacob are my allies, my contemporaries. Suddenly I see Abraham and Isaac going to the altar — and Isaac sacrificing Abraham, not the other way around. Suddenly I understand the past simply because of the present. And one helps the other instead of destroying the other.

March 30, 1976 (72)

There are two ways of writing about suffering — from within and from without. If you write from within, you must write with tears and with blood. You should not show it. You should never show it. But the tears should be there, the anguish should be there.

October 3, 1976 (32)

Literature is actually a matter of obsessions on the one hand and imagery on the other, and every writer has his own imagery, has his own vocabulary, his own code, and the code of Jeremiah is actually my code.

October 7, 1976 (53)

I speak with 3,000 years of history on my shoulders. The stories I want to tell you are the stories of my people. They are not stories I have created. They are stories I re-create.

Literature is an art of saying no to the executioner and of correcting injustice. The executioner kills. I bring back the victim. I tell of the killing.

March 10, 1977 (17)

I don't believe that writers today should write simply to entertain their readers. I believe today literature has a moral dimension. Today literature has a moral imperative. We must change humanity. We must save it. And only the tale of what humanity has done to itself can save it from future catastrophes.

April 27, 1977 (94)

Literature can correct injustices. When I disagree, I write. I tell God, "No, this is not how I see the world." If I agree, why write?

December 30, 1977 (35)

The temptation of every novelist and every storyteller is to tell lies, to tell beautiful lies about situations that are not beautiful at all. This temptation supposes a degree of vanity on the part of the storyteller: that he has found truth. Well, I have not found truth. Therefore all I can do is tell the story. However, the search for truth goes on. And whatever we do in the framework of our history or in the framework of our endeavors I believe is this pursuit of truth.

February 1, 1978 (76)

Fifteen books, almost sixteen now, and I have barely begun. I must share what I know. I must do something with every moment. As a survivor, every day is grace, every moment is a gift.

Spring, 1978 (6)

Do not believe anyone who will tell you that the clever people survived or that those who had motivations survived. It is not true. Survival was an accident. A step in the right direction, in the wrong direction, somebody pushed you, you came a minute too late or too soon — that made the difference. Those who survived, therefore, know they must do something with every minute of their lives. The survivor has to justify his life. And the first justification is testimony. We must be witnesses.

December 5, 1978 (62)

Life is a conflict. Life is not serenity. Serene people do not create works of art. Serene people are not interesting. Contradictions are the price you pay.

March 16, 1979 (98)

I have written nineteen books till now. What do they have in common? Of course, me: I have written them. And I am in all of them. In other words, it is the Jew in me that is in all of these books. Of course, I write about the Jewishness in me or in my heroes for a simple reason: because I am Jewish. In order for me to give you anything — you who are not — I have first to be. I must first see who I am. I must open my own mind here and go deep down, deep down, century after century, back to the origins of inspiration and there find enough words and enough melodies to share with you.

October 30, 1979 (77)

One writes because one can do nothing else. One writes in order to find out not only the words but the silence within the words, not only the stories but the life beyond the stories, a certain darkness, a certain fire, a certain mood. One writes in order to re-create the universe which has been but has vanished since.

March 16, 1980 (91)

I write in French because it was the language I learned at sixteen, and it is valuable to me. Except for non-fiction, I don't try to write English. A language is like a person — it doesn't like infidelity.

April 9, 1980 (9)

THE CREATIVE ACT: SUBJECT

I have made an oath to myself. In every book I write, I must go back over this period — if only for a chapter. And I must constantly ask: What is there lacking in man that he allowed it to happen?

We live in a circle of guilt; no one was untouched. How is it that the experience passed over the world — but failed to leave much of a mark on the conscience of men? . . . The camps were not only an indictment of our present world; they remain an indictment of 2,000 years of Christian civilization.

October 2, 1961 (48)

I do not believe the Jewish people can live without Israel. They couldn't take destruction twice, not in so short a period of time. Therefore my stories deal with Israel.

December 6, 1971 (15)

Silence has to be used in the correct way. I believe the greatest poetry comes from words that are coated in silence.

November 7, 1973 (40)

In 1945 our people had no children and no old men. They had killed our children and our grandparents. To correct history I gave them a name. I gave them a home in my novels.

December 2, 1973 (3)

You write about what you do not have. It is absence that makes literature. It is what you miss that becomes present. Somebody dies and you are shaken by his death. The death inspires you to write. Why? What is the meaning of your writing then? It is not simply that you are overburdened with grief — it is a protest. Instead of giving in to the grief, you take the grief and you say, "I shall build something with it." And then it becomes a protest against death.

October 21, 1975 (67)

I know that many villages were not as beautiful as I make them and that many people were not as saintly as I make them, but that is the least I can do for them: to give them in their purity. Camus once told me, "One must approach mankind not through its ugly common point but through its most exalting opening." I believe that is true for Judaism, too. You can approach Judaism through its ugliness —

[286]

there are ugly sides, I'm sure. There are some ugly Jews, especially those who are ashamed of being Jewish. But if you approach Judaism through its most exalting aspects, you enter quite an adventure, an adventure that I wish I could be worthy of.

October 21, 1975 (67)

All Jewish stories contain the elements of our existence: the persecution that somehow accompanies our existence from the very beginning; the opposition between man and God; and especially the persistence of the Jew. Why is he always there? If God chose to punish and persecute His people all the time, how is it that we are still here?

November 23, 1975 (64)

If my work emphasizes the Talmud and the Bible, it is because I want to bring them back to contemporary society. We have a need for conscience: that is what is lacking now.

March 5, 1976 (44)

Even in my earlier work, except for *Night*, I have not said about the Holocaust what should have been said, what could have been said. What can be said will not be said. We don't know what to do with the subject. But that is exactly the nature of the subject and the nature of the event. We do not know how to handle it. We did not know what to do before it occurred: we were totally disoriented while it occurred; and now after it we have acquired a unique knowledge from it that may crush us. We simply do not know what to do with such knowledge. It goes deep into the nature of man and has extraordinary implications about the relationship between man and men, man and language, man and himself, and, ultimately, man and God. We don't know: at the beginning that is the answer to it, and I am afraid at the end as well.

March 30, 1976 (72)

I believe that testimony or literature or art or history or memory have mainly one task and one duty and one function: to say no to the executioner. Centuries ago it was to say no to death. In our generation I prefer to say no to the executioner. He killed communities — 10,000 communities. So what do I do? My task is to bring them back to life — in words. Yes, only with words. What else do I have?

March 30, 1976 (72)

A Jew is a storyteller; he trics to tell the tale in order to prevent another catastrophe. I speak of Jews because I am Jewish. This is inclusive, not exclusive. Speaking of Judaism is my way of speaking of humanity.

March 11, 1977 (2)

Every tale that I tell, every tale that haunts me is actually a question. Where was

God? Surely, where was God? I have not made peace with Him. But where was man?

November 7, 1977 (54)

To be Jewish today, therefore, is to tell the truth. I have not written enough about the Holocaust. I didn't feel adequate. Not because people don't want to read. It's their loss. To participate in an event and be aware of it is a benediction. If I have not written more it is because the subject is so great, the magnitude so anti-divine.

January 20, 1978 - February 2, 1978 (8)

How did the Holocaust affect my attitude toward religion? In all my books I still ask the question, and I do not have the answer. I try to deepen my questions more and more, to examine them from different views, from different angles. The answer? Maybe one day, when the Messiah will come.

October 28, 1979 (70)

One of the characters who has been present in all my writings is the character of the Messiah, and who is the Messiah, what is the Messiah, if not the embodiment of eternity in the present, the embodiment of eternity in the future. He is waiting for us as long as we are waiting for him.

March 30, 1980 (62)

·

THE CREATIVE ACT: AUDIENCE

I believe that what you need most today is not lessons but stories, but you must see them as experiences. As for my stories, you must see beneath every word the child I was and that perhaps I would still like to be today.

February 28, 1971 (78)

I don't believe the tale of the Holocaust is a morbid one. There are things you must learn there.

February 17, 1972 (45)

My tales are not tragic. I do not seek tragedy. I do not want melancholy. I do not want despair. If I have ever attempted to do something with my words, it is to make them sing, and with them to make you dream, and that is all. I have written books with words and dreams, and they are yours, your dreams in my words.

February 27, 1972 (65)

I do not believe in self-pity. To tell the tale, that is the thing. It gives a dimension to your past when you feel that whatever you have gone through belongs not only to you but to many others. My grandfather said that no one has the right to keep stories to himself.

March 12, 1972 (47)

Do we know the story? Have we heard the story? Are we taking the story and claiming kinship with all the intense moments it contains? Do we claim kinship with all the characters that make up the story and that lived so that we could go on living? That is the question, and the question too is part of the story. What I give is not answers. I try to give tales and stories and questions.

April 24, 1973 (49)

All catastrophes began with words, as did all redemptions. Words can also bring life and hope and — sometimes — joy. God himself used language when He created the universe. Kabbalists will tell you that words, if properly inspired and used, can change the laws of nature and history as well.

October 1, 1975 (63)

All Hasidic tales are full of friendship. And to retell them is to communicate their promise. Listen to our Jewish tales, and you will know what hurts your friend. To listen well is to acquire all knowledge and experience. But who will

[289]

teach modern man how to listen? To listen means to deny solitude, and solitude is the problem of man today.

April 30, 1976 (69)

I am responsible not only for the words I write. I am totally responsible also for the interpretation of my words. Therefore, it is you who ultimately justify my work, not I. If my words are received in an inhuman way, then in a way it is my defeat that you have confirmed. If, on the other hand, my words help move you one step closer to one another and humanize the human being, then it is a kind of reward. We, the storytellers of this generation, seek no other reward.

April 27, 1977 (94)

Art for art's sake does not exist. Literature must have a moral thrust; the reader should be changed. The writer wants to change life from within with words; whatever we have must be shared. With words the writer is overcoming time. Stories regarding the Jewish experience, when deep, are universal.

December 30, 1977 (35)

Often we feel we cannot even talk to the living. We are so surrounded by the dead that we can talk only to them.

March 25, 1979 (95)

There is beauty in the text. There is no greater adventure than an encounter with the text, especially with a text which is three thousand years old, for there you find not only those who wrote it, but also those who have studied it and explored it. In studying the Bible or the Talmud I meet my teachers, whose names I revere to this day. Whether they lived in the sixteenth century or in the twelfth century, I find their trace there in the text. They have left some clues, some hints. I pick them up.

October 30, 1979 (77)

What is a poet? A poet takes words and gives them a destiny. What does a poet do? A poet takes everday words like *bread* or *wine* or *air* or *life* or *death* or *childhood*, and somehow, by putting one after the other and by introducing silence into them, he produces a certain electric current. Suddenly, routine words burn and burst in your heart, in your mind, and in receiving these words you become poetically receptive.

May 24, 1981 (92)

When you have a text, you must resist it. There must be a tension between you and the text. Simple acceptance won't do. The deeper you go, the more tension you need, because the more tension, the more truth. What do you do when you resist the text and you don't understand it? You read it again.

September 13, 1981 (59)

THE CREATIVE ACT: TECHNIQUE

When I write, it is as if I am telling a story. When I wrote *A Beggar in Jerusalem*, I wrote it in one great sweep. And the amazing thing — as I was writing, my lips were moving. The book is a tale because I told it as I wrote it. Afterwards I was hoarse for a week.

March 12, 1972 (47)

In my tradition we have the expression "to be like a bow." You pull the arrow and you are tense, but you don't let the arrow go, ever. The tension must be there; you don't release it. Well, this is what a sentence should be, and this is what a book should be.

April 27, 1977 (94)

I write every book three times. The first draft is handwritten. The second and third I type myself. I always say, "If I take this chapter out, will there still be a book? Will the chapter still be a chapter, if I take this sentence out?" The main thing is never to fall into sentimentality or mellowness. Writing must be stark, austere.

Behind every word I write are ten words I do not write. *Night* was 864 pages; now it is 120. You think those other 744 pages are not there? They are there. You do not see them.

March 16, 1979 (98)

The dialogue is a kind of new genre I have tried to invent to describe certain events that needed a new language. The problem for all those who deal with the period of the Holocaust is that the language itself was corrupted, distorted, destroyed. We had to invent something new, a new way of communication.

March 25, 1979 (95)

YOUTH AND HIS STUDENTS

The missing dimension in Jewish education and Jewish life today is the dimension of beauty. Let our youth see that Judaism is not only a religion, not only a philosophy, not only a structure of ethical values. Judaism is, above all, beauty. There is so much beauty in the Talmud, there is so much beauty in Jewish history and Jewish legends, even in the saddest ones, that one cannot but respond to it. Who are my masters? Victor Hugo or Immanuel Kant? The Midrash, the Aggadah, the Hasidic rebbe and his fervor, the Musarnik and his love for knowledge: they are my teachers, my predecessors. It is their beauty I try to capture and transmit to the young who need beauty to go on living in a society that has none.

November 14, 1970 (55)

Bring to your fight your Judaism, your heritage, and your fervor.

I resent it when anyone tries to tell me that he who chooses Judaism is withdrawing from human society. Judaism is not a restrictive concept. It is an opening to others and mankind.

December 6, 1971 (15)

Whenever I have a chance to have encounters and to tell tales, I prefer to address myself to young people who need these tales more than anything else.

There is only one man more unhappy than all of us. That is a man who has no future. Right? Wrong. Worse is the fate of a man who has no past. Fortunately you have a past. Sometimes it sounds sad. Sometimes it sounds melancholy. But all the time it contains a certain call for beauty and a certain call for humanity. And it always demands a meaning which only you and I and we can give it — and no one else.

And the meaning is in the tale.

February 28, 1972 (75)

I'm concerned about young people. I feel they are lost. We live with the curse of the past and the uncertainty of the future.

December 2, 1973 (3)

Once a child is born it is up to the child to justify his parents' project. I use "project" in the philosophical sense. It is up to the son or the daughter to say to the parents, "You were right." If not, what a tragedy! What a waste, what an absurdity of existence!

October 21, 1975 (67)

[292]

I teach the Holocaust in a very special way. I show my students what they cannot know. I try to communicate a feeling that cannot be communicated.

March 17, 1976 (38)

Protest, yes; fight, yes; demonstrate, yes. Do whatever you can for justice. Do whatever you can against injustice. But I do not believe in violence, not even in violence for justice.

April 30, 1976 (69)

My young friends, I want you to know that if there was one obsession my people had, that obsession was you. The obsession was to bear testimony so that you one day would know what man is capable of, that you one day would know what not to do, that you one day would know what your duties are from the very beginning so that you might one day prevent further catastrophes and further injustices and ugliness. That was the obsession.

April 27, 1977 (94)

It is possible to acquire knowledge and to use that knowledge against mankind. It is possible, if you do not also take into account values, if you do not take into account the human truths. There is no other truth but human truth, and there is nothing in the world except the human being. And there is nothing as important in the world as my fellow man. If you don't know that, all the literature that you may absorb and all the science you learn will only be destructive.

April 27, 1977 (94)

Never has the teaching of any subject been more urgent. The event recedes in mystery; those who survived it are old, tired, anguished. Hitler is being rehabilitated in many quarters, his crimes obliterated. Dozens of books try to "prove" that the Holocaust never existed.

With so few survivors in our midst — and their number is decreasing almost daily — this is the last chance for our generation to study and communicate, to explore and analyze an event that will forever remain a challenge in history and perhaps to history.

The main responsibility, therefore, falls on teachers and schools — especially high schools. The responsibility for teaching the Holocaust also must involve both Jews and non-Jews, and ultimately it will affect both, though not to the same degree. It is impossible today to understand or comprehend what is happening in the world in all fields — human rights, anti-Semitism, Israel and the Middle East, poverty, racism — unless the Holocaust is viewed as a factor in the equation.

October 9, 1977 (86)

To have a degree means nothing, to be an educated man means nothing, if it is not accompanied by moral commitment. Knowledge, in itself, may be anti-human if it lacks ethical dimensions.

Spring, 1978 (6)

To teach is to sensitize to words, to problems, to ideas, to anguish and humanity. Anguish is a strong word, but there is much anguish in the world. And humanity is what you do in response to anguish.

October 13, 1982 (14)

AGAINST DESPAIR

If something should happen to our people, it will signal the end of the world. The next holocaust will be a universal holocaust.

I am very pessimistic, but I still have hope. Hope has never been more possible because it has never been more necessary.

November 24, 1973 (30)

Even in the death camps they danced on *Simhat Torah*, and we must dance today because of so much sadness.

December 21, 1973 (5)

We are entering a dangerous period in history. I fear that mankind is running to suicide. Without Auschwitz, Hiroshima would not have been possible. What happens to the world happens to Jews first.

And yet — and yet — we are mad enough to go on believing in man and his destiny, mad enough to resist despair.

December 15, 1974 (26)

There are all the reasons in the world not to trust man, not to trust history, not to trust civilization, not even to believe in God. And yet we must be capable of refuting all these reasons and go on believing in man, in mankind, in language, in poetry, and in friendship — in friendship above all.

February 18, 1975 (68)

If I am so passionately involved with our children today, it is because we lost so many then. I cannot without a real existential effort recapture my faith in man after that. I would even say my faith in God requires an effort. But not to make that effort would be to yield to the enemy. That was the whole question then: Who sets the rules — we or the enemy? Maybe then we followed the enemy's rules, but now we will not.

April 11, 1975 (74)

When I am in a pessimistic mood, I feel that we are always alone when we fight, that those in power have more power than we, that we have no power. But when I am in a good mood, I say to myself, no, if I manage to remain true to myself, then somehow it works on others, somehow it reverberates, and somehow other people, whether they want it or not, whether they know it or not, benefit from my loyalty to our common principles.

April 30, 1976 (69)

Why go on? From the very beginning of our history we have suffered. If to be Jewish is to suffer, why suffer?

I believe that to be Jewish is not to suffer. If suffering affects you to the point of denial, it is bad. But, if it helps you to make one step forward, the suffering has meaning.

March 15, 1978 (7)

I am pessimistic now. I am pessimistic because I do not trust history. But at the same time, I am optimistic. Out of despair one creates. What else can one do? There is no good reason to go on living, but you must go on living. There is no good reason to bring a child into this world, but you must have children to give the world a new innocence, a new reason to aspire towards innocence.

April 7, 1981 (22)

QUESTIONS AND ANSWERS

Nothing is clear to me. Nothing is solved. Nothing is answered.

December 2, 1973 (3)

An answer satisfies; the question dissatisfies. We can move forward because of the question, not because of the answer. Answers divide people. Questions unite them.

February 15, 1974 (25)

In the beginning my students do not understand the arrogance of answers. The professor is supposed to have answers. After a while they realize there is beauty in questions, more than in answers. There is truth in questions. Questions never provoked a war.

October 3, 1976 (32)

I prefer to take my place on the side of Job, who chose questions and not answers, silence and not speeches. . . . I envy those scholars and thinkers who pride themselves on understanding the tragedy of the Holocaust in terms of an entire people; I myself have not yet succeeded in explaining the tragedy of a single one of its sons.

October 3, 1976 (32)

A rebbe is not someone who gives the answers. A rebbe is someone who shares his questions with you. But then, if they are articulated with enough sincerity, the questions become answers, or at least they become a beginning of an answer.

May 1, 1977 (60)

In Hebrew the word for "question" is *she'elah*, and the *alef lamed* of God's name are part of the fabric of that word. Therefore God is in the question.

February 1, 1978 (76)

SUFFERING

We can choose to love Isaac more than Jacob, or Saul more than David. The Bible always gives us the option to take the other side. And in the Talmud one is always asked: What if the situation were the opposite? Whatever we read, we are forced to read either way — except when it comes to suffering. When it comes to either inflicting or enduring suffering, we can only hope that we will endure rather than afflict. Jewish history has given us that sad privilege.

March 15, 1978 (7)

CHRISTIANITY

As most historians have stated, Christianity's role in the Holocaust should not be underrated. The Final Solution was rooted in the centuries-old Christian hatred of the Jews. . . . Pope John XXIII understood the guilt of the Church — and of Christianity in general. The mass killings took place in a Christian setting. Protestant leaders applauded Hitler — as did their Catholic counterparts. Those who killed . . . felt no tension, no conflict between their Christian faith and their criminal deeds.

June 3, 1974 (50)

Are we, as Christians would say, witnesses to *their* truth? This is what the Christians usually say — that the Jews should live, but live in suffering for having rejected Christ. And we Jews all suffered: they made us suffer. But this is their view, not the Jewish view. We reject suffering.

November 23, 1975 (64)

John XXIII, a saint even in my vocabulary, opened the Church and liberalized it not only because he was a friend of the Jewish people but also because he felt the Catholic Church had failed. It had gone bankrupt. It was inconceivable to him that the Holocaust could occur within Christianity. Germany was a Christian nation — devotedly Christian and Catholic. Therefore John XXIII said we must rethink even Catholicism. And he began. Today's pope walks in the footsteps of Pius XII, not in those of John.

April 13, 1978 (56)

I am worried about this movement of conversion, these crusades. It is a new word with an old meaning. For the Jews the word "crusade" has a terrible meaning. I welcome support of the Moral Majority, but I would like to have the Christian leadership make an open statement for a pluralistic society and that they want to become better Christians, but not at the expense of the Jews. I am not a theologian, I do not want to give them any advice, but I resent their effort to proselytize.

As a Jew I can respect the Christian faith in Christians, the Moslem faith in Moslems — that is the beauty of it.

September 24, 1981 (39)

JEWISH RESISTANCE

There was no death urge. The Jewish religion is against death. Everywhere in the Talmud you are told, "Choose life." Anything that is life is good; anything that is death is evil. The Jews are alien to death; he has never been their friend. Moses was a great man as long as he lived; the moment he died he became impure.

There was resistance in the camps, but mostly along political lines. If in the end the Jews accepted death, it was their only way to protest. What could they do when the whole world had forgotten them? They were in Poland, at Auschwitz, and if they escaped, they knew that the very first Pole they met would turn them in. Most of all, they had no idea the extermination camps existed; they could not conceive that destruction was their destiny.

October 2, 1961 (48)

I have seen photographs of the victims. I looked into their eyes and found not a trace of hate, remorse, or shame. I found pity — pity for mankind, for those who survive. As if to say, "If that is your world, keep it. We do not want it." That is why they did not resist.

December 6, 1971 (15)

JUDAISM

Judaism is not only true; it is also beautiful. The tale of Judaism is its beauty. And when I say beauty, I am aware of the fact that it may cover a lot of territory, even tragedy. I accept it.

November 15, 1968 (73)

This is the substance of Judaism — to remain human in a world that is inhuman.

March 28, 1969 (43)

Because the waiting is long and the reasons for despair are so apparent, waiting cannot be a waiting in and with and for despair, but a waiting turned into celebration, into joy, with song and dream. It must become a celebration itself. And the tale of the celebration is ours.

February 28, 1971 (78)

Hasidism was the most poetic adventure in Jewish history, an adventure based upon beauty, the aesthetic dimension of Judaism.

February 25, 1972 (4)

You cannot be impatient. You must learn to accept responsibility for them all — those Jews you love and those you do not love — simply because, like it or not, they are a part of you, and you are part of them.

March 12, 1972 (47)

The waiting for the Messiah, of course, is one of the cardinal elements of our faith and of our condition. We believe the Messiah has not come yet. And we believe that one day he will come. Who is he? What is he? These are questions for our sages to answer. But I believe that a Jew is he who waits.

April 24, 1973 (49)

Why did the Jews survive when so many ancient peoples perished? The will to survive is tied into a will to bear testimony. The only reason for surviving a concentration camp was the will to break silence.

Do you suppose that this may be why the Jews brought history to the world?

November 7, 1973 (40)

My version of madness is not clinical madness. It is spiritual madness, and it brings redemption rather than negation.

November 7, 1973 (40)

[301]

We Jews are madmen who shout "Do not forget!" We must go on shouting because a tradition of 3,500 years cannot stop with us.

December 21, 1973 (5)

The Jew is linked to whatever happens today, to whatever happened yesterday. You cannot understand humanity if you ignore him.

June 11, 1974 (12)

If you remove the Jew today from his past, if you remove him from his people and place him in the present alone, he cannot survive. He cannot survive either as a Jew or as a human being. A Jew without the past is worse than a man without a future. It is the past that is his treasure. It is the past that is his inspiration. If I have courage to go on living — and today you need the courage to go on living — it is because I remember all the generations that preceded me, or I try to. Otherwise life is not worth living. The name of the secret is memory.

October 21, 1975 (67)

Isaac is almost a contemporary, a companion. Isaac is my friend. Isaac is tragic. The tragic condition of man is in Isaac.

October 21, 1975 (67)

Our enemies in the United Nations have accused the Jewish people of racism. I think I know why. It is not really an attempt to destroy our present. It is an attempt to destroy our past. Maybe they are even helped by some Jews who are not really Jewish. But somehow they instinctively realize that the strength of the Jewish people lies in our memory. And they try to distort, to twist our memory. How better to deprive us of its strength than by turning that memory into a source of shame for us? What is the worst word for a Jew? It is "racism" — because we have been its victims. So what do they say? They say we are racists. I know that they say, "We have nothing against Jews, only against Zionists." Well, Zionists happen to be Jewish too. But that is not really the point. The point is that they want to split us. It is not a new strategy.

November 23, 1975 (64)

I see the pride and fervor that Americans can generate because America is 200 years old. But for God's sake, we are 3,500 years old. Every Abraham here is linked to a man named Abraham who was born 3,500 years ago, and every Moses to another Moses.

I wonder why some of us do not have that quasi-religious and historic fervor that every man and woman of our people should have in the deepest level of their being: that we are not alone in this world and that centuries of Jews stand behind us, around us, in us.

March 17, 1976 (38)

It is eerie. Pharaoh and Stalin used the same arguments and were obsessed by the same paranoia when it came to Jews.

March 17, 1976 (38)

What can you tell a Jew who says, "I do not want my son to suffer any more"? The issue arose mainly in Russia. Communism held an appeal for many Jews in the beginning. What is communism if not messianism without God? It was beautiful. It offered all the prophetic ideas: justice, equality, truth. Why were Jews taken by it? They said, "We must stop suffering, and since we cannot stop it as Jews, we shall stop it as Communists. We shall change history." Except it does not work. When you want to do things without God, it does not work — not even messianism. Communism degenerated. It was degraded, and it became a movement of murder and deceit. But what can you tell such a father? Of course, you can tell him, "You may try. You won't succeed. Maybe *you* want your son to forget his Jewishness, but other people will remind him of it." But I do not want to give the others that much credit and that much strength. I want my children to get their strength from within. And this is the thrust of all the words we try to use.

March 30, 1976 (72)

Let's not allow them to change us. If we remain as we are, they will have to change.

October 14, 1976 (37)

I want the world to be redeemed. The Jew in me seeks redemption, not chastisement — redemption for the whole world, redemption for mankind, and redemption in history.

March 20, 1977 (52)

I think the Jewish tradition is the only one that gives man a second chance. Another tradition believes in being born again. Well, we do not go that far. But we give and accept a second chance. Whatever we do we can do again.

The Messiah will come, we are told, on *Tishah b'Av*, on the ninth day of Av, the day on which we commemorate the destruction of the Temple. Thus the greatest tragedy of our history somehow already contains the beginning of a new era, the Messianic Era. I love the poetic prediction. Among the ten things God created before Creation is not the Messiah, but the name of the Messiah. What this really means is that for two, three, four thousand years a name has been waiting for the person. A name is waiting for the Messiah. And when they meet, we shall all be helped and redeemed.

March 20, 1977 (52)

People who are indifferent, people who do not care, people who are not aware are afraid of paradoxes because they do not see them. A Hasid can assume the paradoxes of life. A Hasid has to be aware. He has to be sensitive. Someone who is not sensitive is not human and cannot be a Hasid.

December, 1977 (71)

We all want to go to Israel. We want to go back to the source because only at the source can we find the truth, motivation, and dreams that make the human being in us possess enough strength to say, "This is beautiful but this is ugly; this is false, but this is truth; this is sad, but this is not; this is life, this is anti-life." The very fact that we do it, say it, sing it, and cherish it means that we are on the side of life and, hopefully, beauty!

January 20 - February 2, 1978 (8)

What are we doing here? If we are a people like all other peoples, with no special meaning attached to our survival, no special mission, then why go on?

January 20 - February 2, 1978 (8)

In our literature we have the expression *Netzah Yisrael*, the eternity of Israel. I never doubted it. Even during the era of night, when I doubted everything else, when I doubted the eternity of man and the eternity of the Eternal, the eternity of the Jewish people somehow was beyond any doubt.

April 16, 1978 (1)

Have we gone through so much, have we survived 3,500 years simply to enter normalcy? I don't believe it. The Jews have represented a moment of turmoil in history, a moment of conscience in the life of nations. We are a Biblical people with a Biblical memory. There is something special and specific for us.

Spring, 1978 (6)

The Jewish people are part of history and, in a way, we transcend history. We are the eternal defiance of logic because we should not be alive. No other people has had so many massacres throughout history.

June 23, 1978 (31)

A good definition of a Jew is he who is both teacher and student — teacher to those who have to be taught, and student at the feet of those who have something to give. I prefer to be a student. In our tradition, when we speak of a "sage," we do not call him a *hakham*. We call him *talmid hakham* — that is, a student of the sage. Thus, one always chooses for himself someone from whom he can learn.

October 28, 1979 (70)

We always try to remember who gave us the message: the God of Israel, the God of history, the God of mankind, the God of Creation. I also believe that the message was entrusted to us by all those whom we have left behind or who left us behind, all the six million Jews who somehow were prevented from living in a guilty world.

October 30, 1979 (77)

Hasidism means to go from place to place, to find a spark here and there and collect all the sparks and offer them to other Jews in gratitude.

November 9, 1979 (96)

The Hasidim take a simple story and endow it with secrets. A simple event is endowed with meaning. Nothing is as simple as you think it is.

November 9, 1979 (96)

What makes a Hasid? A Hasid does everything a good Jew does but with one difference — passion.

November 9, 1979 (96)

Jean-Paul Sartre, a great philosopher and a great humanist, said that man is a useless passion. I do not believe so — not in my tradition. In the Jewish tradition, man's life and fate are never useless. We believe that whatever happens in the world has an effect on the entire world. We believe that the death of one child, Jewish or not Jewish, leaves a scar not only on my memory or yours but on the memory of God, on Creation.

May 31, 1981 (83)

The emphasis in every one of our laws is on man's obligation, on our privilege, on our role in Creation. We say it in the *Kiddush* on Friday evening: God created, but the doing is our doing. *How* you do it is for you to decide.

October 25, 1981 (51)

A Jew is someone who studies the Torah and accepts the Law. How much you accept is very personal. I am not God's policeman.

October 25, 1981 (51)

JEWISH IDENTITY

What is lacking in modern literature by or about Jews is any intensity or even awareness of two criteria — the Holocaust and the creation of the State of Israel. Most Jewish writers lack a deep understanding of either phenomenon as factors in their existence as Jews. Their books cannot be called "Jewish."

March 15, 1966 (87)

To be a Jew, I believe, is to tell the world, to tell history, and to tell God that we are here.

November 15, 1968 (73)

As a child I was much too pious, much too fanatic, obsessed with my own way of viewing Judaism. I did not even know there was anything else but a Hasidic *shtibel*. We had one Reform congregation in Sighet, and I heard about it, but I never went there. Now in retrospect I regret it. I believe all Jews are alike. No matter what denomination they belong to, we all share in our history. To be a Jew is to take upon oneself the fate and the history of the whole Jewish people.

November 15, 1968 (73)

What does it mean to be a Jew? In Hebrew a Jew means *Ivri*. *Ivri*, "Hebrew," comes from the root *ever*, "from the other side." It also comes from the word *avar*, "past." And the next metamorphosis of the word is *ha'avarah*, "transmission." A Jew, an *Ivri*, a Hebrew, is the one who transmits the past to the future. A Jew, I believe, is someone who transmits his own experience to his children or to his friends and, sometimes, to his readers. But transmit he must. Transmit what? And how? I believe that transmission must be total. It must be almost on the level of existence. One transmits one's doubts, one's anguish, one's joy, one's hopes, one's despair, one's nostalgia for the past and hope for the future.

November 15, 1968 (73)

The Jewish Jew — there are also some non-Jewish Jews — cannot live outside the community. He can do all kinds of things alone, but in order to attain his Jewishness he needs the community. "Do not remove yourself from the community" is a cardinal principle. In other religions one must cease to exist as an individual

[306]

before creating his link with the community. In Judaism it is just the opposite. It is only when an individual finds his place and his role and his identity within the community that his identity becomes clearly defined.

November 13, 1971 (81)

I am disturbed by Jews who are indifferent to themselves, indifferent to their past. Our enemy today is within.

June 20, 1973 (28)

To be a Jew without a past is to be less than a Jew. A Jew must accept his past and take it into his future. If we have not learned this, we have not learned anything. If we do not give this sense of history to our children, all we are doing is a comedy.

December 2, 1973 (3)

Too many people talk about the Holocaust. To find the authentic voice I must give the more complete experience of being a Jew. It is not really about suffering. It is about defiance of suffering.

March 5, 1976 (44)

We stood at Sinai together — after having left Egypt together. We are bound by this belief not only to God but to each other as well. We are together now — because we were together then. Thus, Jews never meet for the first time — they meet again. And when they do, something happens to them, both collectively and personally: their very thoughts and emotions are affected.

May 19, 1977 (90)

Do not be a part of other peoples' dreams — but of our own — or our dreams can become nightmares.

December 30, 1977 (35)

I believe the mission of our people is to be the question mark in history.

June 23, 1978 (31)

We have not chosen suffering — it has always been imposed upon us. I believe being a Jew has nothing to do with suffering. If I believed it did, my problems would be much deeper. You can be, ideally, a Jew outside suffering — but practically a Jew is a Jew, and suffers.

June 23, 1978 (31)

Is there a Jewish future in the Diaspora? Yes. Wherever Jews remain Jewish. But I do not restrict their Jewishness. The way a Jew expresses his Jewishness is up to him. I do not deny Reform or any others.

June 23, 1978 (31)

THE UNIVERSALITY
OF THE JEW

Whatever we do for ourselves, we do also for the world. Whatever we do for Israel, we do also for the other peoples. Whatever we do for other racial or ethnic groups, we also do for Jews.

May 11, 1972 (85)

I believe that today no one is more universal than the Jew who is Jewish.

May 11, 1972 (85)

GOD

In one of the many concentration camps, a Jew spoke to God, saying, "Perhaps I am guilty, perhaps we all are, and all deserve punishment. But what are *You* guilty of in meting out to us this terrible punishment?"

1968 (58)

Had Hitler stayed in Poland and exterminated its Jews, without invading Belgium and France, would the free powers have waged war against the Third Reich? In this limited respect, Hitler's intuition did not mislead him. As far as Jews were concerned, his hands were untied.

October 16, 1971 (93)

What man did to man at Auschwitz could not have been done outside of God; in some way He too was at work — was He questioning man? Was He showing His face? What a face! In a sense, at Auschwitz God was afraid — afraid of Himself.

October 30, 1971 (18)

The *Shemoneh Esreh* in the *Amidah* that we say every day is very beautiful, especially if you sing it according to the Wizsnitzer *niggun*. In it we say, "We shall never be ashamed and humiliated because we have faith in You." Once after a lecture in which I spoke about prayer before an audience of religious Jews, a Hasidic Jew came up to me and he said, "I am a Hasid. I am very religious. And I say *Shemoneh Esreh* three times a day. But do you know what I do? I add one little word. I say, 'We shall never be ashamed *that* we have faith in You.' It means that we should never be humiliated for having been confident in You, for having kept our faith in You." And this is the heart of the matter in Judaism. It is the story of our story, of our grandeur, our dream, and our song.

November 13, 1971 (81)

A new attempt must be made to define man's relation to God and man's relation to himself. But I would have man put the accent on his relation to other men; in doing so he would change his relation to God. And a change in our relations to man would involve all our other relationships as well.

April 11, 1975 (74)

I am possessed by a *dybbuk* because of the children. I cannot forgive and never will. I will not forgive mankind, nor will I forgive God. I cannot forgive Him.

October 21, 1975 (67)

I tell students, "If you are angry with God, I respect you. If you love God, I respect you. Indifference I do not respect."

October 3, 1976 (32)

My being Jewish is to me more important than my thinking about God. God can take care of himself.

May 9, 1977 (33)

When the camps were finally liberated, we had not eaten in six days. . . . We had had almost nothing before that, but nothing at all for six days. . . .

Do you know what the Jews did? Before they even ate anything, their first act, instinctively, was to form *minyanim* and say *Kaddish* for the dead.

I would say this to anybody, I would say it in public, I would say this in front of the *Sefer Torah* itself: God did not deserve that *Kaddish*.

December, 1978 (27)

Of course, I go on quarreling with God. If I were to tell you that I believe in God the way I believed when I was a child, I would lie to you. If I would tell you I do not believe at all, I would lie, too. I am still searching for a possibility, for an answer.

December 31, 1978 (34)

In our tradition we may say no to the Messiah although he is the longing of our longing, the dream of our dreams, the rhythm of our heartbeat, the tone of our poem. We may say no to God himself, but always on behalf of His Creation and always from within and not from without.

October 30, 1979 (77)

THE HOLOCAUST

We can talk today of the extermination of millions by H-bombs because the world allowed the extermination of millions by Hitler. Until we ask why the world let Hitler do it, and until we find out why men can act the way they do, everything is in doubt: God, man, morality, life.

October 2, 1961 (48)

What is there for Jews born in the twentieth century to be ashamed of? This century has taught us the very opposite: man failed — the Jew did not; man betrayed — the Jew did not. What was the Holocaust if not the story of man betraying the Jew?

November 14, 1970 (55)

Six million Jews may have died in vain. We have somehow seen the unleashing of a madness in the Nazi Holocaust that is not yet done. We have had Hiroshima, Biafra, and now East Pakistan, and the world is still silent. We seem to be saying, "It was possible then — why not go on?"

October 30, 1971 (18)

If world Jewry had reacted then as it is now reacting to the Soviet situation, there would have been no Holocaust.

October 29, 1972 (20)

What went on *there* was something on the level of history, something on the level of theology, something on the highest level. The Germans wanted not only to kill Jews: they wanted to kill the Jewish past, and they wanted to destroy the Jewish God. The Germans wanted to be god to the Jews, replacing God.

April 24, 1974 (79)

This event because of its magnitude can either crush us or save us. If we forget it, it will crush us. If we remember it, I think it can protect us. That is why in all my books I stress certain themes: the theme of madness — because it was an era of madness; the theme of silence — because maybe only silence can transmit some fragment of the fire each of us took with him; and the theme of laughter. Maybe the whole thing was a farce, a theological farce. Maybe someone is laughing. It is

[311]

not even a tragedy because it is more than a tragedy. It is a huge comedy, a divine comedy.

April 24, 1974 (79)

The Holocaust was the greatest event in my life, and I think the greatest event in the life of my people, and I think the greatest event in the life of mankind. I believe that that event cannot be compared to any other, should not be compared to any other, and should not be invoked in vain. It has a special status. It is a mystery whose parallel may only be the one of Sinai when something was revealed to mankind. Mankind did — or did not — listen. Apparently it did not. And now came the anti-Sinai. The antinomian law prevailed.

February 18, 1975 (68)

What has been written about the Holocaust and the research that has been done on it only covers the surface. Only those who were there will ever know the real story. All the rest is commentary.

March 17, 1976 (38)

One generation ago what happened in Europe showed the abyss between the Jewish people and others. It was a total breakdown. The effect of the Holocaust on the world is serious, and it will be lasting.

March 30, 1976 (72)

Our enemies want to destroy our link to the Holocaust, knowing that somehow, paradoxically, the event that could have destroyed us maintained us alive. That event now constitutes our strength. But that strength is being eroded. The first to attempt to weaken it were not the Arabs. Their masters were the Russians and the other Communist nations when they began systematically to deny any Jewish role in the Holocaust, when they refused to recognize the Jews as victims of Auschwitz, when they claimed that the Jews died as Poles, as Frenchmen, as Ukrainians — but not as Jews. At a commemoration in Auschwitz for the liberation of the camp the Polish government refused to allow the Jewish delegation to say *Kaddish*. Why? It was not simple anti-Semitism. It was a way to deprive us of that memory.

Forty years ago in Russia *Pravda* wrote that Moshe Dayan was like Adolf Eichmann. Why did they say it? They did not want to increase Eichmann's guilt but, on the contrary, to decrease it. If such comparisons can be made, if such distortions can be articulated, and if they are repeated often enough, you know what is happening.

March 30, 1976 (72)

I do not understand how the world can be so indifferent to its own fate. But, then, it was indifferent to ours.

October 3, 1976 (32)

What can be done? Teach I say. Teach and teach again. We need more books and more teaching. We must bring back with dignity the awareness of those events.

We as Jews always have believed that words carry some weight. We take words seriously. Words have become a vehicle for our survival. It makes sense that I want to study, to communicate with my children so they will know so much about life — and death.

October 14, 1976 (37)

The Holocaust makes no sense to me at all — on any level. I do not accept any explanation of the Holocaust in messianic terms. It would be blasphemy. The only response afterwards would have been the coming of the Messiah, but nothing else. If the Messiah had come in 1945, I would have said, "Well, OK. I am grateful" — not to forgive him, but somehow to make up. But nothing less. I do not accept any religious answer. I do not have any answer. Maybe some people do. To me it is still a question, an awesome question.

November 7, 1977 (54)

I try not to make analogies not only because I see the Holocaust as a unique event but because I believe every suffering should be treated as a unique suffering, if it is a collective suffering. By making comparisons we diminish both. So I never make any analogies. The only analogy which perhaps can be made, and I am not making it, is the Etruscan extermination. The entire Etruscan civilization was simply wiped out one day, and nobody knows why. The last child, the language, everything was wiped out. And even there I prefer to study the Etruscans with great sympathy, with great love, as a sweet, generous, collective tragedy, alone. It does not need to be compared to have its greatness.

November 7, 1977 (54)

No one in the whole world cared about the Jewish underground. No one in London, Washington, or Moscow. Not even a message of encouragement was sent. It is clear that no one behaved honorably. The Jews were betrayed by the whole world, yet they went on fighting for that world.

May 5, 1978 (11)

If today we do not have leadership, it is because our leaders were killed when they were ten. If today we do not have moralists, it is because they were murdered when they were six. Imagine them running, aware of the flames. Imagine, but do not look. What they have seen God himself has not seen.

May 5, 1978 (11)

We forget the magnitude of the event. We are not speaking of one thing; we speak of six million times one. We cannot make comparisons; we cannot make theories.

December, 1978 (27)

Why not forget the past? Simply because we can't and still call ourselves human beings. We do not have this Commission simply to remember but to warn. Last time it was the killing of the Jews, then the attempt to annihilate humanity itself. Between the two came the sin of indifference. Today when we hear the word "holocaust" it is preceded by the word "nuclear." If there is to be no new holocaust, first we have to look backward and learn. We hope this mission is a beginning. For if we forget, the next time indifference will no longer be a sin. It will be a judgment.

August 20, 1979 (24)

Do not let your eyes deceive you. No sun ever shines here. Those who perished at Birkenau have not even a cemetery. We are their cemetery.

August 20, 1979 (24)

People will not become anti-Semites today if we invoke the Holocaust in the right way, because automatically an anti-Semite today knows, or should know, that he himself waits in the same line with Himmler and Eichmann. There is no more salon anti-Semitism. Anti-Semitism ends in Auschwitz, and whoever claims he is ready to be an anti-Semite should be ready to accept the view that he is for Auschwitz.

October 28, 1979 (70)

You cannot compare the Holocaust to the massacre of the Armenians by the Turks, to the destruction of the American Indians, or to anything else in history. The event is unique.

We are not all survivors of the Holocaust. If you say that everyone suffered, it means nobody suffered. There were only six million victims of the Holocaust.

A lot of other people died, but they were victims of World War II, not of the Holocaust.

November 9, 1979 (96)

How can a non-Jew who never experienced the suffering of the Jewish victims teach about the Holocaust? The Holocaust is a sacred subject, but sacredness comes from within, not without. One does not need to experience an event to feel its sacredness.

November 9, 1979 (96)

ISRAEL

Israel is not the answer to the Holocaust.

It has always been our destiny to be a question confronting mankind. Israel puzzles the world as a question, not as an answer.

Israel has not solved the problems of the Jews. She is taking responsibility in historic dimensions. If Israel, God forbid, should not survive, this "experiment" will be cursed and damned for dissolving so many Jewish communities throughout the world. So Israel must be a success!

March 28, 1969 (43)

Each side — Arab and Israeli — must respect the other. That is the key word: respect.

November 7, 1973 (40)

Do not ask me, a traumatized Jew, to be pro-Palestinian. I totally identify with Israel and cannot go along with leftist intellectuals who reject it. Perhaps another generation will be free enough to criticize Israel; I cannot.

April 9, 1980 (9)

The United Nations has become a joke, a joke which we should be ashamed of supporting.

Of course we are involved with everything that happens to Israel. Israel *is* a hope. Israel *does* represent something to our people and to mankind — in spite of everything that was done to it. I still believe that in spite of the pressure, in spite of the threats it became the most humane new independent nation in our time. No other nation showed such humanity in times of war as Israel has. And yet, when anything happens, there they are in the United Nations sitting in judgment over Israel. But how dare they! It is difficult to contain one's anger. The representative of Uganda is judging Israel! The ambassador of Russia is judging Israel! An ancient nation of 3,500 years is being judged by dictators.

September 13, 1981 (59)

SOVIET JEWRY

We are not doing our duty as Jews. We are not doing enough for Russian Jews. We do not identify with them. A Jew has no right to make a distinction among the tales he tells — and he has no right to make any distinction between Jews.

We have established a priority system among Jews. We easily gather 100,000 to stand behind Israeli Jews, but we cannot get 10,000 to stand up for the Russian Jews.

I believe in Soviet Jewry, because I believe in man. To be a Jew is an act of faith — an act of generosity. Soviet Jewry is not dead. They will survive as Jews even though they are denied the privilege of living as Jews.

March 28, 1969 (43)

If I should be remembered — I would hope it would be as a messenger of the young Jews of the Soviet Union.

February 12, 1970 (41)

The letters of the Russian Jews to the world sound like historic documents of the fifteenth and sixteenth centuries. I am convinced that these letters will become part of our liturgy, as they already are part of our history. If we do not do our share toward making their revolution a success, we will be guilty in history.

If the Jews of Russia feel that we have abandoned them and have failed them, I am convinced that they will try to commit cultural suicide.

February 25, 1972 (4)

Epilogue

TO OUR CHILDREN

And it came to pass that the great Talmudic scholar Rabbi Shimon bar Yohai and his son Rabbi Eleazar opposed Roman occupation of Judea with such courage that they were sentenced to death. Rejecting martyrdom as an option, they hid in a cave for twelve years. When they emerged, they were shocked. The outside world had not changed. The same people were doing the same things they had done before. It was business as usual. Life went on with its games, temptations, illusions, dangers, and silly victories. Father and son could not believe their eyes. How was all that possible? Had they gone through ultimate trials and burning experiences only to leave no imprint on other people? In their anger, says the Talmud, "whatever they looked upon was reduced to ashes." And then a heavenly voice was heard: "Have you left your hiding place only to destroy my Creation? Go back to your cave." And back they went for another year. When they came out again, Rabbi Eleazar was still angry, but not his father. Comments the Talmud: "Whatever the young Rabbi Eleazar's eyes wounded, the old Rabbi Shimon's eyes healed."

I like this ancient legend for it illustrates the extraordinary challenges which you and we — your older brothers or parents — had to confront and still confront. When the war years were over — with the nightmare lifted in the mist of dawn — we too discovered the outside world with disbelief. It had not changed. History had not altered its course. Human beings were still inhuman, society still cruel, Jews still hated, others jailed, victimized. That your parents were not seized by an irrepressible anger, that they did not yield to impulses to commit violence — and reduce everything to ashes, at least in their minds — remains a source of astonishment to me. Had they set fire to the entire planet, it would not have surprised anyone.

Strange as it may sound, you are angrier than we were. And your anger is healthier than ours might have been. Like Rabbi Shimon bar Yohai, we tried to heal, maybe too soon. But we did so for your sake. Since we chose to have you, we sought to improve the world for you. That your response has been to receive the message and to pass it on has been a source of gratification to us. In other words: your anger — your right to let anger explode — has also been transformed into something else. You, too, have chosen to heal.

Menachem Rosensaft, you and your colleagues belong to a privileged genera-

---

Keynote Address, Plenary Session of the First International Conference of Children of Holocaust Survivors, New York, May 28, 1984. Menachem Z. Rosensaft, son of Hadassah and Josef Rosensaft, presided over the conference. See "Our Older Brother — Josef Rosensaft."

tion. It was you that the enemy sought to destroy. We were only the instruments. You were the enemy's obsession. In murdering living Jews, he wished to prevent you from being born. He knew how vulnerable we Jews are with regard to children. Our history begins with a Jewish child, Isaac, being threatened, but then saved. It continues with Jewish children being massacred by Pharaoh. Nebuchadnezzar and Titus, Haman and Hitler — all our enemies saw our children as the primary target.

For children mean more than innocence; they mean the power of innocence. Children mean more than life; they mean faith in life, justification of life. Therefore, nothing can move us more than Jewish children.

In a New York hospital for years there was a woman nobody knew, a survivor, who would work only in the maternity ward. She would go from room to room visiting the mothers and taking care of their infants. Once, though, someone followed her and watched her in a room with a newborn child. She picked up the child and whispered, but her whisper was heard from one corner of the world to another: "Look, my Jewish people, we have a new child, a new Jewish child." Every Jewish child is therefore more than a child. Every Jewish child is in a way a response to the death of a million Jewish children.

Therefore the children of survivors move me even more than the survivors themselves. They move me to the depth of my being — and beyond. This may hurt or offend you, but whenever I see one of you, I cannot help but see other children through you, beyond you, processions, endless processions of Jewish children walking silently, under distant skies, towards eerie encounters with death.

If every one of my novels contains a Jewish child, it is because I have been, and still am, haunted, literally, by Jewish children — Jewish children who were studying in *heder* or roaming the streets looking for bread and warmth, who were already dead and did not know it. And now they are dead, and the world refuses to know it.

Survivors constitute a category apart. So do you, their children. If your parents had problems with knowledge, you have had to face problems of the imagination. The link between them is inevitably tragic: when knowledge becomes imagination it is as damaging as when imagination assumes the authority of knowledge. God is your witness — and ours — that you tried to know, and I know that you did. You were inspired by compassion for your parents. You wished so much, and sometimes futilely, to alleviate their burden.

It was not easy. In the beginning, your parents could not find the necessary strength to reveal their wounds — not to you, especially not to you. You were too close to them. In many cases they preferred to remain silent with others only because they were afraid you might overhear them, understand them. One young man recently told me that for years he felt a kind of embarrassment, even shame, whenever he would see his father. I understand why. It was because of the suffering involved, the father's suffering. It is uncomfortable for a child to see his father suffer. A father does not wish to appear weak in the eyes of his children. A mother does not wish to show her daughter how humiliated or ugly she might have been in her misery. They feared your pain and perhaps even your judgment. Parents would like their children to feel proud of them and confident in their strength. That is why they could not talk to you and, when they did, why they felt pathetic, incoherent, helpless.

Day after day yours was an extraordinary encounter with your mother, with your father. You must remember all those years of anguish-ridden scrutiny, trying to decode a gesture, a sigh of your parents. You must remember all those days and nights when you feared inadvertently to hurt them with a word, a look, or when you were afraid they would suddenly speak too much and cry — or not speak at all, and cry inwardly.

And yet, you wanted to know them, to know all that had happened to them, not only during the war, but before. Who was your grandfather? Who was your father when he was different? What kind of friends did he have and what ties to whom? Did he love someone else before the war? Another woman, perhaps? Another child? Who was his wife? Did they have children? Who were they? What did they look like? What did your brother look like? Who was your sister? Had she lived, she would be older than you now. But she died. And now, to your father or mother she will forever remain your younger sister.

When other people want to learn about the Holocaust, they look for generalities. They want to learn how it happened, how much, the magnitude, the scope, figures, facts. What you want is something very specific. You want to study that event in its most human dimension. For you, the war has a face — the face of your father, the face of your mother, her eyes on *Shabbat* or after *Shabbat*. You cannot fail to ask yourself the questions; it would not be normal or natural not to ask them. And when you look deeper, your father or mother turns away. When they remember, they are afraid you too may remember.

When you see your father, do you see what he sees? When you see your mother, do you see what she tries to conceal? How do you make them understand that you do understand them? And yet, they know, they must know, that you wish to understand them. There is such a generosity in every one of you — I know it, we all know it — that we too are afraid to cry simply by smiling at you.

What we ask of you, therefore, is not easy. We ask you not to forget what we desperately wanted to remember. We ask you to do what we have tried to do — and more: to keep our tale alive — and sacred. Do not allow it to be trivialized. If we, for so many years, have tried to tell the tale, and we have knocked on every door to do so, your task is to be the guardians of that tale. Do not allow it to be cheapened or diluted. Whatever happened to the Jewish people happened to the Jewish people alone, but only beyond it to other people. Never allow the uniqueness of the Jewish tragedy to be forgotten or distorted. That is your responsibility, and if it happens, it will be your sin. Some people will try to forget or distort it. Do not let them succeed. Always remember that your parents suffered and your grandparents died only because they were Jewish. Just as we have fought forgetfulness, you will have to fight universalization, which dilutes the tragedy and thereby enables those who deny it altogether to erase it, or at least its Jewishness.

In taking it upon yourselves to be our heirs, not only our successors, you also ought to know the price you will pay for your commitment. Several years ago, after a lecture delivered by Menachem, I heard him accused of capitalizing on the Holocaust. Suddenly, I realized what is in store for all of you. One day you will be resented or criticized for your obsessive devotion to the subject. You will be criticized for talking of nothing else or of denying outsiders the right to take part in the debate. You will be accused of seeking to establish a monopoly over the event and even of exploiting it for your own personal or professional benefit. It will hurt you — and I am sorry for that. When you speak about the Holocaust, they will say, "What, again?" But if you do not speak about it, they will say, "Why don't you speak about the Holocaust?" What is the alternative for you or for us? Not to speak? Not to teach? Not to bear witness? Are we to let those who do not know speak and teach instead? Are we to let them vulgarize the event with their stupid, silly, cheap pictures on television?

Remember, my young friends, the responsibility of your parents was solely towards the dead; yours will be towards us. Do not let anyone discourage you in your noble endeavor — and I do believe no project is more noble than yours. It is selfless, compassionate, informative, educational, inspiring.

Endowed with your mission, remain with it, fulfill it. You will need encouragement and strength, and you will discover them among yourselves. Thus I find your being together here a holiday, a celebration. You need each other, and at last you have found one another. Your parents tried to reach out. So will you. Your task is to speak; the task of others is to learn. And if they refuse to learn, so much the worse for them. But do not allow them to pass judgment on you — nobody has that right.

You are very special to me. You represent not only the future, but also the reverberation of the past. The names we have given you belonged to our parents. They are all that has remained from our homes, our customs, our childhood years, our joys, all that has remained from a vanished universe. And that is why we utter them at times with a trembling voice; that is why we love you so.

I know: with these names we may have placed too much of a burden on your shoulders. I know: it may have been wrong to single you out, to deprive you of your childhood by associating you so closely with your dead grandparents. I know: you went from childhood straight to maturity, skipping adolescence. I know: you must have wondered, at times, why your parents chose to bring you into a world filled with dark flames and wounded memories.

Some of you may have suppressed your questions; some of you may have expressed them with anger. Certain cases fill me with an all-consuming sadness: One young man, a son of survivors from Hungary, took his typewriter, bound it to his chest, and went into the ocean. Another one, his age, jumped from a window. Another ordered his parents, "Leave me alone. Don't you see I am dead already?" and withdrew into total seclusion, whispering to himself and his mute tormentors.

But these were exceptions. The great majority of you remain healthy and generous, with a sense of humor, with a sense of literature and culture and humanity. That you are so well-adjusted seems almost abnormal. Logically, most of you should have ended up on the analyst's couch, if not elsewhere. The fact is that you have managed to rechannel your sadness, your anger, your inherited memories into such humanistic endeavors as medicine, law, social action, education, philanthropy. In other words, you are really the worthy children of your parents. They have shown what they can do with their suffering; you are showing what you can do with your observation of their suffering.

In deciding to get married, to have children, to build on ruins, your parents sought to teach history a lesson: that we are not to give up on life, not to give in to despair. And deep down you have felt the need to justify your parents' absurd and persistent faith in life, in faith itself, in history, in society, in humankind.

You ask yourselves, why did they do it? They should have known better. Where did they take the incredible courage and the strength to establish new homes, to get married in the DP camps? Where did they get the courage to continue when even after the war the world remained unforgivably indifferent?

I am convinced that it would have been natural and logical for your parents to have turned their backs on culture and history, to have opted for nihilism, and to have done what Rabbi Shimon bar Yohai and Rabbi Eleazar did: to reduce history to ashes or at least to give it a taste of ashes.

And yet, we have chosen you. And now we are making you responsible for a world you did not create, a world we have created for you with words, a world others destroyed against you and against us. And now you are being summoned to do something with pieces of words, with fragments of our vision, with remnants of our broken, dispersed memories.

We are always telling you that civilization betrayed itself by betraying us, that culture ended in moral bankruptcy, and yet we want you to improve both, not one at the expense of the other.

What have we learned in our adult lives? Let me tell you what I have learned. I have learned that human experiences, whatever their nature, must be shared. I have learned that suffering itself must be conceived as vehicle, not as prison. And I have learned that suffering does not confer privileges; it is what we do with suffering that matters. We will never invoke our suffering simply to create more suffering. Quite the opposite. We invoke it to limit suffering, to curtail it, to eliminate it.

When I was your age, or younger, I was tempted by silence, by madness, and by despair. Like many of my contemporaries I felt like abdicating my role and my place in Creation. I thought the night would never again be followed by day, but only by another night, and that we would therefore have to rewrite the Bible, for we would no longer be able to say "And there was evening and there was morning." We would have to say "and there was evening and there was evening and there was evening" forever. Society, we thought, will forever persecute Jews, will forever torment victims. Yet, we chose to persevere, to use language in spite of language, to invoke reasons to hope in spite of its perils, to give life in spite of death.

How are we to explain to you this act of supreme affirmation? Is it that we refused to grant the enemy any lasting victory? Or that we chose not to let the world be inhabited by killers and bystanders alone?

I do not know the answer. All I know is that somehow an entire generation of Jews has risen from the ashes determined to build on and with ashes: to build new homes for the homeless, new families for the orphans, new words for the mute, new dreams for exiled wanderers.

What dangers do we face? There are some. Do not allow our story to become sentimental. But do not allow it to become rigid either. We shall pursue our intellectual inquiry with integrity. But our pursuit should not be sterile or a source of abstractionism. There is a danger that if we talk too much we shall tire everyone out. People will say, "Enough." If we talk too much, we ourselves may get tired. There is also a danger in survivors and their children meeting too often. And one day, some people will surely sneer, "You are so many. How come?" But whatever the dangers, we must continue. And we shall continue as long as we are here, which means as long as we are here together — and when you are here, even after we are gone.

And so, my friends, I cannot tell you how grateful I am to all of you for being here yesterday, today, and tomorrow. When I speak to others, surely you know that I mean you, all the time. You are my audience, because it is you who matter. Until now, whenever we would meet alone, we listened to each other, sad, proud, but we listened. We listened because we were alone. But now, at last, we can talk freely about our obsessions and share memories and hopes. We have become partners now, united by the same lofty and urgent goal. We are no longer afraid of unshed tears or of unspoken words. Until now you have been our students, perhaps even our disciples. At times, to some of us, you have been our children, troubled and exalted by our desire to see in you more than our children. We saw in you our parents. You became our parents. But now we are closer than ever before because we have spoken and because you have spoken to one another.

We look at one another with pride and gratitude and we think that whatever happened to Abraham and Isaac has happened to us too. The *Akedah*, after all, was not consummated. The testimony of our life and death will not vanish. Our memories will not die with us.

Do you know what we see in you, in all of you? We see in you our heirs, our allies, our younger brothers and sisters. But in a strange way to all of us all of you are our children.

Glossary

GLOSSARY

Aggadah	legends, stories, proverbs, etc., in the Talmud and Midrash that explain the Torah.
Aharit Hayamim	End of Days.
Ahavat Hashem	the love of God by man.
Ahavat Yisrael	love of Israel; love of Jews for Jews.
Aher	the other — applied to one who becomes an apostate.
Akedah	the binding of Isaac for sacrifice to God.
Alef bet (Alef beis)	the Hebrew alphabet; specifically, the first two letters that imply all the rest.
Aliyah	immigration to Israel; also the honor of being called to the reading of the Torah in the synagogue.
Am ha'aretz	an unlearned one.
Amidah	the prayer recited standing up during every service; also called Shemoneh Esreh and Tefillah.
Am Yisrael	the Jewish people.
Am Yisrael Hai	the Jewish people lives; long live the Jewish people.
Ani Maamin	"I believe."
Anokhi	"I am."
Apikoros, (apikores)	unbeliever, heretic.
Apikorsut	heresy.
Ari Hakadosh	Isaac Luria (1534-1572), Kabbalist.
Asarah b'Tevet	tenth day of Tevet, a fast day commemorating the beginning of Nebuchadnezzar's siege of Jerusalem.
Atah bahartanu	"You have chosen us."
Avinu	our father.
Baal teshuvah	one who has returned to Judaism.
Ba'alei hatosafot	authors of the Tosafot commentaries on the Talmud.

[326]

Badhan	troubador, entertainer, jester at weddings.
Bar Mitzvah	a boy who at age thirteen is required to fulfill the commandments.
Barukh haba	"welcome."
Barukh Hashem	"Bless the Lord."
Batlan (pl. batlanim)	an idler, a loafer; unemployed, he is free to study and pray in the synagogue.
Bereshit	Genesis; the beginning.
Besht	acronym for the Baal Shem Tov, the Master of the Good Name, Israel ben Eliezer (1700-1760), the founder of Hasidism.
Bet Din	court of law; rabbinic tribunal.
Bet Din Shel Maalah	the Heavenly Tribunal.
Bet Hamidrash	house of study and prayer.
Bet Hamikdash (Beis Hamikdosh)	The Temple in Jerusalem.
Bet Hillel	school of Hillel.
Bet Shammai	school of Shammai.
Bimah	platform in the synagogue from which the Torah is read.
Bokher (pl. bokherim)	boy.
Brakhah	blessing.
Brit Milah	covenant of circumcision; the circumcision ceremony.
Brihah	name of organized underground rescue operation that brought Jewish survivors from Europe to Eretz Yisrael, 1944-48.
Chutzpah	gall, impudence.
Daven	to pray.
Dayyan	judge of the rabbinic tribunal.
Dayyenu	"It would have been enough."
Din	a law, judgment, legal decision.
Drashah	sermon; a commentary, an exposition, an explication.
Dybbuk	a condemned soul that takes possession of a living person and acts or speaks through him.
Eretz Yisrael	the Land of Israel.
Erev	"on the eve of."
ETZEL	the Irgun Tzeva'i Le'ummi: National Military Organization, underground Jewish organization during British Mandate of Palestine.

Farbrengen	a Hasidic gathering, especially of Lubavitcher Hasidim.
Gadna	Youth Corps in Israel.
Galut	Exile, Diaspora.
Gaon (pl. geonim)	head of academy in post-Talmudic period, especially in Babylonia. Also means genius.
Gemara	part of the Talmud explaining the law as presented in the Mishnah.
Gerush Sepharad	expulsion of the Jews from Spain (1492).
Geulah	redemption.
Golah	See Galut.
Habad	acronym for Hokhmah, Binah, Da'at: wisdom, understanding, knowledge; the name of the Hasidic movement founded by Shneur Zalman of Lyady (1745-1813) and headed in the US by the Lubavitcher Rebbe.
Habayit	the Temple.
Haftarah	selected readings from the Prophets read on the Sabbath and on holidays after the reading from the Pentateuch in the synagogue services.
Haggadah	text recited at the Seder on Passover.
Hakafah (pl. hakafot, hakofes)	circling of the congregation with the scrolls of the law on Simhat Torah.
Halakhah	Jewish law.
Halilah	"God forbid."
Hallel	Psalms 113-118.
Hametz	food and dishes unfit for use on Passover.
Hanukkah	eight-day holiday commemorating defeat of Syrians by the Maccabees (165 B.C.E.) and rededication of the Temple in Jerusalem.
Hashem	the Name (God).
Hasidei Ashkenaz	medieval pietist movement among the Jews of Germany.
Hasidei umot ha'olam	the pious ones of the world.
Hasidut	Hasidism, or the study of Hasidism.
Haskalah	Enlightenment movement (1770s–1880s) promoting the secularization of Jewish life.
"Hatikvah"	"The Hope," national anthem of Israel.
"Hava Nagilah"	"Let us rejoice."
Havdalah	ceremony and blessing concluding the Sabbath and festivals to mark the separation of the sacred from the profane.

Hazal	"our scholars of blessed memory."
Hazer	pig.
Hazzan	cantor.
Heder	Hebrew elementary school; taught children Jewish religious observance.
Heder yinglakh	heder boys.
Hekhsher	rabbinic approval or permission.
Herem	excommunication from the Jewish community.
Heshbon hanefesh	moral stock-taking, self-examination, soul-searching.
Hesped	eulogy.
Hevrah kaddisha	burial society.
Hiddush (pl. hiddushim)	innovation; a new explication of a Talmudic text.
Hillul Hashem	desecration of God's name; blasphemy.
Hitlahavut	enthusiasm, fervor.
Hokhmah	wisdom.
Humash	the Five Books of Moses; the Pentateuch.
Huppah	wedding canopy.
Hurban	see Khourban.
Hurban habayit	Destruction of the Temple.
Kabbalah	Jewish mystical literature, tradition, and thought.
Kabbalat Shabbat	"welcoming of the Sabbath"; the opening Friday night service; precedes the regular evening prayer.
Kaddish	the mourner's prayer; also a prayer recited upon completion of a lesson, a reading from the Bible, a religious discourse.
Kalah (kaleh)	bride.
Kapote	traditional long black coat worn by Eastern European Jews.
Kasher (kosher)	ritually permissible.
Kavvanah	complete devotion or spiritual concentration.
Kavyakhol	an expression for God.
Kedoshim	martyrs.
Kehillah	an organized Jewish community or congregation.
Keter (pl. ketarim)	crowns.
Kever avot	custom of visiting and praying at graves of parents and relatives.

Khourban	the Destruction.
Khourban Bet Hamikdash	Destruction of the Temple.
Kibbutz Galuyyot	the Ingathering of the Exiles.
Kiddush	prayer recited over a cup of wine or hallah to commemorate the Sabbath or a festival.
Kiddush Hashem	the sanctification of God's name; holy martyrdom; also the willingness to act so as to be an honor to Jewry.
Kinnah (pl. kinnot)	lamentation poetry.
Kippah	skullcap, worn by observant Jews.
Klal Yisrael	the whole community of Israel.
Klezmorim	musicians.
Knesset Hagedolah	the Great Assembly.
kofer be'ikor	one who denies God.
Kol Nidrei	prayer chanted on night of Yom Kippur.
Kotel Hamaaravi	the Western Wall.
Lamed-Vovnik	a Just Man, one of thirty-six in every generation upon whom the continued existence of the world depends.
Lehavdil	"not to compare."
Lehayyim	a toast meaning "to life."
LEHI	the Lohamei Herut Israel, Fighters for the Freedom of Israel, the most militant of the Jewish underground groups during the British Mandate; also called the Stern Group.
Maariv	evening prayer.
Maaseh Bereshit	the event of the Creation.
Maaseh Merkavah	the event of the Chariot; prophetic description of the chariot throne in Ezekiel.
Maftir	concluding verses of Sabbath reading from the Pentateuch; also term applied to the reader of these portions.
Maggid (pl. maggidim)	a wandering preacher.
Malakh Hamavet	Angel of Death.
Mashiah	Messiah.
Maskil (pl. maskilim)	adherent of Haskalah movement.
Mattan Torah	the giving of the Law at Sinai.
Matzah	unleavened bread, eaten during Passover.
Megillot genizot	sacred scrolls and other manuscripts hidden away in caves, burial sites, storerooms, etc., like those found in the Cairo Genizah.

Melamed (pl. melamdim)	teacher, usually in elementary school.
Melaveh Malkah	a meal begun at the conclusion of the Sabbath.
Melitz yosher	advocate, defender of the people.
Mensch	a decent human being.
Meshugas	craziness.
Midrash	commentaries, sermons, homilies, Biblical exegesis; consists of Halakhah and Aggadah; also a method of interpreting Scripture.
Mikveh	ritual bath.
Minhah	afternoon prayer service.
Minyan	minimum of ten adult males necessary for a communal prayer service.
Mishegoyim	crazy ones, lunatics.
Mishnah	earliest compilation and codification of Jewish law.
Mitnaged, Misnaged (pl. Mitnagdim, Misnagdim)	opponent of Hasidism.
Mitzvah	a religious commandment; a religious duty; a good deed.
Mohel	ritual circumciser.
Moshe Rabbenu	"our Master Moses."
Motzei Shabbat	the departure of the Sabbath.
Musaf	the added prayer service after the reading of the Torah on the Sabbath and on festivals.
Musar movement	founded by Rabbi Israel Lipkin (Salanter) in the late nineteenth century among Orthodox Jewish groups in Lithuania. It sought to educate the individual toward a strict ethical behavior in the spirit of Halakhah.
Musarnik	an adherent of the Musar movement.
Neilah	prayer concluding Yom Kippur (Day of Atonement) Service.
Neturei Karta	"Guardians of the City"; a small group of religious fanatics, anti-Zionist and anti-Israel.
Niggun (pl. niggunim)	melody.
Olam haba	the world to come.
Olim	immigrants to Israel.
Oneg Shabbat	Joy of the Sabbath; also the name taken by the one hundred historians directed by Emmanuel Ringelblum in the Warsaw Ghetto.
Payes	earlocks.

Pesah	Passover, commemorates the Exodus from Egypt; first of the three annual pilgrim festivals. See Shavuot, Sukkot.
Pikkuah nefesh	the duty to save a life suspends all commandments in the Torah.
Piyyutim	Hebrew liturgical poetry, prayers, litanies.
Posekim	rabbinic authorities and codifiers of Jewish law and practice.
Purim	festival commemorating Jewish victory over Haman as told in the Scroll of Esther.
Purim shpiel	Purim play.
Rabbanim (rabbonim)	rabbis.
Rabbenu	our teacher, our master.
Rabbosai	my masters.
Rebbe	Hasidic rabbi.
Ribono Shel Olam	Master of the Universe.
Rosh Hashanah	the Jewish New Year.
Rosh yeshivah	head of a Talmudic academy.
Ruah Hakodesh	the Holy Spirit.
Sandek	godfather.
Seder	ceremonial meal on the first two nights of Passover.
Sefer Torah	the manuscript scrolls of the Law for public reading in the synagogue.
Seforim (s'forim)	books.
Shabbat (Shabbes)	Sabbath.
Shabbat Hagadol	the Great Sabbath, immediately before Passover.
Shabbat Nahamu	Sabbath of Consolation; the Sabbath immediately following Tishah b'Av.
Shabbat Rosh Hodesh	first Sabbath of the Jewish month.
Shabbat Shirah	Sabbath of Song, when the song of the Israelites at the Red Sea is read.
Shabbat Shuvah	the Sabbath between Rosh Hashanah and Yom Kippur.
Shabbesdik	pertaining to the Sabbath.
Shalachmonos	gifts exchanged during Purim.
Shalosh Regalim	the three pilgrim festivals: Pesah, Shavuot, Sukkot; in ancient times the adult Jew made a pilgrimage to the Temple on these days.

Shalosh Seudot	third Sabbath meal, taking place in the afternoon.
Shammes	beadle.
Shavuot	Festival of Weeks; Pentecost; commemorates the receiving of the Torah at Mt. Sinai; second of the three pilgrim festivals.
She'ilah	question.
Sheino yodea lishol	"One who does not know to ask"; refers to the fourth son of the Hagaddah.
Shekhinah	the Divine Presence.
Shema Yisrael	"Hear, O Israel. The Lord is our God. The Lord is One"; the central principle of Judaism; variously translated: "Hear, O Israel. God is our God. God is One."
Shemoneh Esreh	see Amidah.
Shiur	a study lesson; a study session (of the Talmud).
Shivah	seven days of mourning following the burial of a close relative.
Shlihim	emissaries.
Shliteh	"May he have a long, good life"; usually follows reference to a living Hasidic rebbe or a prominent Torah scholar.
Shofar	ram's horn, sounded on the New Year and other occasions.
Shoihet (pl. shohtim)	ritual slaughterer.
Shokl	shaking, nodding, rocking motions made while praying.
Shpiel	play; a theatrical (see Purim).
Shpieler	player, actor.
Shtetl (pl. shtetlakh)	little Jewish town or village in Eastern Europe.
Shtibel	Hasidic synagogue, often only a small room.
Shtreimel	a black, fur-trimmed hat worn by the very Orthodox and by Hasidism.
Shul	synagogue.
Siddur	daily and Sabbath prayer book.
Sidrah	the weekly portion of the Torah, normally read on the Sabbath.
Simhat Torah	"Rejoicing of the Law"; the last day of the Sukkot festival; celebrates the end of the weekly Pentateuch readings in the synagogue and the beginning of the new yearly cycle.
Smikhah	rabbinical ordination.

Sukkah	booth, hut, tabernacle used for Sukkot.
Sukkot	the Festival of the Booths; Tabernacles; commemorates the huts in which the Children of Israel lived in the wilderness after the Exodus; last of the three pilgrim festivals.
Tafrit	menu.
Tallit (tallis, pl. tallesim)	ritual prayer shawl.
Talmid hakham (pl. talmidei hakhamim)	a rabbinic scholar, an expert on the Talmud.
Tannaim	sages; scholars and teachers of the Mishnaic period.
Taryag mitzvot	the 613 mitzvot of the Torah.
Tehiyyat hametim	Resurrection of the dead.
Tefillah (pl. tefillot)	prayers; see Amidah.
Tefillin	phylacteries.
Tehillim	Psalms.
Teshuvah	repentance, return.
Tikkun	restoration; reparation; restitution; reintegration.
Tishah b'Av	the ninth day of Av; commemorates the destruction of the Temples of Jerusalem.
Tishbi	Elijah the Prophet.
Tosefta	addition or supplement to the Mishnah and following its order.
Traif	ritually unclean.
Tu Bishvat	the day marking the festival of the New Year of Trees; Jewish Arbor Day.
Tzaddik (pl. tzaddikim)	a righteous man.
Tzedakah	righteousness; charity; justice.
Viddui	confession of sins; the last confession before death.
Yad Vashem	national research and documentation center in Israel, dedicated to the perpetuation of the memory of the martyrs and heroes of the Holocaust.
Yahrzeit	annual anniversary of death.
Yarmulka	skullcap, worn by observant Jews.
Yeshivah (pl. yeshivot)	Talmudic school of higher education.
Yeshivah bokher	Yeshivah student.
Yetzer hara	Evil Spirit.
Yidden	Jews.

Yiddelakh	Jews (diminutive).
Yinglakh	boys.
Yizkor	"May He remember"; first word of Ashkenazi prayer commemorating the dead.
Yom Hashoah	Day of Remembrance (commemorates victims of the Holocaust).
Yom Tov (yontif)	holiday, festival.
Zahal	Israel Defence Forces.
Z"l	"Of blessed memory."
Zekhut	privilege, merit.
Zemirot	songs sung during Shabbat meals.
Zohar	principal book of Kabbalah; the Book of Splendor.

Complete
Bibliography

CONTENTS

Bibliographies 1-13 and 16 are arranged by title. Bibliographies 14 and 15 are arranged by author. See "A Note to the Reader."

KEY TO SYMBOLS

A Adaptation from the original source.

A-I Adaptation of the original article interview into the question-and-answer format.

B Bibliography.

P Published version, unrevised.

R Revision of the original source; extensive structural and other changes, including those involved in A.

T Title supplied by the editor, where none previously existed.

NT New title supplied by the editor; replaces the original.

U Never before published; transcripts are not here considered published material.

* Programs produced on *The Eternal Light* series, presented by the National Broadcasting Co. Radio Network, prepared under the auspices of the Jewish Theological Seminary of America, written and narrated by Elie Wiesel.

B 1
LECTURES/ESSAYS

"The Adventure of Hasidism." Lecture, Congregation Shaarey Zedek, Southfield, Mich.,
29 Feb. 1972. (R,T,U)

"Answer to a Young Boy." Lecture, National Press Club, Washington, D.C., 11 April
1983. (R,T,U)

"Are We Worthy of the Story?" Lecture, Temple Beth Israel, Phoenix, Ariz., 24 April
1973. (R,T,U)

"The Burden on Jewish Youth." Lecture, Olin-Sang Institute, Oconomowoc, Wis., Summer 1966. (A,U)

"The Crisis of Hope." 1975 Leo Baeck Memorial Lecture, Westchester Reform Temple,
Scarsdale, N.Y., 4 Dec. 1975. (R,U)

"The Dream of a Moral Society." Fourth Annual Holocaust Lecture, Vanderbilt
University, Nashville, Tenn., 1 Dec. 1981. (R,T,U)

"The Endless Chain." Lecture, Temple Emanuel, Chicago, Ill., 5 Oct. 1975 (R,T,U)

"The Eternal Question of Suffering and Evil." Lecture, Dartmouth College, Hanover,
N.H., 7 Nov. 1977. (R,U)

"Exile and the Human Condition." Lecture, International Young Presidents Organization,
Madrid, Spain, April 1980. (A,NT,U)

"The Gates of the Holocaust." See B 16-G. (A,T)

"Hear, O Israel." See B 16-F. (A)

"The Holocaust as Literary Inspiration." See B 16-H. (R)

"The Holocaust: One Generation After." Lecture, University of Illinois, Circle Campus,
Chicago, Ill., 13 April 1978. (R,U)

"A Jew Today." Lecture, Niles Township Jewish Congregation, Skokie, Ill., 5 Dec. 1978.
(R,U)

"Knowing and Not Knowing: In the Footsteps of Shimon Dubnow." Lecture, Yale Law
School, New Haven, Conn. 15 Nov. 1982. (R,T,U)

"Myth and History." See B 16-K. (R)

"The New Anti-Semitism." Lecture, Glencoe, Ill., sponsored by Moriah Congregation,
Deerfield, Ill., 11 April 1981. (R,U)

"New Beginnings." Lecture, Westchester Reform Temple, Scarsdale, N.Y., 2 Dec. 1976.
(R,U)

"The Power of Separation." Lecture, Temple Beth Am, Los Angeles, Cal., Dec. 1977.
(R,T,U)

"The Question of God." Lecture, Olin-Sang Institute, Oconomowoc, Wis., Summer
1966. (A,U)

"Questions for *Shabbat*." Lecture, Temple Emanuel, Chicago, Ill., 10 Oct. 1969. (R,U)

"The Relevance of Hasidism Today" Lecture, Temple Beth Am, Los Angeles, Cal., Dec.
1977. (R,U)

"Return to the Past." Lecture, Temple Anshe Sholom, Olympia Fields, Ill., 28 Oct. 1979. (R,T,U)

"The Storyteller's Prayer." Lecture, Washington University, St. Louis, Mo., 18 Feb. 1970. (R,T,U)

"The Story Within." Lecture, B'nai B'rith Hillel Foundation, Toronto, Canada, 2 March 1977. (R,T,U)

"The Tale of Soviet Jewry." Lecture, Congregation Shaarey Zedek, Southfield, Mich., Feb. 1971. (R,T,U)

"There Must Be a Difference." Lecture, Temple Judea, Tarzana, Cal., 11 April 1975. (R,NT,U)

"The Tradition of *Dayyenu*." Lecture upon receiving Distinguished Service Award from National Federation of Jewish Men's Clubs, 8 May 1973. (A,T,U)

"The Trial of Man." Lecture, Loyola University, Chicago, Ill., sponsored by Moriah Congregation, Deerfield, Ill., 12 April 1980. (R,T,U)

"Where Is Hope?" Lecture, University of Oregon, 11 April 1975. (R,NT,U)

ADDRESSES/STATEMENTS

"Apostles for Humanity." Transcript, American Broadcasting Co. *Nightline*, ABC-TV Network, 19 June 1981, 5-6. (A,U)

"Art and Culture after the Holocaust." See B 16-A. (R)

"Between Hope and Fear." *City College Alumnus*, Oct. 1973, 6-8. Commencement address, City College of New York, 11 June 1973. (R)

"Between Protest and Belief." Statement, Temple Sholom, Chicago, Ill., 25 Oct. 1981. (R,U)

"Blessed Be the Madmen — and Their Friends." Address, American Friends of Haifa University, N.Y., 3 Oct. 1974. (A,T,U)

"The Call to Remember." Address, 38th Commemorative Memorial Observance for the Six Million Martyrs and the Heroic Fighters of the Warsaw Ghetto, Congregation Shaare Tikvah, Chicago, Ill., 12 April 1981. (A,T,U)

"Escape from Justice: Nazi War Criminals in America." Transcript, American Broadcasting Co. *News Closeup*, ABC-TV Network, 13 Jan. 1980, 50-51. (A,U)

"The Eternal Flame." Statement upon receiving the First International Spertus Award, Chicago, Ill., 7 Oct. 1976. (R,T,U)

"Facing the Present." Commencement address, Brandeis University, Waltham, Mass., 25 May 1980. (R,T,U)

Farewell Address at the Western Wall. World Gathering of Jewish Holocaust Survivors, Closing Ceremony at the Western Wall, Jerusalem, 18 June 1981. (U)

"The Fiery Shadow — Jewish Existence out of the Holocaust." See B 16-B. (R)

"The First Survivor." Statement, Niles Township Jewish Congregation, Skokie, Ill., 7 Dec. 1980. (A,T,U)

"Freedom of Conscience — A Jewish Commentary." See B 16-C. (A)

"If Only I Could Dance." Address, Brussels I: The First World Conference on Soviet Jewry, Brussels, Belgium, 23 Feb. 1971. (T,U)

"Israel Twenty Years Later." See B 16-I. (R)

"Jewish Sovereignty." Address, United Jewish Appeal, Washington, D.C., 15 May 1980. (A,T,U)

"The Jewish Tradition of Learning: A Personal View." See B 16-J. (A)

"Judaism, *Shabbat*, and Our Common Fate." Commencement address, Manhattanville College, Purchase, N.Y., 27 May 1972. (R,T,U)

"*Klal Yisrael*: The Community of All Israel." Statement, United Jewish Appeal *Campaign Supplement*, March 1977, 4-5. (NT)

"Knowledge and Morality." Commencement address, Fairfield University, Fairfield, Conn., 22 May 1983. (R,T,U)

"Lily Edelman." Eulogy delivered at funeral of Lily Edelman, who died 22 Jan. 1981. (T,U)

"Listen to the Wind." Statement made at Auschwitz, 1 Aug. 1979. (R,T,U)

"Living What We Are." Statement upon receiving American Liberties Medallion at 66th Annual Meeting of American Jewish Committee, N.Y., 4 May 1972. (A,T,U)

"The Massacre in Lebanon." Statement, *The New York Times*, 22 Sept. 1982, A 16. (NT)

"The Meaning of Munich." Address United Jewish Appeal, N.Y., 14 Dec. 1972. (R,T,U)

"Meyer Weisgal: Jewish Legend." Eulogy delivered at memorial service at Central Synagogue, N.Y., 17 Nov. 1977. Weisgal died 29 Sept. 1977, in Rehovot, Israel. (T,U)

"On Revolutions in Culture and the Arts." See B 16-L. (R)

"The Open Question." Statement, Temple Sholom, Chicago, Ill., 25 Oct. 1981. (R,T,U)

"Our Older Brother — Josef Rosensaft." Eulogy for Josef Rosensaft, who died 10 Sept. 1975. Translated from the Yiddish by Irving Abrahamson. (T,U)

"Pope John Paul II in Poland." Transcript, Columbia Broadcasting System News *Special Report*, CBS-TV Network, 7 June 1979, 6. (A,U)

"The Problem Is Knowledge." See: Cohn, Robert A. "The Novelist Whose Speeches Set Souls on Fire." *St. Louis Jewish Light*, 15 March 1978, 16. (A,T)

"Saving the Branches of the Tree." Statement upon receiving the Shazar Prize, Jerusalem, 5 May 1980. Translated from the Hebrew by David Weinstein. (R,T,U)

"The School and Survival." Address, Dropsie College, Philadelphia, Pa., 24 May 1983. (R,T,U)

"A Sense of Victory." Address, Brussels II: The Second World Conference on Soviet Jewry, Brussels, Belgium, 17 Feb. 1976. (R,T,U)

"Solidarity March." Statement, March for Soviet Jewry, N.Y., 1967. (T)

"This Is History." Statement, Niles Township Jewish Congregation, Skokie, Ill., 7 Dec. 1980. (A,T,U)

"The Three Times I Saw Jerusalem." Address, World Federation of Bergen-Belsen Associations, Jerusalem, 9 July 1970. (R,U)

"To Antek." Speech delivered at open-air assembly of visitors to the Kibbutz Lohamei Haghettaot during World Gathering of Jewish Holocaust Survivors, Israel, 16 June 1981. Translated from the Yiddish by Eli Pfefferkorn. (T,U)

"To Our Children." Keynote address, Plenary Session, First International Conference of Children of Holocaust Survivors, N.Y., 28 May 1984. (R,U)

"To the Danish Fighters for Freedom." Address, Tribute to the Danes through Scholarships in Israel, N.Y., 15 Oct. 1972. (A,U)

"Toward a Philosophy of Jewish Existence." See B 16-O. (R)

"The Tradition Remembered." Statement, the New School for Social Research, N.Y., 8 May 1977. (A,U)

"A Tribute." Statement introducing Prof. Saul Lieberman upon inauguration of Chair of Talmudic Studies in his honor at Bar-Ilan University, N.Y., 4 June 1980. (U)

B 3
PAMPHLETS

A. *And Thou Shalt Teach Your Children*. Baltimore: Baltimore Hebrew College, 1973. First Louis L. Kaplan Convocation Lecture, Baltimore Hebrew College, 23 Oct. 1973. (R,T)

B. *From Holocaust to Rebirth*. New York: Council of Jewish Federations and Welfare Funds, 1970. The Herbert R. Abeles Memorial Address, 39th General Assembly of the Council of Jewish Federations and Welfare Funds, Kansas City, Mo., 14 Nov. 1970. (R)

C. *Let Us Celebrate*. New York: United Jewish Appeal, April 1979. Address, UJA National Conference, 9 Dec. 1978. (R)

D. *Our Jewish Solitude*. New York: United Jewish Appeal, 1975. Address upon receiving First David Ben-Gurion Award from United Jewish Appeal, N.Y., 11 Dec. 1975. (A)

E. *Think Higher*. New York: United Jewish Appeal, 1977. Address, Fourth International Meeting of UJA, Kennedy Center, Washington, D.C., 29 Nov. 1977. (A)

F. *Two Images, One Destiny*. New York: United Jewish Appeal, 1974. Address, Jewish Agency Assembly, Jerusalem, June 1974. (R)

SHORT FORMS

"The Absence of Hate." See B 16-N, p. 272. (A,T)

"Action for Soviet Jewry." B 3-B, pp. 10-12. (A,T)

"An Act of Faith." *Tarbut*, 36 (Spring 1978): 17. Response on receiving the King Solomon Award, America-Israel Cultural Foundation, N.Y., 20 Nov. 1977. (A,NT)

"Appearance and Reality." Remarks, Congregation Am Shalom, Glencoe, Ill., 11 Nov. 1979. (A,T,U)

"A Body of Work." See: Weisman, John. "Storyteller Elie Wiesel Weaving His Spell at a Local Synagogue." *Detroit Free Press*, 12 March 1972, sec. B, p. 5. (A,T)

"Bringing the Messiah." See: Richards, David. "Elie Wiesel: Voice of the Holocaust . . . Weaving His Themes through a Looking Glass, Darkly." *Washington* (D.C.) *Star-News*, 7 May 1984, C 1, C 4. (A,T)

"The Burning Pillow." Lecture, Wooster, Ohio, 30 Oct. 1979. (A,T,U)

"Choosing to Speak." Transcript, *The Eternal Light*, Chapter 1388, 23 March 1980.* (R,NT,U)

"A Continuous Miracle." Transcript, *The Eternal Light*, Chapter 1349, 25 March 1979.* (A,T,U)

"Declaration of Brussels II." Declaration at Second World Conference on Soviet Jewry, Brussels, Belgium, 17 Feb. 1976. (U)

"Do Not Be Afraid, My Servant Jacob." Lecture, Congregation Shaarey Zedek, Southfield, Mich., Feb. 1971. (R,T,U)

"Dr. Alexander Paritzky." Message, Boston Rally for Soviet Jewry, 12 Dec. 1982. (T,U)

"Encounter with Mr. Rudenko." Remarks made during lectures at Loyola University, Chicago, Ill., 12 March 1980, and in Seattle, Wash., week of 13 Sept. 1981. (R,T,U)

"Eternal Beginning." Lecture, Congregation Shaarey Zedek, Southfield, Mich., 20 March 1977. (R,U)

"The Faces of War: *Yom Kippur*, 1973." Statement, Oct. 1973. (R,T,U)

"Facing the Questions." See: Wershba, Joseph. "An Author Asks Why the World Let Hitler Do It." *New York Post*, 2 Oct. 1961, 30. (A,T)

"Fathers and Sons." See: Larson, Roy. "Elie Wiesel Keeps the Songs of His Fathers Alive." *Chicago Sun-Times*, 20 June 1973, sec. 2, p. 2. (A,T)

"The First Dialogue." Lecture, Washington University, St. Louis, Mo., 1 Feb. 1978. (R,T,U)

"The Forger." Lecture, Niles Township Congregation, Skokie, Ill., 7 Dec. 1980. (A,T,U)

"For the Sake of Our Children." See B 16-P. (R,T)

"Friendship." See B 16-D.

"God Must Obey." See B 16-E, p. 6. (T)

"Golda Meir Remembered." Transcript, *The Eternal Light*, National Broadcasting Co. Television Network, 4 Oct. 1981. (A,U)

"A *Hanukkah* Story." *Jewish Daily Forward*, 10 Dec. 1969, 4. +

"The Haunted House." Transcript, *The Eternal Light*, Chapter 1039, 14 Feb. 1971.*
(A,T,U)

"The Holocaust and the Anguish of the Writer." City University of New York Graduate School Symposium on "The Holocaust Century: Implications and Anxieties," 22 March 1973. (R,U)

"How Does One Write?" Lecture, Temple Beth Israel, Phoenix, Ariz., 24 April 1972. (A,T,U)

"The Idea of Transmission." Lecture, Temple Israel, Los Angeles, Cal., 15 Nov. 1968. (A,T,U)

"Imagining Jewish History." See: Berkowitz, William. "Central Issues Are Explored in Wiesel Dialogue," *The Jewish Week-American Examiner*, week of 14 June 1981, 23. (A,T)

"The Impenetrable Shield." See: Savan, Jakki. "Elie Wiesel: He Tries to Defeat the Executioner with Words." *St. Louis Jewish Light*, 17 March 1976, 7. Remarks made during address, 75th Anniversary Celebration of Jewish Federation of St. Louis, 22 Feb. 1976. (A,T,U)

"Indifference Is the Enemy." See B 16-Q, p. 15. (A,T)

"In Search of Integrity." Lecture, Temple B'nai Abraham, Livingston, N.J., 17 March 1974. (R,T,U)

"The Interview." Lecture, 92nd Street YMHA, N.Y., 3 Nov. 1977. (A,T,U)

"It Ends with Others." Lecture, Congregation Shaarey Zedek, Southfield, Mich., 20 March 1977. (A,T,U)

"It Has Never Been Simple." Lecture, B'nai B'rith Hillel Foundation, Toronto, Canada, 2 March 1977. (R,T,U)

"Jeremiah's Lesson." Address, first workshop meeting to establish the U.S. Holocaust Memorial Council Museum, Washington, D.C., 22 Sept. 1982. (A,T,U)

"Kafka" Lecture, Wooster, Ohio, 30 Oct. 1979. (A,T,U)

"The Last *Maggid*." Address, United Jewish Appeal, N.Y., 14 Dec. 1972. (R,T,U)

"The Legacy." Written Testament of Survivors passed on to the Second Generation, World Gathering of Jewish Holocaust Survivors, Closing Ceremony at the Western Wall, Jerusalem, 18 June 1981. Translated from the Yiddish and the French by Menachem Z. Rosensaft. (U)

"Let Him Remember." See B 16-P. (R,T)

"Look Further." Lecture, Rochester, N.Y., 24 April 1974. (R,T,U)

"Mankind Is the Target." Lecture, 92nd Street YMHA, N.Y., 3 Nov. 1977. (A,T,U)

"A Message to the Free Wallenberg Committee." N.Y., 18 Jan. 1980. (U)

"A Moral Victory." Lecture, Washington University, St. Louis, Mo., 18 Feb. 1970. (A,T,U)

"Moshe the Water Carrier." See B 16-E, p. 7. (T)

"My First Teachers." Transcript, *The Eternal Light*, Chapter 1111, 1 April 1973.*
(A,T,U)

"My Friend Eliahu Amiqam." Remarks made during address "On the Alienation of Our Youth," United Synagogue Convention, Kiamesha Lake, N.Y., 15 Nov. 1971. (R,T,U)

"My Teacher." Remarks introducing Prof. Saul Lieberman, honored by Histadruth Ivrith

+ All entries marked with the + have been translated from the Yiddish by Eva Zeitlin Dobkin.

and *Hadoar Hebrew Weekly* for his fifty years of scholarship and research, N.Y., 13 Feb. 1977. (A,T,U)

"My Teachers after the War." Transcript, *The Eternal Light*, Chapter 1113, 15 April 1973.* (A,T,U)

"My Teacher's Desk." Address, Dropsie College, Philadelphia, Pa., 24 May 1983. (A,T,U)

"My Teachers during the Tempest." Transcript, *The Eternal Light*, Chapter 1112, 8 April 1973.* (A,T,U)

"The New Law." See B 16-P. (A,T)

"A *Niggun* for *Shabbat*." Address, 40th General Assembly of the Council of Jewish Federations and Welfare Funds, Pittsburgh, Pa, 13 Nov. 1971. (R,T,U)

"An Open Letter to Parents Everywhere." *The New York Times*, 20 May 1974, 14. Full page advertisement.

"An Open Letter to President Giscard d'Estaing of France." *The New York Times*, 20 Jan. 1977, 12. Full page advertisement.

"The Owner." See B 16-E, p. 5. (A,T)

"The Passionate Tradition." Lecture, 92nd Street YMHA, N.Y., 3 Nov. 1977. (R,T,U)

"The Plight of the Falashas." Letter, Rally for Ethiopian Jewry, Lincoln Synagogue, N.Y., 11 April 1982. Quoted in *Jewish Telegraphic Agency Daily News Bulletin*, 16 April 1982, 4.

"The Presence of God." See B 16-O. (A,T)

"The Price of Courage." Lecture, Congregation Kol Ami, Chicago, Ill., 22 Nov. 1973. (R,T,U)

"The Problem of Jerusalem." Address upon receiving the American Liberties Medallion at 66th Annual Meeting of the American Jewish Committee, N.Y., 4 May 1972. (A,T,U)

"The Promise." See B 16-E, pp. 5-6. (T)

"The Pure Fire." Presentation of the Remembrance Award of World Federation of Bergen-Belsen Associations to Uri Zvi Greenberg, Jerusalem, 3 July 1973. Translated from the Hebrew by David Weinstein. (R,T,U)

"The Questioners." See B 16-E, p. 10. (T)

"The Reporter." Lecture, 92nd Street YMHA, N.Y., 3 Nov. 1977. (A,T,U)

"A Response to a Letter from the Falashas." *Present Tense*, Summer 1979, 10.

"The Sermon at Hell's Gate." *Jewish Daily Forward*, 5 Oct. 1965, 4. +

"The Silence of Man and God." Lecture, Colloquium of Scholars, California Lutheran College, Thousand Oaks, Cal., 27 April 1977. (A,T,U)

"A Spark of Holiness." See B 16-E, p. 8. (T)

"The Story of a Story." See B 16-M.

"The Tale of Arab Jewry." Lecture, Congregation Shaarey Zedek, Southfield, Mich., Feb. 1971. (R,T,U)

"Teacher and Student." Kent State-Jackson State Memorial Lecture, Stanford University, Stanford, Cal., 30 April 1976. (A,T,U)

"Teachers and Friends." Transcript, *The Eternal Light*, Chapter 1114, 22 April 1973.* (R,T,U)

"A Teacher's Reward." See B 3-E, p. 4. (A,T)

"The Test of Evil." Lecture, Wooster, Ohio, 30 Oct. 1979. (A,T,U)

"Think Higher." See B 3-E, pp. 1-2. (A)

"A Time to Write." Lecture, Niles Township Jewish Congregation, Skokie, Ill., 5 Dec. 1978. (A,T,U)

"To a Jewish Friend in France." *The New York Times*, 16 Oct. 1980, B. 24. Full page advertisement.

"To Correct Injustice." Lecture, Congregation Kol Ami, Chicago, Ill., 22 Nov. 1973. (A,T,U)

"To Our Falasha Brothers and Sisters." *Release* (A Report from American Association for Ethiopian Jews), Summer 1984, 1. Letter dated 13 June 1984.

"To Tell the Story." Lecture, Seattle, Wash., 10 March 1977. (A,T,U)

"The Wall." See: Weisman, John. "Storyteller Elie Wiesel Weaving His Spell at a Local Synagogue." *Detroit Free Press*, 12 March 1972, sec. B, p. 5. (A,T)

"Within and Without." Lecture, Temple Beth Am, Los Angeles, Cal., Dec. 1977. (A,T,U)

"The World of Bernard Malamud." Presentation of Jewish Heritage Award to Bernard Malamud, B'nai B'rith Commission on Adult Jewish Education, N.Y., 20 Feb. 1977. (T,U)

"The Writer and His Obsessions." Lecture, Colloquium of Scholars, California Lutheran College, Thousand Oaks, Cal., 27 April 1977. (A,U)

NEWSPAPER ARTICLES

"And Jacob Still Dreams." *London Jewish Chronicle*, 24 Feb. 1978, 25. + +

"Because of You." *Jewish Daily Forward*, 11 May 1961, 4. + (NT)

"Cantor Riesel's Letter." *Jewish Daily Forward*, 27 Dec. 1967, 4. + (NT)

"The Courage of the Danes." *Jewish Daily Forward*, 29 Nov. 1961, 4. + (NT)

"The Day of Judgment." *Jewish Daily Forward*, 11 April 1961, 4. +

"A Day of Shame in Skokie." *Newsday*, 20 June 1978, 45.

"The Death Sentence." *Jewish Daily Forward*, 30 April 1962, 2. +

"Diaspora Jewry and Criticism of Israel." *London Jewish Chronicle*, 29 June 1979, 20. (NT)

"Does the Holocaust Lie beyond the Reach of Art?" *The New York Times*, 17 April 1983, sec. 2, pp. 1, 12.

"Eichmann's Insolence." *Jewish Daily Forward*, 3 May 1961, 4. + (NT)

"Eichmann's Son." *Jewish Daily Forward*, 30 March 1961, 4. +

"Encounter with Samuel Beckett." *Jewish Daily Forward*, 1969. Translated from the Yiddish by Irving Abrahamson.

"Forgotten at Belsen." *Jewish Daily Forward*, 17 Aug. 1970, 2. + (NT)

"German Justice." *Jewish Daily Forward*, 22 Dec. 1961, 4. +

"I Wrote This Play out of Despair." *The New York Times*, 14 March 1976, sec. 2, p. D 5.

"A Jew Defends Eichmann." *Jewish Daily Forward*, 27 Feb. 1961, 2. + (NT)

"Jewish Atheist: A Quarrel with God." *Baltimore Jewish Times*, 9 April 1965, 20-21.

"The 'Jewish State' at Belsen." *Jewish Daily Forward*, 13 Aug. 1965, 2. +

"A Journey Not Taken: 1977." *London Jewish Chronicle*, 6 Jan. 1978, 19. (NT)

"Mass Murderer in California." *Jewish Daily Forward*, 10 March 1958, 4. + (NT)

"The Memorial for Sighet." *Jewish Daily Forward*, 31 May 1963, 2. +

"Miami: Distant Echoes." *The New York Times*, Special Travel Section, 9 Oct. 1983, 50, 52.

"The Missionary Menace." *London Jewish Chronicle*, 8 Feb. 1980, 23. + + (R)

"New Victims." *Jewish Daily Forward*, 13 July 1961, 4. +

"No Punishment Befitting the Crime." *Jewish Daily Forward*, 4 June 1962, 4. + (N,T)

"People without Memories." *London Jewish Chronicle*, 24 Feb. 1984, 21. + +

"The Plot That Failed." *Jewish Daily Forward*, 28 July 1964, 2. +

"The Problem of the Russian Dropouts." *London Jewish Chronicle*, 29 June 1979, 20. (NT)

"The Promise of Jerusalem: 1977." *London Jewish Chronicle*, 6 Jan. 1978, 19. + + (NT)

"The Saints of Warsaw." *Jewish Daily Forward*, 27 April 1968, 4. + (NT)

+ +   All entries marked with + + have been translated from the French by Sidney Lightman.

"Some Reasons for Hope." *London Jewish Chronicle*, 19 Sept. 1980, 23. + + (R)

"To a Young Rebel." *Washington Post*, 18 Feb. 1971, C 1, C 10.

"Trivializing the Holocaust: Semi-Fact and Semi-Fiction." *The New York Times*, 16 April 1978, sec. 2, pp. 1, 29.

"The Unknown Soldier: 1977." *London Jewish Chronicle*, 6 Jan. 1978, 19. + + (NT)

"The Victims of Injustice Must Be Cared For." *Los Angeles Times*, Opinion, 8 July 1979, 1, 3.

"Voices against Moscow." *London Jewish Chronicle*, 18 July 1980, 19. + +

"Voices of Hate." *London Jewish Chronicle*, 10 Sept. 1982, 23. Translated from the French by Lionel Simmonds.

"What the Pope Omitted to Say." *London Jewish Chronicle*, 2 Nov. 1979, 26.

"While Hausner Spoke." *Jewish Daily Forward*, 13 April 1961, 4. +

"Why Slepak Needs Our Help." *London Jewish Chronicle*, 12 March 1982, 25. + +

"Yesterday's Victims Forgotten, Struggle Is On for Today's." *Los Angeles Times*, 19 Sept. 1980, Part 2, p. 7. Translated from the French by Dan Jacobson.

ARTICLES IN PERIODICALS

"At the Western Wall." *Hadassah Magazine*, July 1967, 4-5. (R)

"Brief Encounter." *Jewish Heritage*, Spring 1966, 4-6.

"Conversation with Nelly Sachs." *Jewish Heritage*, Spring 1968, 30-33. Translated from the Yiddish by Hillel Halkin.

"Faces of a Slaughtered People: Captions for an Exhibit on the Holocaust." *National Jewish Monthly*, Jan. 1973, 6, 8. Address, opening of exhibit of photographs marking 30th anniversary of the Holocaust, B'nai B'rith Headquarters, Washington, D.C., 16 Oct. 1972. (A)

"Forty Years After: Remembering Babi Yar." *Hadassah Magazine*, Aug.-Sept. 1981, 14-15. Translated from the French by Madeline Stifel.

"Golda at 75." *Hadassah Magazine*, Jan. 1973, 6-7, 25-26. Interview held on 21 June 1971. (A, NT)

"Hasidism and Man's Love of Man." *Jewish Heritage*, Fall/Winter 1972, 6-12. Address, B'nai B'rith Commission on Adult Jewish Education, N.Y., 20 Feb. 1972. Article appears here in its original form, as adapted by Elie Wiesel from the transcript of a dialogue between him and Abraham J. Heschel on "Hasidism: What It Is Not: What It Is." Questions and answers are published here for the first time.

"Israel Was Alone." *Hadassah Magazine*, May 1969, 7, 40. Originally included in the French edition of *A Beggar in Jerusalem* but omitted from the American edition.

"Let Us Remember, Let Us Remember." *Journal of Warsaw Ghetto Resistance Organization* (1973): 9-10. Address on the 30th anniversary of Warsaw Ghetto Uprising, Temple Emanu-El, N.Y., 29 April 1973. (A)

"Memory — and Building a Moral Society." *Face to Face: An Interreligious Bulletin* 6 (Spring 1979): 35-37. Address upon receiving Anti-Defamation League Joseph Prize for Human Rights, N.Y., 19 Nov. 1978. (A, NT)

"The Novelist as Teacher." *The New Leader*, 8 Dec. 1975, 19-20. Translated from the French by Norman Jacobs.

"On Being a Jew." *Jewish Heritage*, Summer 1967, 51-55. Commencement address, Jewish Theological Seminary, N.Y., 4 June 1967.

"On Jewish Values in the Post-Holocaust Future." *Judaism* 16 (Summer 1967): 281-99. Transcript of proceedings of a symposium sponsored by *Judaism*, 26 March 1967. (A)

"On Teaching Jewish Identity." *Jewish Education* 43 (Winter/Spring 1975): 8-13. Keynote address, Plenary Session of 32nd Annual Pedagogic Conference, sponsored by Board of Jewish Education of Greater New York, 17 March 1974. (R)

"On the Alienation of Our Youth." Address, United Synagogue Convention, 15 Nov. 1971. Abridged version appears in *United Synagogue Review* 24 (Jan. 1972): 13, 29. Unabridged version is given here. (R,U)

"Reb Aaron Zeitlin, of Blessed Memory." *Yiddish* 1 (Winter 73/74): 2-3. Translated from the Yiddish by Joseph C. Landis.

"Remembrance at Bergen-Belsen." *Hadassah Magazine*, Sept. 1965, 9, 16. Translated from the Hebrew by David Segal.

"Salvation Will Come from Our Children." *Social Education* 47 (Nov./Dec. 1983): 488. Translated from the French by Margaret Berkey.

"*Simhat Torah* in Moscow." *Hadassah Magazine*, Oct. 1968, 3, 25. (A)

"Telling the Tale." *Dimensions in American Judaism* 2 (Spring 1968): 9-12. Address, 49th General Assembly of Union of American Hebrew Congregations, Nov. 1967.

"Then and Now: The Experiences of a Teacher." *Social Education* 42 (April 1978): 10-15. Transcript of address, National Invitational Conference of Anti-Defamation League of B'nai B'rith and the National Council for the Social Studies, N.Y., 9 Oct. 1977. (R)

"A Tribute to Jerusalem." *Tarbut*, Spring 1968, 4. Address, America-Israel Cultural Foundation, N.Y., 21 Jan. 1968.

"Warsaw '43." *Hadassah Magazine*, April 1973, 10, 46.

"Words from a Witness." *Conservative Judaism* 21 (Spring 1967): 40-48. Address, Rabbinical Assembly Convention, Toronto, Canada, 16 May 1966. (R)

BOOK REVIEWS

"Allies Fiddled As Jews Burned." Review of *While Six Million Died: A Chronicle of American Apathy*, by Arthur D. Morse, and *The Holocaust: The Destruction of European Jewry, 1933-1945*, by Nora Levin. *Hadassah Magazine*, March 1968, 16-17. (A)

"All Jews Are Survivors." Review of *The Chocolate Deal*, by Haim Gouri. *Hadassah Magazine*, May 1968, 19.

"All Was Lost, Yet Something Was Preserved." Review of *The Chronicle of the Lodz Ghetto, 1941-1944*, edited by Lucjan Dobroszycki. *The New York Times Book Review*, 19 Aug. 1984, 1, 23-25.

"At the End, a Miracle." Review of *The House of Ashes*, by Oscar Pinkus. *The New York Times Book Review*, 6 Sept. 1964, 4-5.

"Auschwitz: An Incident." Review of *Incident at Vichy*, by Arthur Miller. *Hadassah Magazine*, March 1965, 11-12.

"Auschwitz — Another Planet." Review of *Auschwitz*, by Bernd Naumann. *Hadassah Magazine*, Jan. 1967, 15-16.

"The Doomed and the Defiant." Review of *Heavy Sand*, by Anatoli Rybakov. *Washington Post Book World*, 26 April 1981, 4, 12. Translated from the French by Michael Dirda.

"A Dream of the Past." Review of *Two Tales: Betrothed & Edo and Enam*, by S.Y. Agnon. *Chicago Sun-Times Book Week*, 25 Sept. 1966, 8.

"Even Those Who Survived Are Partly Lost." Review of *The Agunah*, by Chaim Grade. *The New York Times Book Review*, 1 Sept. 1974, 5-6. (A)

"Everybody's Victim." Review of *The Painted Bird*, by Jerzy Kosinski. *The New York Times Book Review*, 31 Oct. 1965, 5, 46.

"Fighting for a New Nation." Review of *The State of the Jews*, by Marie Syrkin. *Washington Post Book World*, 3 Aug. 1980, 1-2. Translated from the French by Michael Dirda. (A)

"From Ancient Truths, Petrakis Creates a Modern Greek Tragedy." Review of *Days of Vengeance*, by Harry Mark Petrakis. *Chicago Tribune Book World*, 7 Aug. 1983, sec. 13, p. 31.

"From Exile to Exile." Review of *Other People's Houses*, by Lore Segal. *The Nation*, 25 April 1966, 494-95.

"Gypsy's Tale a Still-burning Ember of the Holocaust." Review of *The Eighth Sin*, by Stefan Kanfer. *Los Angeles Times Book Review*, 28 May 1978, 1, 4.

"In God's Image." Review of *Der Vidershtand fun Yiddn in Gettos un Lagern* (The Spiritual Resistance of the Jews in the Ghettos and Concentration Camps), by Menashe Unger. *Jewish Daily Forward*, 7 Dec. 1969, sec. II, p. 11.+ (T)

"In the Face of Barbarians a Victory of Spirit." Review of *The Terezin Requiem*, by Josef Bor. *The New York Times Book Review*, 27 Oct. 1963, 4, 69.

"Legacy of Evil." Review of *The 28th Day of Elul*, by Richard M. Elman. *The New York Times Book Review*, 28 May 1967, 4, 34.

"The Lives of Three Trottas." Review of *The Radetzky March*, by Joseph Roth. *The New York Times Book Review*, 3 Nov. 1974, 70.

"The Magic of Malamud." Review of *Idiots First*, by Bernard Malamud. *Hadassah Magazine*, Nov. 1963, 18. (T)

"The Man from Kikl." Review of *Meyer Weisgal. . . . So Far: An Autobiography*, by Meyer Weisgal. *The New York Times Book Review*, 27 Feb. 1972, 6-7. (T)

"Mao Tse-tung Is Not a Jew — Yet." Review of *The Jews: A Fictional Venture into the Follies of Anti-Semitism*, by Roger Peyrefitte. *Washington Post Book World*, 31 Dec. 1967, 7.

"Nobel Laureate Forges a World of Mystery." Review of *The Issa Valley*, by Czeslaw Milosz. *Chicago Tribune Book World*, 31 May 1981, sec. 7, p. 1.

"No Market for Jews." Review of *The Mission*, by Hans Habe. *Hadassah Magazine*, Sept. 1966, 12-13.

"Resistance in Hell." Review of *The Fighting Ghettos*, edited by Meyer Barkai. *The New Leader*, 5 Aug. 1963, 21-22. (R)

"Reviewing Jacobo Timerman." Review of *Prisoner Without a Name, Cell Without a Number*, by Jacobo Timerman. *Hadassah Magazine*, June-July 1981, 22.(NT)

"The Riddle of Israel Kastner." Review of *The Man Who Played God*, by Robert St. John. *Hadassah Magazine*, Nov. 1963, 12-13. (T)

"The Savage Olympic Game." Review of *The Blood of Israel: The Massacre of the Israeli Athletes, The Olympics, 1972*, by Serge Groussard. *The New York Times Book Review*, 8 June 1975, 4-5.

"A *Shtetl* Grows in Brooklyn." Review of *The Chosen*, by Chaim Potok. *Hadassah Magazine*, April 1967, 13.

"The Telling of the War." Reviews of *The Upstairs Room*, by Johanna Reis; *I Was There*, by Hans Peter Richter; *From Ice Set Free*, by Bruce Clements; *I Am Rosemarie*, by Marietta Moskin; *Petros' War*, by Alki Zei; *When Hitler Stole Pink Rabbit*, by Judith Kerr; *Till the Break of Day*, by Maia Wojciechowska. *The New York Times Book Review*, 5 Nov. 1972, 3, 22.

"Unanswerable Questions." Review of *Into That Darkness*, by Gitta Sereny. *Midstream*, Nov. 1975, 73-75. (R)

"Victims of God." Review of *Selected Stories by I.L. Peretz*, edited by Irving Howe and Eliezer Greenberg. *The New Republic*, 21 Sept. 1974, 26-27. (A)

"Voice from the Graveyard." Review of *Blood from the Sky*, by Piotr Rawicz. *The New Leader*, 11 May 1964, 25-26.

"The War against the Children." Review of *Herod's Children*, by Ilse Aichinger, *Hadassah Magazine*, Nov. 1963, 19. (T)

"Was Kurt Gerstein a Saint in Nazi Clothing?" Review of *A Spy For God: The Ordeal of Kurt Gerstein*, by Pierre Joffroy. *The New York Times Book Review*, 4 April 1971, 1, 44-45.

"The World of the *Shtetl*." Review of *The Samurai of Vishogrod: The Notebooks of Jacob Marateck*, retold by Shimon and Anita Wincelberg. *The New Leader*, 24 May 1976, 13-14. Translated from the French by Norman Jacobs.

FOREWORDS AND AFTERWORDS

"Across and beyond the Centuries." Afterword to *Biblical Themes in World Literature*, by
   Sol Liptzin. New York: Schocken, 1984. (T)
"Built with Memories." Introduction to *Village of the Brothers: Memoirs of the Members
   of Kfar Ahim*, compiled by Rivka Guber. New York: Shengold Publishers, Inc., 1979.
   Introduction is dated 8 Jan. 1974. (T)
"A Few Words about Raoul Wallenberg." Preface to *With Raoul Wallenberg in Budapest:
   Memories of the War in Hungary*, by Per Anger. New York: Holocaust Library, 1981.
"Four Days in Jerusalem." Introduction to *From Holocaust to Redemption: Bearing
   Witness*, edited by Sam E. Bloch. New York: World Gathering of Jewish Holocaust
   Survivors, 1984. Translated from the French by Richard Howard.
"I Envy Him His Memories." Introduction to *The Liberation of Jerusalem: The Battle of
   1967*, by Uzi Narkiss. London: Vallentine, Mitchell and Co., Ltd., 1983. Translated
   from the French by Martha Hauptman. (T)
"The Jewish Writer." Foreword to *The Literature of American Jews*, edited by Theodore
   L. Gross. New York: Free Press, 1973. (T)
"A Lost Universe." Foreword to *Piety and Perseverance: Jews from the Carpathian
   Mountains*, by Herman Dicker. New York: Sepher-Hermon Press, 1981. (T)
"The Mystery and the Fear." Foreword to *Jews and Christians after the Holocaust*, edited
   by Abraham J. Peck. Philadelphia: Fortress Press, 1982. (T)
"The Name in Jewish History." Foreword to *From Generation to Generation: How to
   Trace Your Jewish Genealogy and Personal History*, by Arthur Kurzweil. New York:
   William Morrow and Co., Inc., 1980. (T)
"Now We Know." Epilog to *Genocide in Paraguay*, edited by Richard Arens.
   Philadelphia: Temple University Press, 1976. Translated from the French by
   Raymond Federman.
"On the Stage of History." Introduction to *In the Land of Light: Israel, a Portrait of Its
   People*, by Rodney Smith. New York: Houghton Mifflin, 1983. (T)
"The Ring of Truth." Foreword to *On the Tip of a Mast*, by Yehuda Elberg. New York:
   Shulsinger Brothers, 1974. Translated from the Yiddish by Irving Abrahamson. (T)
"Songs and Silences." Foreword to *To Find an Image*, by Jean Edelman. New York:
   Nathan Edelman, 1967. Translated from the French by Lily and Nathan Edelman. (T)
"The Story Remains the Same." Foreword to *Voices from the Holocaust*, edited by Sylvia
   Rothchild. New York: New American Library, 1981. Translated from the French by
   Stanley Hochman. (R,T)
"Two Voices in One." Introduction to *Journey toward the Roots*, by Hans Juergensen. St.

[356]

Petersburg, Fla.: Valkyrie Press, 1976. Introduction is dated New York, March 1976. Translated from the French by Steven Rubin and Hans Juergensen. (T)

"Under the Sign of Fidelity." Foreword to *A Vanished World*, by Roman Vishniac. New York: Farrar, Straus & Giroux, 1983. Translated from the French by Richard Howard. (T)

"Witness to Betrayal." Introduction to *On Both Sides of the Wall: Memoirs from the Warsaw Ghetto*, by Vladka Meed. New York: Holocaust Library, 1979. Newly translated from the Yiddish by Steven Meed. Introduction was originally written in 1971 for the first English edition (Israel: Ghetto Fighters' House, Publishers, 1972). (T)

"A Word of Gratitude." Foreword to *Honor the Promise: America's Commitment to Israel*, by Robert F. Drinan. New York: Doubleday and Co., Inc., 1977.

TELEVISION SCRIPTS

"Elie Wiesel's Jerusalem." Transcript of Canadian Broadcasting Corp.-TV, Easter 1979. (A)

"The Itinerary of Elie Wiesel: From Sighet to Jerusalem." Transcript of National Broadcasting Co. *The Eternal Light*, NBC-TV Network, 21 May 1972. (A)

B 10
DRAMA

A Black Canopy A Black Sky. New York: Hadassah, 1968. Translated from the Yiddish by Harry Gersh. Elie Wiesel's first play, performed in 1968 to mark the 25th anniversary of the Warsaw Ghetto Uprising. (U)

THE BOOKS: GENESIS AND COMMENTARY

Ani Maamin

Letter to James H. Silberman, 25 Sept. 1973. 2 pp. (Typewritten.) (U)
"Question and Quest." Transcript, *The Eternal Light*, Chapter 1159, 12 May 1974.*
 (R,T,U)

A Beggar in Jerusalem

Letter to the Publisher. Book jacket, 1968
"The Madmen of Sighet." *Commentary*, May, 1968, 38-41.
"Encounter with Jerusalem." Transcript, *The Eternal Light*, Chapter 1019, 14 June 1970.*
 (A,T,U)
"The Adventure of Jerusalem." Lecture, Temple Sinai, Hollywood, Fla., 28 Feb. 1972.
 (R,T,U)

The Gates of the Forest

"A Simple Dialogue." Excerpt from statement marking thirty years of Rebbe Menahem
 Schneerson's leadership of the Lubavitch movement, N.Y., 28 Jan. 1980. (T,U)

The Jews of Silence

"The Song of Russian Jewry." Transcript, *The Eternal Light*, Chapter 1018, 7 June 1970.*
 (R,T,U)

A Jew Today

Cromie, Robert. "*A Jew Today* and Its Author." *Book Beat*, television broadcast, 16 Dec.
 1978; taped 5 Dec. 1978, Chicago, Ill. (A,T,U)
"Encounter with Christianity." Question and answer session, Moriah Congregation,
 Deerfield, Ill., 27 March 1982. (A,T,U)

Legends of Our Time

"The Tale of the Tale." Transcript, *The Eternal Light*, Chapter 1017, 31 May 1970.*
(R,T,U)

"Mordecai Shoshani." Transcript, *The Eternal Light*, Chapter 1040, 21 Feb. 1971.*
(A,T,U)

Messengers of God

"Messengers through Time." Transcript, *The Eternal Light* , Chapter 1234, 4 April 1976.*
(A,T,U)

"Whose Messengers Are We?" Transcript, *The Eternal Light*, Chapter 1237, 25 April
1976.* (A,T,U)

"The Jew and the Human Condition." Transcript, *The Eternal Light*, Chapter 1272, 24
April 1977.* (A,T,U)

Night

"The Deportation." Opening of *Un di Velt Hot Geshvign*. Translated from the Yiddish by
Eli Pfefferkorn.

"The End and the Beginning." Last chapter of *Un di Velt Hot Geshvign*. Translated from
the Yiddish by Eli Pfefferkorn.

"The Call to Life." Transcript, *The Eternal Light*, Chapter 1016, 24 May 1970.* (R,T,U)

The Oath

Letter to James H. Silberman, 30 March 1973. 2 pp. (Typewritten.) (U)

"A Kingdom of Fire." Transcript, *The Eternal Light*, Chapter 1158, 5 May 1974.* (R,U)

One Generation After

Letter to James H. Silberman, 3 April 1970. 3 pp. (Typewritten.) (U)

Souls on Fire

Letter to James H. Silberman, 14 April 1971. 5 pp. (Typewritten.) (U)

"The Baal Shem Tov." Transcript, *The Eternal Light*, Chapter 1073, 20 Feb. 1972.*
(A,T,U)

"Levi Yitzhak of Berditchev." Transcript, *The Eternal Light*, Chapter 1074, 27 Feb.
1972.* (R,T,U)

"Back to the Source." Lecture, Temple Sinai, Hollywood, Fla., 28 Feb. 1972. (A,T,U)

"Israel of Rizhin." Transcript, *The Eternal Light*, Chapter 1075, 5 March 1972.* (A,T,U)

"Menahem Mendel of Kotzk." Transcript, *The Eternal Light*, Chapter 1076, 12 March
1972.* (R,T,U)

The Testament

Letter to James H. Silberman, 15 April 1980. 2 pp. (Typewritten.) (U)

"Words Are the Link." Lecture, Boston University, 10 Nov. 1980. (A,T,U)

"The Story of *The Testament*." Lecture, Niles Township Jewish Congregation, Skokie, Ill., 7 Dec. 1980. (R,T,U)

"Origins of *The Testament*." Transcript, *The Eternal Light*, Chapter 1435, 10 May 1981.* (R,T,U)

"Paltiel Kossover's Search." Transcript, *The Eternal Light*, Chapter 1436, 17 May 1981.* (A,U)

"The Mark." Transcript, *The Eternal Light*, Chapter 1436, 17 May 1981.* (A,T,U)

"The Watchman and the Poet." Transcript, *The Eternal Light*, Chapter 1436, 17 May 1981.* (R,T,U)

"Against God and Man." Transcript, *The Eternal Light*, Chapter 1438, 31 May 1981.* (A,T,U)

The Trial of God

"The Story of *The Trial of God*." Lecture, Loyola University, Chicago, Ill., sponsored by Moriah Congregation, Deerfield, Ill., 12 April 1980. (A,T,U)

Zalmen, or The Madness of God

"My Song of Songs." Statement, first performance, Arena Stage, Washington, D.C., 8 May 1974. (T)

"A Tale of Defiance." Transcript, *The Eternal Light*, Chapter 1192, 9 March 1975.* (A,T,U)

"The Story of *Zalmen*." Lecture, B'nai B'rith Hillel Foundation, Toronto, Canada, 2 March 1977. (R,T,U)

PRESIDENT'S COMMISSION ON THE HOLOCAUST

"Against Extrapolation." Closing statement, transcript, *Proceedings, President's Commission on the Holocaust*, Commission Meeting, Washington, D.C., 24 April 1979, 125-26. (A,T,U)

"The Focus Is Memory." *Report to the President*. Washington: President's Commission on the Holocaust, 1979, i-iv. Introductory letter to President Jimmy Carter, 27 Sept. 1979. (T)

"For the Sake of History and Justice." Address to the Main Commission for Investigation of Hitlerite Crimes in Poland; Warsaw, 30 July 1979. (T,U)

"The Holocaust: Beginning or End?" In *Days of Remembrance: National Civic Holocaust Commemoration Ceremony*. Washington: President's Commission on the Holocaust, 1979. Address, Capitol Rotunda, Washington, D.C., 24 April 1979.

"Plea for the Boat People." *Congressional Record-Senate*, 27 June 1979, S 8753. See: "Southeast Asia Refugee Tragedy." (U)

"Presentation of the Report of the President's Commission on the Holocaust to the President of the United States." *Report to the President*. Washington: President's Commission on the Holocaust, 1979, Appendix F, pp. 33-34. Statement, the Rose Garden, the White House, Washington, D.C., 27 Sept. 1979.

"A Quest for Memory and Justice." Opening statement, transcript, *Proceedings, President's Commission on the Holocaust*, Commission Meeting, Washington, D.C., 15 Feb. 1979, 2-8. (A,T,U)

"To Deepen Memory." Opening statement, transcript, *Proceedings, President's Commission on the Holocaust*, Commission Meeting, Washington, D.C., 7 June 1979, 2-6. (A,T,U)

B 13
UNITED STATES HOLOCAUST MEMORIAL COUNCIL

"Man's Right to Be Remembered." Transcript, *Proceedings, United States Holocaust Memorial Council*, Council Meeting, Washington, D.C., 28 May 1980, pp. 5-10. An edited version appears in *Congressional Record*, 4 June 1980, E 2722-23. (A,T,U)

"Meeting Again." Transcript, welcoming address, International Liberators Conference, United States Department of State, Washington, D.C., 26 Oct. 1981. See also: *Congressional Record*, 6 Nov. 1981, E 5189-90. (U)

"Protest against Iran." News Release, United States Holocaust Memorial Council, Washington, D.C., 7 July 1983. (T)

Remarks on Anti-Semitism and on the Revisionists. Transcript, *Proceedings, United States Holocaust Memorial Council*, Council Meeting, N.Y., 10 Dec. 1980, 156-57. (A,T,U)

"Remembering the Holocaust." In *Days of Remembrance 1981*. Washington: United States Holocaust Memorial Council, 1981. Address, Remembrance Day observance, the White House, 30 April 1981. (R)

"Setting Precedent for History." Transcript, *Proceedings, United States Holocaust Memorial Council*, Council Meeting, N.Y., 10 Dec. 1980, 106-9. (A,T,U)

"The Temple of Fire." Transcript, *Proceedings, United States Holocaust Memorial Council*, Council Meeting, Washington, D.C., 2 Dec. 1982, 3-6, 11-12. (A,T,U)

"Thank You, the American People." Statement, Museum Transfer ceremony, United States Capitol, Washington, D.C., 13 April 1983. (R,T,U)

"To the Liberators of the Camps." In *International Liberators Conference, 1981*. Washington, United States Holocaust Memorial Council, 1981. Letter to the International Liberators Conference, United States Department of State, Washington, D.C., 26-29 Oct. 1981.

"We Must Remember." Address, Remembrance Day observance, Capitol Rotunda, Washington, D.C., 30 April 1984. (R,T,U)

"What Will Remain." Transcript, *Proceedings, United States Holocaust Memorial Council*, Council Meeting, Washington, D.C., 2 Dec. 1982, 112-14. (A,T,U)

"Why We Teach." Statement, Remembrance Day observance, the White House , 20 April 1982. (T,U)

EXPLORATIONS AND EXPLANATIONS

Abrahamson, Irving. "The Great Adventure." Interview, Congregation Am Shalom, Glencoe, Ill., 16 April, 1978. (A,T,U)

Ages, Arnold. "Writer Elie Wiesel Sums Up His Message: Life is Destructible, More Evil Than Good." *The Canadian Jewish Press*, 18 Jan. 1979, 4. (A-I, NT)

Agmon, Yaacov. "A Writer's Fears." *Israel Magazine*, April 1970, 54-55. (A, NT)

Baras, Barbara. "The Writer and His Universe." *Young Israel Viewpoint*, 29 April 1971, 13. (Publication of National Council of Young Israel, N.Y.) (A, T)

"Being an American." Statement, Horace M. Kallen Memorial Symposium on "What does being an American mean to you in this Bicentennial Year?" Staten Island Community College, Staten Island, N.Y., 18 Feb. 1976. (A, U)

Berkowitz, William. "My Father's *Tallis*." *The Jewish Week-American Examiner*, week of 14 June 1981, pp. 22-23. (A,T)

"Beyond Survival." *European Judaism*, 6 (Winter 1971/72): 4-10. Discussion participants: Elie Wiesel, Eugene Heimler, Michael Goulston, Anthony Rudolf. (A)

Cargas, Harry James. "What Is a Jew?" *U.S. Catholic/Jubilee*, Sept. 1971, pp. 26, 28-31. (A)

Clark, Don. "What Is to Be Done?" *Bostonia* (Boston University Alumni Magazine), Spring 1978, 44-45. (A-I, NT)

Cromie, Robert. "*A Jew Today* and its Author." *Book Beat*, television broadcast, 16 Dec. 1978; taped 5 Dec. 1978, Chicago, Ill. (T,U)

Dresner, Samuel. "The Jewish Condition." Dialogue, Glencoe, Ill., under auspices of Moriah Congregation, Deerfield, Ill., 28 March 1982. (A,T,U)

Edelman, Lily. "The Use of Words and the Weight of Silence." *National Jewish Monthly*, Nov. 1973, 5-18. (A, NT)

Fine, Ellen S. "A Sacred Realm." *Centerpoint*, 4, no. 1 (Fall 1980): 19-25. (A, NT)

Flender, Harold. "The Key to the Mystery." *Women's American ORT Reporter*, March/April 1970, 4-6. (A, NT)

Harazim, Dorritt. "Israel's Dilemmas." *Veja* (Brazil), 8 Sept. 1982, 3-6. (A)

"A High Point in History." Transcript of dialogue, Cathedral Church of St. John the Divine, N.Y., 7 Dec. 1975. (A,T,U)

Hirsch, Kathleen. "On Silence, Words, and Salvation." *World* (Boston University), 15 Oct. 1980, 2. (A, NT)

Hurwitz, Donald. "The Silence between Question and Answer." *Together* (Hillel Foundation, University of Maryland), March 1974, 7-8. (A-I)

"Inner Geography and Outer." Question and answer session, Staten Island Community College, Staten Island, N.Y., 28 April 1975. (A,T,U)

Koppel, Gene, and Henry Kaufmann. *A Small Measure of Victory*. Tucson: University of Arizona, 1974. Interview taped 25 April 1973. (A)

Kresh, Paul. "Giving and Receiving." *UJA World*, 1972, 17. (A-I, NT)

Kurzweil, Arthur. "Confronting Questions." *Hadassah Magazine*, Dec. 1978, 16-17, 47-48. (A-I, NT)

Larson, Roy. "The Story Saves." *Chicago Sun-Times*, 9 Oct. 1976, 46. (A-I, NT)

Nadel, Ira. "In the Shadow of Flames." Interview, Canadian Broadcasting Corp. *Audience*, 29 Sept. 1979. (A,NT,U)

Questions and Answers: At Brandeis-Bardin, 1978. Interview and question and answer session, Brandeis-Bardin Institute, Simi Valley, Cal., 22 Jan. 1978. Interviewers: Dennis Prager and Joseph Telushkin. (A,U)

Questions and Answers: At the University of Oregon, 1975. Question and answer session, University of Oregon, Eugene, Ore., 10 April 1975. (A,U)

Questions and Answers: At Washington University, 1978. Question and answer session, Washington University, St. Louis, Mo., 1 Feb. 1978. (A,U)

Questions and Answers: At Willamette University, 1977. Question and answer session, Willamette University, Salem, Ore., 10 March 1977. (A,U)

Reichek, Morton A. "Out of the Night." *Present Tense*, Spring 1976, 41-47. (A-I, NT)

Remsberg, Bonnie. "Before the End of History — and After." *Some of My Best Friends*, Chicago, Ill., Channel 5-TV, 28 June 1981. Taped 9 April 1981. (A,T,U)

Reynolds, Frank. "In Spite of Everything." Transcript, American Broadcasting Co., Inc. *Directions*, ABC-TV, 18 June 1978 (A,NT,U)

————. "The Lesson of Auschwitz." Transcript, American Broadcasting Co., Inc. *Directions*, ABC-TV, 25 June 1972. (A,NT,U)

Salomon, Michel. "The Jews of Silence." *Conservative Judaism* 21 (Spring 1967): 49-53. Translated from the French by Navah Harlow. Originally appeared in *L'Arche*, Oct. 1966. (NT)

Scott, Will, and Tommy Ehrbar. "Witness of the Holocaust." *Kenyon College Alumni Bulletin*, Summer 1982, 7-9. (A, NT)

Szonyi, David M., and Bennet Zurofsky. "Tales Change People." *Rutgers Daily Targum*, *Critiques*, 3 Dec. 1970, 7. (A, NT)

Walker, Heidi Anne. "How and Why I Write." *Journal of Education* (Boston University) 162 (Spring, 1980): 57-63. (A, NT)

Wiesel, Elie. "Golda at 75." *Hadassah Magazine*, Jan. 1973, 6-7, 25-26. Interview held 21 June 1971. (A, NT)

B 15
QUOTES AND COMMENTS

1. Abrahamson, Irving. "The Great Adventure." Interview, Congregation Am Shalom, Glencoe, Ill., 16 April 1978. (A,T,U)
2. Abramson, Shelley. "Why Elie Wiesel Writes and Talks, and Why a New Generation Listens." *The Oregonian Forum*, 11 March 1977.
3. Brenner, Betty. "Jewish Author's Focus: Meaning of Life, Faith." *Flint* (Mich.) *Journal*, 2 Dec. 1973, Arts Section.
4. Brin, Herb. "Wiesel's Warning: 'Last Chance to Save Soviet Jews.'" *Los Angeles Heritage-Southwest Jewish Press*, 25 Feb. 1972, 1, 6.
5. *California Orange County Jewish Heritage*, 21 Dec. 1973, 4. Remarks quoted from lecture given at Temple Beth Sholom, 9 Dec. 1973.
6. Clark, Don. "What Is to Be Done?" *Bostonia* (Boston University Alumni Magazine), Spring 1978, 44-45. (A-I, NT)
7. Cohn, Robert A. "Elie Wiesel: The Novelist Whose Speeches Set Souls on Fire." *St. Louis Jewish Light*, 15 March 1978, 16.
8. DeKovner-Mayer, Barbara. "Man in Search of Meaning." *Israel Today*, 20 Jan.-2 Feb. 1978, 8-9.
9. Dupont, Joan. "Elie Wiesel: The Man Who Will Not Let Others Forget." *International Herald Tribune*, 9 April 1980.
10. Eckman, Fern Marja. "Out of the Inferno." *New York Post Magazine*, 10 Dec. 1968, 55.
11. Farrell, Dave. "Holocaust Survivor Sees Return of Madness That Killed Millions." *Palo Alto Times*, 5 May 1978, 8.
12. Fields, Sidney. "Indifference Is the Sin." *New York Daily News*, 11 June 1974, 51.
13. Fiske, Edward B. "Elie Wiesel: Archivist with a Mission." *The New York Times*, 31 Jan. 1973, Part II, p. M 35, M 64.
14. Freedman, Samuel G. "Elie Wiesel Teaches Lessons of Anguish." *The New York Times*, 13 Oct. 1982, B1, B2.
15. Gantz, Paula. "Author Emphasizes Jewish Past." *Cornell Daily Sun*, 6 Dec. 1971, 6.
16. Gerson, Allan. "Notes of a Survivor's Son." *The Jerusalem Post*, 3 July 1981, 5. Remarks made at Kibbutz Lohamei Haghettaot (Fighters of the Warsaw Ghetto), the Museum of the Holocaust, 16 June 1981, during the First World Gathering of Jewish Holocaust Survivors.
17. Goodman, Howard. "Jewish Author Re-creates Stories of Camps' Victims." *Oregon Statesman*, 10 March 1977.
18. Harpur, Tom. "A Survivor of Auschwitz Asks Why God Permits Suffering." *Toronto Star*, 30 Oct. 1971, 9.
19. Hurwitz, Donald. "The Silence between Question and Answer." *Together* (Hillel Foundation, University of Maryland), March 1974, 7-8.

20. Hyer, Marjorie. "Young Jews Stir World Conscience." *Staten Island Advance*, 29 Oct. 1972.

21. "Jewish Holocaust Survivors Plan International Gathering in Israel." *Jewish Press* (N.Y.), 7 March 1980, 62.

22. Kakutani, Michiko. "Elie Wiesel: No Answers, Only Questions." *The New York Times*, 7 April 1981, Arts/Entertainment, C 11.

23. Kamm, Henry. "Marchers with Food Aid Get No Cambodian Response." *The New York Times*, 7 Feb. 1980, A 3.

24. Kanfer, Stefan. "Never Forget, Never Forgive." *Time*, 20 Aug. 1979, 32-33.

25. Kass, Marcia. "Stirring Up the Past." *Argus/Dimension*, 15 Feb. 1974, 3.

26. Kobren, Gerri. "From Auschwitz, a Message of the Joy of Life." *Baltimore Sun*, 15 Dec. 1974. Remarks made during lecture, 8 Dec. 1974.

27. Kurzweil, Arthur. "Confronting Questions." *Hadassah Magazine*, Dec. 1978, 16-17, 47-48.(A-I, NT)

28. Larson, Roy. "Elie Wiesel Keeps the Songs of His Fathers Alive." *Chicago Sun-Times*, 20 June 1973, sec. 2, p. 2.

29. _____. "The Story Saves." *Chicago Sun-Times*, 9 Oct. 1976, 46. (A-I, NT)

30. _____. "Wiesel Returns from Israel Fearing Final Holocaust." *Chicago Sun-Times*, 24 Nov. 1973, 38.

31. Levi, Lucille. "Jews Question Mark of History." *Jewish* (Manchester, England) *Gazette*, 23 June 1978, 10.

32. McCain, Nina. "Elie Wiesel: Witness to Evil." *Boston Globe*, 3 Oct. 1976, 1.

33. Montalvo, Gilda, and David Myers. "A Hasidic Storyteller." *Scholastic* (Notre Dame), 9 May 1977, 11.

34. Peck, Abraham. "Still Searching for an Answer." *Chicago Sun-Times*, 31 Dec. 1978, Views, 4. Remarks taped 5 Dec. 1978.

35. Reiss, Leni. "Wiesel Casts Spell; Captivates Audience." *Phoenix Jewish News*, 30 Dec. 1977, 5.

36. Richards, David. "Elie Wiesel: Voice of the Holocaust . . . Weaving His Themes through a Looking Glass, Darkly." *Washington* (D.C.) *Star News*, 7 May 1974, C 1, C 4.

37. Rosenberg, Neil D. "In Memory: Jews Recall Holocaust." *Milwaukee Journal*, 14 Oct. 1976. Remarks quoted in review of speech delivered 13 Oct. 1976.

38. Savan, Jakki. "Elie Wiesel: He Tries to Defeat the Executioner with Words." *St. Louis Jewish Light*, 17 March 1976, 7. Address, 75th Anniversary Celebration of Jewish Federation of St. Louis, 22 Feb. 1976.

39. Scheier, Philip R. "Wiesel Blasts Sale of AWACS." *Seattle Jewish Transcript*, 24 Sept. 1981, 5A.

40. Sharp, Christopher. "Wiesel on the Holocaust: 'America Turned Its Back.'" *Women's Wear Daily*, 7 Nov. 1973, 34.

41. Shear, Natalie P. "Elie Wiesel: A Destiny of His Own." *Washington* (D.C.) *Jewish Week*, 12 Feb. 1970. Article quoted in B'nai B'rith News Release, 6 March 1970, 1-2.

42. Shenker, Israel. "The Concerns of Elie Wiesel: Today and Yesterday." *The New York Times*, 10 Feb. 1970, 48.

43. Sky, Doris. "Huge Crowd Thrilled by Wiesel Address." *Denver Intermountain Jewish News*, 28 March 1969, sec. A, p. 14.

44. Stroud, Jerri. "Vision of Being a Jew." *St. Louis Post-Dispatch*, 5 March 1976, 3D.

45. "Survivor Tells Jews: Remember." *Omaha World-Herald*, 17 Feb. 1972, 2.
46. Wallace, Andrew. "Wiesel Makes Holocaust Meaningful to Youths." *Philadelphia Inquirer*, 16 Oct. 1971, sec. 4, p. 4.
47. Weisman, John. "Storyteller Elie Wiesel Weaving His Spell at a Local Synagogue." *Detroit Free Press*, 12 March 1972, sec. B, p. 5.
48. Wershba, Joseph. "An Author Asks Why the World Let Hitler Do It." *New York Post*, 2 Oct. 1961, 30
49. Wiesel, Elie. "Are We Worthy of the Story?" Lecture, Temple Beth Israel, Phoenix, Ariz., 24 April 1973. (U)
50. ————. "Art and Culture after the Holocaust." See B 16-A, p. 406.
51. ————. "Between Protest and Belief." Statement, Temple Sholom, Chicago, Ill., 25 Oct. 1981. (A,U)
52. ————. "Eternal Beginning." Lecture, Congregation Shaarey Zedek, Southfield, Mich., 20 March 1977. (U)
53. ————. "The Eternal Flame." Statement upon receiving First Spertus International Award, Chicago, Ill., 7 Oct. 1976. (U)
54. ————. "The Eternal Question of Suffering and Evil." Lecture, Dartmouth College, Hanover, N.H., 7 Nov. 1977. (U)
55. ————. *From Holocaust to Rebirth.* See B 3, pp. 9, 10.
56. ————. "The Holocaust: One Generation After." Lecture, University of Illinois, Circle Campus, Chicago, Ill., 13 April 1978. (R,U)
57. ————. "The Holocaust and the Anguish of the Writer." Statement, City University of New York Graduate School Symposium on "The Holocaust Century: Implications and Anxieties," 22 March 1973. (U)
58. ————. "Jewish Legends." Film lecture. See B 16-E, p. 6.
59. ————. "The Jewish Response to Suffering." Lecture, Seattle, Wash., week of 13 Sept. 1981. (U)
60. ————. "Jewish Tales — A Message for Humanity: Hasidism." Transcript, *The Eternal Light*, Chapter 1274, 1 May 1977, 4.* (U)
61. ————. "A Jewish Writer in Search of His Characters: A Modern Pilgrimage." Transcript, *The Eternal Light*, Chapter 1389, 30 March 1980, 8.* (U)
62. ————. "A Jew Today." Lecture, Niles Township Jewish Congregation, Skokie, Ill., 5 Dec. 1978. (A,U)
63. ————. Lecture, American Friends of Haifa University, N.Y., 1 Oct. 1975. (A,T,U)
64. ————. Lecture, Beth El Temple, Harrisburg, Pa., 23 Nov. 1975. (U)
65. ————. Lecture, Central Florida Jewish Community Council, Orlando, Fla., 27 Feb. 1972. (R,U)
66. ————. Lecture, Cornell University, Ithaca, N.Y., 5 Dec. 1971. (U)
67. ————. Lecture, Great Neck Synagogue, Great Neck, N.Y., 21 Oct. 1975. (U)
68. ————. Lecture, Lehigh University, Bethlehem, Pa., 18 Feb. 1975. (U)
69. ————. Lecture, Stanford University, Stanford, Cal., 30 April 1976. Kent State-Jackson State Memorial Lecture. (U)
70. ————. Lecture, Temple Anshe Sholom, Olympia Fields, Ill., 28 Oct. 1979. (A,U)
71. ————. Lecture, Temple Beth Am, Los Angeles, Cal., Dec. 1977. (U)
72. ————. Lecture, Temple Beth El, Birmingham, Mich., 30 March 1976. (U)
73. ————. Lecture, Temple Israel, Los Angeles, Cal., 15 Nov. 1968. (U)
74. ————. Lecture, Temple Judea, Tarzana, Cal., 11 April 1975. (U)

75. _____. Lecture, Temple Sinai, Hollywood, Fla., 28 Feb. 1972. (U)

76. _____. Lecture, Washington University, St. Louis, Mo., 1 Feb. 1978. (U)

77. _____. Lecture, Wooster, Ohio, 30 Oct. 1979. (U)

78. _____. "Letters to the Young." Transcript, *The Eternal Light*, Chapter 1041, 28 Feb. 1971, 1-2, 3, 8.* (A,U)

79. _____. "Look Further." Lecture, Rochester, N.Y., 24 April 1974. (U)

80. _____. "The Meaning of Munich." Address, United Jewish Appeal, N.Y., 14 Dec. 1972. (R,U)

81. _____. "A *Niggun* for *Shabbat*." Comment during address, 40th General Assembly of the Council of Jewish Federations and Welfare Funds, Pittsburgh, Pa., 13 Nov. 1971. (U)

82. _____. "On Revolutions in Culture and the Arts." See B 16-L, p. 84.

83. _____. "Paltiel Kossover's Discovery." Transcript, *The Eternal Light*, Chapter 1438, 31 May 1981, 3.* (U)

84. _____. Questions and Answers: At the University of Oregon, 1975. Question and answer session, University of Oregon, Eugene, Ore., 10 April 1975. (U)

85. _____. Statement, American Jewish Congress National Biennial Convention, Cleveland, Ohio, 10-14 May 1972. American Jewish Congress News Release, 11 May 1972.

86. _____. Statement, National Invitational Conference of Anti-Defamation League of B'nai B'rith and the National Council for the Social Studies, N.Y., 9 Oct. 1977. (U)

87. _____. Statement on receiving First B'nai B'rith Heritage Award from B'nai B'rith Commission on Adult Jewish Education. B'nai B'rith Press Release, 15 March 1966.

88. _____. "The Story of *The Testament*." Lecture, Niles Township Jewish Congregation, Skokie, Ill., 7 Dec. 1980. (U)

89. _____. "Tales of Anguish." Transcript, *The Eternal Light*, Chapter 1191, 2 March 1975.* (A,U)

90. _____. *Think Higher*. See B 3-E, p. 1. (P)

91. _____. "What I Must Do." Transcript, *The Eternal Light*, Chapter 1387, 16 March 1980.* (A,T,U)

92. _____. "What Is a Poet?" Transcript, *The Eternal Light*, Chapter 1437, 24 May 1981* (A,T,U)

93. _____. "Why Should People Care?" See B 16-Q, p. 17.

94. _____. "The Writer and His Obsessions." Lecture, Colloquium of Scholars, California Lutheran College, Thousand Oaks, Cal., 27 April 1977. (U)

95. _____. "A Writer's Invention." Transcript, *The Eternal Light*, Chapter 1349, 25 March 1979.* (A,T,U)

96. "Wiesel Lauds Lubavitch, Talks to Holocaust Educators." *Detroit Jewish News*, 9 Nov. 1979, 40. Remarks from lecture given 6 Nov. 1979.

97. "Wiesel Re-visits Auschwitz During Holocaust Commission's East European Tour." *St. Louis Jewish Light*, 15 Aug. 1979.

98. Winerip, Mike. "Holocaust Left Him Gentle and Angry." *Miami Herald*, 16 March 1979, 1 E.

99. Young, Mort. Press release, 31 Oct. 1973.

B 16

OTHER SOURCES

A. "Art and Culture after the Holocaust." In *Auschwitz: Beginning of a New Era? Reflections on the Holocaust*, edited by Eva Fleischner, 403-15. New York: Ktav; Cathedral of St. John the Divine; Anti-Defamation League, 1977. Opening address, International Symposium on the Holocaust, Cathedral of St. John the Divine, N.Y., 3 June 1974.

B. "The Fiery Shadow — Jewish Existence out of the Holocaust." In *Jewish Existence in an Open Society*, edited by Baruch Cohon, 39-49. Los Angeles: Ward Ritchie Press, 1970. Address, 25th Anniversary Convocation of Jewish Centers Association of Los Angeles, 6 May 1968.

C. "Freedom of Conscience — A Jewish Commentary." In *Religious Liberty in the Crossfire of Creeds*, edited by Franklin H. Littell, 638-49. Philadelphia: Ecumenical Press, 1978. Address, Bicentennial Conference on Religious Liberty, Philadelphia, Pa., 27 April 1976.

D. "Friendship." In *Through the Sound of Many Voices: Writings Contributed on the Occasion of the 70th Birthday of W. Gunther Plaut*, edited by Jonathan V. Plaut, 2-7. Toronto: Lester and Orpen Dennys, Ltd., 1982.

E. "God Must Obey," and others. In *Teachers' Study Guide: Jewish Legends*.Film lecture. New York: Catholic Archdiocese of New York and Anti-Defamation League of B'nai B'rith, 1968.

F. "Hear, O Israel." In *Great Religions of the World*, edited by Merle Severy, 173-91 passim. Washington: National Geographic Society, 1978.

G. "The Holocaust and the Future." In *The Holocaust: Its Meaning for Christians And Jews*, 7-16. St Louis: National Conference of Christians and Jews, 1976. Lecture, National Conference of Christians and Jews, St. Louis, Mo., 3 Nov. 1976.

H. "The Holocaust as Literary Inspiration." In *Dimensions of the Holocaust*, 5-19. Evanston: Northwestern University, 1977. Lecture, Northwestern University, 28 March 1977.

I. "Israel Twenty Years Later." In *The Impact of Israel on American Jewry — 20 Years Later*, 71-76. New York: American Histadrut Cultural Exchange Institute, 1969. Address, American Histadrut Cultural Exchange Institute, N.Y., 23 April 1968.

J. "The Jewish Tradition of Learning: A Personal View." In *Proceedings Princeton Conference II: What the Modern Jew Needs to Know: A National Conference on Informal Adult Learning*, 1-15. Princeton: B'nai B'rith Commission on Adult Jewish Education, 1977. Address, B'nai B'rith Commission on Adult Jewish Education, 22 Oct. 1977.

K. "Myth and History." In *Myth Symbol and Reality*, edited by Alan M. Olson, 20-30. Boston University Studies in Philosophy and Religion, vol. 1. Notre Dame: University of Notre Dame Press, 1980. Lecture, Harvard University, March 1978.

L. "On Revolutions in Culture and the Arts." In *Revolutionary Directions in Intellectual and Cultural Production: Their Consequences for the Higher Learning*, 77-87. New York: Research Foundation of City University of New York, 1975. Keynote address, symposium on "Revolutions in Culture and the Arts," Tenth Anniversary Convocation of the Graduate School of City University of New York, 4 May 1973.

M. "The Story of a Story." In *Wonders: Writings and Drawings for the Child in Us All*, edited by Jonathan Cott and Mary Gimbel, 610-12. New York: Summit Books, 1980. Translated from the French by Mary Gimbel.

N. "Talking and Writing and Keeping Silent." In *The German Church Struggle and the Holocaust*, edited by Franklin H. Littell and Hubert G. Locke, 269-77. Detroit: Wayne State University Press, 1974. Address, First International Scholars' Conference, Wayne State University, Detroit, Mich., 18 March 1970.

O. "Toward a Philosophy of Jewish Existence." In *Discussion Proceedings: 25th Anniversary Convocation of Jewish Centers Association of Los Angeles*, edited by Baruch Cohon, 17-24. Los Angeles: Ward Ritchie Press, 1970. Panelist speaker, 7 May 1968.

P. "Why Remember?" *Vancouver* (B.C.) *Jewish Western Bulletin*, 14 Dec. 1978, 25-32, 34. Lecture, Schara Tzedeck Synagogue, Vancouver, B.C., 6 May 1978.

Q. "Why Should People Care?" Prologue to *A Consuming Fire: Encounters with Elie Wiesel and the Holocaust*, by John K. Roth. Atlanta: John Knox Press, 1979. The prologue was originally delivered as a lecture at the Interntional Symposium on Human Rights, Retardation and Research, Washington, D.C., 16 Oct. 1971. (A,T)

DIRECTORY

Abbreviations for works by Elie Wiesel

ABIJ	A Beggar in Jerusalem
AJT	A Jew Today
AM	Ani Maamin
LOOT	Legends of Our Time
MOG	Messengers of God
N	Night
OGA	One Generation After
SOF	Souls on Fire
TGOTF	The Gates of the Forest
TJOS	The Jews of Silence
TO	The Oath
TT	The Testament
TTOG	The Trial of God
Z	Zalmen

The B notations following each entry refer to the Complete Bibliography. The roman numerals followed by the arabic numerals locate each work by volume and page.

INDEX

(The letter H is used for Holocaust and the letter W for Wiesel.)

Sachs, Nelly, II: 48-51, 125
Sadat, Anwar el-, I: 163, 359-60; II: 9, 205
St. John, Robert, II: 271
St. Louis, I: 120, 150; III: 145
Sakharov, Andrei, II: 166
The Samurai of Vishogrod, II: 331-32
Sand, Mikhail, II: 204
Sartre, Jean-Paul, I: 52, 255, 380; II: 69, 70, 96; III: 222, 305
Satmar Hasidim, I: 237; III: 82
Saturday Evening Post, II: 226
Saudi Arabia, I: 199
Schindler, Oskar, III: 193
Schneerson, Menahem, III: 63
Schneider, Alan, III: 95
Scholem, Gershom, III: 222, 236
Schwarz-Bart, André, II: 190, 202; III: 73-74, 199
Segal, Lore, II: 285-86
Selected Stories of I.L. Peretz, II: 321-23
Sereny, Gitta, II: 329-30
Servatius, Robert, II: 171, 177
The Seven Beauties (film), I: 317
Shakespeare, I: 288
Shammai, II: 166
Sharf, Mendel, II: 171
Shazar, Zalman, II: 206
Shcharansky, Anatoly, II: 166, 240, 247; III: 193
Shema Yisrael, I: 279; II: 14, 57, 261
Shevet Yehudah, I: 146
Shimon bar Yohai, III: 319, 323
Shneour, Zalman, I: 320
Shneur Zalman of Lyadi, I: 358
Shoshani, Mordecai, I: 291; II: 21, 39; III: 66, 270
Shukeiry, Ahmed, I: 237; II: 189, 193
Shulhan Arukh, II: 261
Siegel, Bernard, II: 16
Sighet, I: 14, 15, 89, 129, 289; II: 3, 150; III: 1-9, 40, 54, 65, 68
Sigheter Hasidim, III: 82
Silberman, James H., letters to: on *Ani Maamin*, III: 91-92; on *One Generation After*, III: 75-76; on *Souls on Fire*, III, 77-79; on *The Oath*, III: 88-89; on *The Testament*, III, 114-15
Silence: of Birkenau, I, 114; of the dead, I: 30; defined, I, 55; of God, I, 27, 31, 54, 110, 144 and III: 93, 228-29, 267; of Hasidic masters, II, 255; of H, I, 13; in Jewish history, I, 54; mystical, I, 56, 57, 239 and II, 111; of the silent tradition, I, 56; opposition to, I, 54-55, 148, 192, 206, 211, 212, 214,

238, 247, II, 68, 82, 109, 116, 121, 154, 235, 385, and III, 162, 265, 283, 284, 289; weight of, I, 21, 45-46, 57 and II, 83, 119; and words, II, 18 and III, 268, 285; 286; in W's work and Sinai, I, 273; of the world, III, 267; of the world during H, I, 31, 34, 54, 55, 110; writer's responsibility for, II, 65
Silone, Ignazio, II: 91
Sinai, III: 307; and all Jews, I, 132; and anti-Sinai, I, 44, 240; and H, I, 35, 43-44, 211 and III, 312; mystery of, I, 280; silence of, I, 306-307
Sinai Campaign, II: 200, 216
Singer, Isaac Bashevis, III: 225
Six-Day War, I: 34, 236, 237, 253, 295; II: 1, 187, 189, 193-94, 195; III: 37-38, 67
Sklare, Marshall, II: 189
Skokie, Illinois, I: 149, 159-60, 161
Slavic peoples, III: 182
Slepak, Vladimir, II: 240, 246-47; III: 193
Smith, Rodney, II: 391-92
Sobibor, II: 104
Solzhenitsyn, Aleksandr, I: 21, 281
Sonderkommando, I: 53, 119, 136-37, 211
Song of My Slaughtered People, II: 91
Sophie's Choice (film), II: 124
Sorbonne, II: 21, 112
Soviet Jewry, III: 8, 316
Soviet Writers' Union, II: 338
Spain, I: 132
Speer, Albert, II: 69
Spinoza, Baruch, I: 324, 359
The Spiritual Resistance of the Jews in the Ghettos and Concentration Camps, II: 307-8
A Spy for God, II: 309-11
SS, I: 134, 182
Stalin, Josef, I: 379; III: 114, 118, 120, 208, 266
Stangl, Franz, II: 329-30
The State of the Jews, II: 336-37
Stauffenberg, Klaus von, I: 127
Steiner, George I: 203; II: 121
Steiner, Jean-François, I: 230
Stern group (Lehi), II: 22
Streicher, Julius, I: 33
Strochlitz, Sigmund, III: 164
Styron, William, II: 124
Subjects and themes: I: 39, 50, 311 and III: 197, 311; God, I, 48, 206 and II, 58; Hasidism, II, 255 and III, 77-79; H, I, 46, 47, 271-72 and II, 83, 106; Israel, III, 286; Jerusalem, III, 210; Jewish history, I, 13-14, 57-58 and II, 77, 107; Judaism, I, 37 and II, 84; madness, I, 310; Messiah, III, 93, 244,

CREDITS

"The Absence of Hate," quoted from lecture "Talking and Writing and Keeping Silent."
Reprinted from *The German Church Struggle and the Holocaust*, edited by Franklin H.
Littell and Hubert G. Locke. Reprinted by permission of the Wayne State University
Press. Copyright: 1974.

"An Act of Faith." Reprinted by permission of *Tarbut*, published by America-Israel
Cultural Foundation, Inc.

And Thou Shalt Teach Your Children. Reprinted by permission of Baltimore Hebrew
College.

"Art and Culture after the Holocaust," in *Auschwitz: Beginning of a New Era? Reflections
on the Holocaust*, edited by Eva Fleischner. Copyright © 1977 by Ktav. Reprinted by
permission.

"Before the End of History — and After." *Some of My Best Friends*, P. #3887, adapted and
used by permission of WMAQ-TV, Chicago, Ill.

"Between Hope and Fear." Copyright © October, 1973, *City College Alumnus*. Reprinted
by permission.

"Beyond Survival." Reprinted by permission of *European Judaism*.

A Black Canopy A Black Sky. Copyright © 1968 by Hadassah, The Women's Zionist
Organization of America, Inc. Reprinted by permission.

"Brief Encounter." Reprinted from *Jewish Heritage*. Copyright © 1966 by the
Commission on Adult Jewish Education of B'nai B'rith International.

"Conversation with Nelly Sachs." Reprinted from *Jewish Heritage*. Copyright © 1968 by
the Commission on Audlt Jewish Educaton of B'nai B'rith International.

"A Day of Shame in Skokie." Article first appeared in *Newsday*, June 20, 1978.

"The Doomed and the Defiant." Copyright © 1981 by *Book World, The Washington Post*.
Reprinted by permission.

"A Dream of the Past." Copyright © 1966 by the *Chicago Sun-Times*. Reprinted by
permission.

"Elie Wiesel Keeps the Songs of His Fathers Alive." Copyright © 1973 by the *Chicago
Sun-Times*. Excerpt reprinted by permission.

"Faces of a Slaughtered People." Copyright © 1973 by B'nai B'rith. Reprinted by
permission from the *National Jewish Monthly*.

"The Fiery Shadow — Jewish Existence out of the Holocaust," in *Jewish Existence in an
Open Society*, edited by Baruch Cohon. Copyright © 1970 by Jewish Centers
Association of Los Angeles. Reprinted by permission.

"Fighting for a New Nation." Copyright © 1980 by *Book World, The Washington Post*.
Reprinted by permission.

"For the Sake of Our Children," in "Why Remember?" Reprinted by permission of *Jewish
Western Bulletin*.

"Freedom of Conscience — A Jewish Commentary," in *Religious Liberty in the Crossfire*